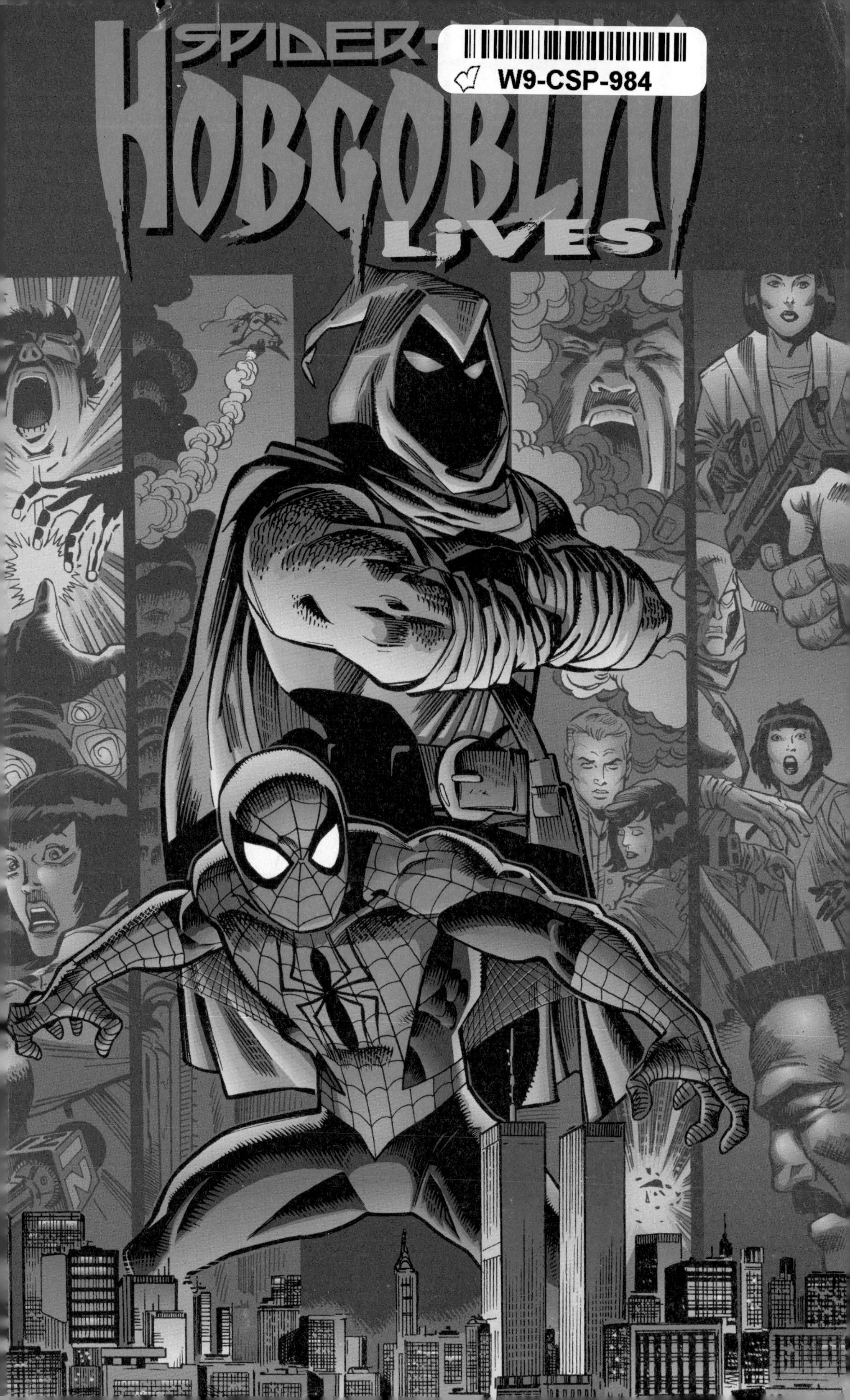
SPIDER-
HOBGOBLIN
LIVES

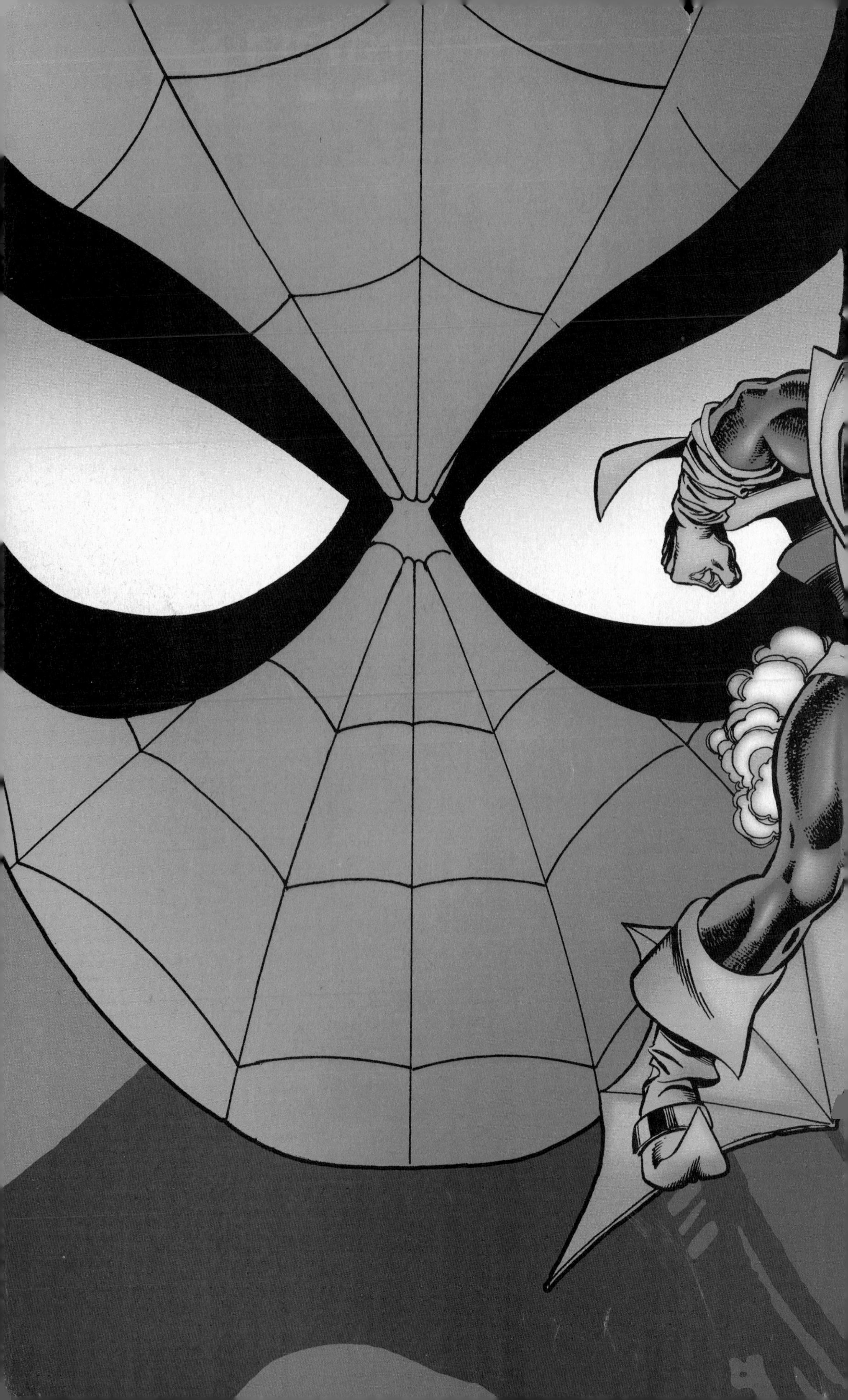

Writers
ROGER STERN *and* **GLENN GREENBERG**
Pencilers
RON FRENZ *and* **LUKE ROSS**
Inkers
AL MILGROM, GEORGE PÉREZ, JEROME MOORE, SCOTT HANNA *and* **BOB MCLEOD**
Colorists
CHRISTIE SCHEELE, JOE ANDREANI *and* **JOHN KALISZ**
Letterers
JIM NOVAK *and* **RICHARD STARKINGS & COMICRAFT'S LIZ AGRAPHIOTIS**
Editors
GLENN GREENBERG, TOM BREVOORT *and* **RALPH MACCHIO**

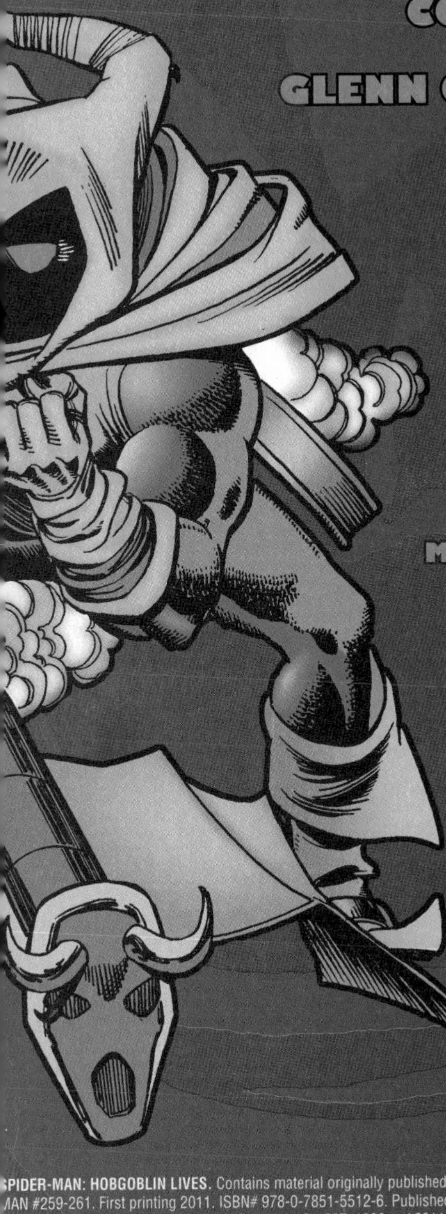

Cover Artist:
JOHN ROMITA
Cover Colorist:
ATOMIC PAINTBRUSH

Collection Editor & Designer
JOHN BARBER
Editorial Assistants
JAMES EMMETT *and* **JOE HOCHSTEIN**
Assistant Editors
NELSON RIBEIRO *and* **ALEX STARBUCK**
Editors, Special Projects
MARK D. BEAZLEY *and* **JENNIFER GRÜNWALD**
Senior Editor, Special Projects
JEFF YOUNGQUIST
Research
ROB LONDON
Production
RYAN DEVALL *and* **COLORTEK**
Senior Vice President of Sales
DAVID GABRIEL
SVP of Brand Planning & Communications
MICHAEL PASCIULLO

Editor in Chief
AXEL ALONSO
Chief Creative Officer
JOE QUESADA
Publisher
DAN BUCKLEY
Executive Producer
ALAN FINE

SPIDER-MAN: HOBGOBLIN LIVES. Contains material originally published in magazine form as SPIDER-MAN: HOBGOBLIN LIVES #1-3, and PETER PARKER, THE SPECTACULAR SPIDER-MAN #259-261. First printing 2011. ISBN# 978-0-7851-5512-6. Published by MARVEL WORLDWIDE, INC., a subsidiary of MARVEL ENTERTAINMENT, LLC. OFFICE OF PUBLICATION: 135 West 50th Street, New York, NY 10020. **Printed in the U.S.A.** ALAN FINE, EVP - Office of the President, Marvel Worldwide, Inc. and EVP & CMO Marvel Characters B.V.; DAN BUCKLEY, Publisher & President - Print, Animation & Digital Divisions; JOE QUESADA, Chief Creative Officer; JIM SOKOLOWSKI, Chief Operating Officer; DAVID BOGART, SVP of Business Affairs & Talent Management; TOM BREVOORT, SVP of Publishing; C.B. CEBULSKI, SVP of Creator & Content Development; DAVID GABRIEL, SVP of Publishing Sales & Circulation; MICHAEL PASCIULLO, SVP of Brand Planning & Communications; JIM O'KEEFE, VP of Operations & Logistics; DAN CARR, Executive Director of Publishing Technology; JUSTIN F. GABRIE, Director of Publishing & Editorial Operations; SUSAN CRESPI, Editorial Operations Manager; ALEX MORALES, Publishing Operations Manager; STAN LEE, Chairman Emeritus. For information regarding advertising in Marvel Comics or on Marvel.com, please contact John Dokes, SVP Integrated Sales and Marketing, at jdokes@marvel.com. For Marvel subscription inquiries, please call 800-217-9158. **Manufactured between 4/7/2011 and 4/26/2011 by QUAD/GRAPHICS, DUBUQUE, IA, USA.**

10 9 8 7 6 5 4 3 2 1

APPROVED BY THE COMICS CODE AUTHORITY

One of the greatest mysteries in Spider-Man's long and colorful crime fighting career has just become unsolved!

The trial of Jason Macendale – the current Hobgoblin – sets off a chain of events that will culminate in blackmail, corruption, political maneuvering and murder! And lurking in the shadows, presiding over all of it, is a man thought to be long dead, thought to be nothing more than an unpleasant memory... the original Hobgoblin, returning to the New York crime scene after a long absence!

But the original Hobgoblin was discovered to be Daily Bugle investigative reporter Ned Leeds, who was murdered in Berlin several years ago! Can it be that Ned has somehow come back from the dead? Is it possible that he never truly died? Or... was he never really the Hobgoblin at all?

The Hobgoblin lives... and Spider-Man's days may be numbered!

[redacted]

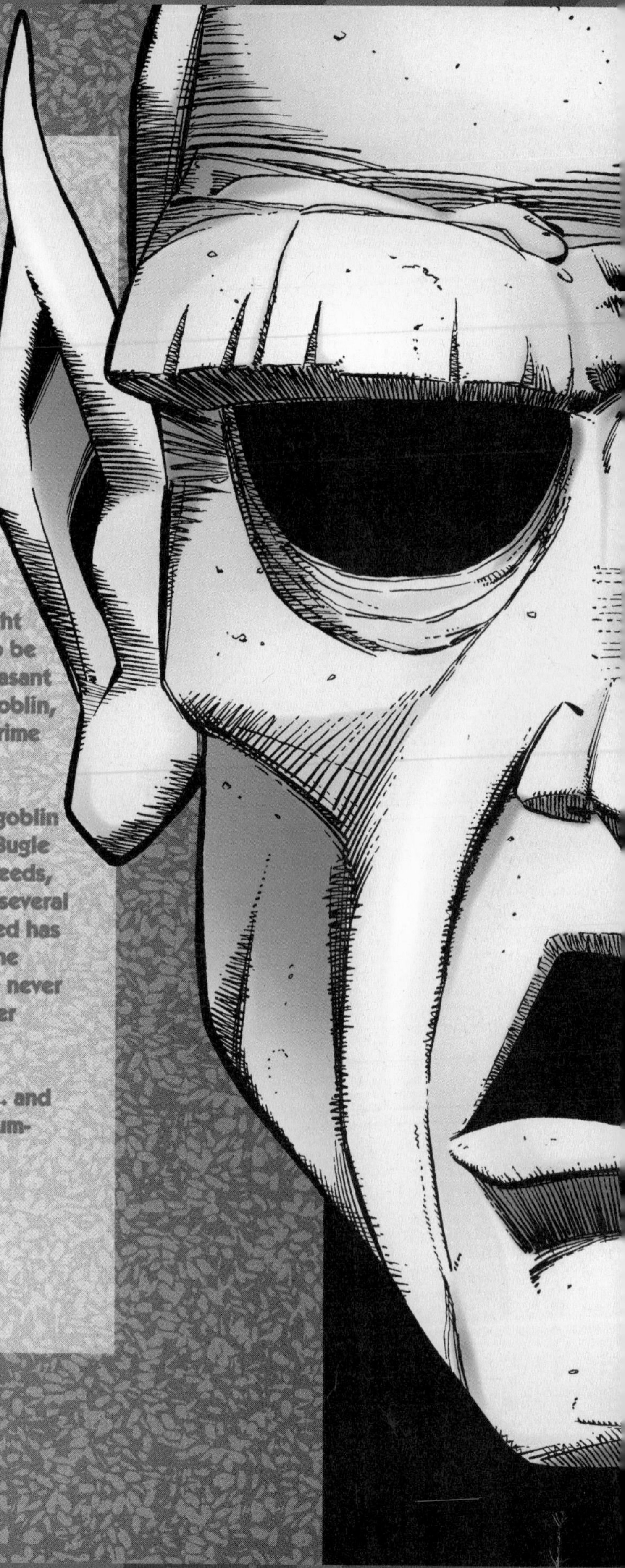

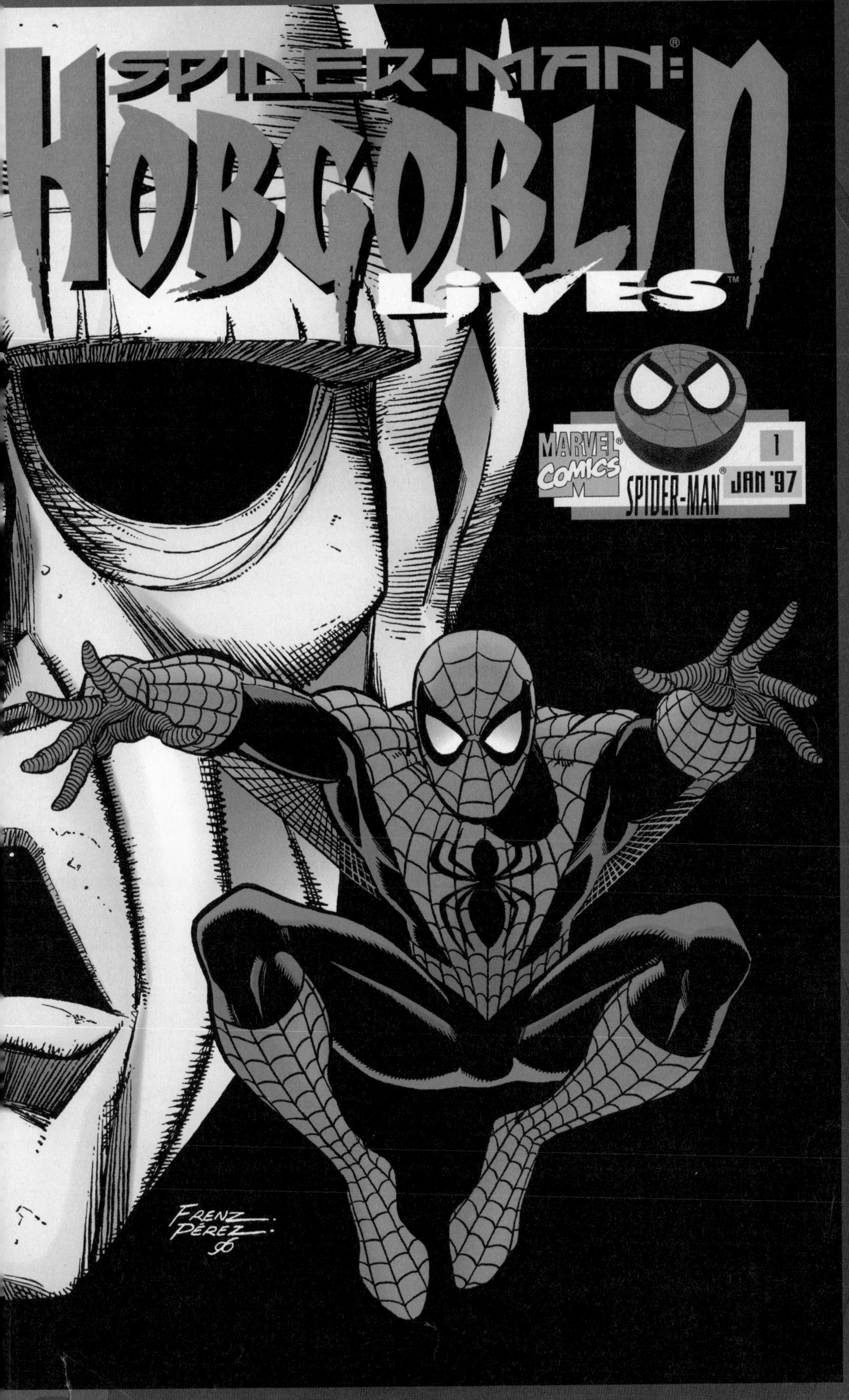
SPIDER-MAN:
HOBGOBLIN
LIVES
MARVEL COMICS
1
SPIDER-MAN
JAN '97
FRENZ
PÉREZ
96

SPIDER-MAN: HOBGOBLIN LIVES™

Roger Stern — WRITER

Ron Frenz & George Pérez — ARTISTS

Jim Novak — LETTERER

Christie Scheele — COLORIST

Glenn Greenberg & Tom Brevoort — EDITORS

Bob Harras — EDITOR IN CHIEF

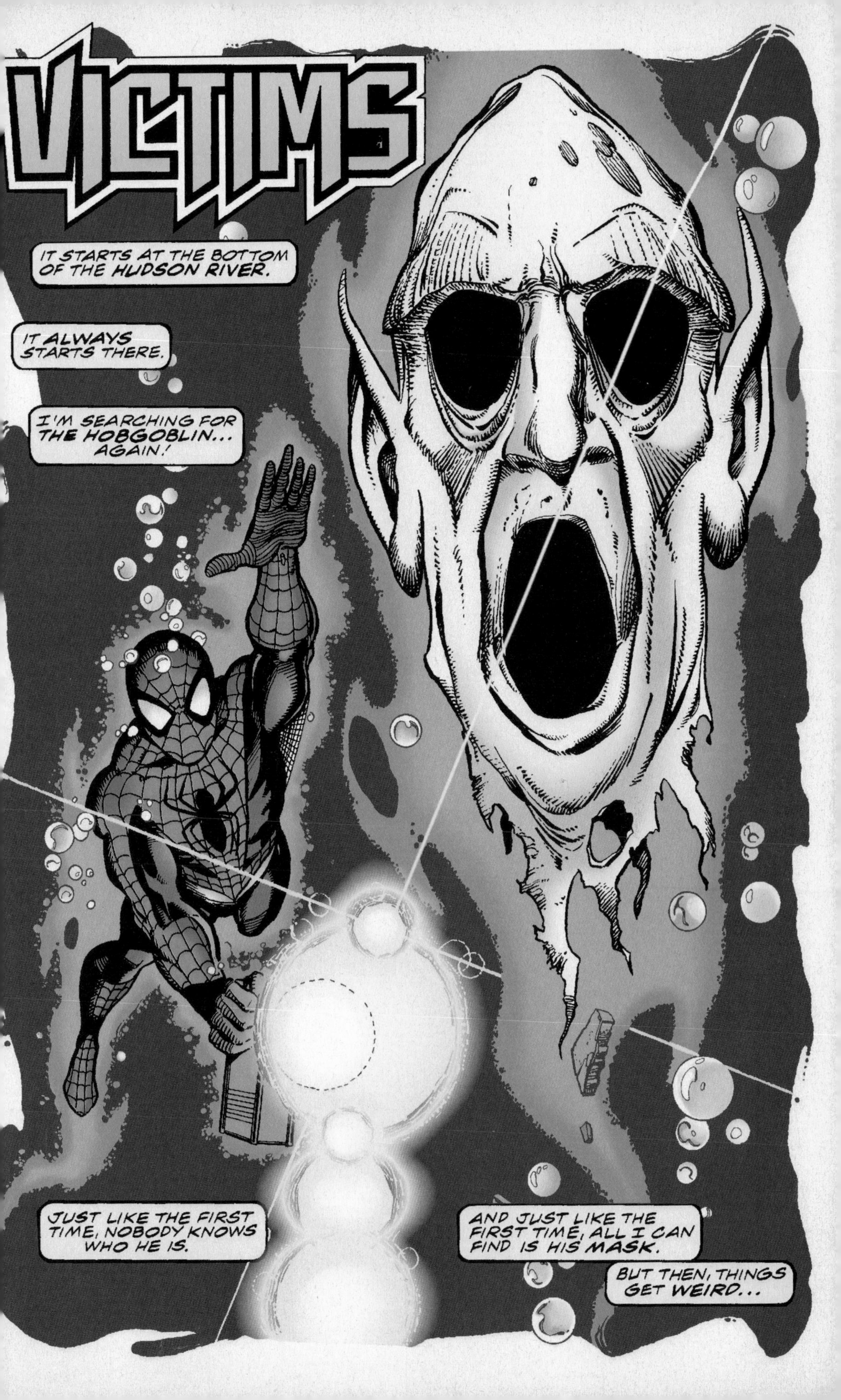
VICTIMS
IT STARTS AT THE BOTTOM OF THE HUDSON RIVER.
IT ALWAYS STARTS THERE.
I'M SEARCHING FOR THE HOBGOBLIN... AGAIN!
JUST LIKE THE FIRST TIME, NOBODY KNOWS WHO HE IS.
AND JUST LIKE THE FIRST TIME, ALL I CAN FIND IS HIS MASK.
BUT THEN, THINGS GET WEIRD...

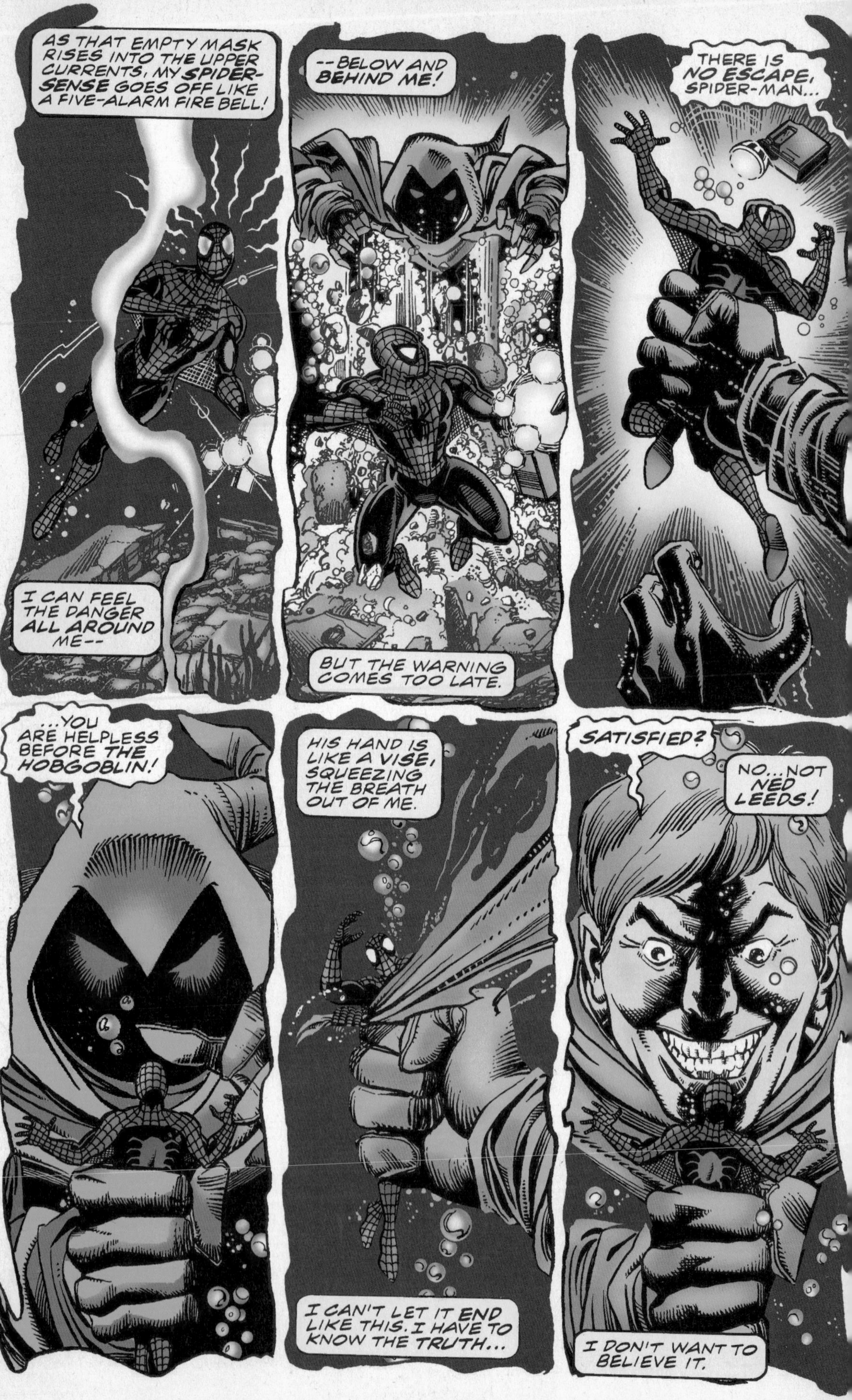

AS THAT EMPTY MASK RISES INTO THE UPPER CURRENTS, MY SPIDER-SENSE GOES OFF LIKE A FIVE-ALARM FIRE BELL!
I CAN FEEL THE DANGER ALL AROUND ME--
--BELOW AND BEHIND ME!
BUT THE WARNING COMES TOO LATE.
THERE IS NO ESCAPE, SPIDER-MAN...
...YOU ARE HELPLESS BEFORE THE HOBGOBLIN!
HIS HAND IS LIKE A VISE, SQUEEZING THE BREATH OUT OF ME.
I CAN'T LET IT END LIKE THIS. I HAVE TO KNOW THE TRUTH...
SATISFIED?
NO...NOT NED LEEDS!
I DON'T WANT TO BELIEVE IT.

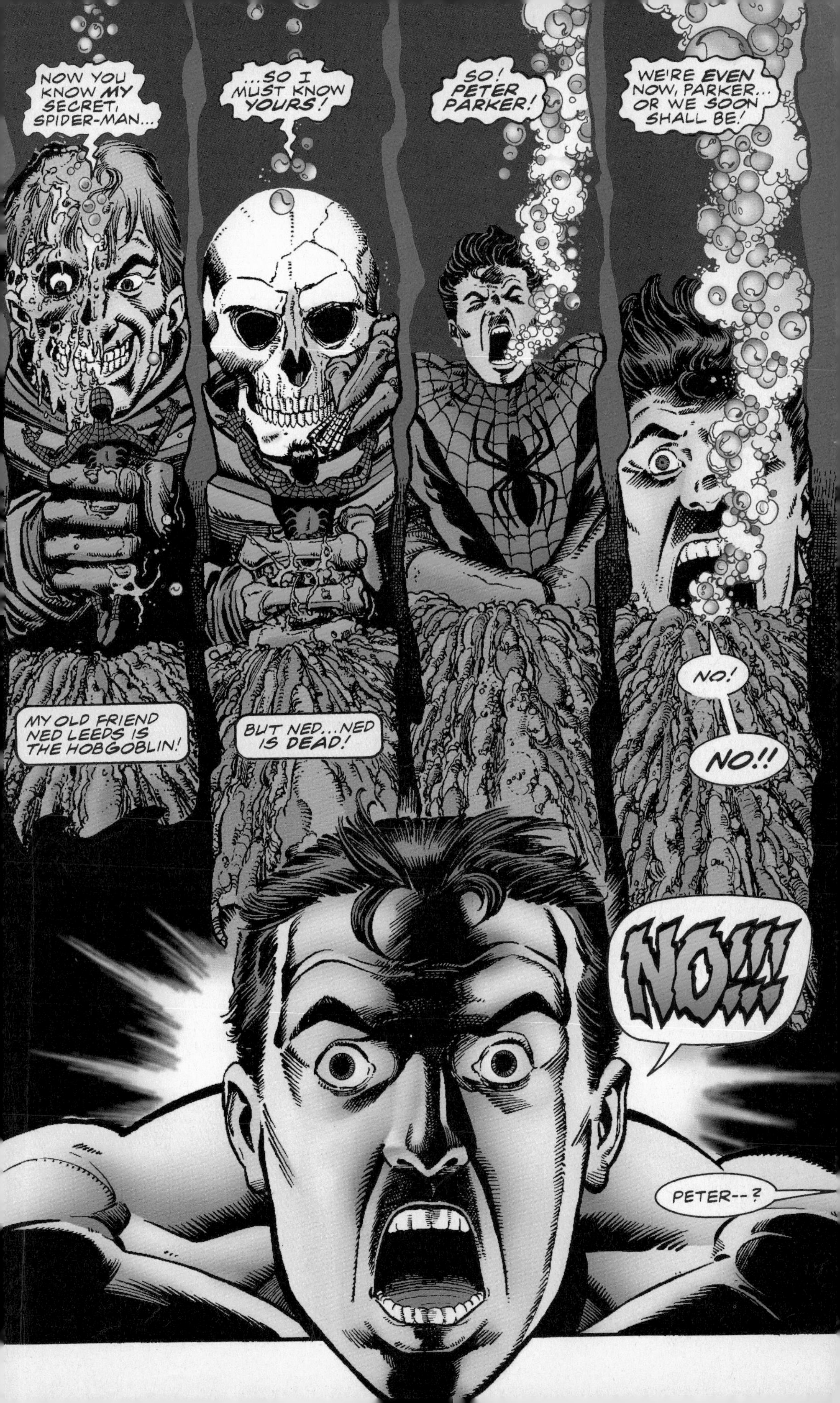
NOW YOU KNOW MY SECRET, SPIDER-MAN...
MY OLD FRIEND NED LEEDS IS THE HOBGOBLIN!
...SO I MUST KNOW YOURS!
BUT NED...NED IS DEAD!
SO! PETER PARKER!
WE'RE EVEN NOW, PARKER... OR WE SOON SHALL BE!
NO!
NO!!
NO!!!
PETER--?

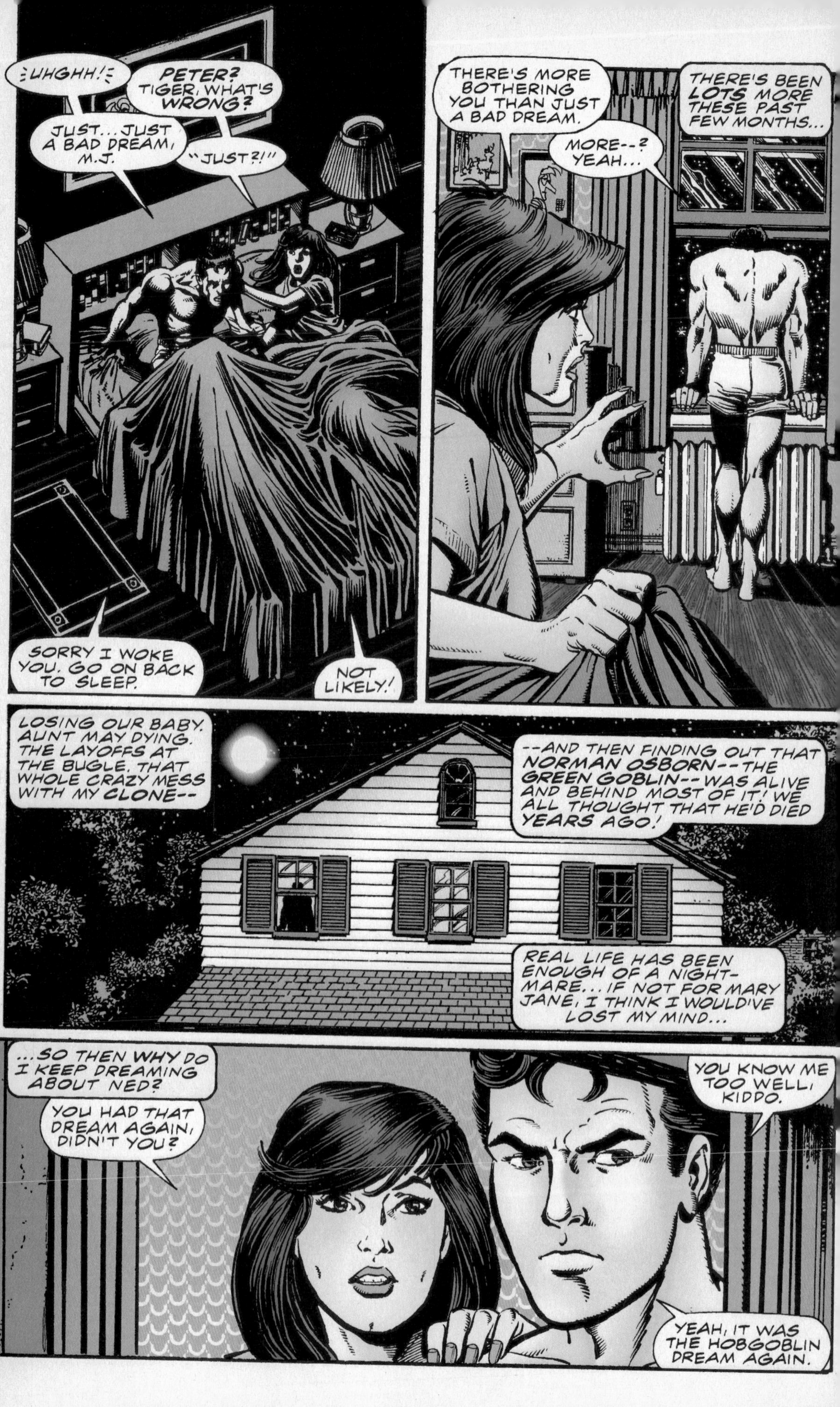
UHGHH!
PETER? TIGER, WHAT'S WRONG?
JUST... JUST A BAD DREAM, M.J.
"JUST?!"
SORRY I WOKE YOU. GO ON BACK TO SLEEP.
NOT LIKELY!
THERE'S MORE BOTHERING YOU THAN JUST A BAD DREAM.
MORE--? YEAH...
THERE'S BEEN LOTS MORE THESE PAST FEW MONTHS...
LOSING OUR BABY. AUNT MAY DYING. THE LAYOFFS AT THE BUGLE. THAT WHOLE CRAZY MESS WITH MY CLONE--
--AND THEN FINDING OUT THAT NORMAN OSBORN--THE GREEN GOBLIN--WAS ALIVE AND BEHIND MOST OF IT! WE ALL THOUGHT THAT HE'D DIED YEARS AGO!
REAL LIFE HAS BEEN ENOUGH OF A NIGHT-MARE... IF NOT FOR MARY JANE, I THINK I WOULD'VE LOST MY MIND...
...SO THEN WHY DO I KEEP DREAMING ABOUT NED?
YOU HAD THAT DREAM AGAIN, DIDN'T YOU?
YOU KNOW ME TOO WELL, KIDDO.
YEAH, IT WAS THE HOBGOBLIN DREAM AGAIN.

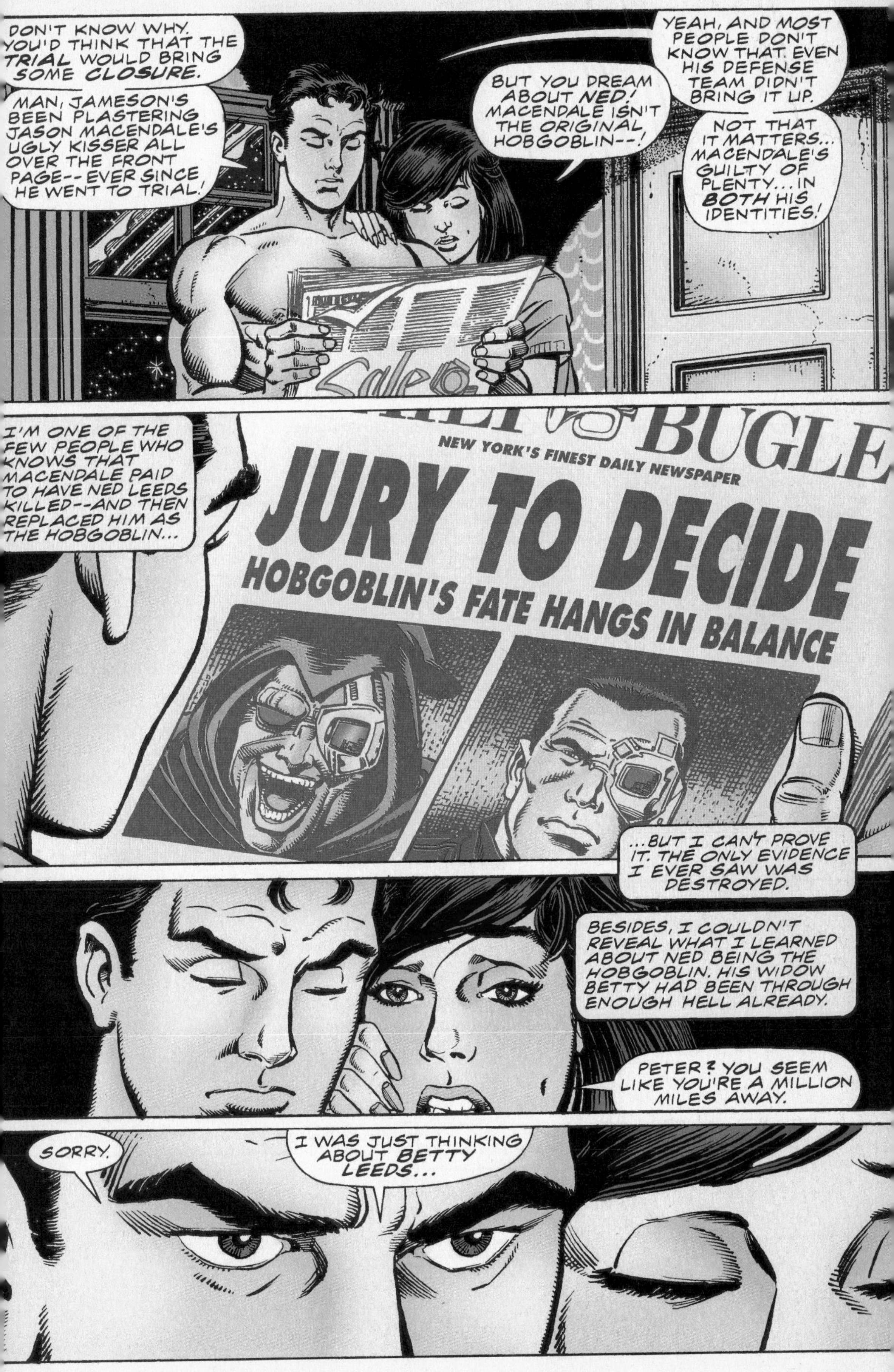
DON'T KNOW WHY. YOU'D THINK THAT THE TRIAL WOULD BRING SOME CLOSURE.
MAN, JAMESON'S BEEN PLASTERING JASON MACENDALE'S UGLY KISSER ALL OVER THE FRONT PAGE-- EVER SINCE HE WENT TO TRIAL!
BUT YOU DREAM ABOUT NED! MACENDALE ISN'T THE ORIGINAL HOBGOBLIN--!
YEAH, AND MOST PEOPLE DON'T KNOW THAT. EVEN HIS DEFENSE TEAM DIDN'T BRING IT UP.
NOT THAT IT MATTERS... MACENDALE'S GUILTY OF PLENTY... IN BOTH HIS IDENTITIES!
I'M ONE OF THE FEW PEOPLE WHO KNOWS THAT MACENDALE PAID TO HAVE NED LEEDS KILLED--AND THEN REPLACED HIM AS THE HOBGOBLIN...
BUGLE
NEW YORK'S FINEST DAILY NEWSPAPER
JURY TO DECIDE
HOBGOBLIN'S FATE HANGS IN BALANCE
...BUT I CAN'T PROVE IT. THE ONLY EVIDENCE I EVER SAW WAS DESTROYED.
BESIDES, I COULDN'T REVEAL WHAT I LEARNED ABOUT NED BEING THE HOBGOBLIN. HIS WIDOW BETTY HAD BEEN THROUGH ENOUGH HELL ALREADY.
PETER? YOU SEEM LIKE YOU'RE A MILLION MILES AWAY.
SORRY.
I WAS JUST THINKING ABOUT BETTY LEEDS...

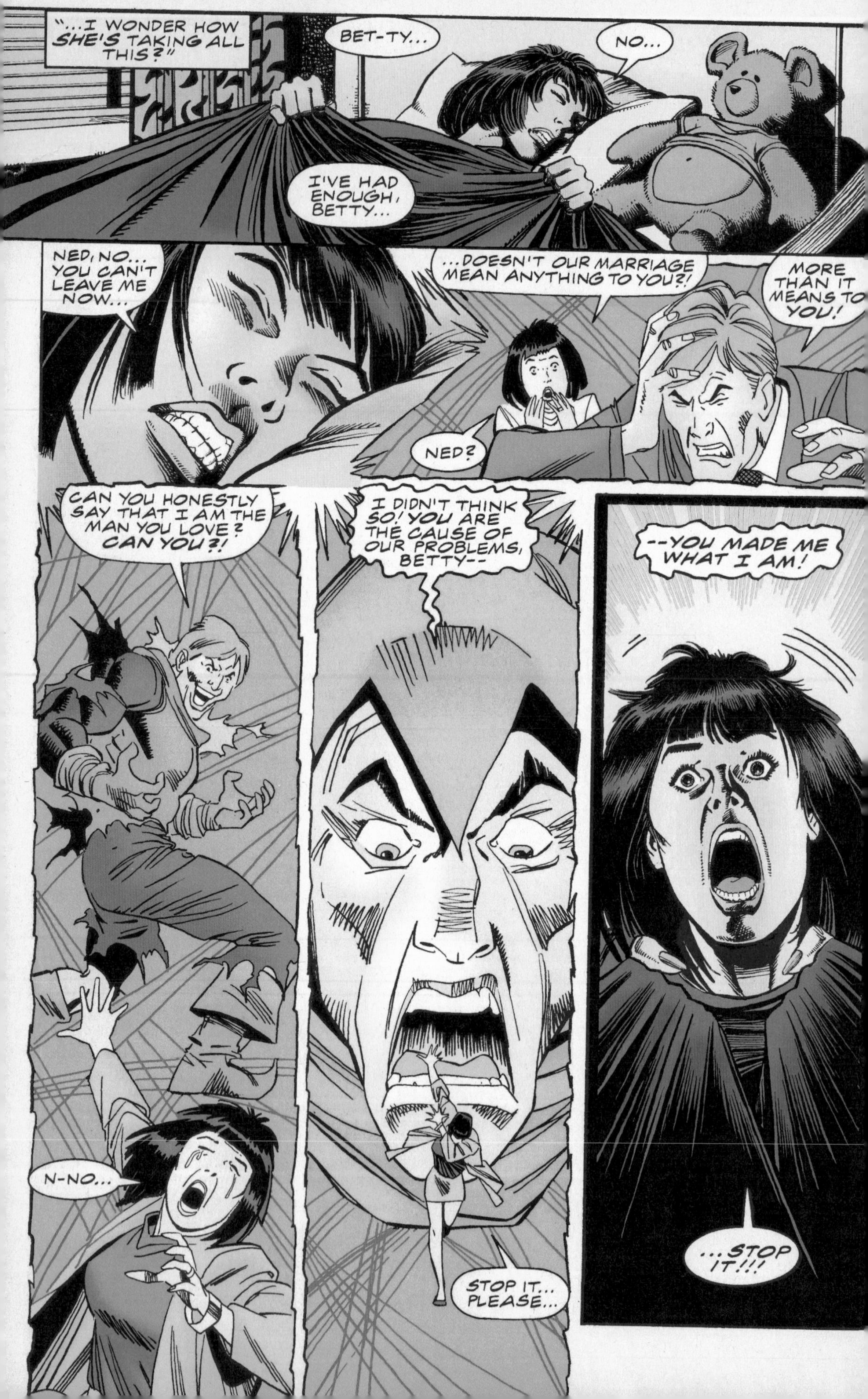
"...I WONDER HOW SHE'S TAKING ALL THIS?"
BET-TY...
NO...
I'VE HAD ENOUGH, BETTY...
NED, NO... YOU CAN'T LEAVE ME NOW...
...DOESN'T OUR MARRIAGE MEAN ANYTHING TO YOU?!
MORE THAN IT MEANS TO YOU!
NED?
CAN YOU HONESTLY SAY THAT I AM THE MAN YOU LOVE? CAN YOU?!
N-NO...
I DIDN'T THINK SO! YOU ARE THE CAUSE OF OUR PROBLEMS, BETTY--
STOP IT... PLEASE...
--YOU MADE ME WHAT I AM!
...STOP IT!!!

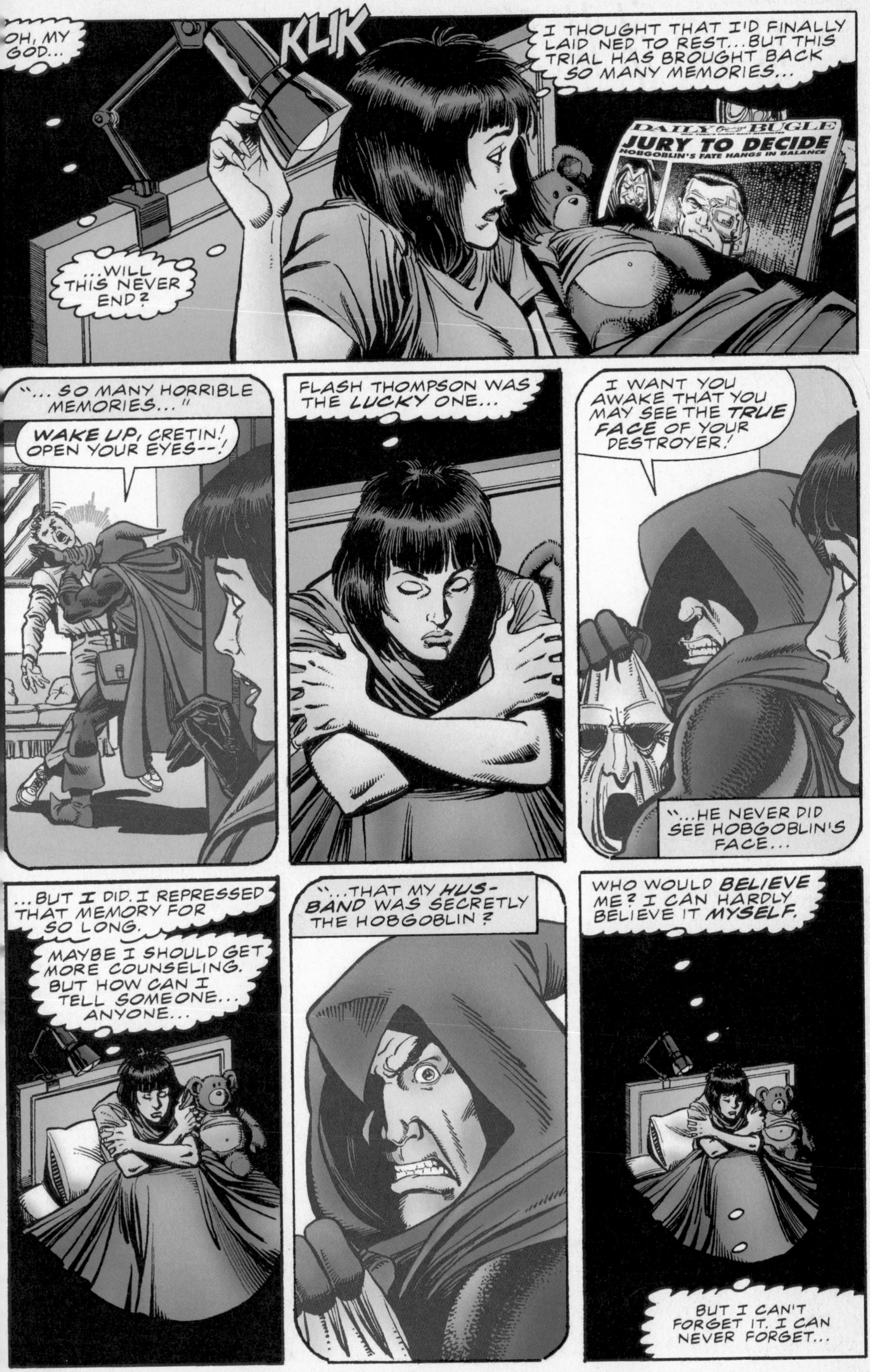
OH, MY GOD...
KLIK
I THOUGHT THAT I'D FINALLY LAID NED TO REST... BUT THIS TRIAL HAS BROUGHT BACK SO MANY MEMORIES...
DAILY BUGLE
JURY TO DECIDE
HOBGOBLIN'S FATE HANGS IN BALANCE
...WILL THIS NEVER END?
"... SO MANY HORRIBLE MEMORIES..."
WAKE UP, CRETIN! OPEN YOUR EYES--!
FLASH THOMPSON WAS THE LUCKY ONE...
I WANT YOU AWAKE THAT YOU MAY SEE THE TRUE FACE OF YOUR DESTROYER!
"...HE NEVER DID SEE HOBGOBLIN'S FACE...
...BUT I DID. I REPRESSED THAT MEMORY FOR SO LONG.
MAYBE I SHOULD GET MORE COUNSELING. BUT HOW CAN I TELL SOMEONE... ANYONE...
"...THAT MY HUSBAND WAS SECRETLY THE HOBGOBLIN?
WHO WOULD BELIEVE ME? I CAN HARDLY BELIEVE IT MYSELF.
BUT I CAN'T FORGET IT. I CAN NEVER FORGET...

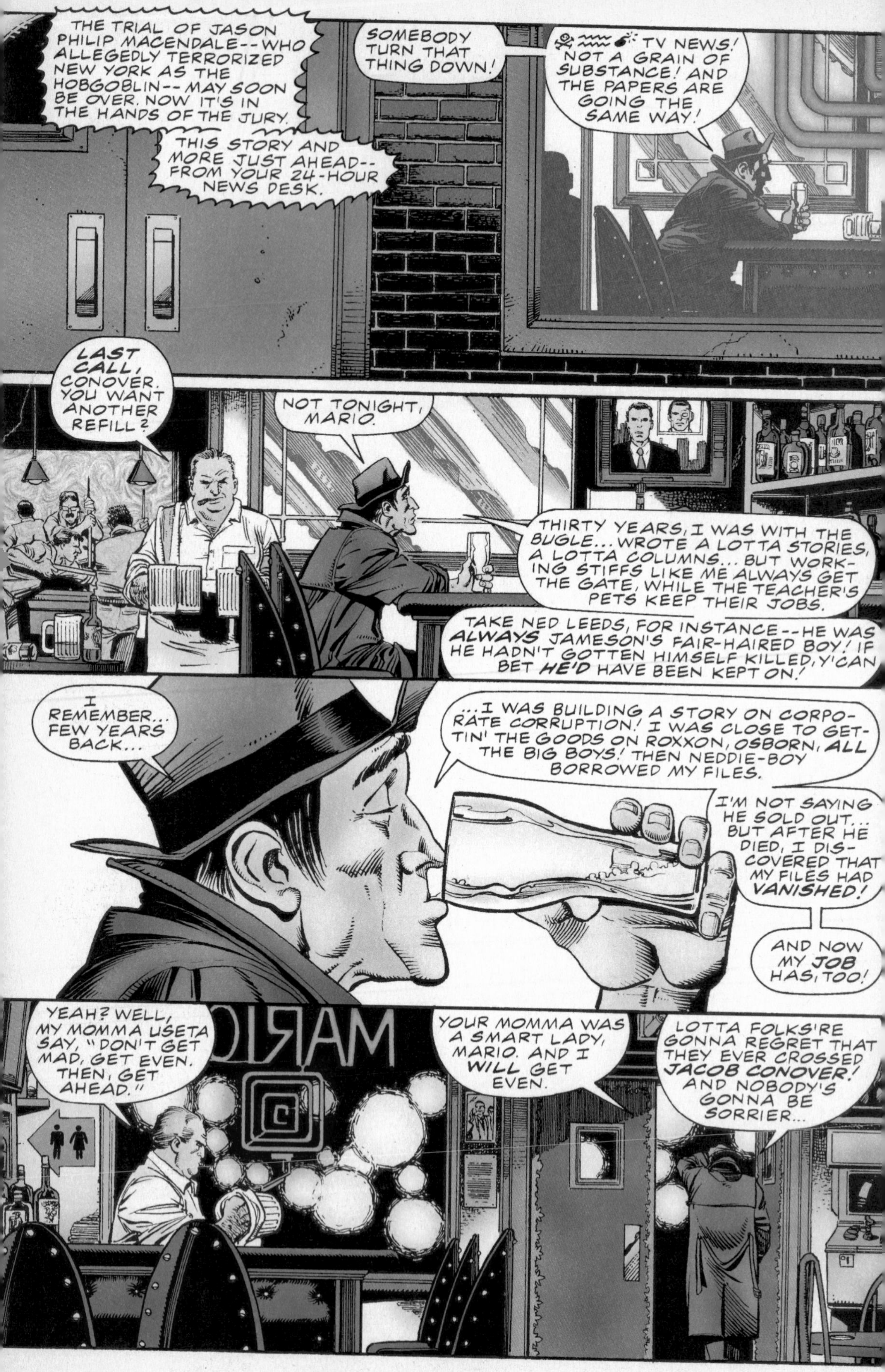
THE TRIAL OF JASON PHILIP MACENDALE--WHO ALLEGEDLY TERRORIZED NEW YORK AS THE HOBGOBLIN--MAY SOON BE OVER. NOW IT'S IN THE HANDS OF THE JURY.
THIS STORY AND MORE JUST AHEAD--FROM YOUR 24-HOUR NEWS DESK.
SOMEBODY TURN THAT THING DOWN!
TV NEWS! NOT A GRAIN OF SUBSTANCE! AND THE PAPERS ARE GOING THE SAME WAY!
LAST CALL, CONOVER. YOU WANT ANOTHER REFILL?
NOT TONIGHT, MARIO.
THIRTY YEARS, I WAS WITH THE BUGLE... WROTE A LOTTA STORIES, A LOTTA COLUMNS... BUT WORKING STIFFS LIKE ME ALWAYS GET THE GATE, WHILE THE TEACHER'S PETS KEEP THEIR JOBS.
TAKE NED LEEDS, FOR INSTANCE--HE WAS ALWAYS JAMESON'S FAIR-HAIRED BOY! IF HE HADN'T GOTTEN HIMSELF KILLED, Y'CAN BET HE'D HAVE BEEN KEPT ON!
I REMEMBER... FEW YEARS BACK...
...I WAS BUILDING A STORY ON CORPORATE CORRUPTION! I WAS CLOSE TO GETTIN' THE GOODS ON ROXXON, OSBORN, ALL THE BIG BOYS! THEN NEDDIE-BOY BORROWED MY FILES.
I'M NOT SAYING HE SOLD OUT... BUT AFTER HE DIED, I DISCOVERED THAT MY FILES HAD VANISHED!
AND NOW MY JOB HAS, TOO!
YEAH? WELL, MY MOMMA USETA SAY, "DON'T GET MAD, GET EVEN. THEN, GET AHEAD."
YOUR MOMMA WAS A SMART LADY, MARIO. AND I WILL GET EVEN.
LOTTA FOLKS'RE GONNA REGRET THAT THEY EVER CROSSED JACOB CONOVER! AND NOBODY'S GONNA BE SORRIER...

"...THAN *J. JONAH JAMESON!*"

WHERE'S THE JUSTICE?

EVEN IF MACENDALE GETS THE MAXIMUM, IT DOESN'T BRING BACK THE PEOPLE HE'S KILLED.

TOO MANY GOOD MEN DIE...

...TOO MANY LIKE NED LEEDS.

JONAH? ARE YOU STILL UP?

YOU WEREN'T GOING TO SMOKE THAT--?

NOT IF YOU DON'T WANT ME TO, DEAR. WHAT'S WEIGHING ON YOUR MIND THIS TIME?

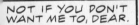

THE HOBGOBLIN TRIAL. REMEMBER I TOLD YOU...

"...ABOUT THE TIME HOBGOBLIN TRIED TO BLACK-MAIL ME? AND HOW THAT BLASTED SPIDER-MAN INTER-VENED? I WASN'T ABOUT TO BE BEHOLDEN TO HIM...

...SO I SECRETLY ASSIGNED NED LEEDS TO INVESTI-GATE THE HOBGOBLIN.

IF ONLY I'D INSIST-ED THAT HE STICK TO THAT ASSIGN-MENT...INSTEAD OF LETTING HIM RUN OFF TO BERLIN.

I WISH I COULD BELIEVE THAT, MARLA. BUT WHEN I THINK OF ALL THE HEARTACHE AND GRIEF BETTY SUFFERED AFTER NED DIED...

I LET HIM GO TO HIS DEATH.

JONAH, IT'S NOT YOUR FAULT--!

I CAN NEVER BRING HER HUSBAND BACK...

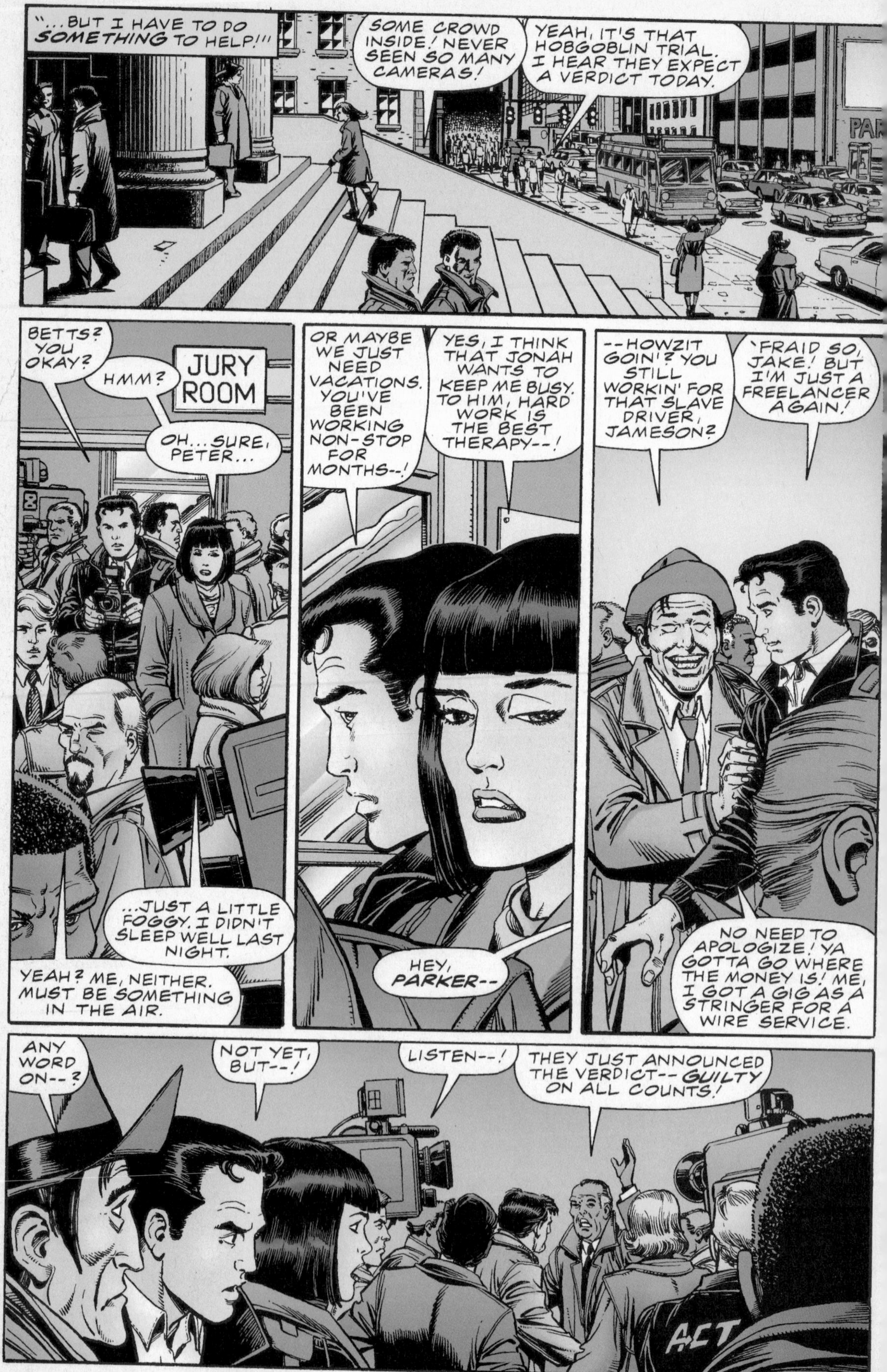
"...BUT I HAVE TO DO SOMETHING TO HELP!"
SOME CROWD INSIDE! NEVER SEEN SO MANY CAMERAS!
YEAH, IT'S THAT HOBGOBLIN TRIAL. I HEAR THEY EXPECT A VERDICT TODAY.
PAR
BETTS? YOU OKAY?
HMM?
JURY ROOM
OH... SURE, PETER...
...JUST A LITTLE FOGGY. I DIDN'T SLEEP WELL LAST NIGHT.
YEAH? ME, NEITHER. MUST BE SOMETHING IN THE AIR.
OR MAYBE WE JUST NEED VACATIONS. YOU'VE BEEN WORKING NON-STOP FOR MONTHS--!
YES, I THINK THAT JONAH WANTS TO KEEP ME BUSY. TO HIM, HARD WORK IS THE BEST THERAPY--!
HEY, PARKER--
--HOWZIT GOIN'? YOU STILL WORKIN' FOR THAT SLAVE DRIVER, JAMESON?
`FRAID SO, JAKE! BUT I'M JUST A FREELANCER AGAIN!
NO NEED TO APOLOGIZE! YA GOTTA GO WHERE THE MONEY IS! ME, I GOT A GIG AS A STRINGER FOR A WIRE SERVICE.
ANY WORD ON--?
NOT YET, BUT--!
LISTEN--!
THEY JUST ANNOUNCED THE VERDICT--GUILTY ON ALL COUNTS!
ACT

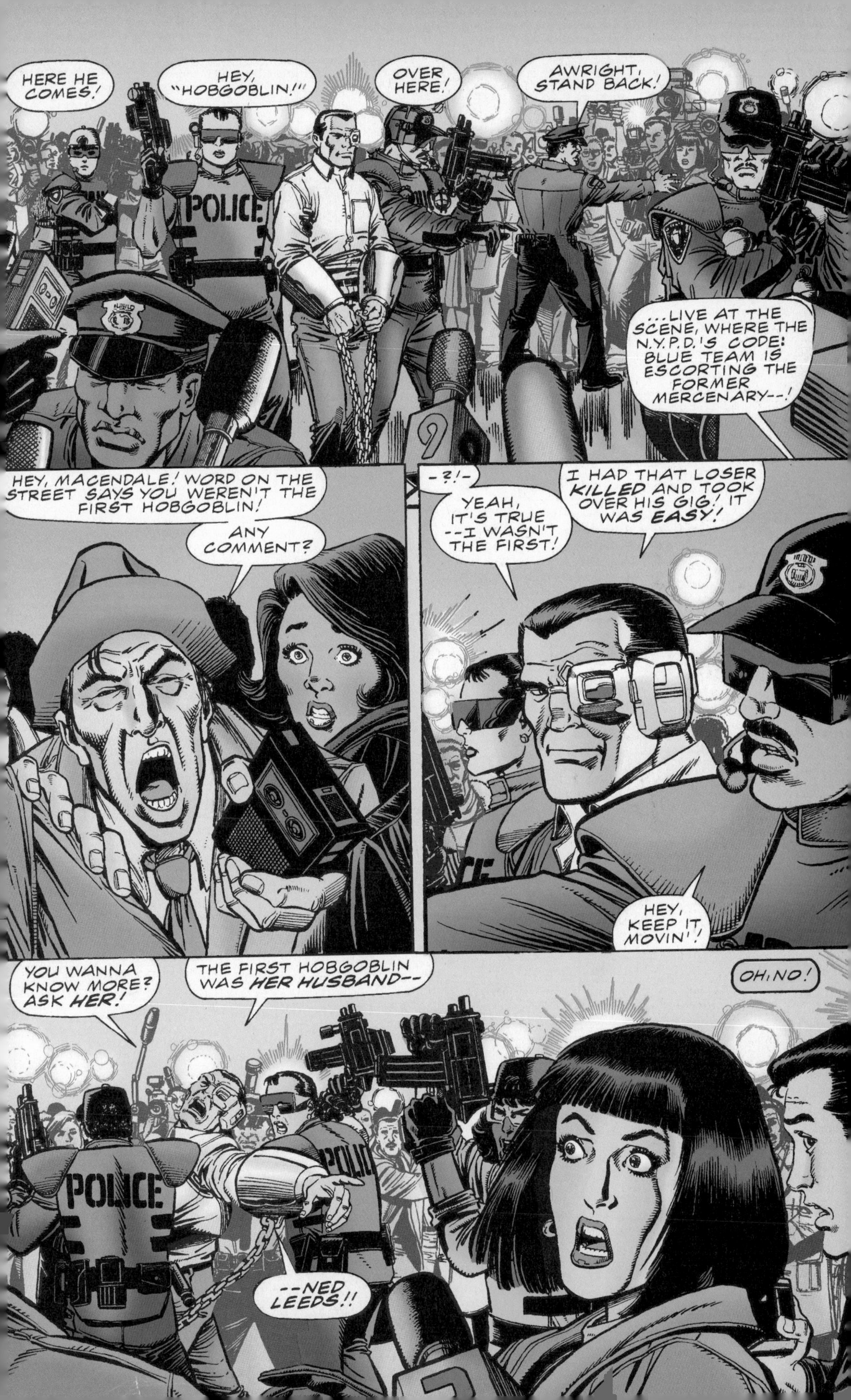
HERE HE COMES!
HEY, "HOBGOBLIN!"
OVER HERE!
AWRIGHT, STAND BACK!
...LIVE AT THE SCENE, WHERE THE N.Y.P.D.'S CODE: BLUE TEAM IS ESCORTING THE FORMER MERCENARY--!
HEY, MACENDALE! WORD ON THE STREET SAYS YOU WEREN'T THE FIRST HOBGOBLIN!
ANY COMMENT?
-?!-
YEAH, IT'S TRUE --I WASN'T THE FIRST!
I HAD THAT LOSER KILLED AND TOOK OVER HIS GIG! IT WAS EASY!
HEY, KEEP IT MOVIN'!
YOU WANNA KNOW MORE? ASK HER!
THE FIRST HOBGOBLIN WAS HER HUSBAND--
OH, NO!
--NED LEEDS!!

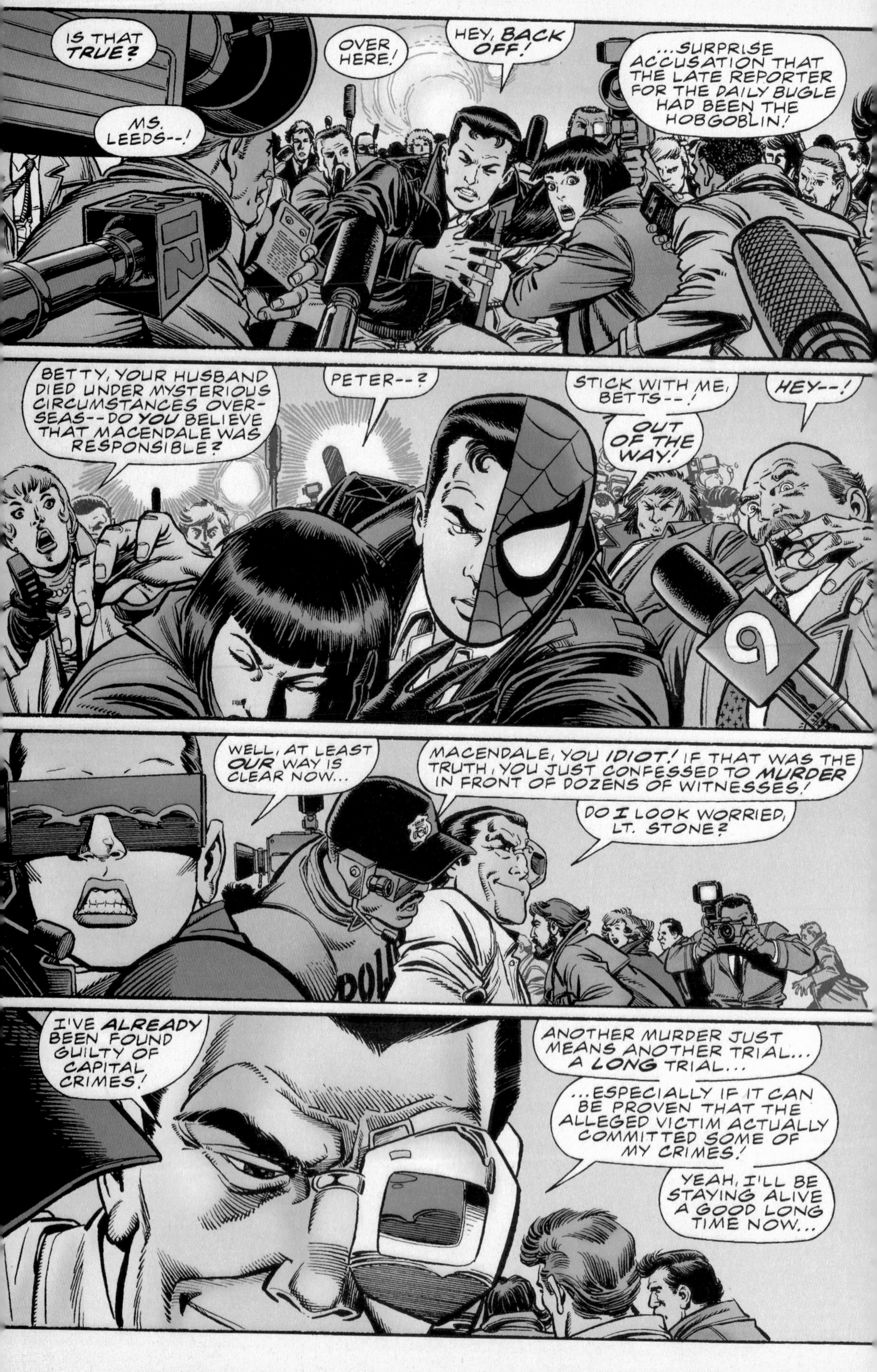
IS THAT TRUE?
MS. LEEDS--!
OVER HERE!
HEY, BACK OFF!
...SURPRISE ACCUSATION THAT THE LATE REPORTER FOR THE DAILY BUGLE HAD BEEN THE HOBGOBLIN!
BETTY, YOUR HUSBAND DIED UNDER MYSTERIOUS CIRCUMSTANCES OVERSEAS--DO YOU BELIEVE THAT MACENDALE WAS RESPONSIBLE?
PETER--?
STICK WITH ME, BETTS--!
OUT OF THE WAY!
HEY--!
WELL, AT LEAST OUR WAY IS CLEAR NOW...
MACENDALE, YOU IDIOT! IF THAT WAS THE TRUTH, YOU JUST CONFESSED TO MURDER IN FRONT OF DOZENS OF WITNESSES!
DO I LOOK WORRIED, LT. STONE?
I'VE ALREADY BEEN FOUND GUILTY OF CAPITAL CRIMES!
ANOTHER MURDER JUST MEANS ANOTHER TRIAL... A LONG TRIAL...
...ESPECIALLY IF IT CAN BE PROVEN THAT THE ALLEGED VICTIM ACTUALLY COMMITTED SOME OF MY CRIMES!
YEAH, I'LL BE STAYING ALIVE A GOOD LONG TIME NOW...

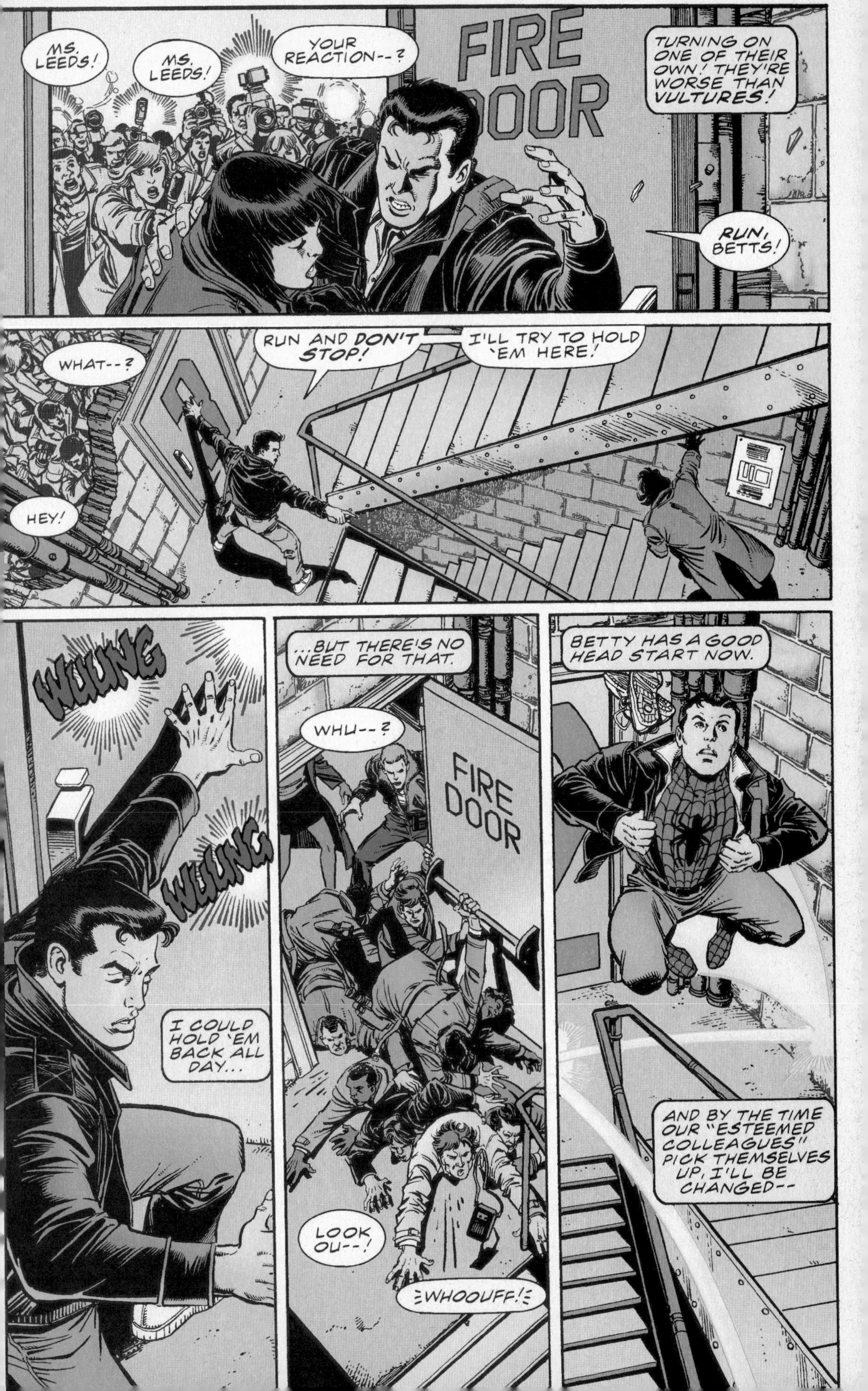
MS. LEEDS!
MS. LEEDS!
YOUR REACTION--?
FIRE DOOR
TURNING ON ONE OF THEIR OWN! THEY'RE WORSE THAN VULTURES!
RUN, BETTS!
WHAT--?
RUN AND DON'T STOP!
I'LL TRY TO HOLD 'EM HERE!
HEY!
WUUNG
WUUNG
I COULD HOLD 'EM BACK ALL DAY...
...BUT THERE'S NO NEED FOR THAT.
WHU--?
FIRE DOOR
LOOK OU--!
WHOOUFF!
BETTY HAS A GOOD HEAD START NOW.
AND BY THE TIME OUR "ESTEEMED COLLEAGUES" PICK THEMSELVES UP, I'LL BE CHANGED--

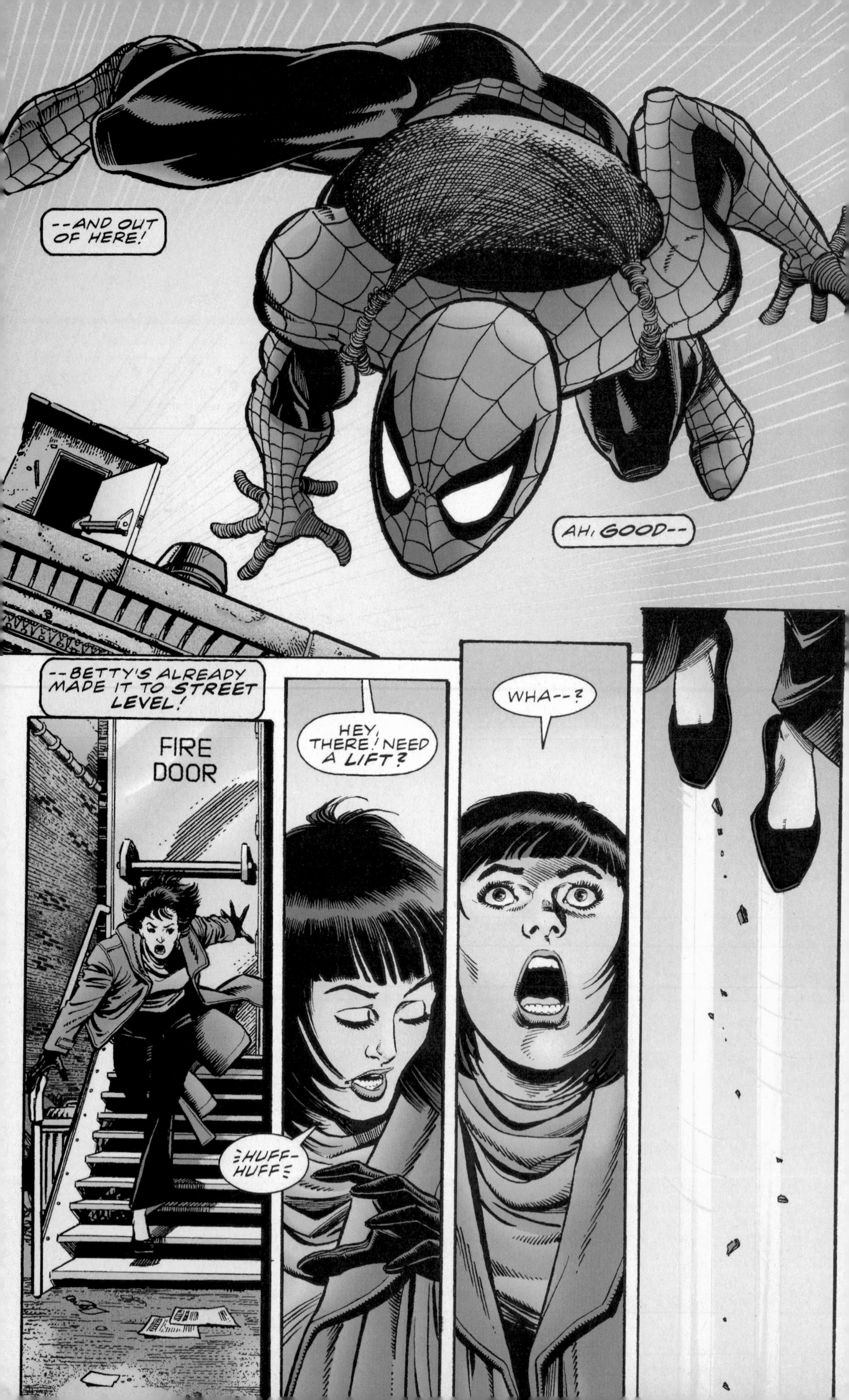
--AND OUT OF HERE!
AH, GOOD--
--BETTY'S ALREADY MADE IT TO STREET LEVEL!
FIRE DOOR
HUFF-HUFF
HEY, THERE! NEED A LIFT?
WHA--?

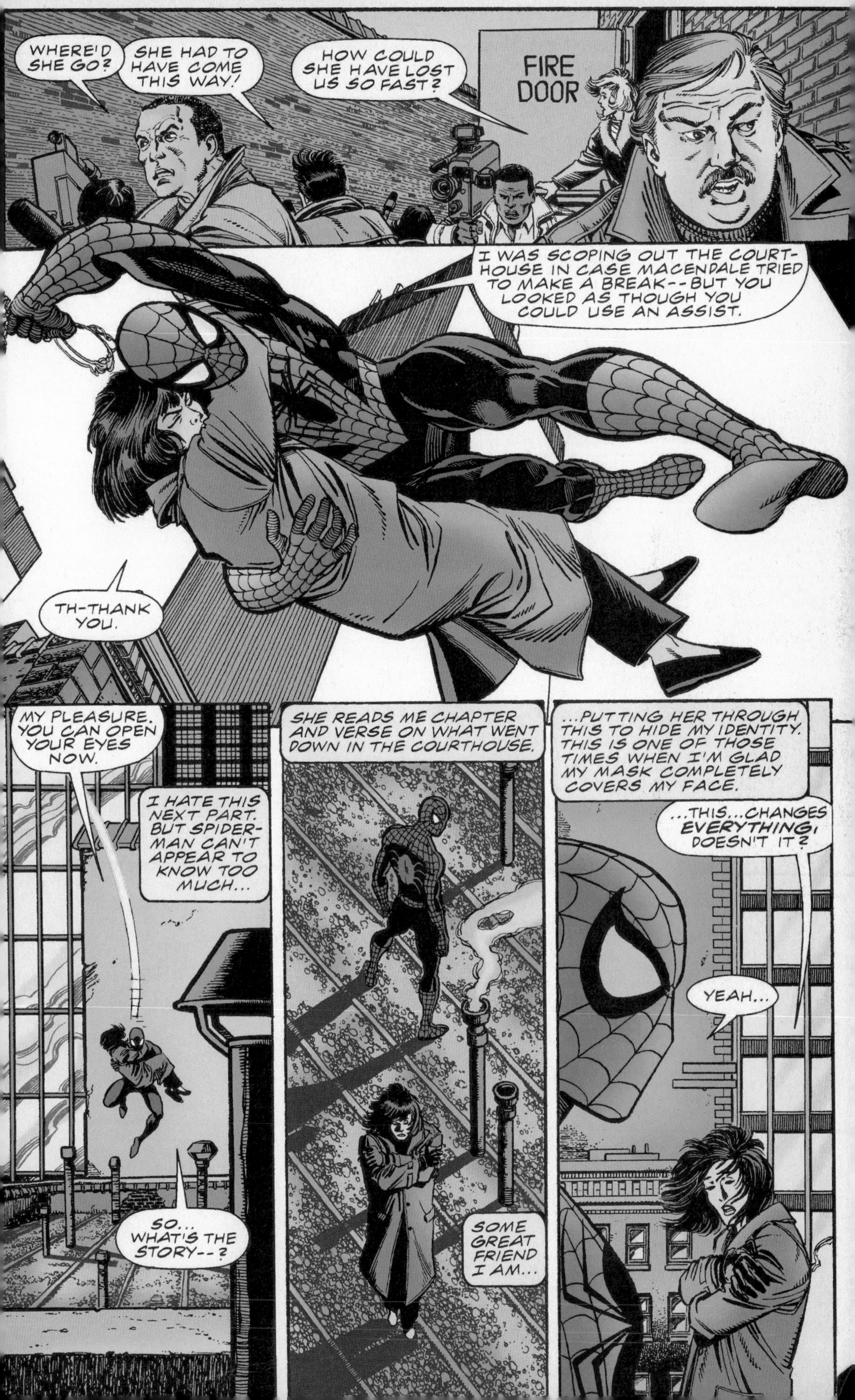

WHERE'D SHE GO?
SHE HAD TO HAVE COME THIS WAY!
HOW COULD SHE HAVE LOST US SO FAST?
FIRE DOOR
I WAS SCOPING OUT THE COURT-HOUSE IN CASE MACENDALE TRIED TO MAKE A BREAK--BUT YOU LOOKED AS THOUGH YOU COULD USE AN ASSIST.
TH-THANK YOU.
MY PLEASURE. YOU CAN OPEN YOUR EYES NOW.
I HATE THIS NEXT PART. BUT SPIDER-MAN CAN'T APPEAR TO KNOW TOO MUCH...
SO... WHAT'S THE STORY--?
SHE READS ME CHAPTER AND VERSE ON WHAT WENT DOWN IN THE COURTHOUSE.
SOME GREAT FRIEND I AM...
...PUTTING HER THROUGH THIS TO HIDE MY IDENTITY. THIS IS ONE OF THOSE TIMES WHEN I'M GLAD MY MASK COMPLETELY COVERS MY FACE.
...THIS...CHANGES EVERYTHING, DOESN'T IT?
YEAH...

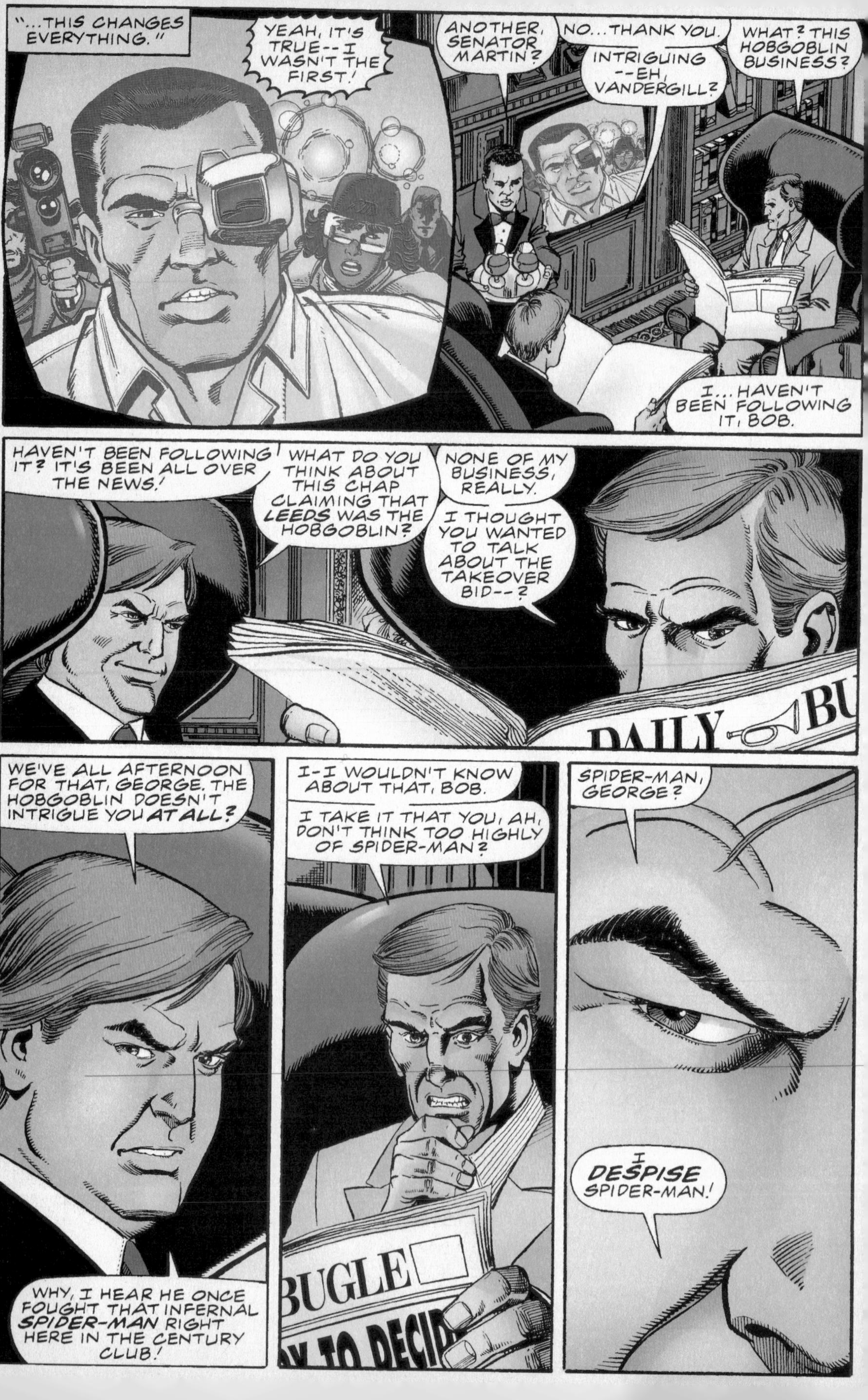
"...THIS CHANGES EVERYTHING."
YEAH, IT'S TRUE--I WASN'T THE FIRST!
ANOTHER, SENATOR MARTIN?
NO...THANK YOU.
INTRIGUING --EH, VANDERGILL?
WHAT? THIS HOBGOBLIN BUSINESS?
I... HAVEN'T BEEN FOLLOWING IT, BOB.
HAVEN'T BEEN FOLLOWING IT? IT'S BEEN ALL OVER THE NEWS!
WHAT DO YOU THINK ABOUT THIS CHAP CLAIMING THAT LEEDS WAS THE HOBGOBLIN?
NONE OF MY BUSINESS, REALLY.
I THOUGHT YOU WANTED TO TALK ABOUT THE TAKEOVER BID--?
DAILY BU
WE'VE ALL AFTERNOON FOR THAT, GEORGE. THE HOBGOBLIN DOESN'T INTRIGUE YOU AT ALL?
WHY, I HEAR HE ONCE FOUGHT THAT INFERNAL SPIDER-MAN RIGHT HERE IN THE CENTURY CLUB!
I-I WOULDN'T KNOW ABOUT THAT, BOB.
I TAKE IT THAT YOU, AH, DON'T THINK TOO HIGHLY OF SPIDER-MAN?
BUGLE
SPIDER-MAN, GEORGE?
I DESPISE SPIDER-MAN!

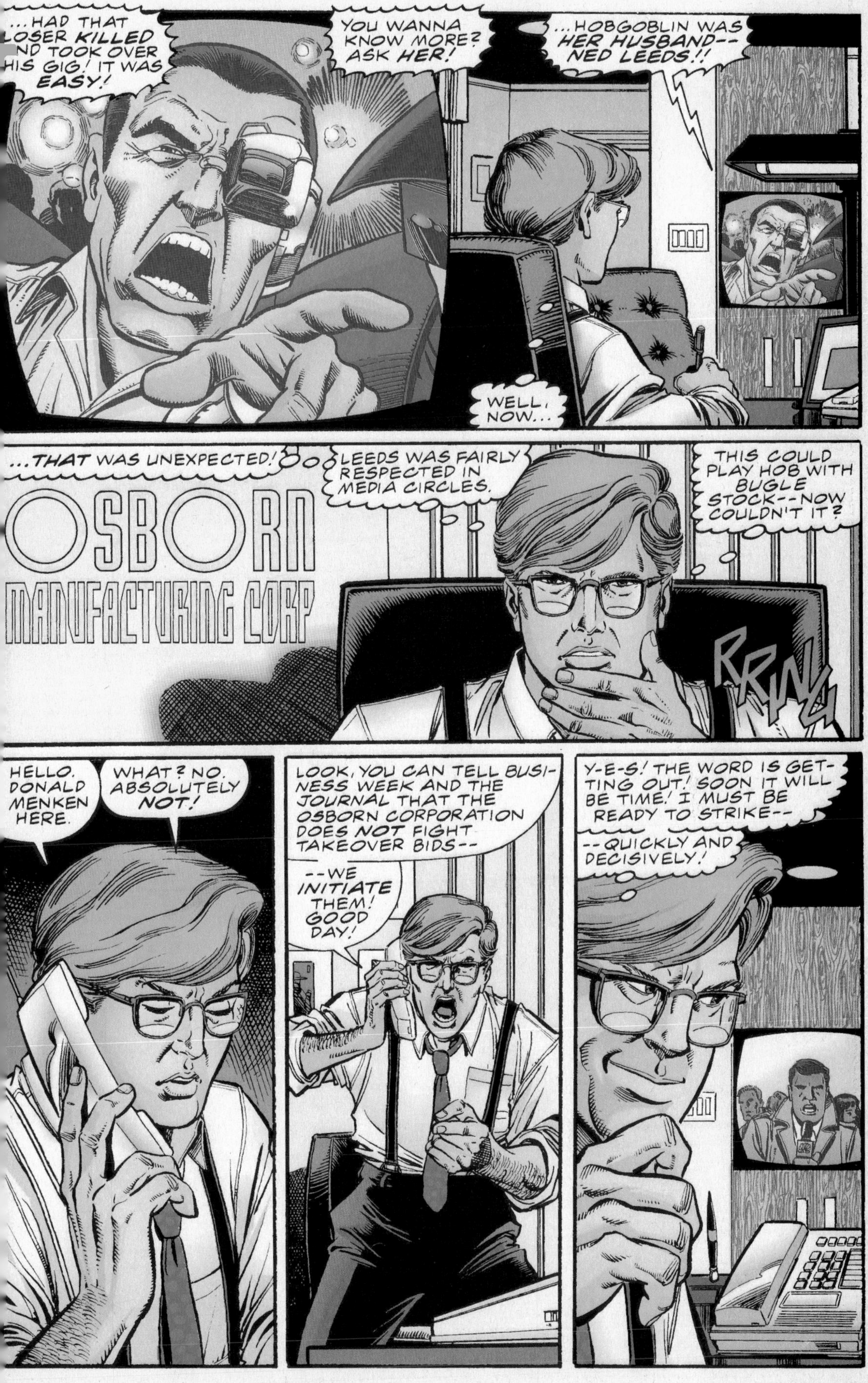
...HAD THAT LOSER KILLED AND TOOK OVER HIS GIG! IT WAS EASY!
YOU WANNA KNOW MORE? ASK HER!
...HOBGOBLIN WAS HER HUSBAND--NED LEEDS!!
WELL, NOW...
...THAT WAS UNEXPECTED!
LEEDS WAS FAIRLY RESPECTED IN MEDIA CIRCLES.
THIS COULD PLAY HOB WITH BUGLE STOCK--NOW COULDN'T IT?
OSBORN MANUFACTURING CORP
RRRING
HELLO. DONALD MENKEN HERE.
WHAT? NO. ABSOLUTELY NOT!
LOOK, YOU CAN TELL BUSINESS WEEK AND THE JOURNAL THAT THE OSBORN CORPORATION DOES NOT FIGHT TAKEOVER BIDS--
--WE INITIATE THEM! GOOD DAY!
Y-E-S! THE WORD IS GETTING OUT! SOON IT WILL BE TIME! I MUST BE READY TO STRIKE--
--QUICKLY AND DECISIVELY!

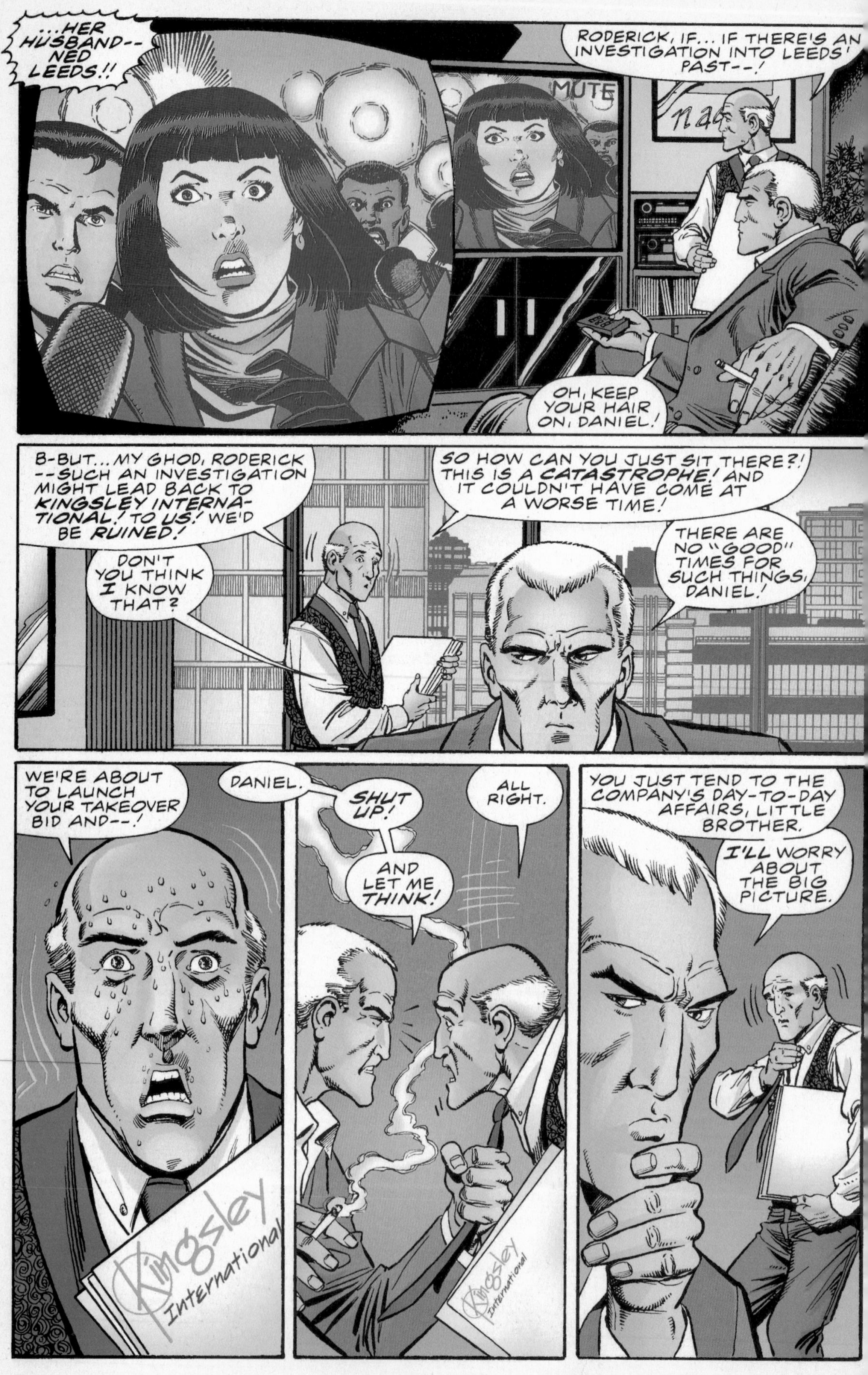
...HER HUSBAND--NED LEEDS!!
MUTE
RODERICK, IF... IF THERE'S AN INVESTIGATION INTO LEEDS' PAST--!
OH, KEEP YOUR HAIR ON, DANIEL!
B-BUT... MY GHOD, RODERICK --SUCH AN INVESTIGATION MIGHT LEAD BACK TO KINGSLEY INTERNATIONAL! TO US! WE'D BE RUINED!
DON'T YOU THINK I KNOW THAT?
SO HOW CAN YOU JUST SIT THERE?! THIS IS A CATASTROPHE! AND IT COULDN'T HAVE COME AT A WORSE TIME!
THERE ARE NO "GOOD" TIMES FOR SUCH THINGS, DANIEL!
WE'RE ABOUT TO LAUNCH YOUR TAKEOVER BID AND--!
Kingsley International
DANIEL.
SHUT UP!
AND LET ME THINK!
ALL RIGHT.
Kingsley International
YOU JUST TEND TO THE COMPANY'S DAY-TO-DAY AFFAIRS, LITTLE BROTHER.
I'LL WORRY ABOUT THE BIG PICTURE.

...SURPRISE ACCUSATION THAT THE LATE REPORTER FOR THE DAILY BUGLE HAD BEEN THE HOBGOBLIN!

POLICE SOURCES CONFIRM THE EXISTENCE OF AT LEAST ONE PREVIOUS "HOBGOBLIN"--

--ONE SAMUEL "LEFTY" DONOVAN, WHO DIED WHILE FIGHTING SPIDER-MAN-- BUT THEY ARE SO FAR REFUSING COMMENT ABOUT LEEDS.

HMM!

COMPUTER!

YES, DOCTOR HARROW?

ACCESS ARCHIVAL FOOTAGE OF SPIDER-MAN-- CHECKING FOR OPPONENT: HOBGOBLIN.

COMPARE FOOTAGE IMMEDIATELY BEFORE AND AFTER THE DATE RECORDED FOR THE DEATH OF ONE NED LEEDS.

RUNNING...

...SIGNIFICANT DIFFERENCES NOTED IN BODY LANGUAGE AND FIGHTING STYLE.

YES, THEY ARE DIFFERENT MEN. EVEN A *FOOL* COULD SEE THAT--

--ONCE HE KNEW WHAT TO LOOK FOR. AND ALL THE FOOLS WILL BE LOOKING FOR IT NOW.

BAH! NO WONDER MACEN-DALE WAS CAPTURED!

MY OPERATIONS BEDEVILED SPIDER-MAN FOR YEARS--

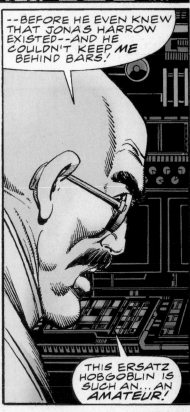

--BEFORE HE EVEN KNEW THAT JONAS HARROW EXISTED--AND HE COULDN'T KEEP *ME* BEHIND BARS!

THIS ERSATZ HOBGOBLIN IS SUCH AN... AN *AMATEUR!*

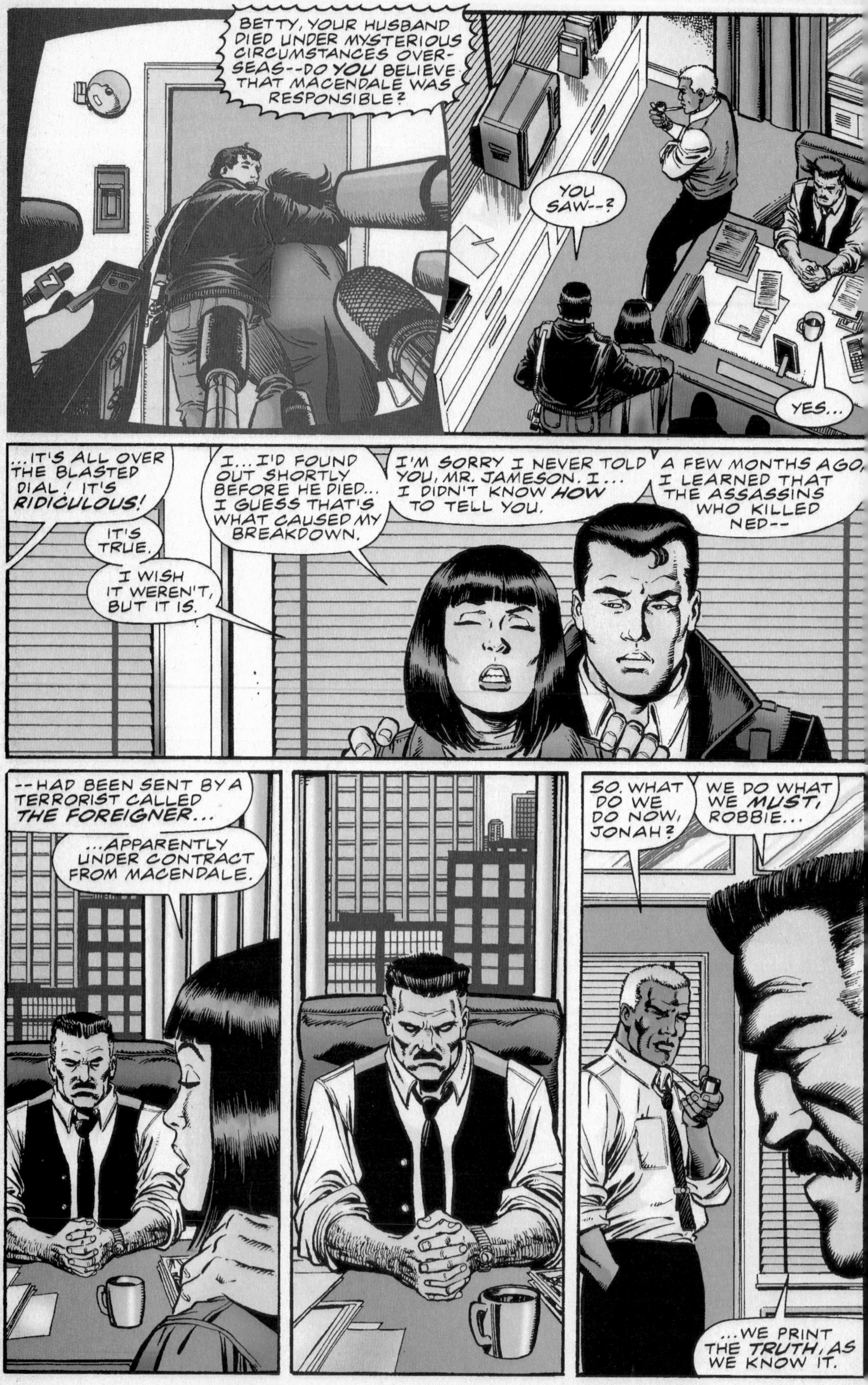

BETTY, YOUR HUSBAND DIED UNDER MYSTERIOUS CIRCUMSTANCES OVER-SEAS--DO YOU BELIEVE THAT MACENDALE WAS RESPONSIBLE?
YOU SAW--?
YES...
...IT'S ALL OVER THE BLASTED DIAL! IT'S RIDICULOUS!
IT'S TRUE.
I WISH IT WEREN'T, BUT IT IS.
I... I'D FOUND OUT SHORTLY BEFORE HE DIED... I GUESS THAT'S WHAT CAUSED MY BREAKDOWN.
I'M SORRY I NEVER TOLD YOU, MR. JAMESON. I... I DIDN'T KNOW HOW TO TELL YOU.
A FEW MONTHS AGO, I LEARNED THAT THE ASSASSINS WHO KILLED NED--
--HAD BEEN SENT BY A TERRORIST CALLED THE FOREIGNER...
...APPARENTLY UNDER CONTRACT FROM MACENDALE.
SO. WHAT DO WE DO NOW, JONAH?
WE DO WHAT WE MUST, ROBBIE...
...WE PRINT THE TRUTH, AS WE KNOW IT.

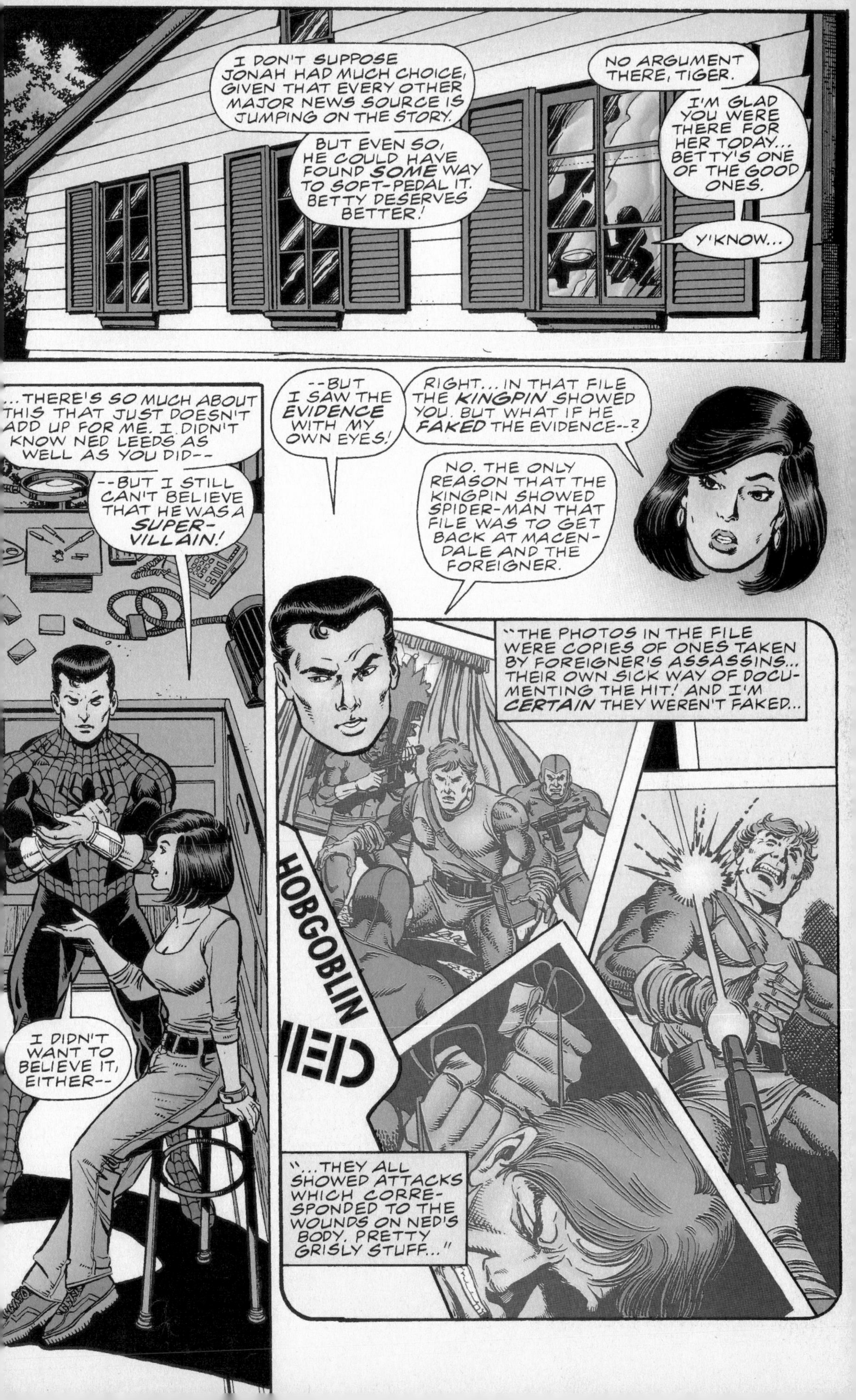
I DON'T SUPPOSE JONAH HAD MUCH CHOICE, GIVEN THAT EVERY OTHER MAJOR NEWS SOURCE IS JUMPING ON THE STORY.
BUT EVEN SO, HE COULD HAVE FOUND SOME WAY TO SOFT-PEDAL IT. BETTY DESERVES BETTER!
NO ARGUMENT THERE, TIGER.
I'M GLAD YOU WERE THERE FOR HER TODAY... BETTY'S ONE OF THE GOOD ONES.
Y'KNOW...
...THERE'S SO MUCH ABOUT THIS THAT JUST DOESN'T ADD UP FOR ME. I DIDN'T KNOW NED LEEDS AS WELL AS YOU DID--
--BUT I STILL CAN'T BELIEVE THAT HE WAS A SUPER-VILLAIN!
--BUT I SAW THE EVIDENCE WITH MY OWN EYES!
RIGHT... IN THAT FILE THE KINGPIN SHOWED YOU. BUT WHAT IF HE FAKED THE EVIDENCE--?
NO. THE ONLY REASON THAT THE KINGPIN SHOWED SPIDER-MAN THAT FILE WAS TO GET BACK AT MACENDALE AND THE FOREIGNER.
"THE PHOTOS IN THE FILE WERE COPIES OF ONES TAKEN BY FOREIGNER'S ASSASSINS... THEIR OWN SICK WAY OF DOCUMENTING THE HIT! AND I'M CERTAIN THEY WEREN'T FAKED...
HOBGOBLIN
NED
I DIDN'T WANT TO BELIEVE IT, EITHER--
"...THEY ALL SHOWED ATTACKS WHICH CORRESPONDED TO THE WOUNDS ON NED'S BODY. PRETTY GRISLY STUFF..."

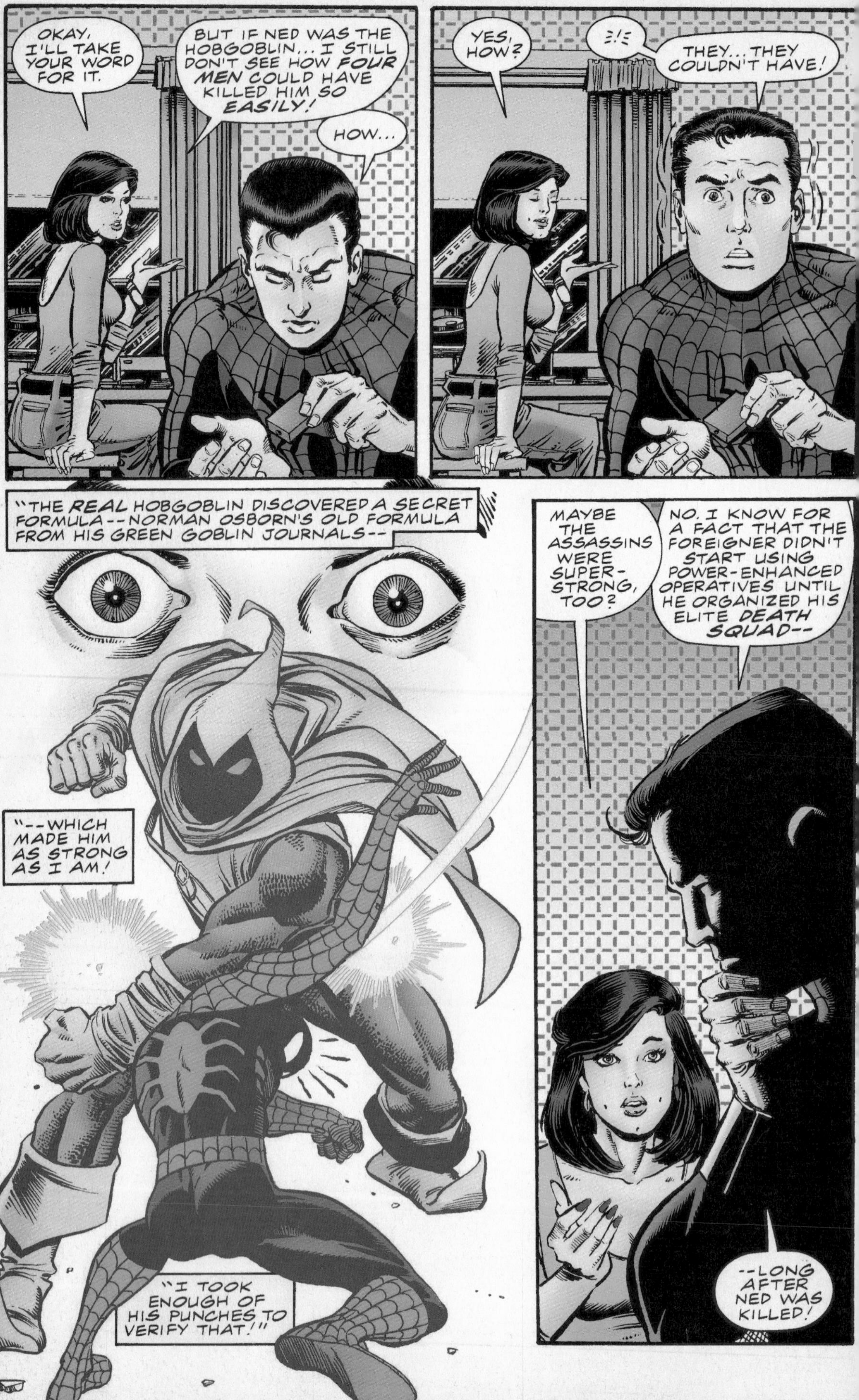
OKAY, I'LL TAKE YOUR WORD FOR IT.
BUT IF NED WAS THE HOBGOBLIN... I STILL DON'T SEE HOW FOUR MEN COULD HAVE KILLED HIM SO EASILY!
HOW...
YES, HOW?
!!
THEY... THEY COULDN'T HAVE!
"THE REAL HOBGOBLIN DISCOVERED A SECRET FORMULA--NORMAN OSBORN'S OLD FORMULA FROM HIS GREEN GOBLIN JOURNALS--
"--WHICH MADE HIM AS STRONG AS I AM!
"I TOOK ENOUGH OF HIS PUNCHES TO VERIFY THAT!"
MAYBE THE ASSASSINS WERE SUPER-STRONG, TOO?
NO. I KNOW FOR A FACT THAT THE FOREIGNER DIDN'T START USING POWER-ENHANCED OPERATIVES UNTIL HE ORGANIZED HIS ELITE DEATH SQUAD--
--LONG AFTER NED WAS KILLED!

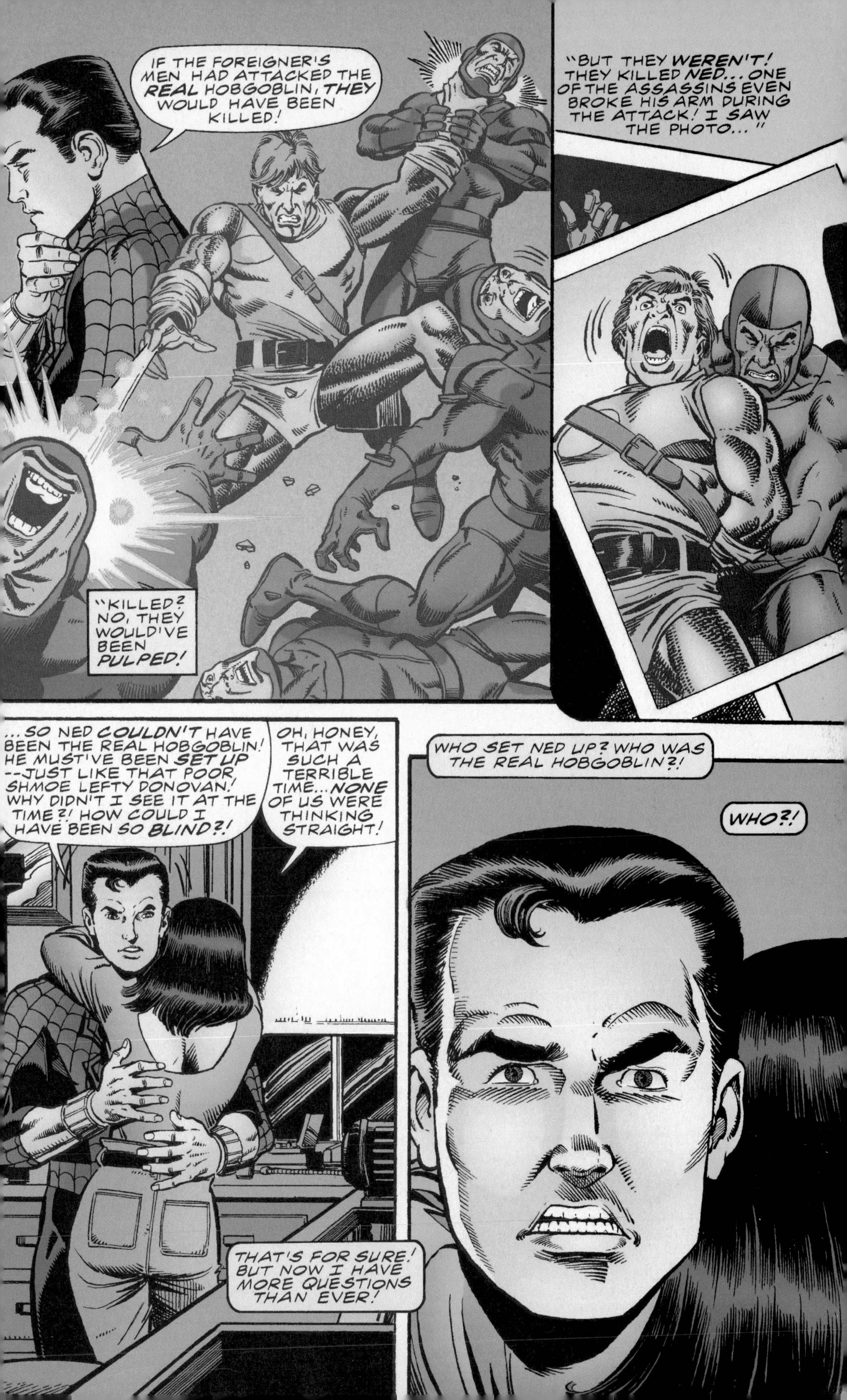
IF THE FOREIGNER'S MEN HAD ATTACKED THE REAL HOBGOBLIN, THEY WOULD HAVE BEEN KILLED!
"KILLED? NO, THEY WOULD'VE BEEN PULPED!
"BUT THEY WEREN'T! THEY KILLED NED... ONE OF THE ASSASSINS EVEN BROKE HIS ARM DURING THE ATTACK! I SAW THE PHOTO..."
...SO NED COULDN'T HAVE BEEN THE REAL HOBGOBLIN! HE MUST'VE BEEN SET UP --JUST LIKE THAT POOR SHMOE LEFTY DONOVAN! WHY DIDN'T I SEE IT AT THE TIME?! HOW COULD I HAVE BEEN SO BLIND?!
OH, HONEY, THAT WAS SUCH A TERRIBLE TIME... NONE OF US WERE THINKING STRAIGHT!
THAT'S FOR SURE! BUT NOW I HAVE MORE QUESTIONS THAN EVER!
WHO SET NED UP? WHO WAS THE REAL HOBGOBLIN?!
WHO?!

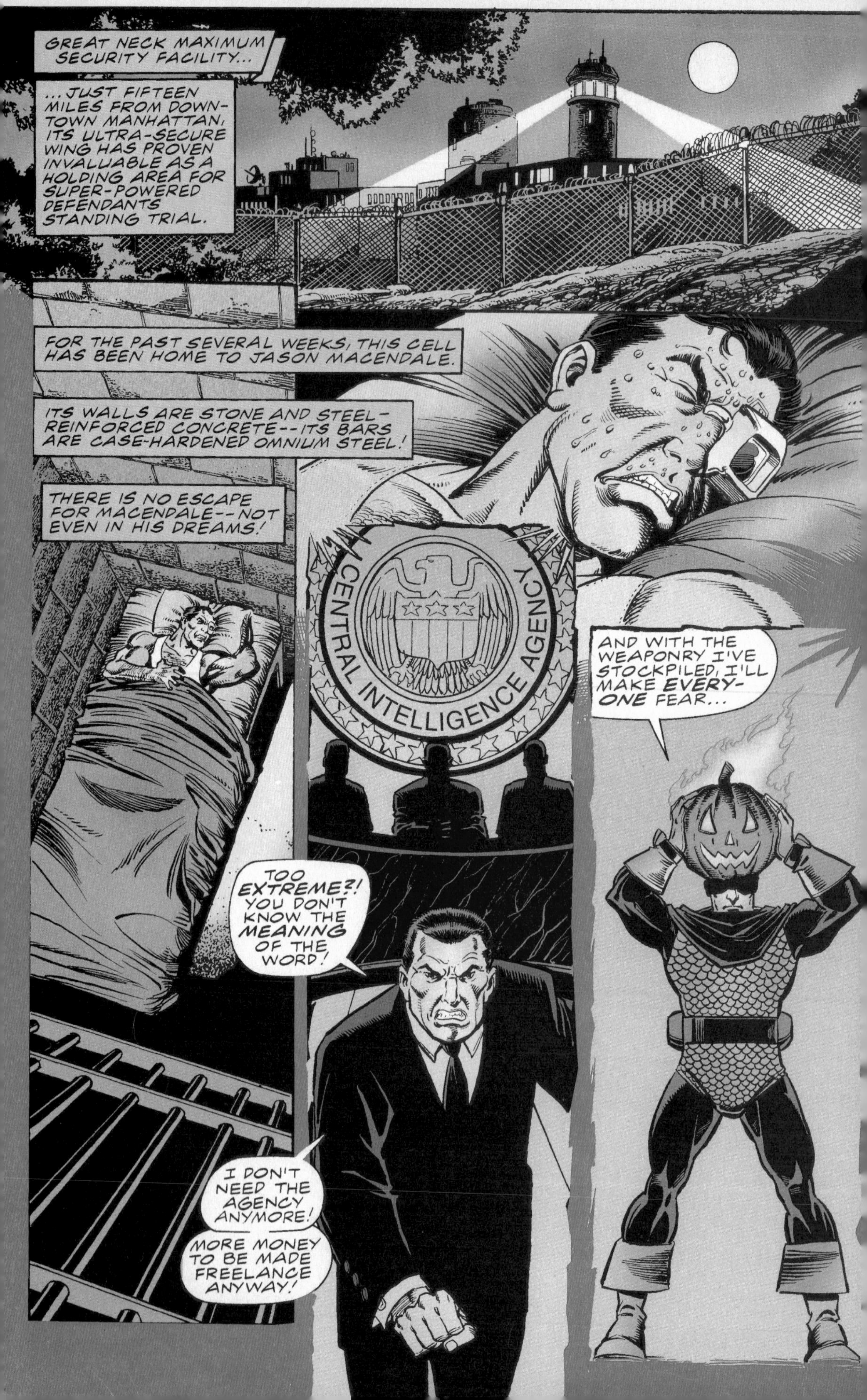
GREAT NECK MAXIMUM SECURITY FACILITY...
...JUST FIFTEEN MILES FROM DOWN-TOWN MANHATTAN, ITS ULTRA-SECURE WING HAS PROVEN INVALUABLE AS A HOLDING AREA FOR SUPER-POWERED DEFENDANTS STANDING TRIAL.
FOR THE PAST SEVERAL WEEKS, THIS CELL HAS BEEN HOME TO JASON MACENDALE.
ITS WALLS ARE STONE AND STEEL-REINFORCED CONCRETE--ITS BARS ARE CASE-HARDENED OMNIUM STEEL!
THERE IS NO ESCAPE FOR MACENDALE--NOT EVEN IN HIS DREAMS!
CENTRAL INTELLIGENCE AGENCY
TOO EXTREME?! YOU DON'T KNOW THE MEANING OF THE WORD!
I DON'T NEED THE AGENCY ANYMORE!
MORE MONEY TO BE MADE FREELANCE ANYWAY!
AND WITH THE WEAPONRY I'VE STOCKPILED, I'LL MAKE EVERY-ONE FEAR...

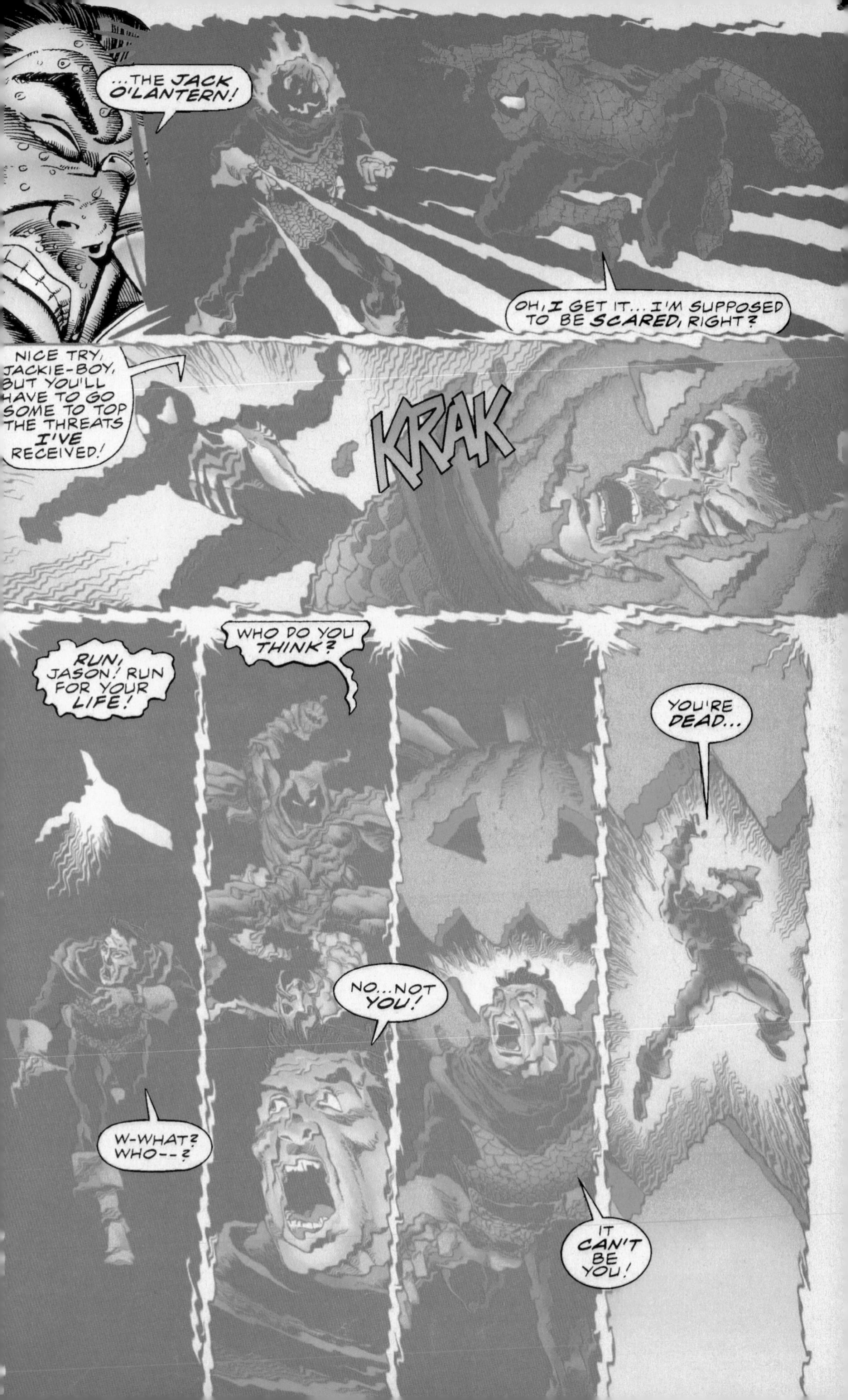

...THE JACK O'LANTERN!
OH, I GET IT... I'M SUPPOSED TO BE SCARED, RIGHT?
NICE TRY, JACKIE-BOY, BUT YOU'LL HAVE TO GO SOME TO TOP THE THREATS I'VE RECEIVED!
KRAK
RUN, JASON! RUN FOR YOUR LIFE!
W-WHAT? WHO--?
WHO DO YOU THINK?
NO...NOT YOU!
IT CAN'T BE YOU!
YOU'RE DEAD...

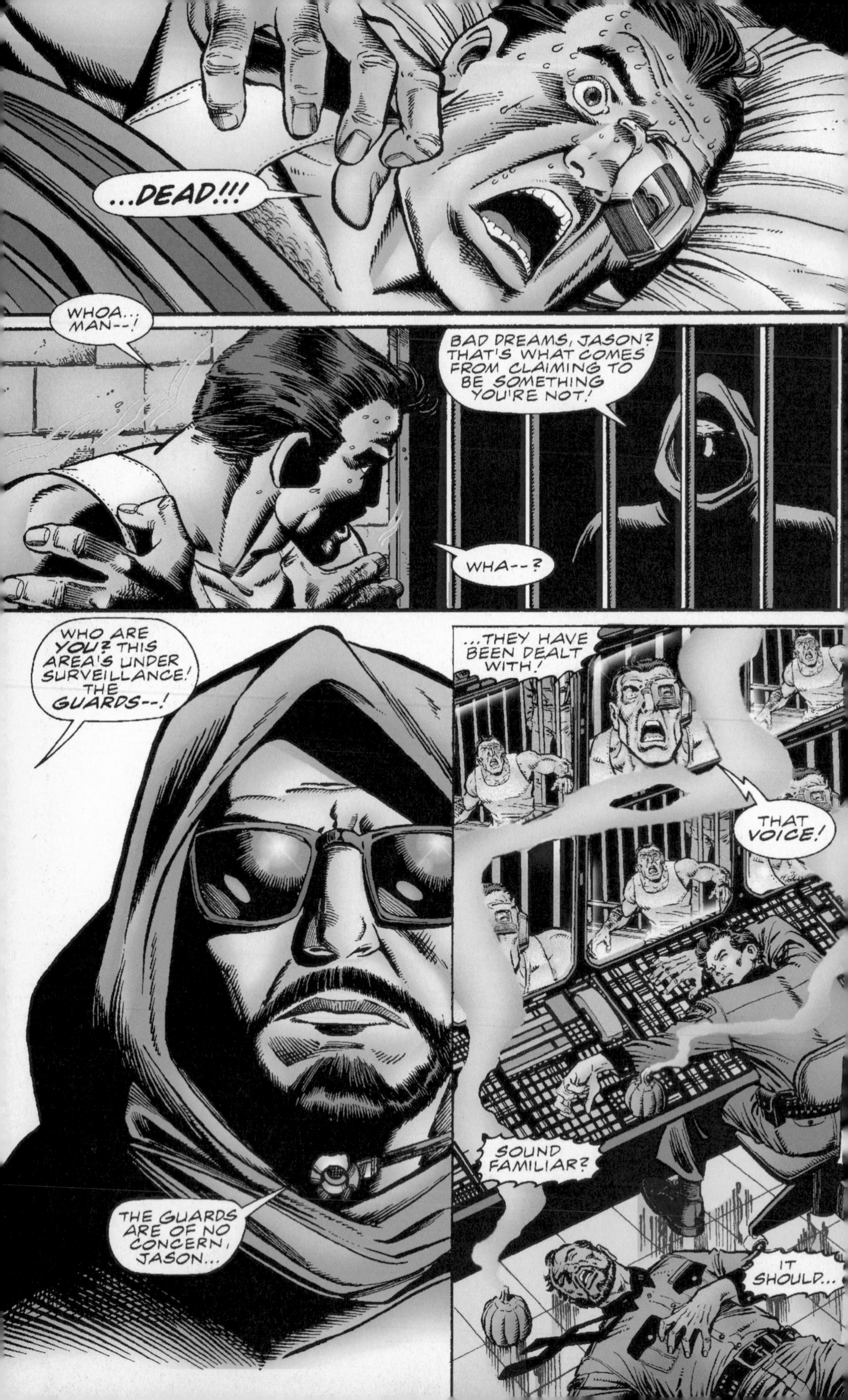

...DEAD!!!
WHOA... MAN--!
BAD DREAMS, JASON? THAT'S WHAT COMES FROM CLAIMING TO BE SOMETHING YOU'RE NOT!
WHA--?
WHO ARE YOU? THIS AREA'S UNDER SURVEILLANCE! THE GUARDS--!
THE GUARDS ARE OF NO CONCERN, JASON...
...THEY HAVE BEEN DEALT WITH!
THAT VOICE!
SOUND FAMILIAR?
IT SHOULD...

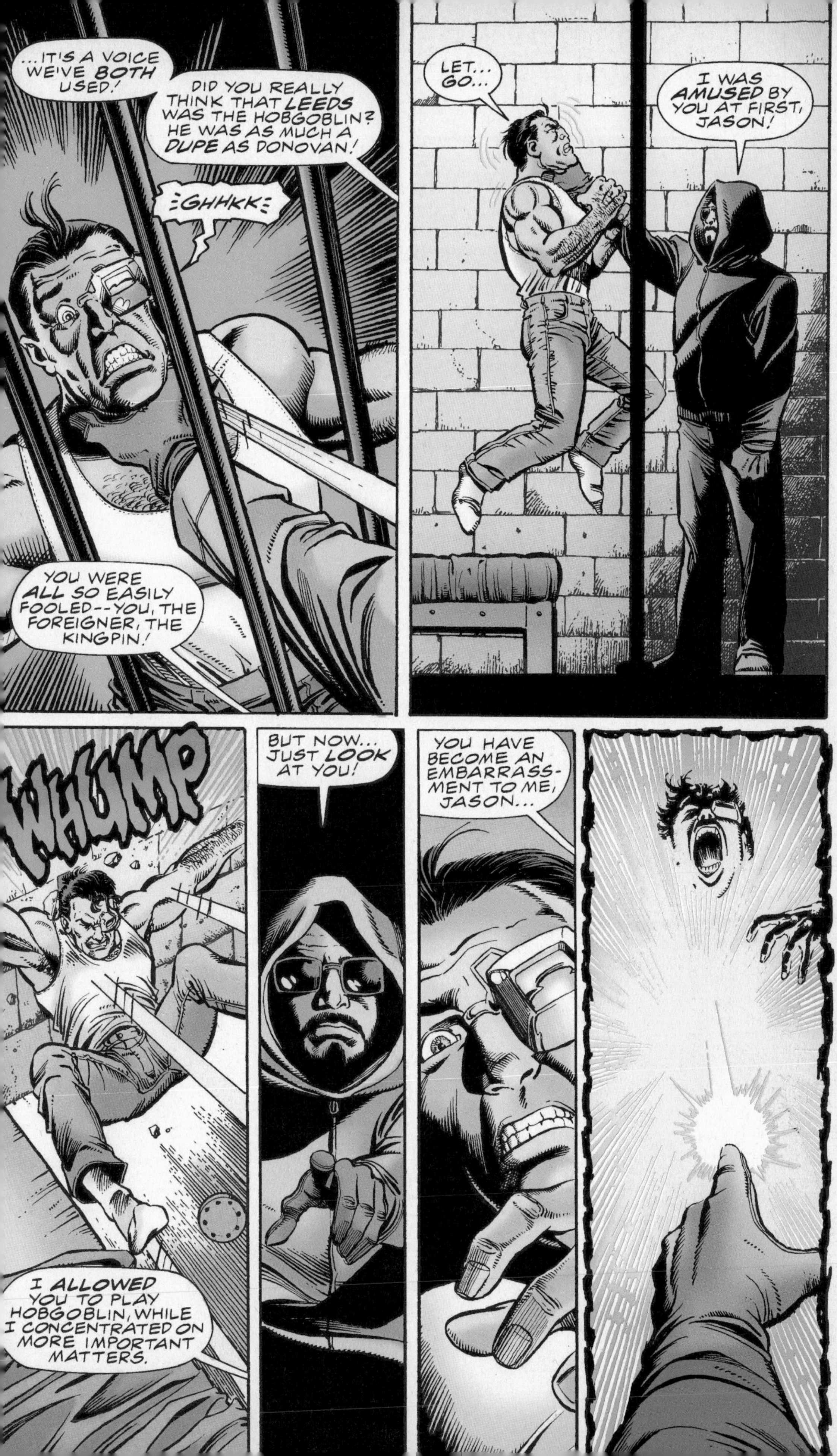
...IT'S A VOICE WE'VE BOTH USED!
DID YOU REALLY THINK THAT LEEDS WAS THE HOBGOBLIN? HE WAS AS MUCH A DUPE AS DONOVAN!
GHHKK
YOU WERE ALL SO EASILY FOOLED--YOU, THE FOREIGNER, THE KINGPIN!
LET... GO...
I WAS AMUSED BY YOU AT FIRST, JASON!
WHUMP
I ALLOWED YOU TO PLAY HOBGOBLIN, WHILE I CONCENTRATED ON MORE IMPORTANT MATTERS.
BUT NOW... JUST LOOK AT YOU!
YOU HAVE BECOME AN EMBARRASS-MENT TO ME, JASON...

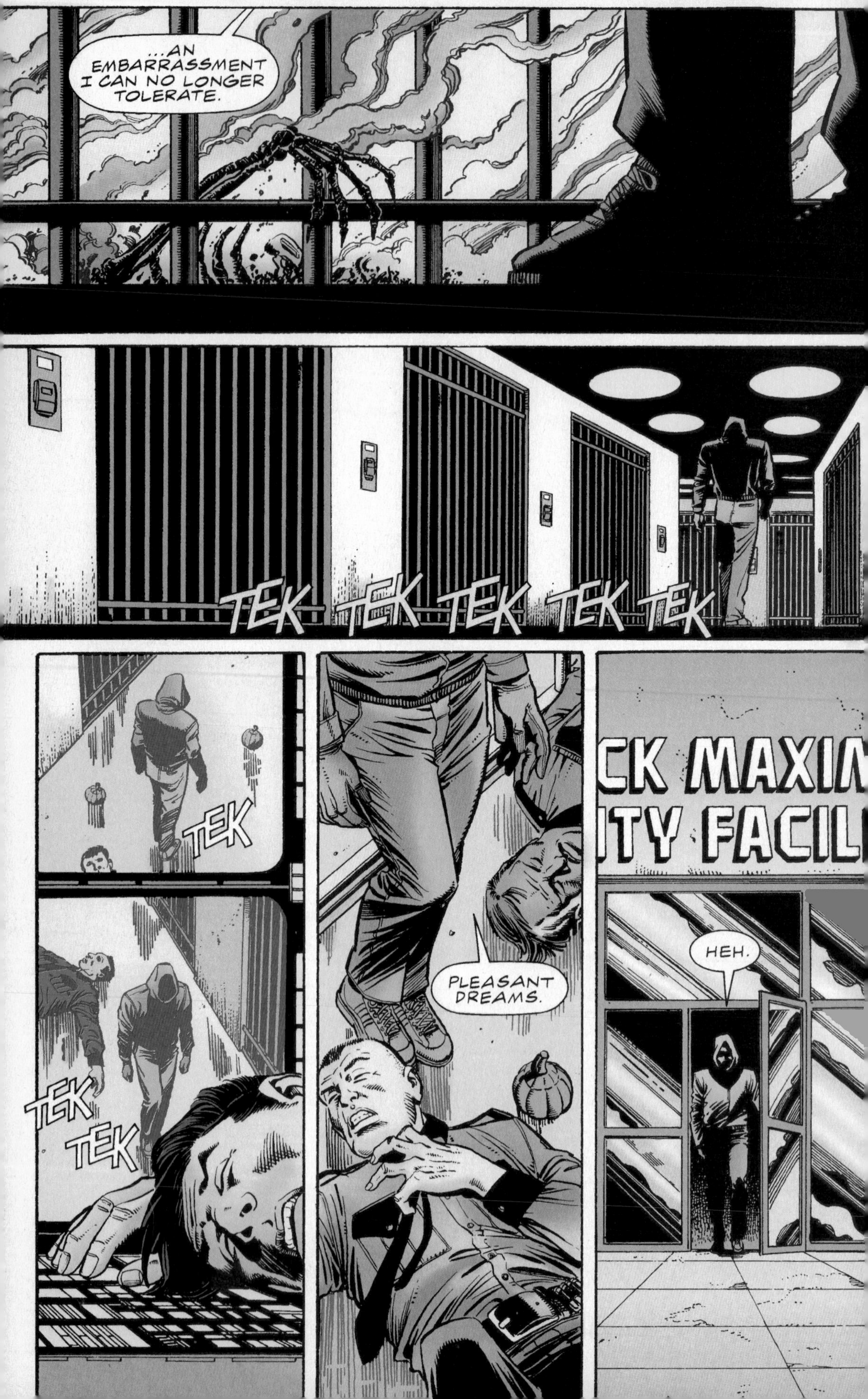
...AN EMBARRASSMENT I CAN NO LONGER TOLERATE.
TEK TEK TEK TEK TEK
TEK
TEK
TEK
PLEASANT DREAMS.
CK MAXIM
ITY FACIL
HEH.

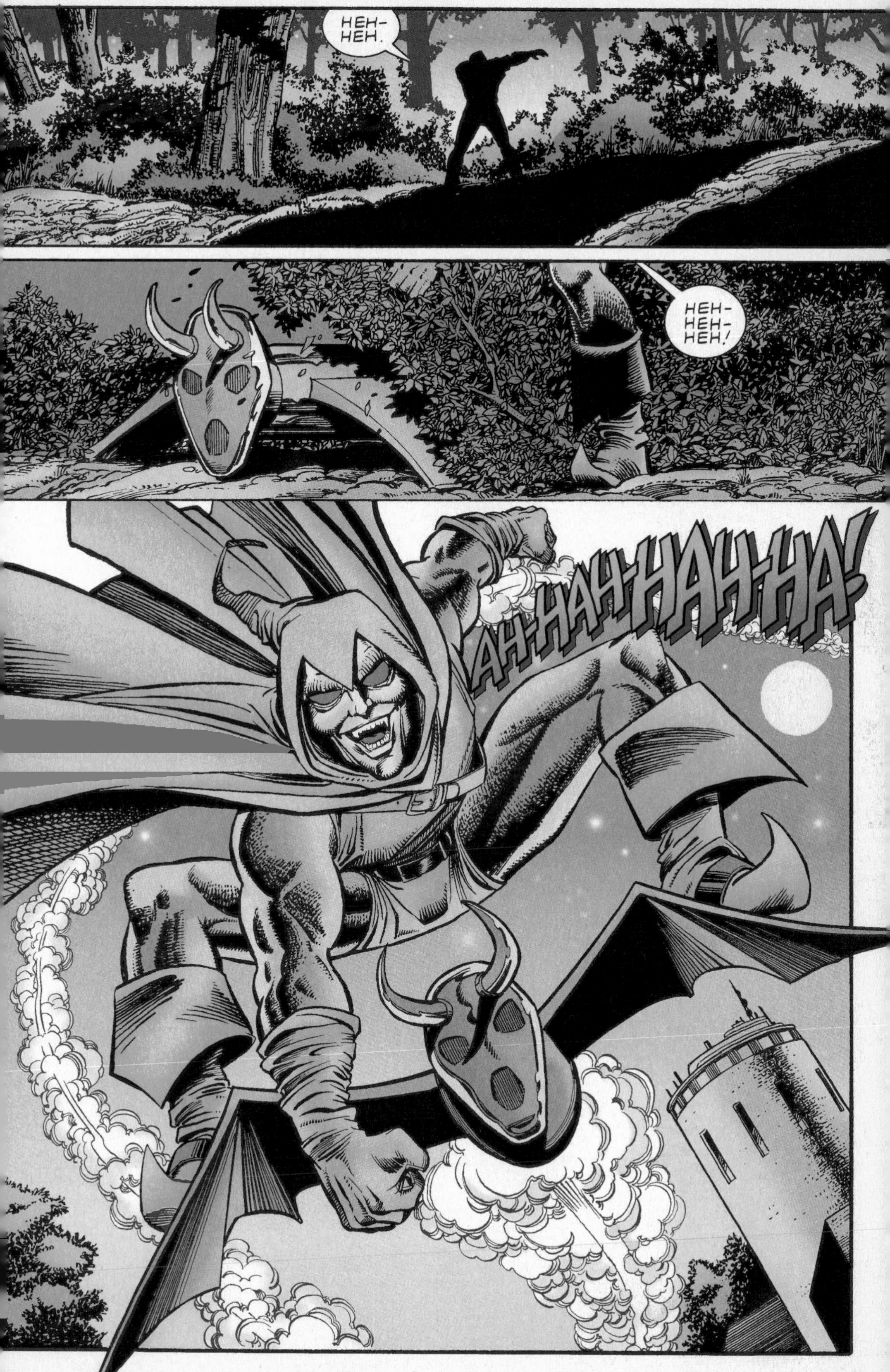
HEH-
HEH.
HEH-
HEH-
HEH!
AH-HAH-HAH-HAH-HA!

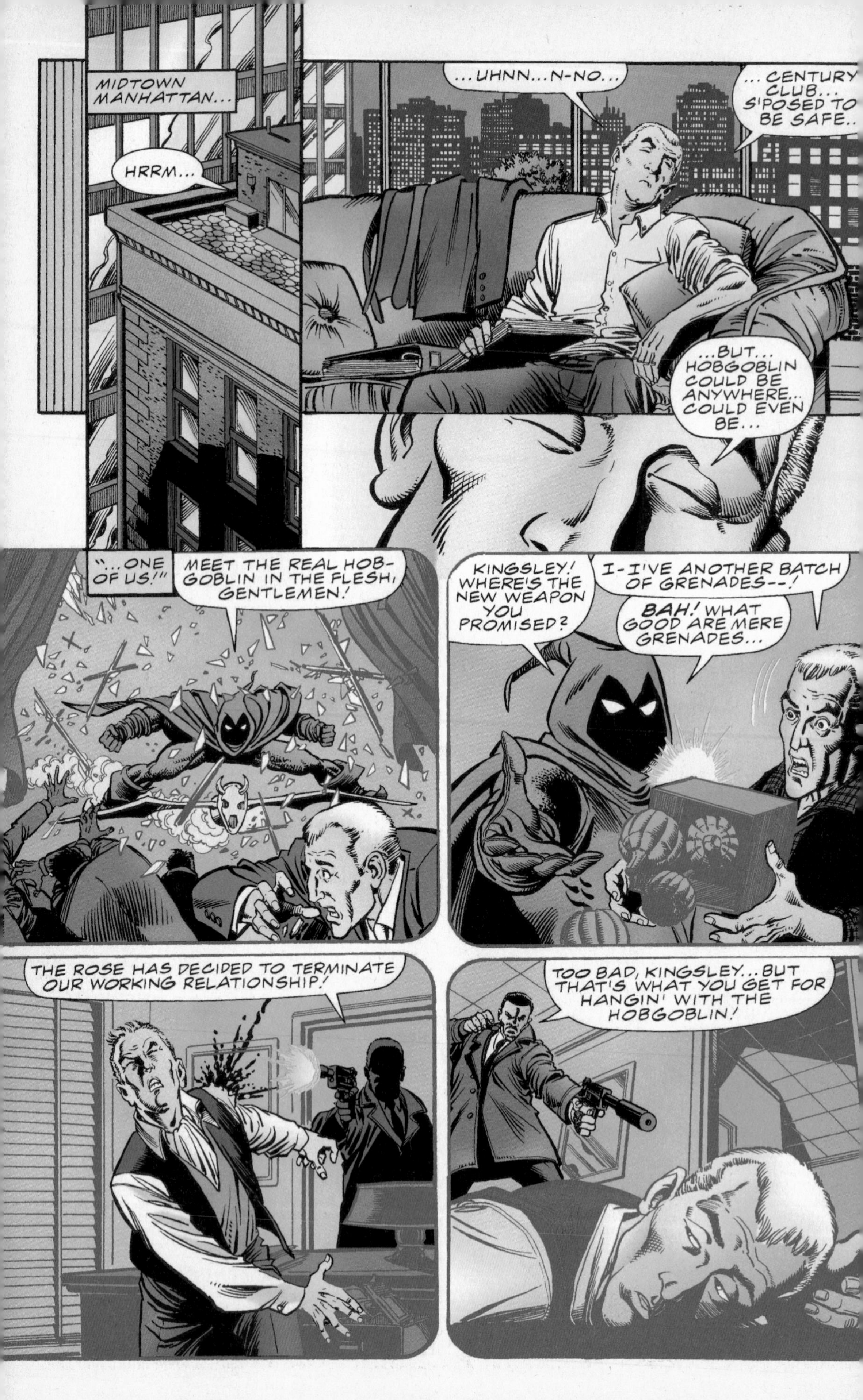
MIDTOWN MANHATTAN...
HRRM...
...UHNN...N-NO...
...CENTURY CLUB... S'POSED TO BE SAFE..
...BUT... HOBGOBLIN COULD BE ANYWHERE... COULD EVEN BE...
"...ONE OF US!"
MEET THE REAL HOB-GOBLIN IN THE FLESH, GENTLEMEN!
KINGSLEY! WHERE'S THE NEW WEAPON YOU PROMISED?
I-I'VE ANOTHER BATCH OF GRENADES--!
BAH! WHAT GOOD ARE MERE GRENADES...
THE ROSE HAS DECIDED TO TERMINATE OUR WORKING RELATIONSHIP!
TOO BAD, KINGSLEY...BUT THAT'S WHAT YOU GET FOR HANGIN' WITH THE HOBGOBLIN!

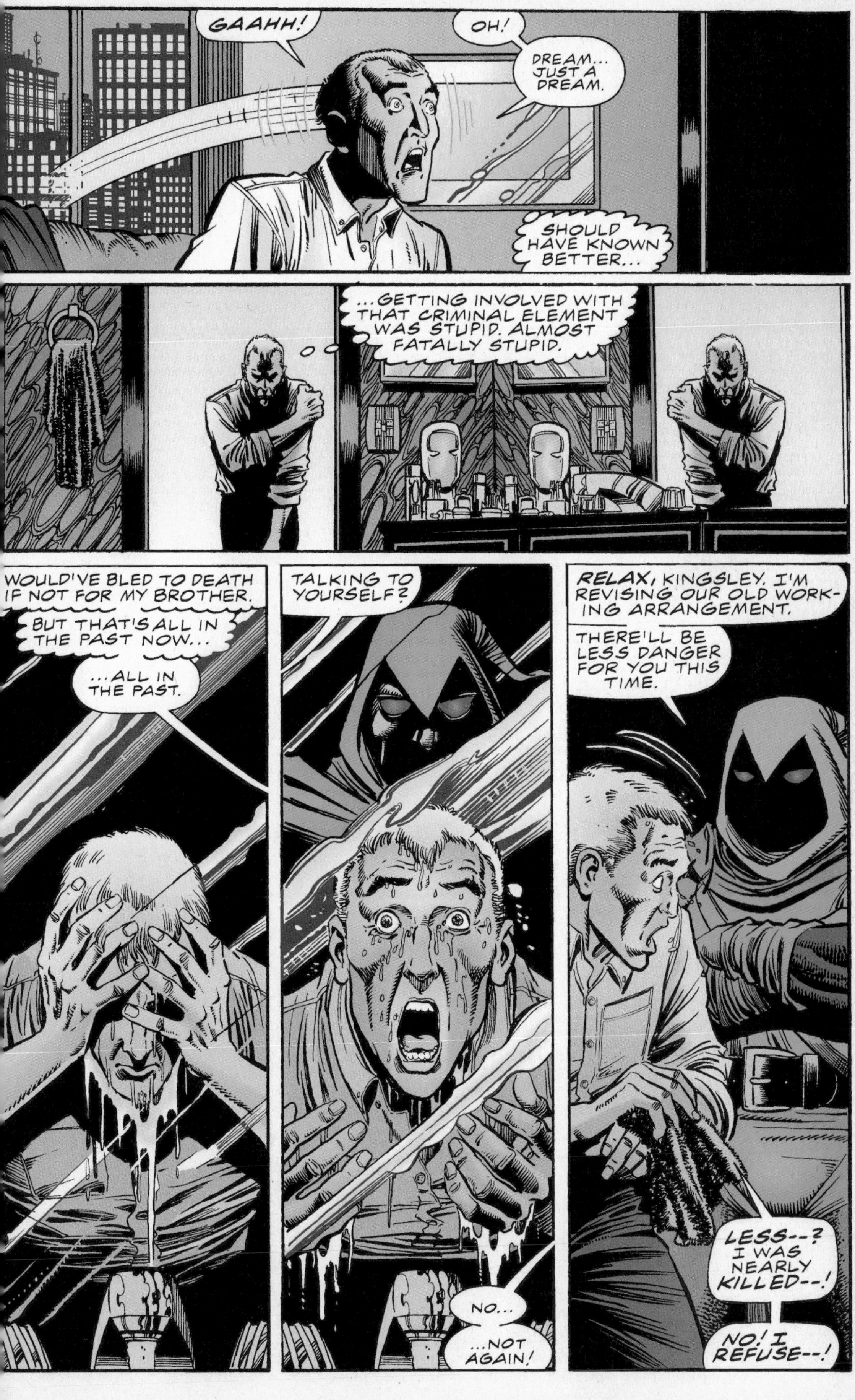
GAAHH!
OH!
DREAM... JUST A DREAM.
SHOULD HAVE KNOWN BETTER...
...GETTING INVOLVED WITH THAT CRIMINAL ELEMENT WAS STUPID. ALMOST FATALLY STUPID.
WOULD'VE BLED TO DEATH IF NOT FOR MY BROTHER.
BUT THAT'S ALL IN THE PAST NOW...
...ALL IN THE PAST.
TALKING TO YOURSELF?
NO...
...NOT AGAIN!
RELAX, KINGSLEY. I'M REVISING OUR OLD WORKING ARRANGEMENT.
THERE'LL BE LESS DANGER FOR YOU THIS TIME.
LESS--? I WAS NEARLY KILLED--!
NO! I REFUSE--!

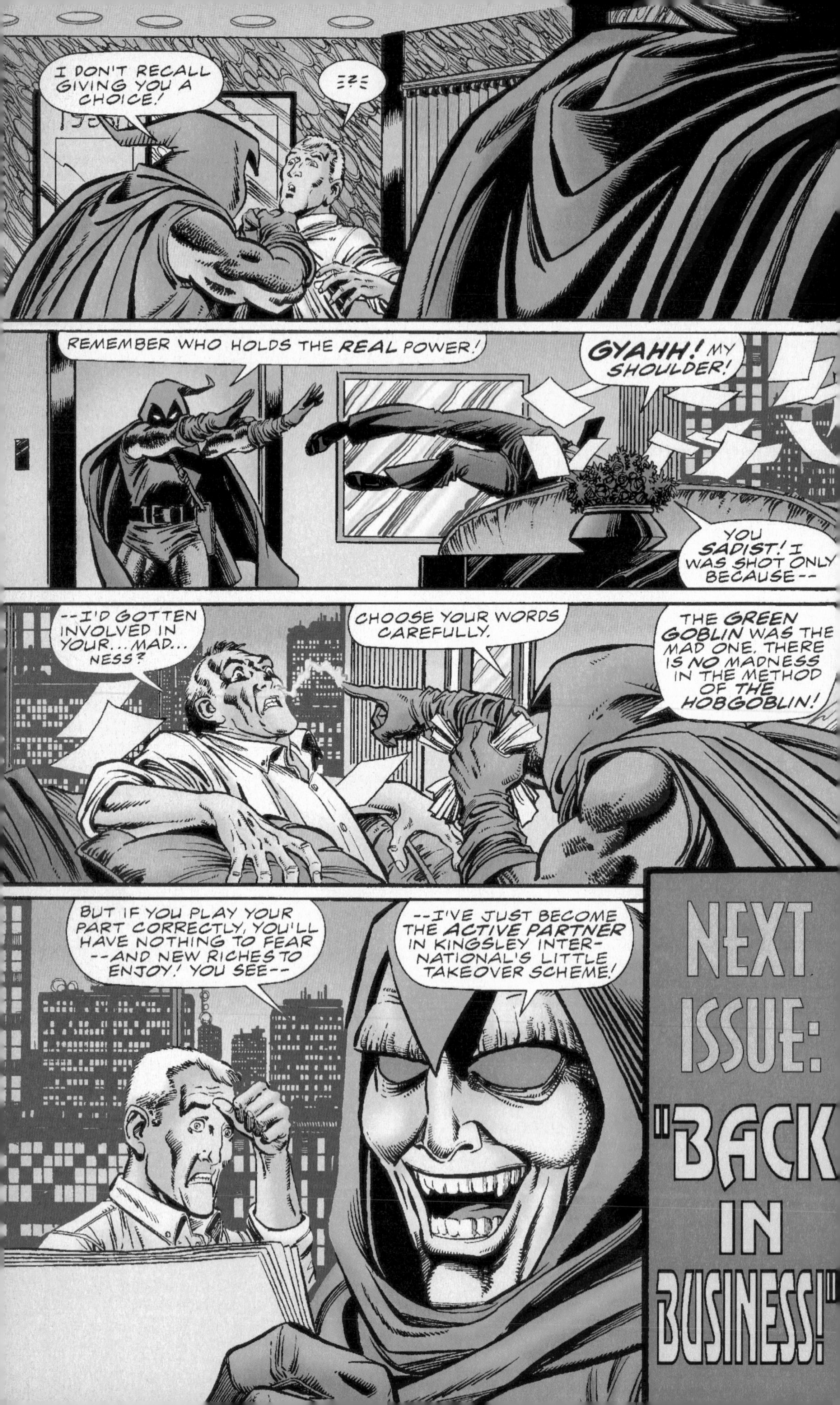

I DON'T RECALL GIVING YOU A CHOICE!
?
REMEMBER WHO HOLDS THE REAL POWER!
GYAHH! MY SHOULDER!
YOU SADIST! I WAS SHOT ONLY BECAUSE--
--I'D GOTTEN INVOLVED IN YOUR...MAD... NESS?
CHOOSE YOUR WORDS CAREFULLY.
THE GREEN GOBLIN WAS THE MAD ONE. THERE IS NO MADNESS IN THE METHOD OF THE HOBGOBLIN!
BUT IF YOU PLAY YOUR PART CORRECTLY, YOU'LL HAVE NOTHING TO FEAR --AND NEW RICHES TO ENJOY! YOU SEE--
--I'VE JUST BECOME THE ACTIVE PARTNER IN KINGSLEY INTER-NATIONAL'S LITTLE TAKEOVER SCHEME!
NEXT ISSUE:
"BACK IN BUSINESS!"

HOBGOBLIN LIVES  SOURCES

 Page 1
Spider-Man searched the Hudson River for signs of the Hobgoblin following their battle in AMAZING SPIDER-MAN #251

 Page 5
Jason Macendale was captured in SPIDER-MAN #69

 Page 7
Betty Brant believed that she saw the Hobgoblin unmasked in AMAZING SPIDER-MAN #288

 Page 8
Jacob Conover was fired from the Daily Bugle in AMAZING SPIDER-MAN #416

 Page 9
J. Jonah Jameson first appeared in AMAZING SPIDER-MAN #1; he and select members of the Century Club were confronted by the Hobgoblin in AMAZING SPIDER-MAN #249

 Page 16
Senator Robert Martin first appeared in SPECTACULAR SPIDER-MAN #38. George Vandergill was featured in AMAZING SPIDER-MAN #249-250

 Page 17
Donald Menkin first appeared in AMAZING SPIDER-MAN #239

 Page 18
Roderick Kingsley first appeared in SPECTACULAR SPIDER-MAN #43; a brother was first mentioned in AMAZING SPIDER-MAN #250

 Page 19
The late Lefty Donovan was manipulated into posing as the Hobgoblin in AMAZING SPIDER-MAN #245. Doctor Jonas Harrow first appeared in AMAZING SPIDER-MAN #114

 Page 20
Betty learned of the Foreigner's connection to her husband's death in WEB OF SPIDER-MAN #91-92

 Page 21
As Spider-Man, Peter saw the evidence in AMAZING SPIDER-MAN #289

 Page 22
The original Hobgoblin gained his super-strength in SPECTACULAR SPIDER-MAN #85. The Foreigner first used super-powered operatives in WEB OF SPIDER-MAN #91-92

 Page 25
As Jack O'Lantern, Macendale first fought Spider-Man in SPECTACULAR SPIDER-MAN #56

 Page 30
Kingsley was present at the Century Club encounter with the Hobgoblin in AMAZING SPIDER-MAN #249; he was shown consorting with the Hobgoblin in AMAZING SPIDER-MAN #283; he was shot by an agent of the Rose in WEB OF SPIDER-MAN #29

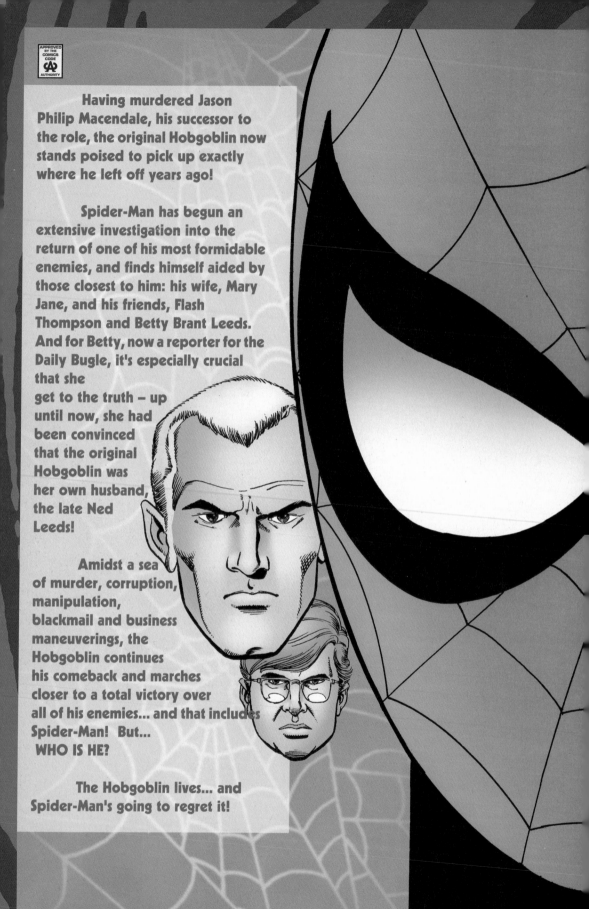

Having murdered Jason Philip Macendale, his successor to the role, the original Hobgoblin now stands poised to pick up exactly where he left off years ago!

Spider-Man has begun an extensive investigation into the return of one of his most formidable enemies, and finds himself aided by those closest to him: his wife, Mary Jane, and his friends, Flash Thompson and Betty Brant Leeds. And for Betty, now a reporter for the Daily Bugle, it's especially crucial that she get to the truth – up until now, she had been convinced that the original Hobgoblin was her own husband, the late Ned Leeds!

Amidst a sea of murder, corruption, manipulation, blackmail and business maneuverings, the Hobgoblin continues his comeback and marches closer to a total victory over all of his enemies... and that includes Spider-Man! But... WHO IS HE?

The Hobgoblin lives... and Spider-Man's going to regret it!

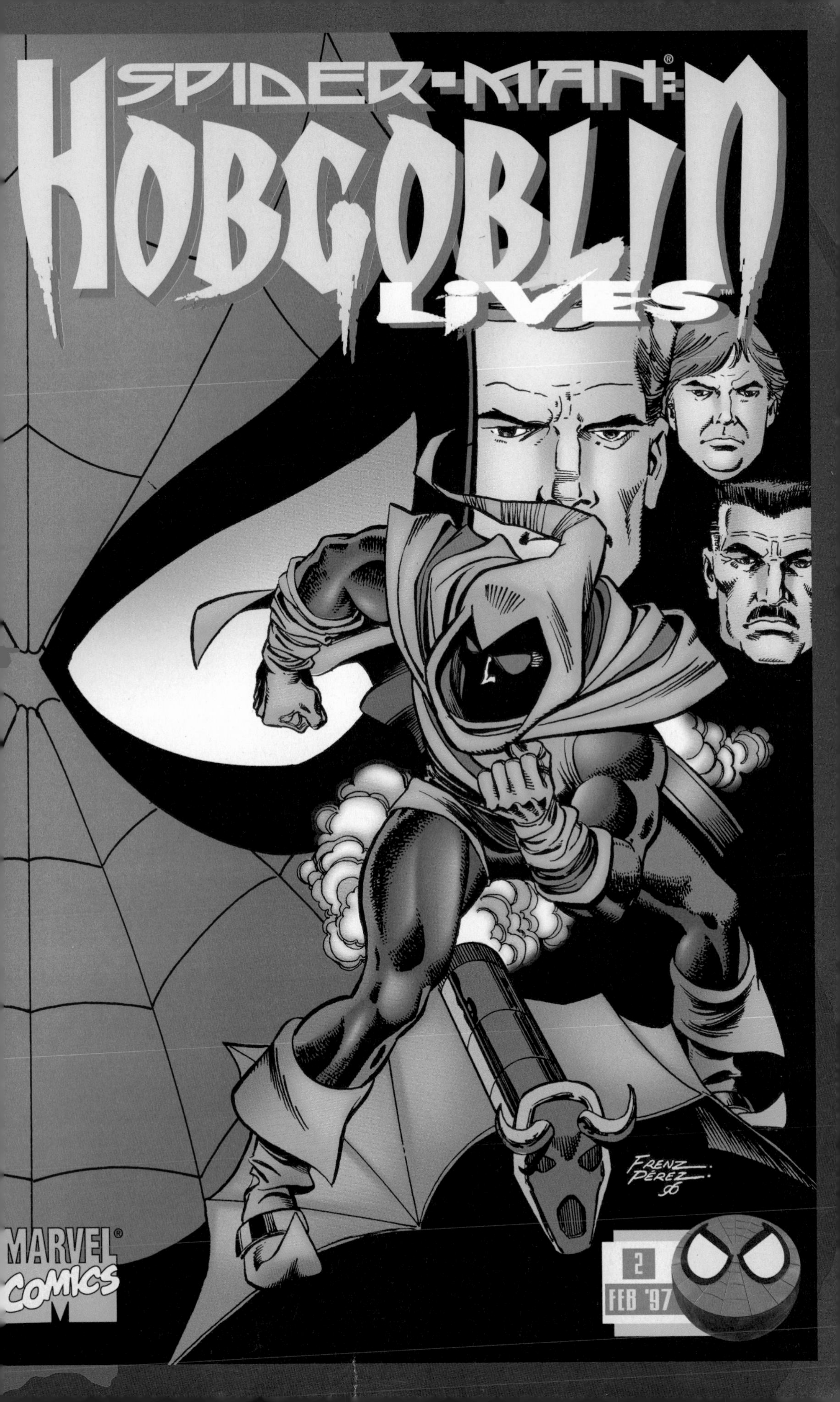

SPIDER-MAN®:
HOBGOBLIN
LIVES™
FRENZ
PÉREZ
96
MARVEL®
COMICS
2
FEB '97

SPIDER-MAN: HOBGOBLIN LIVES

Roger Stern — WRITER

Ron Frenz, Jerome Moore & Scott Hanna — ARTISTS

Jim Novak — LETTERER

Joe Andreani — COLORIST

Glenn Greenberg & Tom Brevoort — EDITORS

Bob Harras — EDITOR IN CHIEF

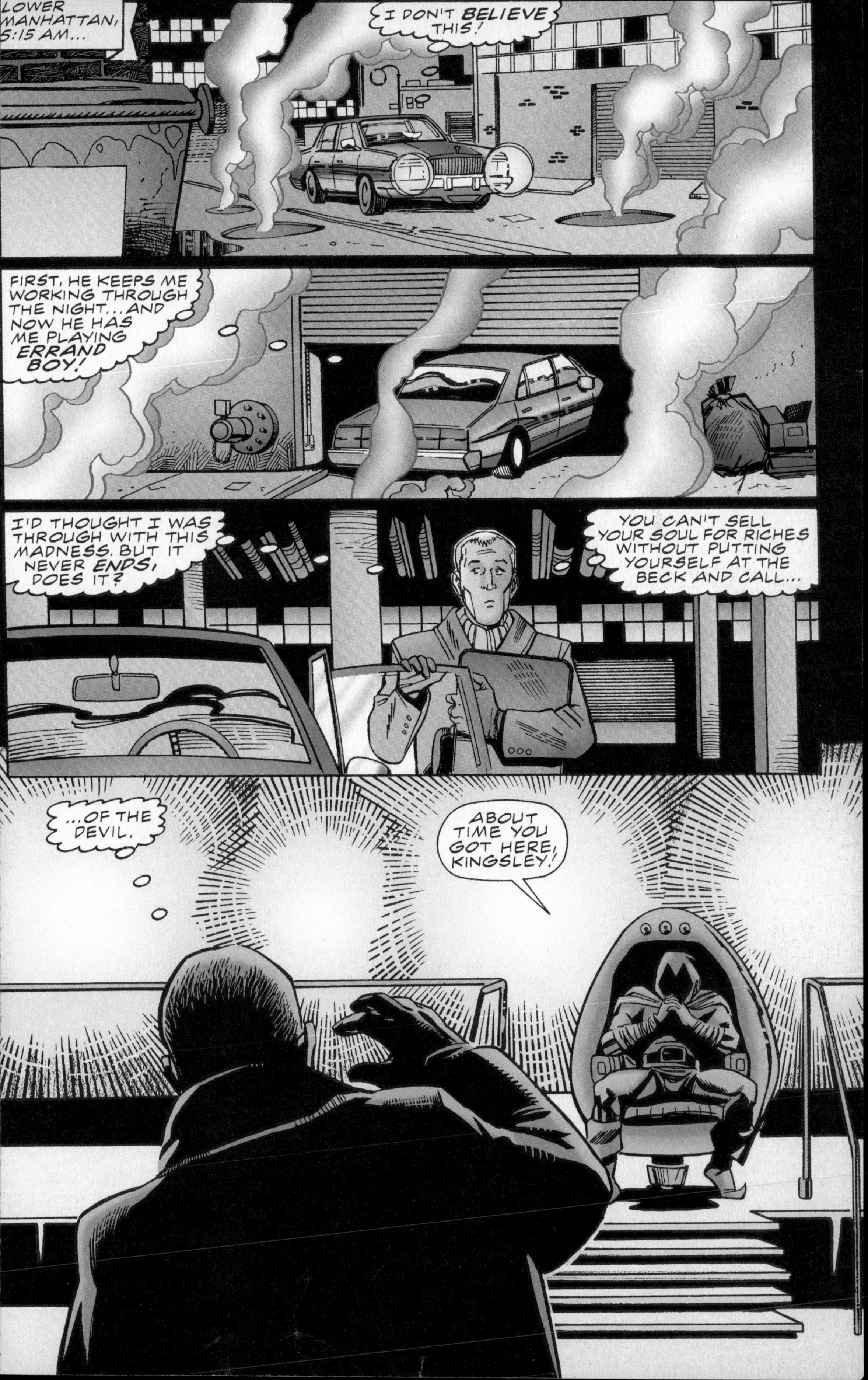
LOWER MANHATTAN, 5:15 AM...
I DON'T BELIEVE THIS!
FIRST, HE KEEPS ME WORKING THROUGH THE NIGHT... AND NOW HE HAS ME PLAYING ERRAND BOY!
I'D THOUGHT I WAS THROUGH WITH THIS MADNESS. BUT IT NEVER ENDS, DOES IT?
YOU CAN'T SELL YOUR SOUL FOR RICHES WITHOUT PUTTING YOURSELF AT THE BECK AND CALL...
...OF THE DEVIL.
ABOUT TIME YOU GOT HERE, KINGSLEY!

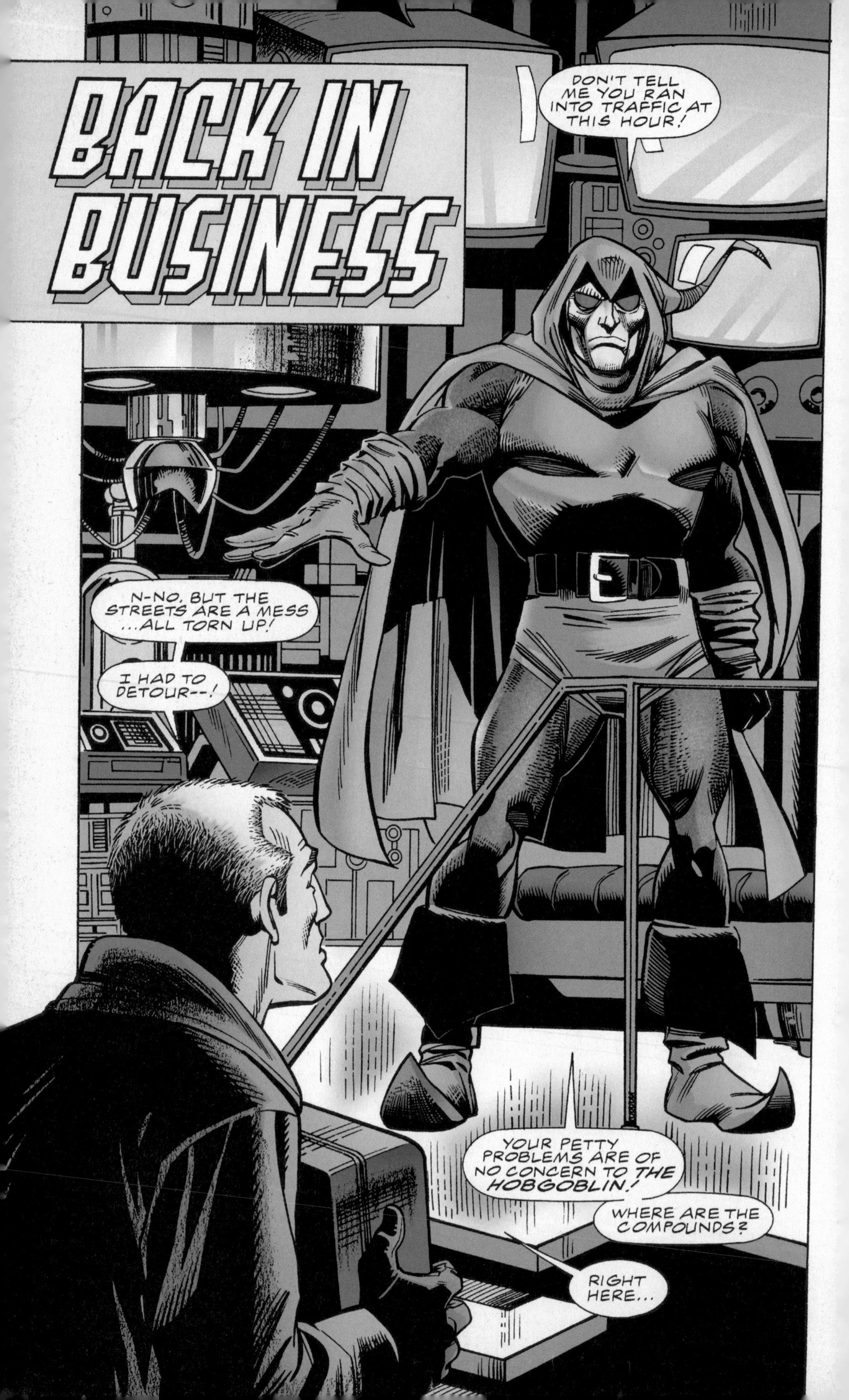
BACK IN BUSINESS
DON'T TELL ME YOU RAN INTO TRAFFIC AT THIS HOUR!
N-NO, BUT THE STREETS ARE A MESS ...ALL TORN UP!
I HAD TO DETOUR--!
YOUR PETTY PROBLEMS ARE OF NO CONCERN TO THE HOBGOBLIN!
WHERE ARE THE COMPOUNDS?
RIGHT HERE...

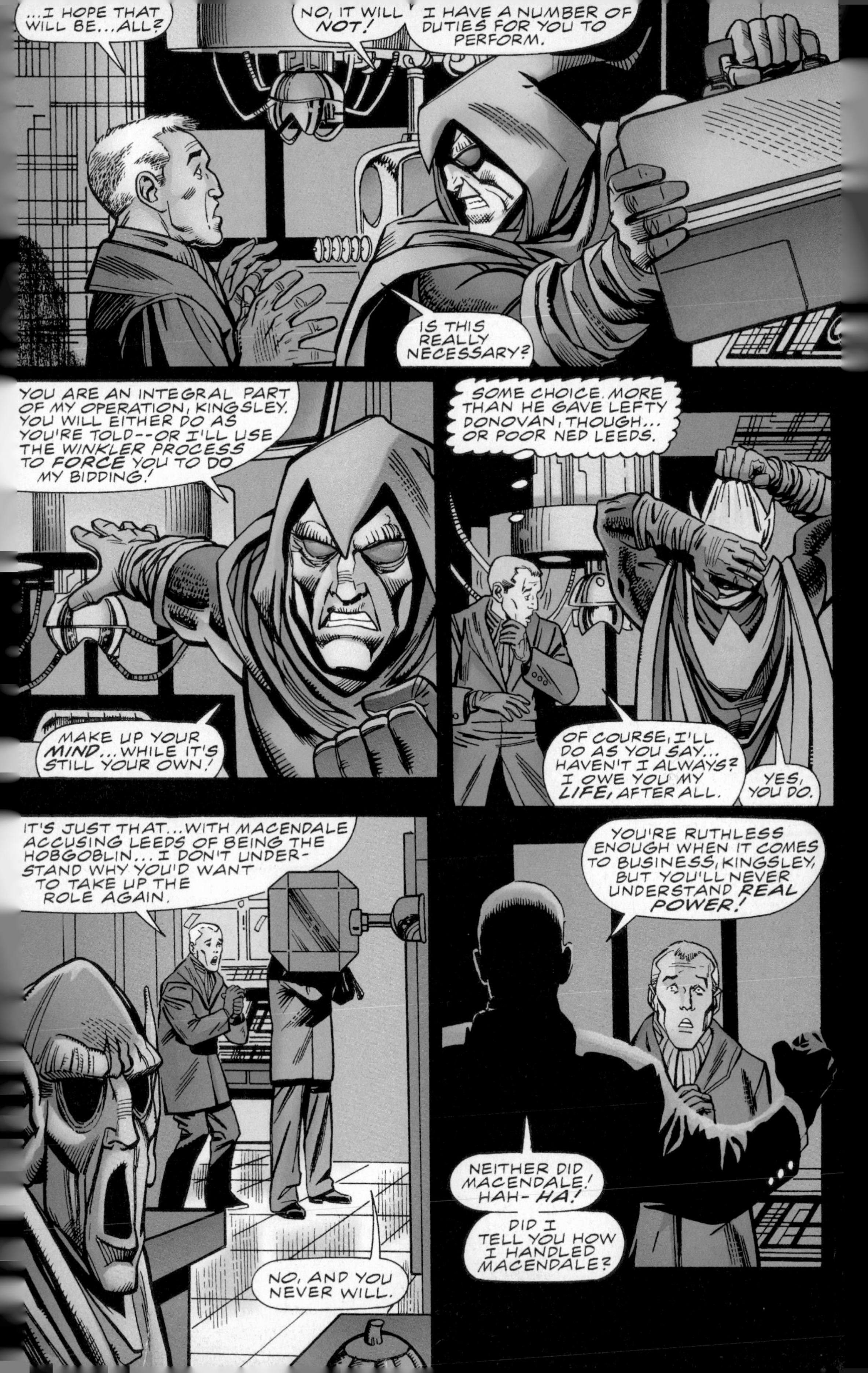
...I HOPE THAT WILL BE...ALL?
NO, IT WILL NOT!
I HAVE A NUMBER OF DUTIES FOR YOU TO PERFORM.
IS THIS REALLY NECESSARY?
YOU ARE AN INTEGRAL PART OF MY OPERATION, KINGSLEY. YOU WILL EITHER DO AS YOU'RE TOLD--OR I'LL USE THE WINKLER PROCESS TO FORCE YOU TO DO MY BIDDING!
MAKE UP YOUR MIND... WHILE IT'S STILL YOUR OWN!
SOME CHOICE. MORE THAN HE GAVE LEFTY DONOVAN, THOUGH... OR POOR NED LEEDS.
OF COURSE, I'LL DO AS YOU SAY... HAVEN'T I ALWAYS? I OWE YOU MY LIFE, AFTER ALL.
YES, YOU DO.
IT'S JUST THAT... WITH MACENDALE ACCUSING LEEDS OF BEING THE HOBGOBLIN... I DON'T UNDERSTAND WHY YOU'D WANT TO TAKE UP THE ROLE AGAIN.
NO, AND YOU NEVER WILL.
YOU'RE RUTHLESS ENOUGH WHEN IT COMES TO BUSINESS, KINGSLEY, BUT YOU'LL NEVER UNDERSTAND REAL POWER!
NEITHER DID MACENDALE! HAH-HA!
DID I TELL YOU HOW I HANDLED MACENDALE?

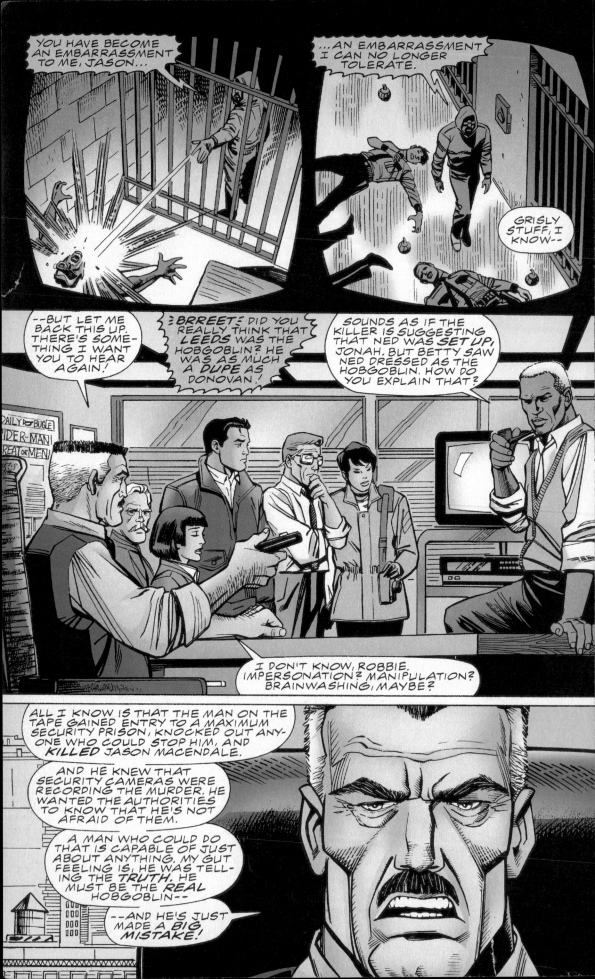

YOU HAVE BECOME AN EMBARRASSMENT TO ME, JASON...

...AN EMBARRASSMENT I CAN NO LONGER TOLERATE.

GRISLY STUFF, I KNOW--

--BUT LET ME BACK THIS UP. THERE'S SOMETHING I WANT YOU TO HEAR AGAIN!

≥BRREET≤ DID YOU REALLY THINK THAT LEEDS WAS THE HOBGOBLIN? HE WAS AS MUCH A DUPE AS DONOVAN!

SOUNDS AS IF THE KILLER IS SUGGESTING THAT NED WAS SET UP, JONAH. BUT BETTY SAW NED DRESSED AS THE HOBGOBLIN. HOW DO YOU EXPLAIN THAT?

I DON'T KNOW, ROBBIE. IMPERSONATION? MANIPULATION? BRAINWASHING, MAYBE?

ALL I KNOW IS THAT THE MAN ON THE TAPE GAINED ENTRY TO A MAXIMUM SECURITY PRISON, KNOCKED OUT ANYONE WHO COULD STOP HIM, AND KILLED JASON MACENDALE.

AND HE KNEW THAT SECURITY CAMERAS WERE RECORDING THE MURDER. HE WANTED THE AUTHORITIES TO KNOW THAT HE'S NOT AFRAID OF THEM.

A MAN WHO COULD DO THAT IS CAPABLE OF JUST ABOUT ANYTHING. MY GUT FEELING IS, HE WAS TELLING THE TRUTH. HE MUST BE THE REAL HOBGOBLIN--

--AND HE'S JUST MADE A BIG MISTAKE!

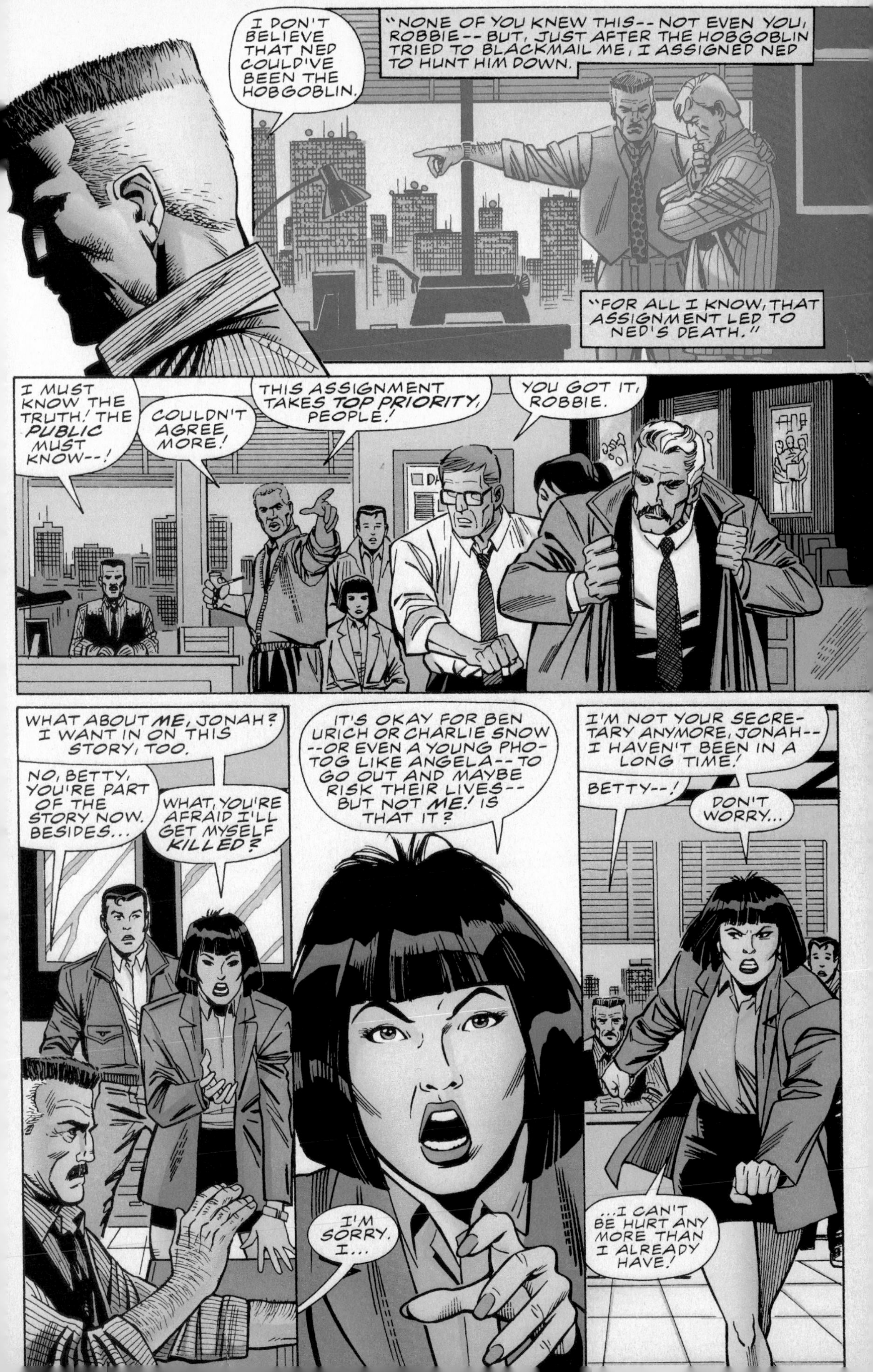
I DON'T BELIEVE THAT NED COULD'VE BEEN THE HOBGOBLIN.
"NONE OF YOU KNEW THIS-- NOT EVEN YOU, ROBBIE-- BUT, JUST AFTER THE HOBGOBLIN TRIED TO BLACKMAIL ME, I ASSIGNED NED TO HUNT HIM DOWN.
"FOR ALL I KNOW, THAT ASSIGNMENT LED TO NED'S DEATH."
I MUST KNOW THE TRUTH! THE PUBLIC MUST KNOW--!
COULDN'T AGREE MORE!
THIS ASSIGNMENT TAKES TOP PRIORITY, PEOPLE!
YOU GOT IT, ROBBIE.
WHAT ABOUT ME, JONAH? I WANT IN ON THIS STORY, TOO.
NO, BETTY, YOU'RE PART OF THE STORY NOW. BESIDES...
WHAT, YOU'RE AFRAID I'LL GET MYSELF KILLED?
IT'S OKAY FOR BEN URICH OR CHARLIE SNOW --OR EVEN A YOUNG PHOTOG LIKE ANGELA-- TO GO OUT AND MAYBE RISK THEIR LIVES-- BUT NOT ME! IS THAT IT?
I'M SORRY. I...
I'M NOT YOUR SECRETARY ANYMORE, JONAH-- I HAVEN'T BEEN IN A LONG TIME!
BETTY--!
DON'T WORRY...
...I CAN'T BE HURT ANY MORE THAN I ALREADY HAVE!

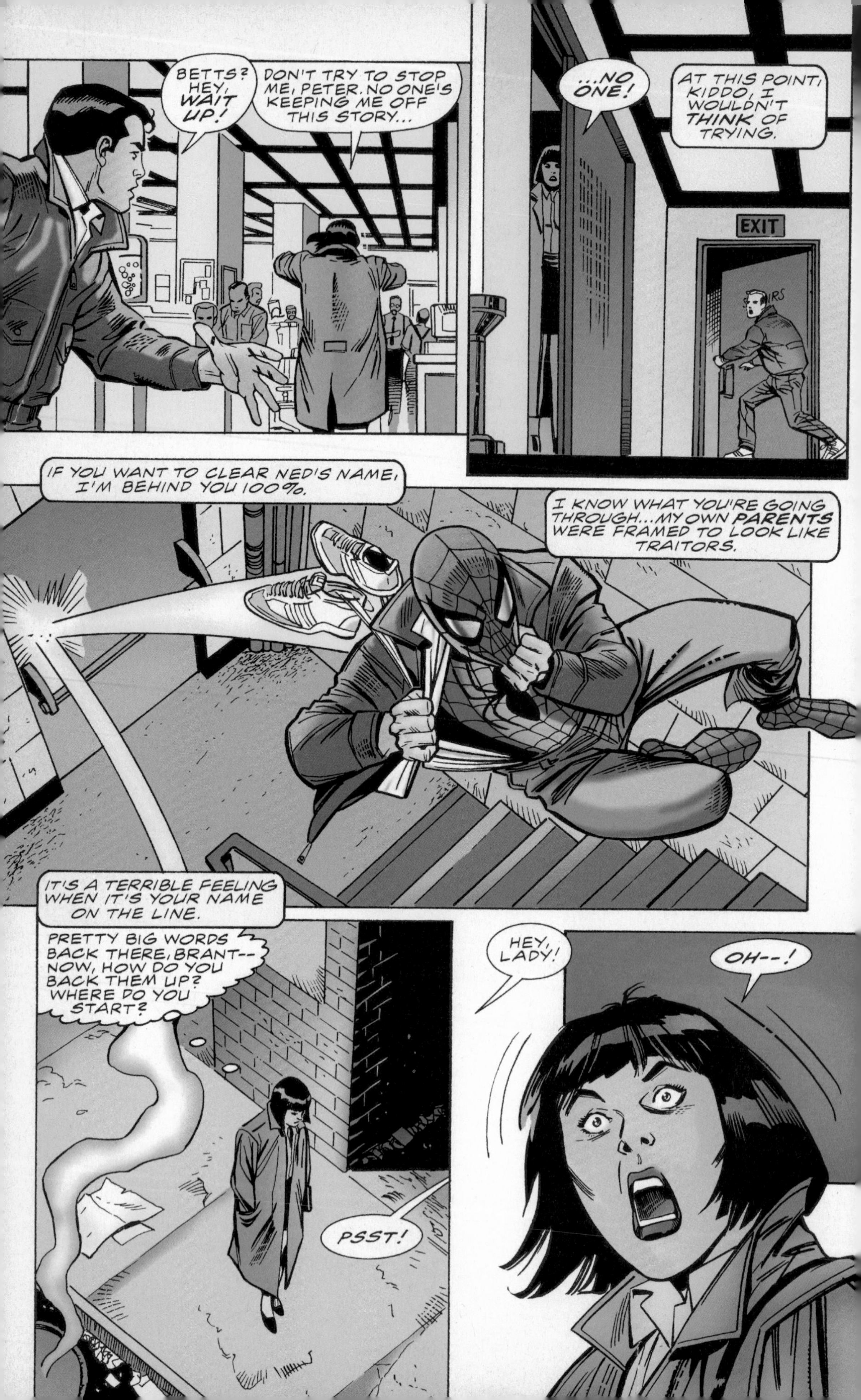
BETTS? HEY, WAIT UP!
DON'T TRY TO STOP ME, PETER. NO ONE'S KEEPING ME OFF THIS STORY...
...NO ONE!
AT THIS POINT, KIDDO, I WOULDN'T THINK OF TRYING.
EXIT
IF YOU WANT TO CLEAR NED'S NAME, I'M BEHIND YOU 100%.
I KNOW WHAT YOU'RE GOING THROUGH...MY OWN PARENTS WERE FRAMED TO LOOK LIKE TRAITORS.
IT'S A TERRIBLE FEELING WHEN IT'S YOUR NAME ON THE LINE.
PRETTY BIG WORDS BACK THERE, BRANT-- NOW, HOW DO YOU BACK THEM UP? WHERE DO YOU START?
PSST!
HEY, LADY!
OH--!

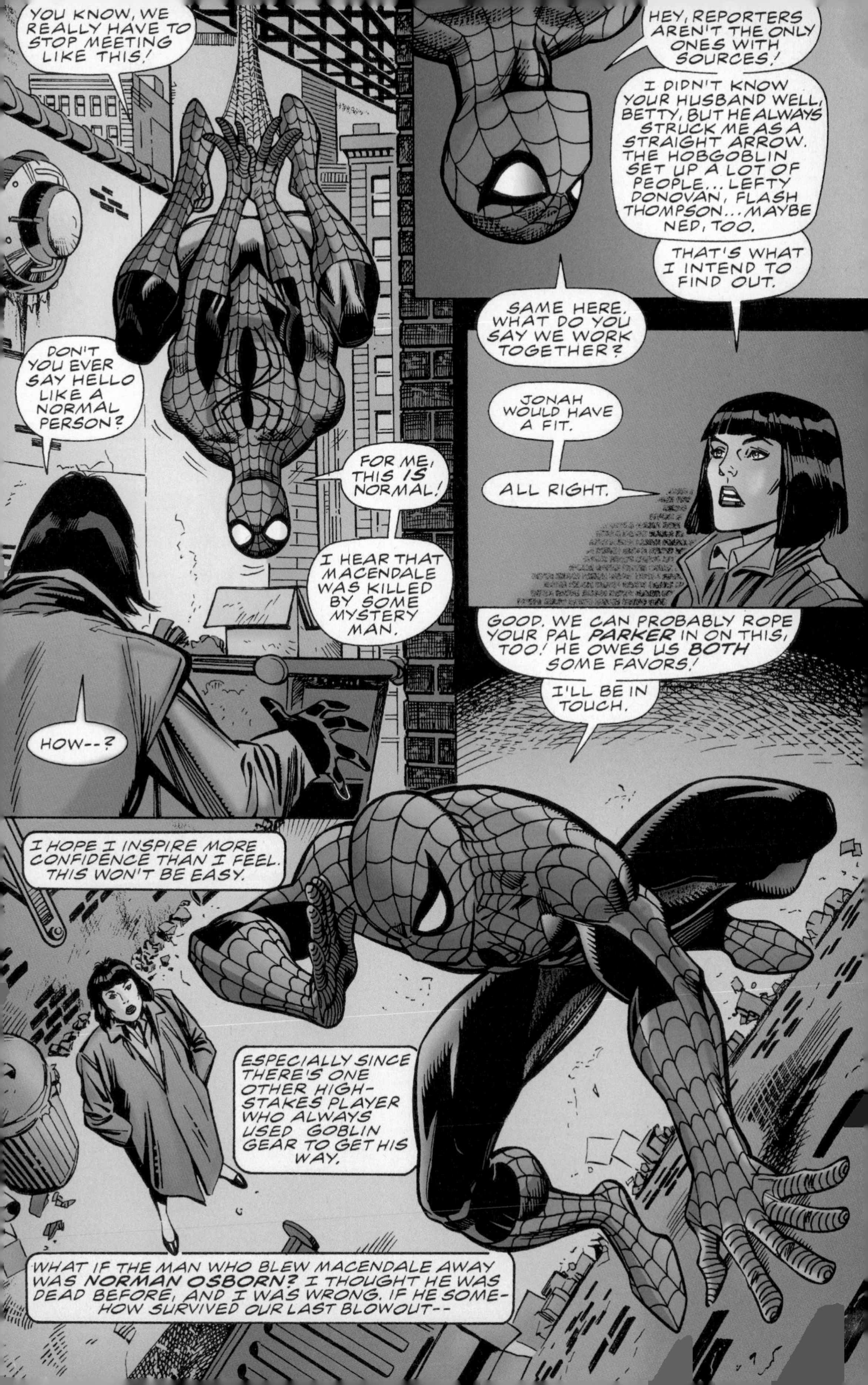

YOU KNOW, WE REALLY HAVE TO STOP MEETING LIKE THIS!
DON'T YOU EVER SAY HELLO LIKE A NORMAL PERSON?
FOR ME, THIS IS NORMAL!
I HEAR THAT MACENDALE WAS KILLED BY SOME MYSTERY MAN.
HOW--?
HEY, REPORTERS AREN'T THE ONLY ONES WITH SOURCES!
I DIDN'T KNOW YOUR HUSBAND WELL, BETTY, BUT HE ALWAYS STRUCK ME AS A STRAIGHT ARROW. THE HOBGOBLIN SET UP A LOT OF PEOPLE... LEFTY DONOVAN, FLASH THOMPSON... MAYBE NED, TOO.
THAT'S WHAT I INTEND TO FIND OUT.
SAME HERE. WHAT DO YOU SAY WE WORK TOGETHER?
JONAH WOULD HAVE A FIT.
ALL RIGHT.
GOOD. WE CAN PROBABLY ROPE YOUR PAL PARKER IN ON THIS, TOO! HE OWES US BOTH SOME FAVORS!
I'LL BE IN TOUCH.
I HOPE I INSPIRE MORE CONFIDENCE THAN I FEEL. THIS WON'T BE EASY.
ESPECIALLY SINCE THERE'S ONE OTHER HIGH-STAKES PLAYER WHO ALWAYS USED GOBLIN GEAR TO GET HIS WAY.
WHAT IF THE MAN WHO BLEW MACENDALE AWAY WAS NORMAN OSBORN? I THOUGHT HE WAS DEAD BEFORE, AND I WAS WRONG. IF HE SOMEHOW SURVIVED OUR LAST BLOWOUT--

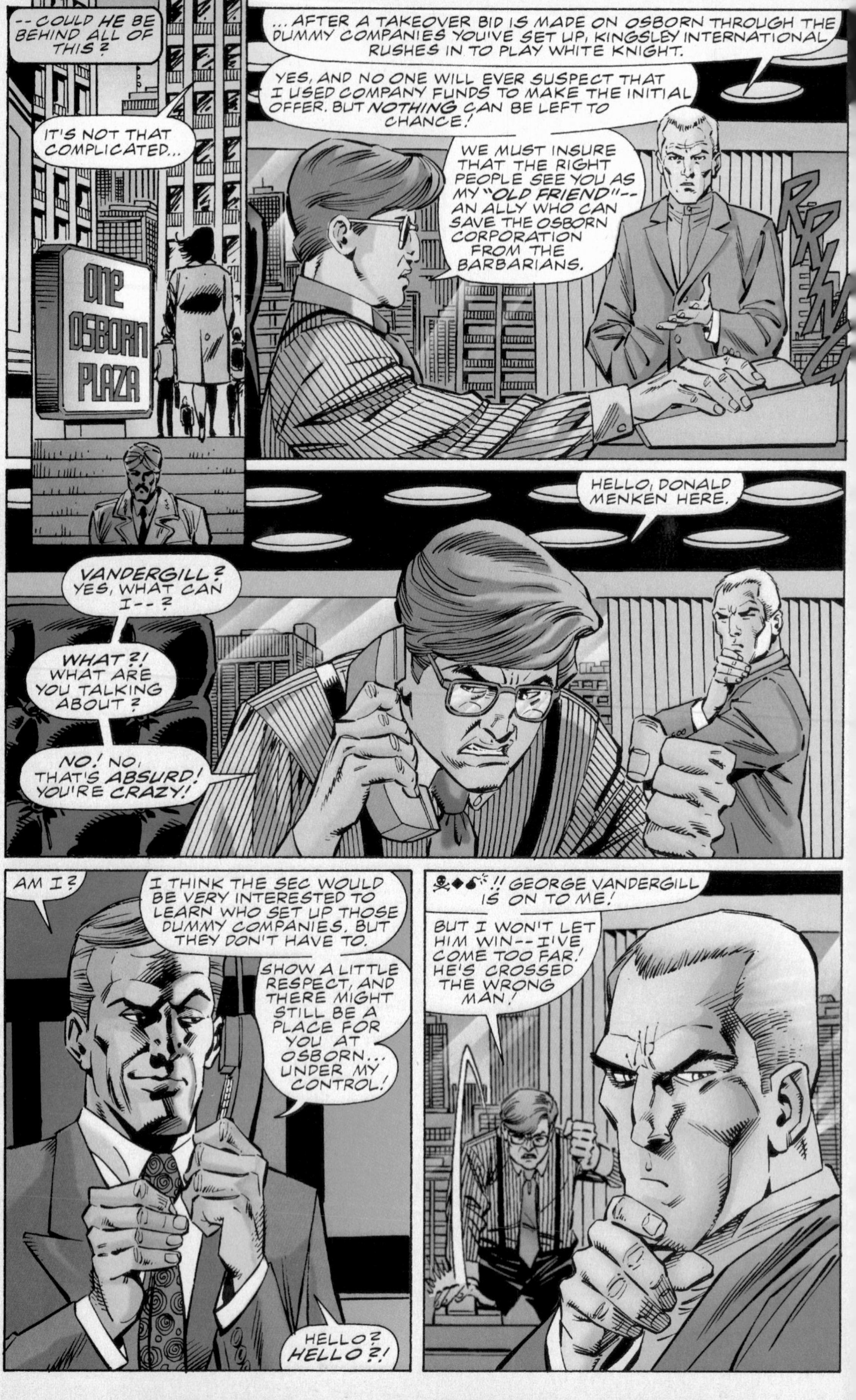
--COULD HE BE BEHIND ALL OF THIS?
IT'S NOT THAT COMPLICATED...
...AFTER A TAKEOVER BID IS MADE ON OSBORN THROUGH THE DUMMY COMPANIES YOU'VE SET UP, KINGSLEY INTERNATIONAL RUSHES IN TO PLAY WHITE KNIGHT.
YES, AND NO ONE WILL EVER SUSPECT THAT I USED COMPANY FUNDS TO MAKE THE INITIAL OFFER. BUT NOTHING CAN BE LEFT TO CHANCE!
WE MUST INSURE THAT THE RIGHT PEOPLE SEE YOU AS MY "OLD FRIEND"--AN ALLY WHO CAN SAVE THE OSBORN CORPORATION FROM THE BARBARIANS.
RRRNG
HELLO, DONALD MENKEN HERE.
VANDERGILL? YES, WHAT CAN I--?
WHAT?! WHAT ARE YOU TALKING ABOUT?
NO! NO, THAT'S ABSURD! YOU'RE CRAZY!
AM I?
I THINK THE SEC WOULD BE VERY INTERESTED TO LEARN WHO SET UP THOSE DUMMY COMPANIES. BUT THEY DON'T HAVE TO.
SHOW A LITTLE RESPECT, AND THERE MIGHT STILL BE A PLACE FOR YOU AT OSBORN... UNDER MY CONTROL!
HELLO? HELLO?!
☠◆💣!! GEORGE VANDERGILL IS ON TO ME!
BUT I WON'T LET HIM WIN--I'VE COME TOO FAR! HE'S CROSSED THE WRONG MAN!

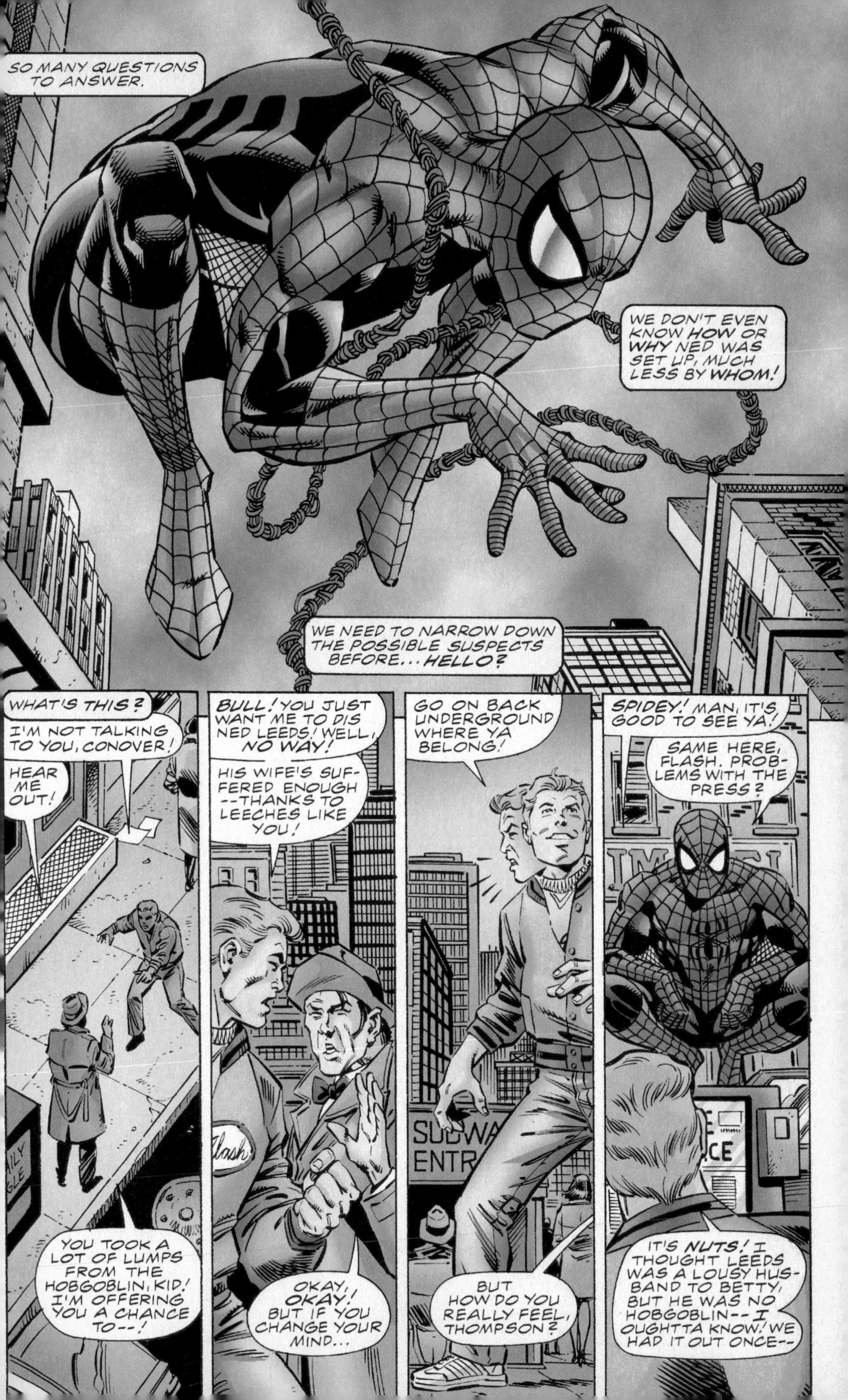
SO MANY QUESTIONS TO ANSWER.
WE DON'T EVEN KNOW HOW OR WHY NED WAS SET UP, MUCH LESS BY WHOM!
WE NEED TO NARROW DOWN THE POSSIBLE SUSPECTS BEFORE... HELLO?
WHAT'S THIS?
I'M NOT TALKING TO YOU, CONOVER!
HEAR ME OUT!
YOU TOOK A LOT OF LUMPS FROM THE HOBGOBLIN, KID! I'M OFFERING YOU A CHANCE TO--!
BULL! YOU JUST WANT ME TO DIS NED LEEDS! WELL, NO WAY!
HIS WIFE'S SUFFERED ENOUGH --THANKS TO LEECHES LIKE YOU!
OKAY, OKAY! BUT IF YOU CHANGE YOUR MIND...
GO ON BACK UNDERGROUND WHERE YA BELONG!
BUT HOW DO YOU REALLY FEEL, THOMPSON?
SPIDEY! MAN, IT'S GOOD TO SEE YA!
SAME HERE, FLASH. PROBLEMS WITH THE PRESS?
IT'S NUTS! I THOUGHT LEEDS WAS A LOUSY HUSBAND TO BETTY, BUT HE WAS NO HOBGOBLIN--I OUGHTTA KNOW! WE HAD IT OUT ONCE--

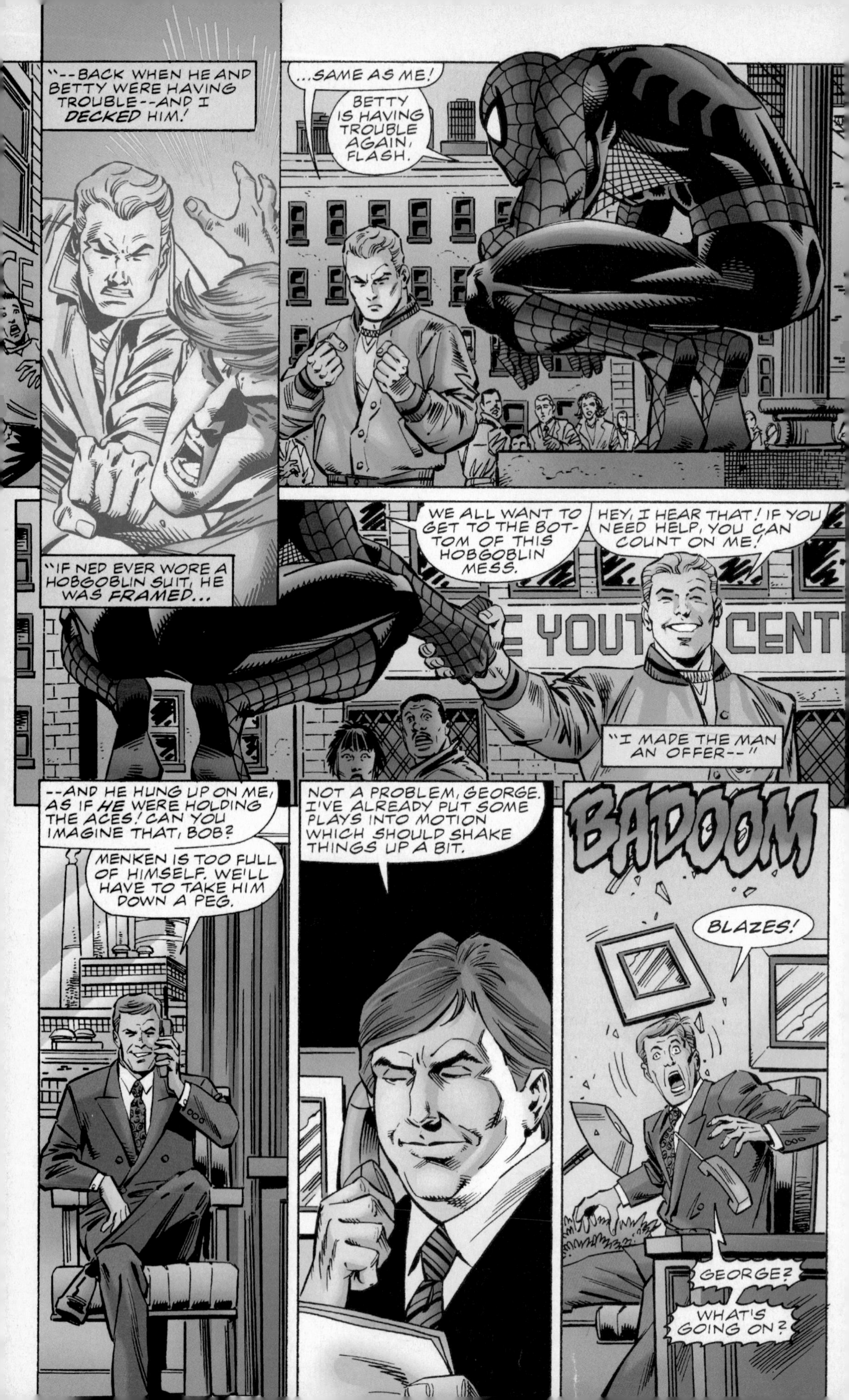
"--BACK WHEN HE AND BETTY WERE HAVING TROUBLE--AND I DECKED HIM!
"IF NED EVER WORE A HOBGOBLIN SUIT, HE WAS FRAMED...
...SAME AS ME!
BETTY IS HAVING TROUBLE AGAIN, FLASH.
WE ALL WANT TO GET TO THE BOTTOM OF THIS HOBGOBLIN MESS.
HEY, I HEAR THAT! IF YOU NEED HELP, YOU CAN COUNT ON ME!
E YOUT CENT
"I MADE THE MAN AN OFFER--"
--AND HE HUNG UP ON ME, AS IF HE WERE HOLDING THE ACES! CAN YOU IMAGINE THAT, BOB?
MENKEN IS TOO FULL OF HIMSELF. WE'LL HAVE TO TAKE HIM DOWN A PEG.
NOT A PROBLEM, GEORGE. I'VE ALREADY PUT SOME PLAYS INTO MOTION WHICH SHOULD SHAKE THINGS UP A BIT.
BADOOM
BLAZES!
GEORGE?
WHAT'S GOING ON?

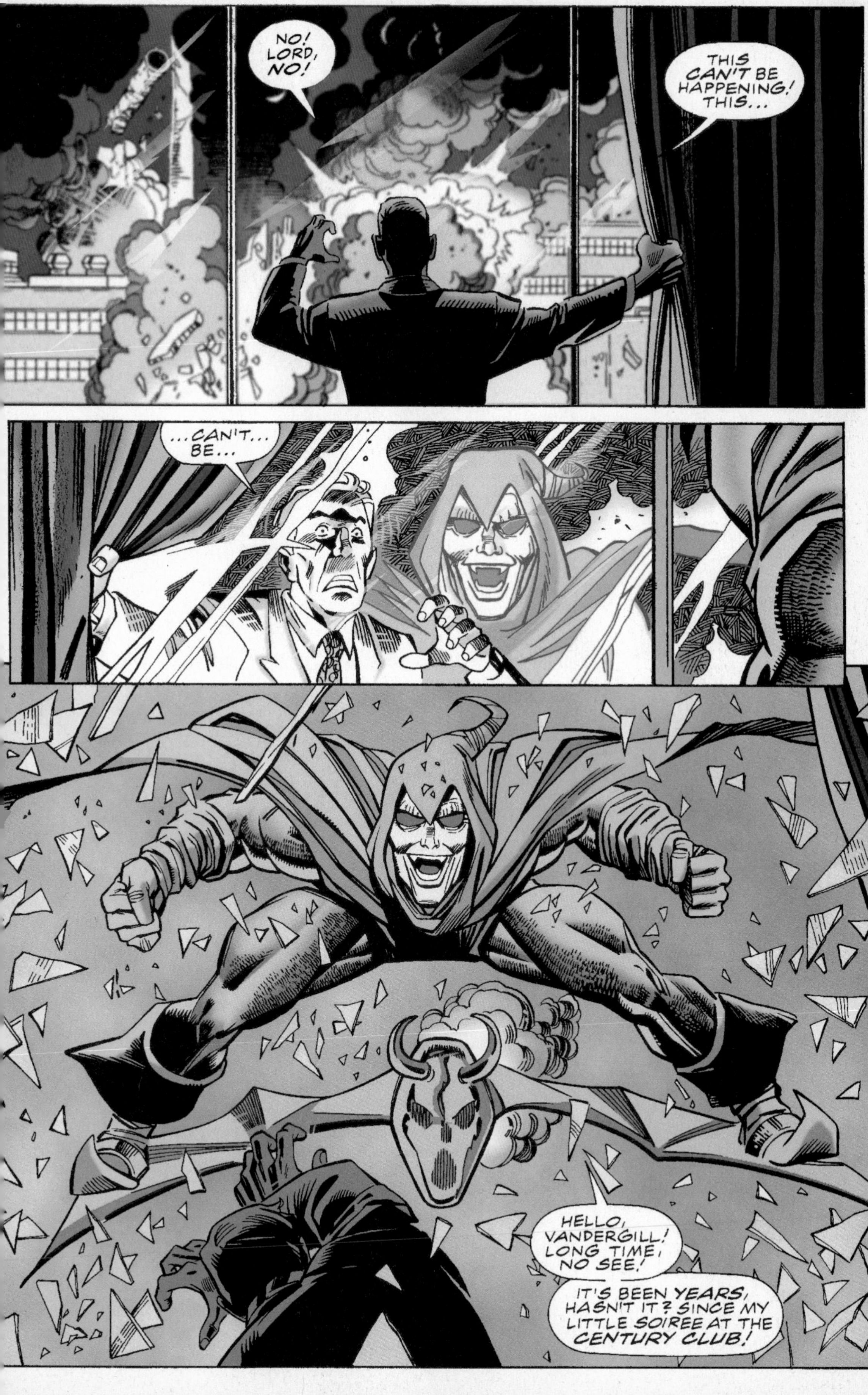

NO! LORD, NO!
THIS CAN'T BE HAPPENING! THIS...
...CAN'T... BE...
HELLO, VANDERGILL! LONG TIME, NO SEE!
IT'S BEEN YEARS, HASN'T IT? SINCE MY LITTLE SOIREE AT THE CENTURY CLUB!

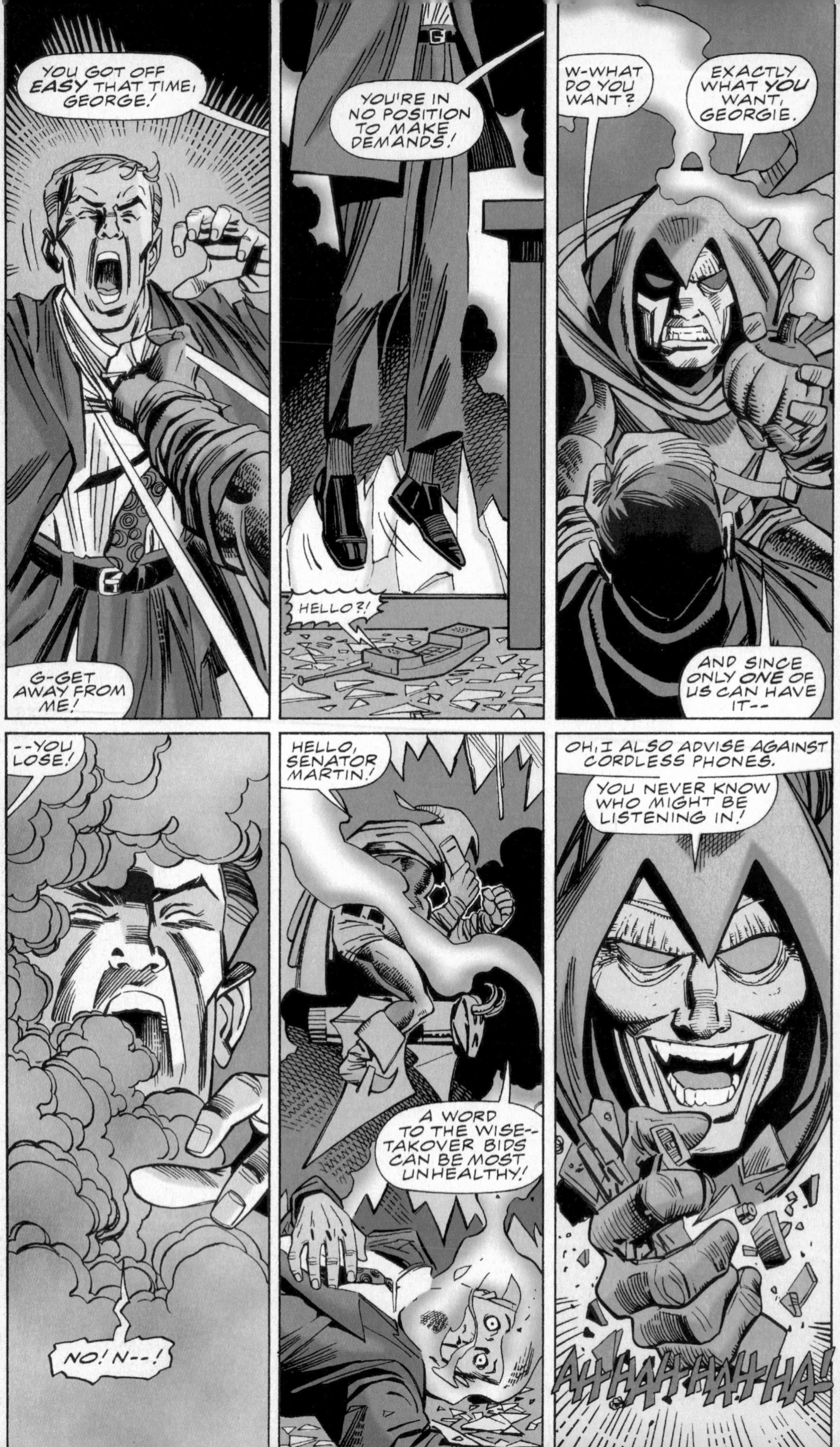
YOU GOT OFF EASY THAT TIME, GEORGE!
G-GET AWAY FROM ME!
YOU'RE IN NO POSITION TO MAKE DEMANDS!
HELLO?!
W-WHAT DO YOU WANT?
EXACTLY WHAT YOU WANT, GEORGIE.
AND SINCE ONLY ONE OF US CAN HAVE IT--
--YOU LOSE!
NO! N--!
HELLO, SENATOR MARTIN!
A WORD TO THE WISE--TAKEOVER BIDS CAN BE MOST UNHEALTHY!
OH, I ALSO ADVISE AGAINST CORDLESS PHONES.
YOU NEVER KNOW WHO MIGHT BE LISTENING IN!
AHHAHHAHHA!

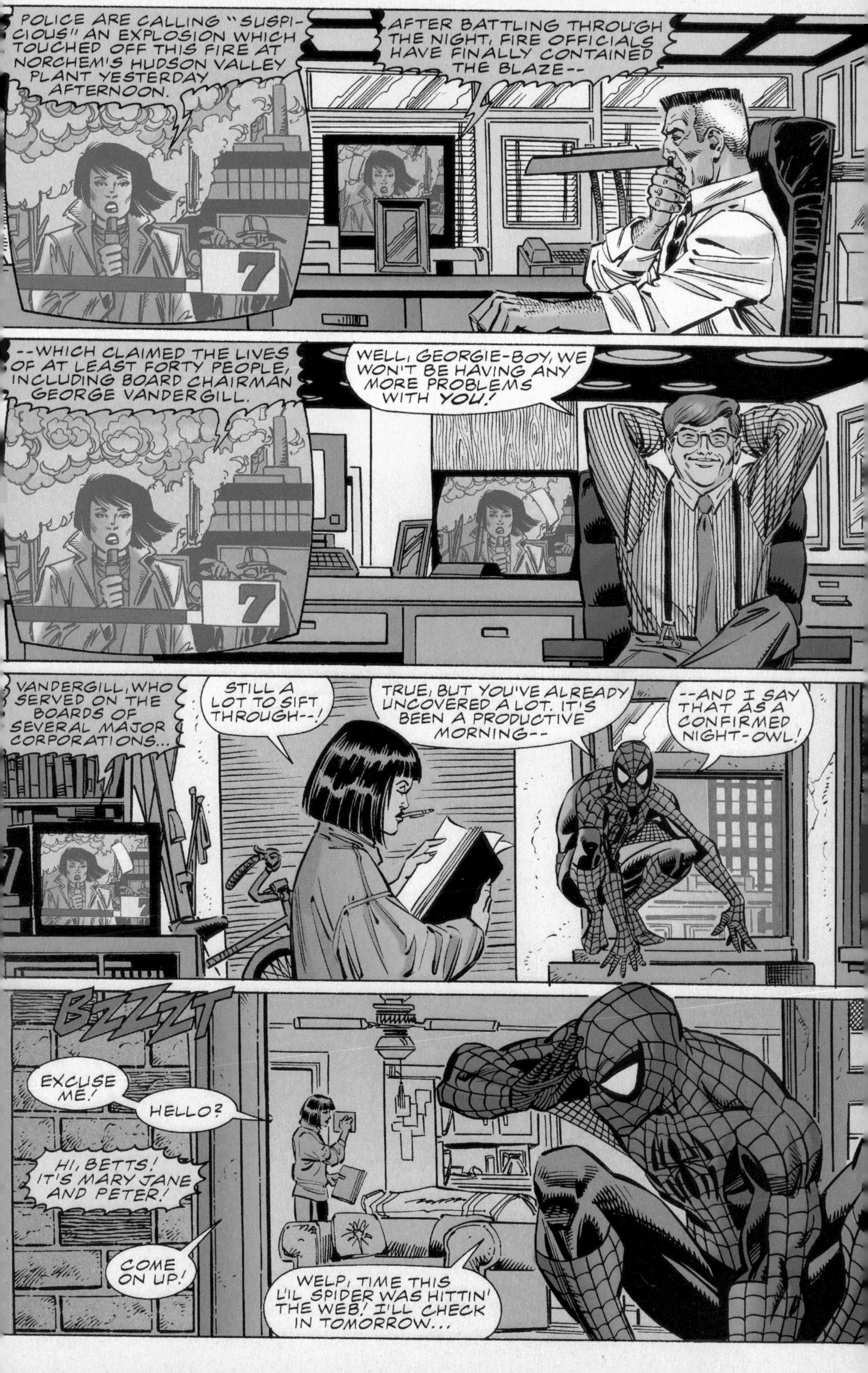
POLICE ARE CALLING "SUSPICIOUS" AN EXPLOSION WHICH TOUCHED OFF THIS FIRE AT NORCHEM'S HUDSON VALLEY PLANT YESTERDAY AFTERNOON.
AFTER BATTLING THROUGH THE NIGHT, FIRE OFFICIALS HAVE FINALLY CONTAINED THE BLAZE--
7
--WHICH CLAIMED THE LIVES OF AT LEAST FORTY PEOPLE, INCLUDING BOARD CHAIRMAN GEORGE VANDERGILL.
WELL, GEORGIE-BOY, WE WON'T BE HAVING ANY MORE PROBLEMS WITH YOU!
7
VANDERGILL, WHO SERVED ON THE BOARDS OF SEVERAL MAJOR CORPORATIONS...
STILL A LOT TO SIFT THROUGH--!
TRUE, BUT YOU'VE ALREADY UNCOVERED A LOT. IT'S BEEN A PRODUCTIVE MORNING--
--AND I SAY THAT AS A CONFIRMED NIGHT-OWL!
BZZZT
EXCUSE ME!
HELLO?
HI, BETTS! IT'S MARY JANE AND PETER!
COME ON UP!
WELP, TIME THIS L'IL SPIDER WAS HITTIN' THE WEB! I'LL CHECK IN TOMORROW...

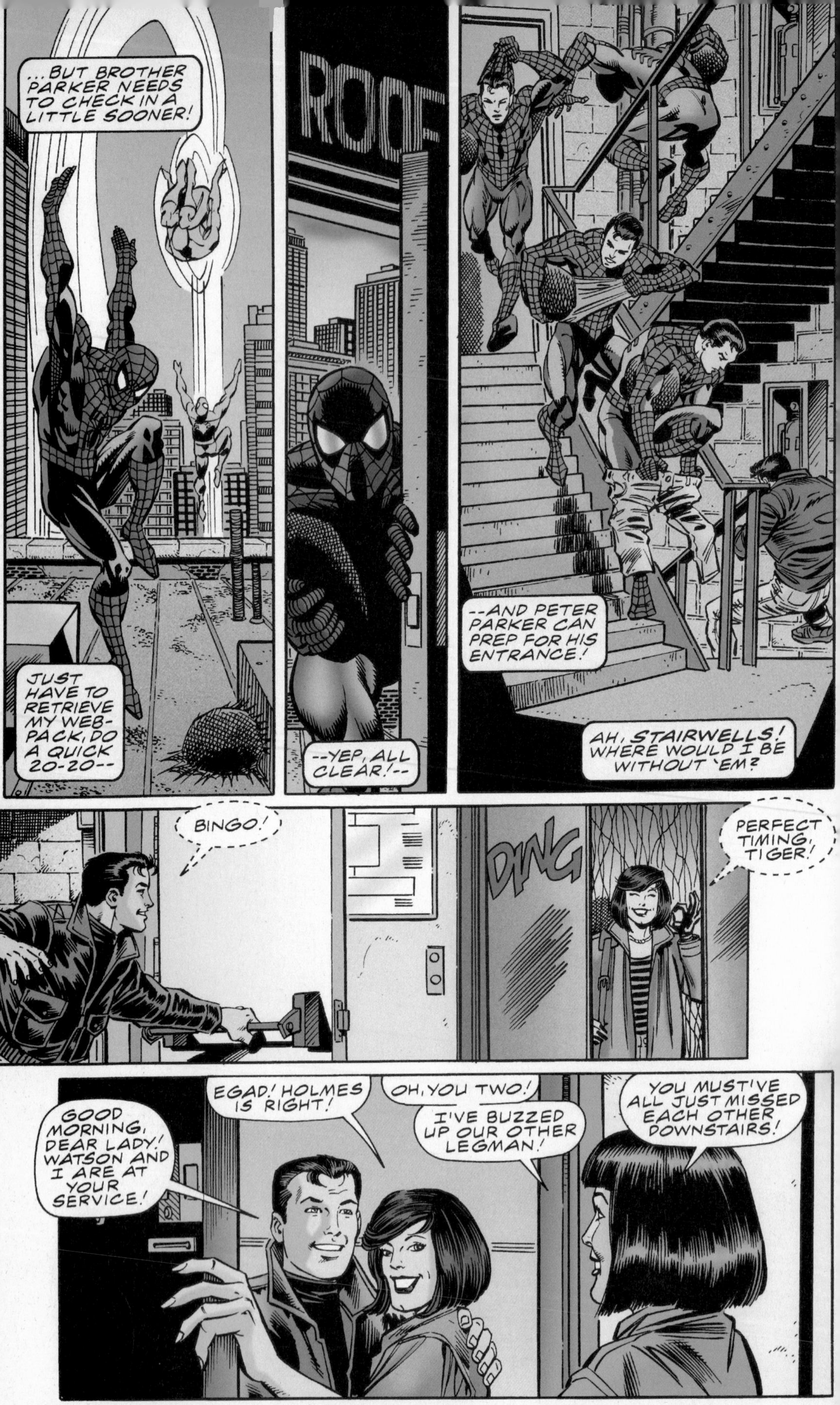
...BUT BROTHER PARKER NEEDS TO CHECK IN A LITTLE SOONER!
JUST HAVE TO RETRIEVE MY WEB-PACK, DO A QUICK 20-20--
ROOF
--YEP, ALL CLEAR!--
--AND PETER PARKER CAN PREP FOR HIS ENTRANCE!
AH, STAIRWELLS! WHERE WOULD I BE WITHOUT 'EM?
BINGO!
DING
PERFECT TIMING, TIGER!
GOOD MORNING, DEAR LADY! WATSON AND I ARE AT YOUR SERVICE!
EGAD! HOLMES IS RIGHT!
OH, YOU TWO!
I'VE BUZZED UP OUR OTHER LEGMAN!
YOU MUST'VE ALL JUST MISSED EACH OTHER DOWNSTAIRS!

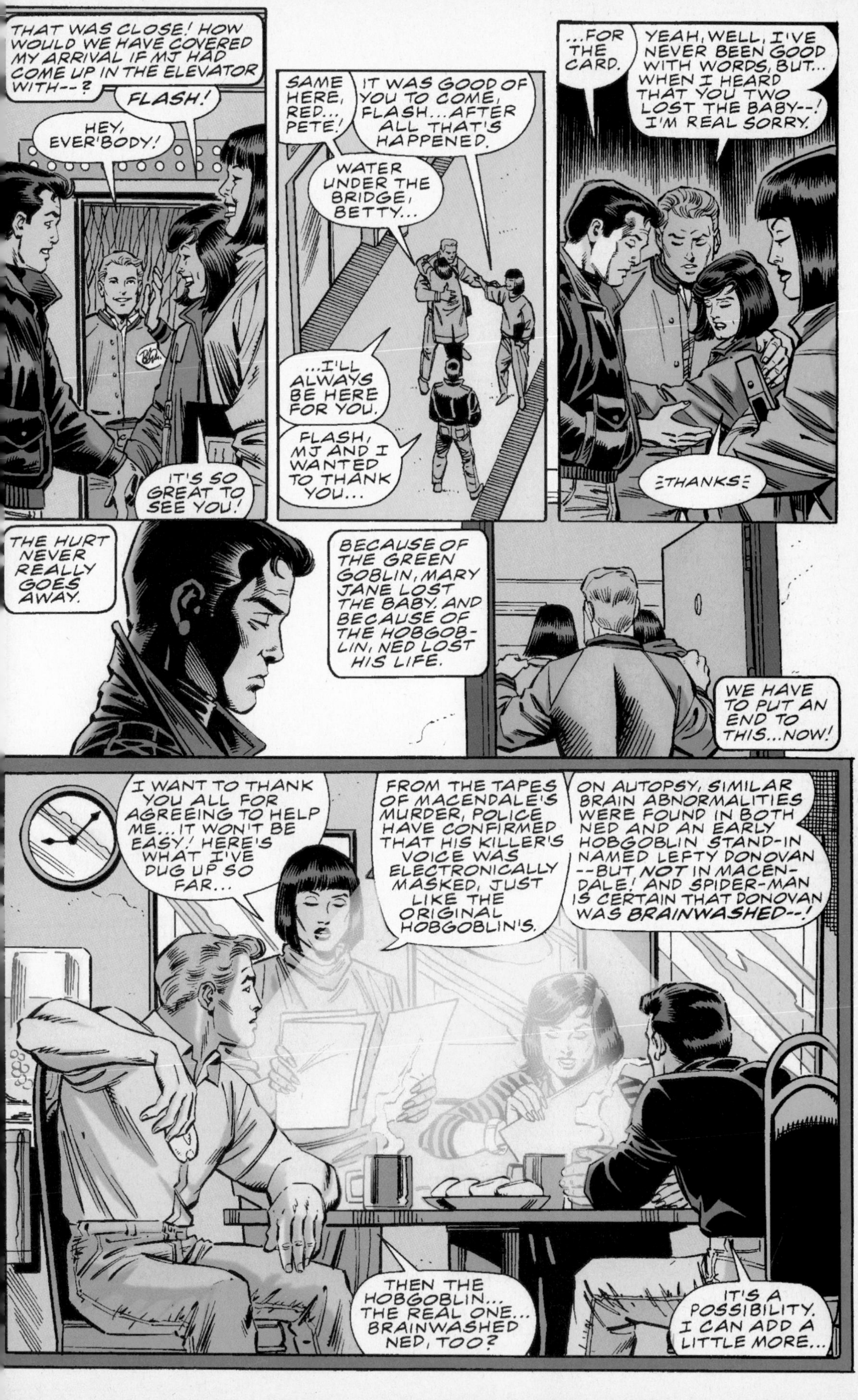
THAT WAS CLOSE! HOW WOULD WE HAVE COVERED MY ARRIVAL IF MJ HAD COME UP IN THE ELEVATOR WITH--?
FLASH!
HEY, EVER'BODY!
IT'S SO GREAT TO SEE YOU!
SAME HERE, RED... PETE!
IT WAS GOOD OF YOU TO COME, FLASH... AFTER ALL THAT'S HAPPENED.
WATER UNDER THE BRIDGE, BETTY...
...I'LL ALWAYS BE HERE FOR YOU.
FLASH, MJ AND I WANTED TO THANK YOU...
...FOR THE CARD.
YEAH, WELL, I'VE NEVER BEEN GOOD WITH WORDS, BUT... WHEN I HEARD THAT YOU TWO LOST THE BABY--! I'M REAL SORRY.
THANKS
THE HURT NEVER REALLY GOES AWAY.
BECAUSE OF THE GREEN GOBLIN, MARY JANE LOST THE BABY. AND BECAUSE OF THE HOBGOBLIN, NED LOST HIS LIFE.
WE HAVE TO PUT AN END TO THIS...NOW!
I WANT TO THANK YOU ALL FOR AGREEING TO HELP ME...IT WON'T BE EASY! HERE'S WHAT I'VE DUG UP SO FAR...
FROM THE TAPES OF MACENDALE'S MURDER, POLICE HAVE CONFIRMED THAT HIS KILLER'S VOICE WAS ELECTRONICALLY MASKED, JUST LIKE THE ORIGINAL HOBGOBLIN'S.
ON AUTOPSY, SIMILAR BRAIN ABNORMALITIES WERE FOUND IN BOTH NED AND AN EARLY HOBGOBLIN STAND-IN NAMED LEFTY DONOVAN --BUT NOT IN MACENDALE! AND SPIDER-MAN IS CERTAIN THAT DONOVAN WAS BRAINWASHED--!
THEN THE HOBGOBLIN... THE REAL ONE... BRAINWASHED NED, TOO?
IT'S A POSSIBILITY. I CAN ADD A LITTLE MORE...

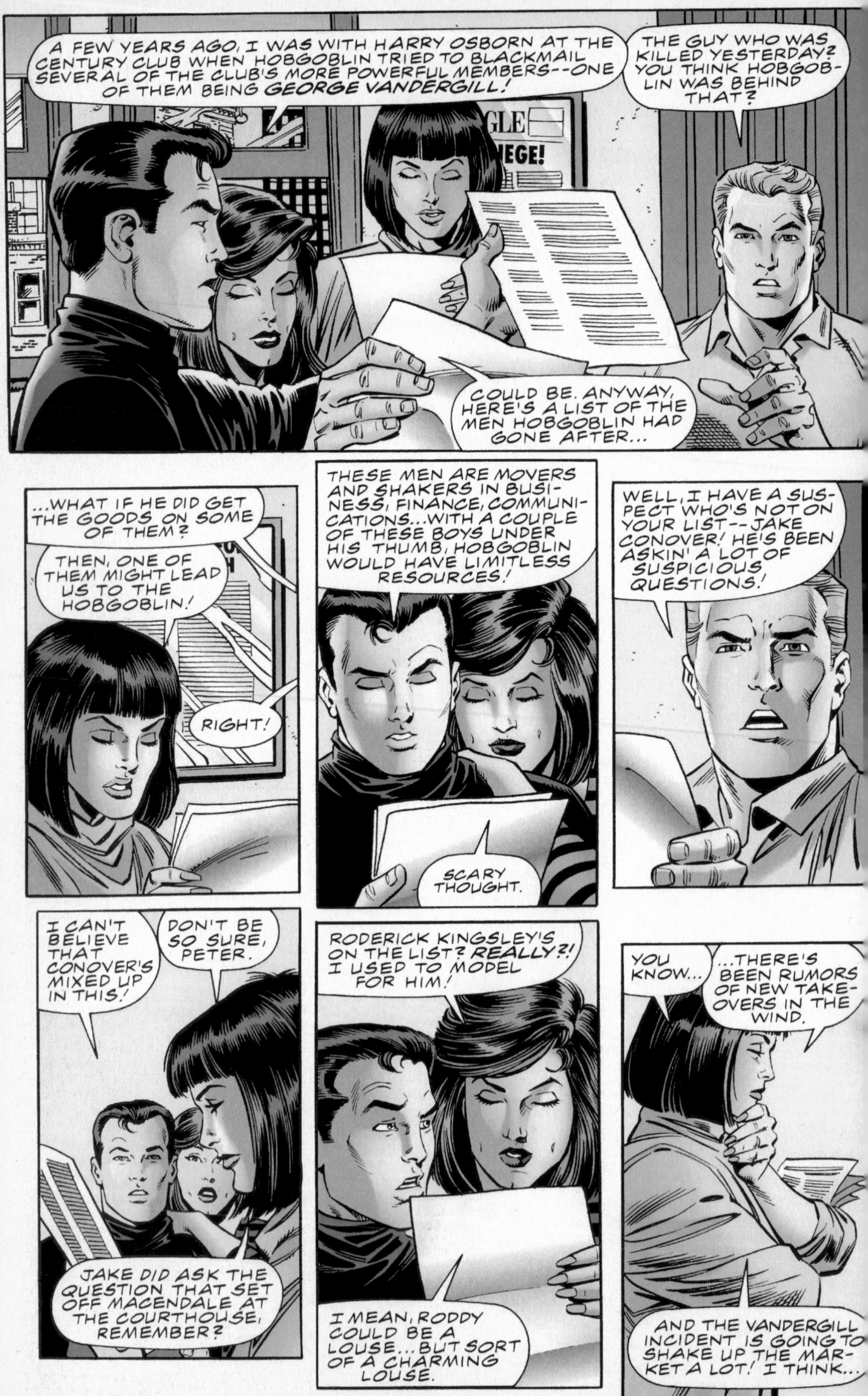
A FEW YEARS AGO, I WAS WITH HARRY OSBORN AT THE CENTURY CLUB WHEN HOBGOBLIN TRIED TO BLACKMAIL SEVERAL OF THE CLUB'S MORE POWERFUL MEMBERS--ONE OF THEM BEING *GEORGE VANDERGILL!*
THE GUY WHO WAS KILLED YESTERDAY? YOU THINK HOBGOBLIN WAS BEHIND THAT?
COULD BE. ANYWAY, HERE'S A LIST OF THE MEN HOBGOBLIN HAD GONE AFTER...
...WHAT IF HE DID GET THE GOODS ON SOME OF THEM?
THEN, ONE OF THEM MIGHT LEAD US TO THE HOBGOBLIN!
RIGHT!
THESE MEN ARE MOVERS AND SHAKERS IN BUSINESS, FINANCE, COMMUNICATIONS... WITH A COUPLE OF THESE BOYS UNDER HIS THUMB, HOBGOBLIN WOULD HAVE LIMITLESS RESOURCES!
SCARY THOUGHT.
WELL, I HAVE A SUSPECT WHO'S NOT ON YOUR LIST--JAKE CONOVER! HE'S BEEN ASKIN' A LOT OF SUSPICIOUS QUESTIONS!
I CAN'T BELIEVE THAT CONOVER'S MIXED UP IN THIS!
DON'T BE SO SURE, PETER.
JAKE DID ASK THE QUESTION THAT SET OFF MACENDALE AT THE COURTHOUSE, REMEMBER?
RODERICK KINGSLEY'S ON THE LIST? *REALLY?!* I USED TO MODEL FOR HIM!
I MEAN, RODDY COULD BE A LOUSE... BUT SORT OF A CHARMING LOUSE.
YOU KNOW...
...THERE'S BEEN RUMORS OF NEW TAKEOVERS IN THE WIND.
AND THE VANDERGILL INCIDENT IS GOING TO SHAKE UP THE MARKET A LOT! I THINK...

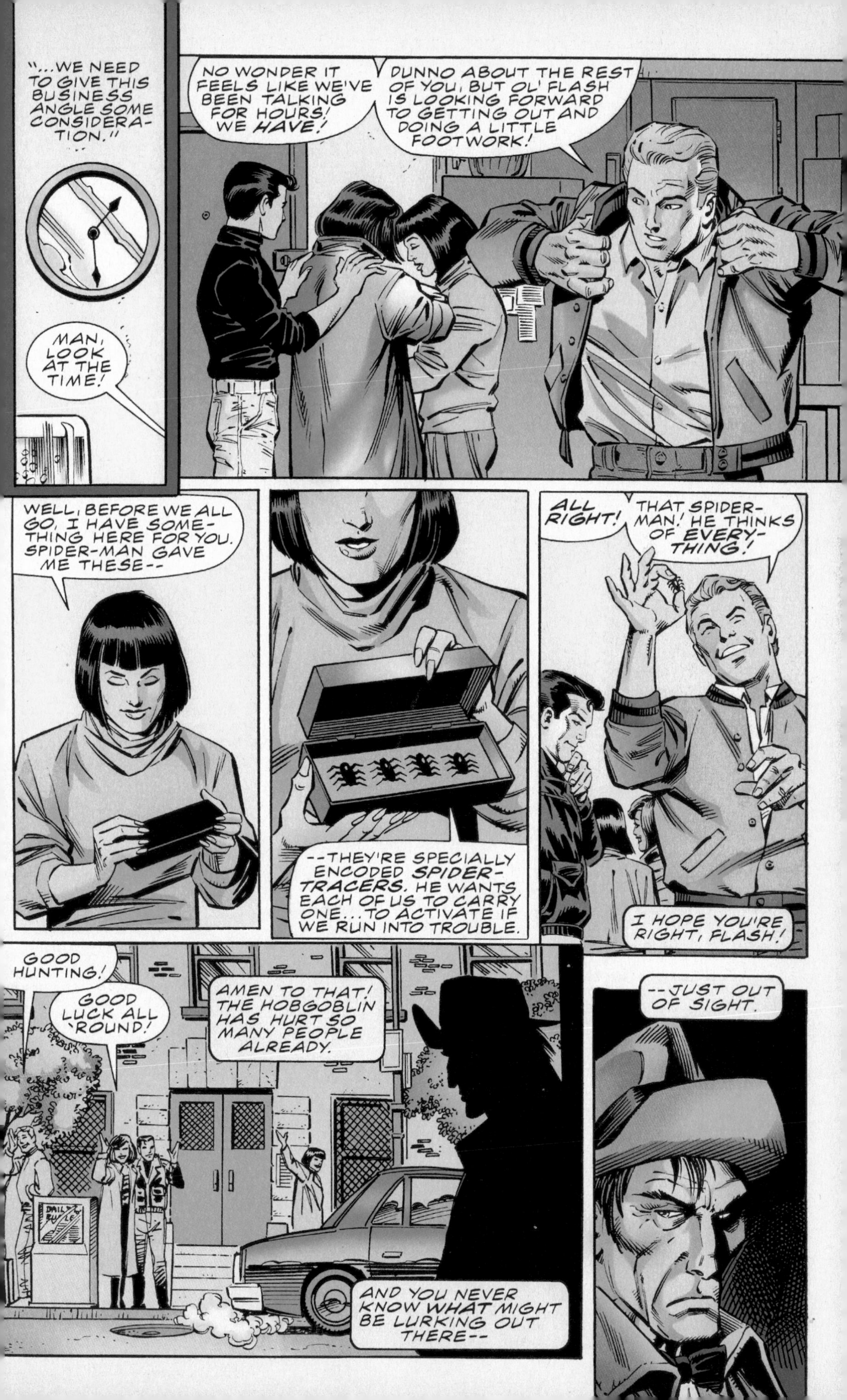
"...WE NEED TO GIVE THIS BUSINESS ANGLE SOME CONSIDERA-TION."
MAN, LOOK AT THE TIME!
NO WONDER IT FEELS LIKE WE'VE BEEN TALKING FOR HOURS! WE HAVE!
DUNNO ABOUT THE REST OF YOU, BUT OL' FLASH IS LOOKING FORWARD TO GETTING OUT AND DOING A LITTLE FOOTWORK!
WELL, BEFORE WE ALL GO, I HAVE SOME-THING HERE FOR YOU. SPIDER-MAN GAVE ME THESE--
--THEY'RE SPECIALLY ENCODED SPIDER-TRACERS. HE WANTS EACH OF US TO CARRY ONE... TO ACTIVATE IF WE RUN INTO TROUBLE.
ALL RIGHT!
THAT SPIDER-MAN! HE THINKS OF EVERY-THING!
I HOPE YOU'RE RIGHT, FLASH!
GOOD HUNTING!
GOOD LUCK ALL 'ROUND!
AMEN TO THAT! THE HOBGOBLIN HAS HURT SO MANY PEOPLE ALREADY.
AND YOU NEVER KNOW WHAT MIGHT BE LURKING OUT THERE--
--JUST OUT OF SIGHT.

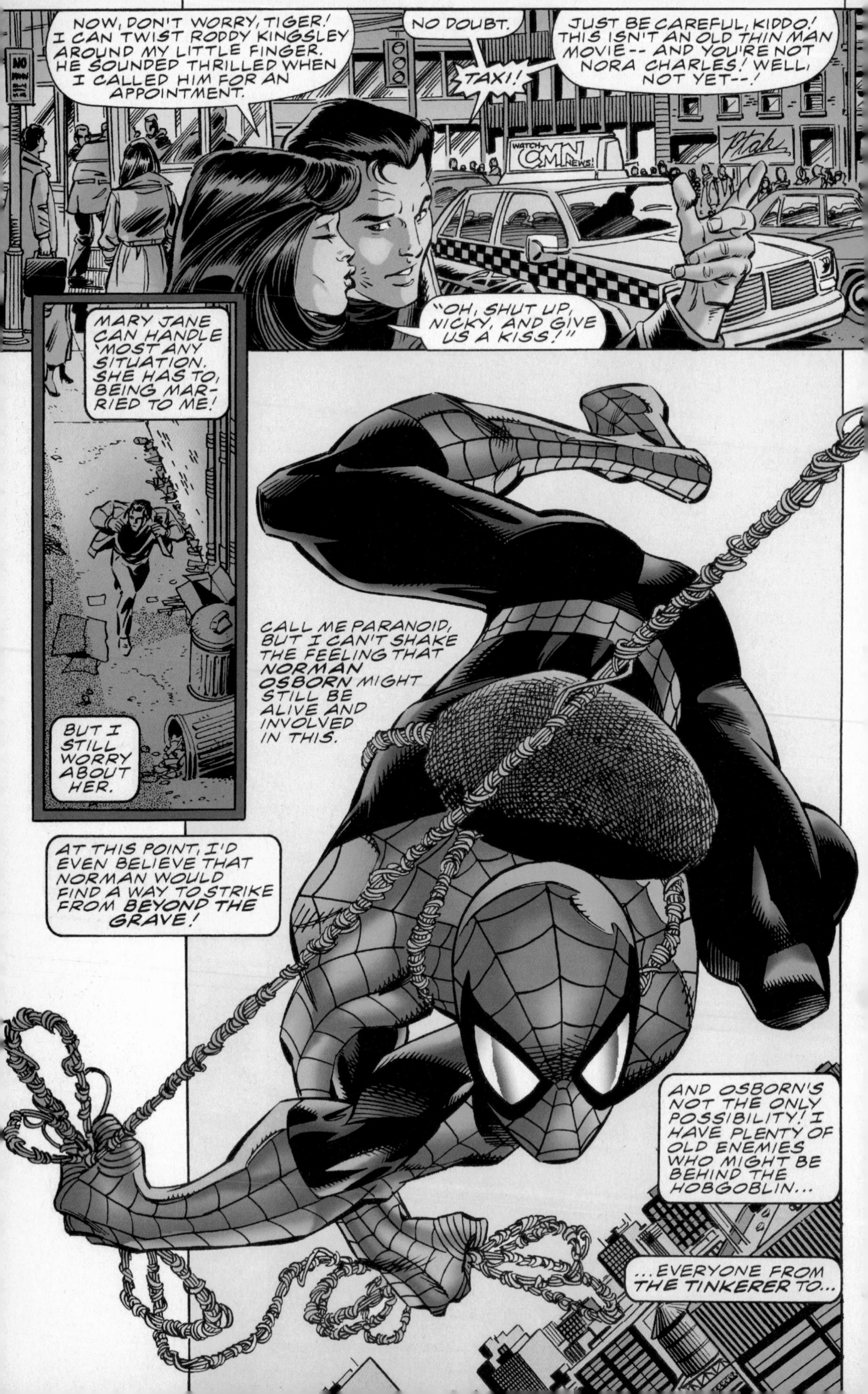
NOW, DON'T WORRY, TIGER! I CAN TWIST RODDY KINGSLEY AROUND MY LITTLE FINGER. HE SOUNDED THRILLED WHEN I CALLED HIM FOR AN APPOINTMENT.
NO DOUBT.
TAXI!
JUST BE CAREFUL, KIDDO! THIS ISN'T AN OLD THIN MAN MOVIE -- AND YOU'RE NOT NORA CHARLES! WELL, NOT YET--!
"OH, SHUT UP, NICKY, AND GIVE US A KISS!"
WATCH CMN NEWS!
MARY JANE CAN HANDLE 'MOST ANY SITUATION. SHE HAS TO, BEING MARRIED TO ME!
BUT I STILL WORRY ABOUT HER.
CALL ME PARANOID, BUT I CAN'T SHAKE THE FEELING THAT NORMAN OSBORN MIGHT STILL BE ALIVE AND INVOLVED IN THIS.
AT THIS POINT, I'D EVEN BELIEVE THAT NORMAN WOULD FIND A WAY TO STRIKE FROM BEYOND THE GRAVE!
AND OSBORN'S NOT THE ONLY POSSIBILITY! I HAVE PLENTY OF OLD ENEMIES WHO MIGHT BE BEHIND THE HOBGOBLIN...
...EVERYONE FROM THE TINKERER TO...

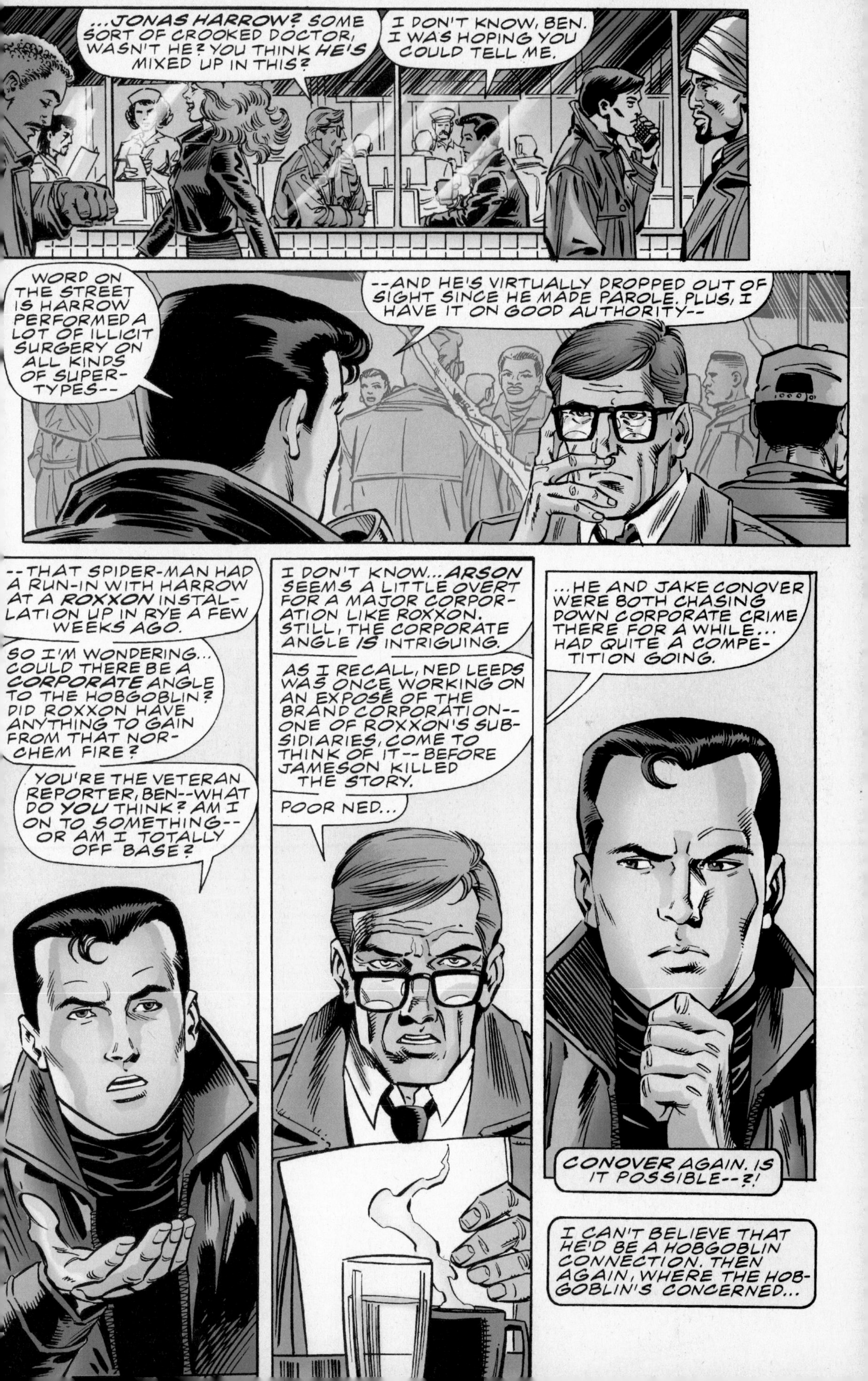
...JONAS HARROW? SOME SORT OF CROOKED DOCTOR, WASN'T HE? YOU THINK HE'S MIXED UP IN THIS?
I DON'T KNOW, BEN. I WAS HOPING YOU COULD TELL ME.
WORD ON THE STREET IS HARROW PERFORMED A LOT OF ILLICIT SURGERY ON ALL KINDS OF SUPER-TYPES--
--AND HE'S VIRTUALLY DROPPED OUT OF SIGHT SINCE HE MADE PAROLE. PLUS, I HAVE IT ON GOOD AUTHORITY--
--THAT SPIDER-MAN HAD A RUN-IN WITH HARROW AT A ROXXON INSTALLATION UP IN RYE A FEW WEEKS AGO.
SO I'M WONDERING... COULD THERE BE A CORPORATE ANGLE TO THE HOBGOBLIN? DID ROXXON HAVE ANYTHING TO GAIN FROM THAT NORCHEM FIRE?
YOU'RE THE VETERAN REPORTER, BEN--WHAT DO YOU THINK? AM I ON TO SOMETHING--OR AM I TOTALLY OFF BASE?
I DON'T KNOW... ARSON SEEMS A LITTLE OVERT FOR A MAJOR CORPORATION LIKE ROXXON. STILL, THE CORPORATE ANGLE IS INTRIGUING.
AS I RECALL, NED LEEDS WAS ONCE WORKING ON AN EXPOSÉ OF THE BRAND CORPORATION--ONE OF ROXXON'S SUBSIDIARIES, COME TO THINK OF IT--BEFORE JAMESON KILLED THE STORY.
POOR NED...
...HE AND JAKE CONOVER WERE BOTH CHASING DOWN CORPORATE CRIME THERE FOR A WHILE... HAD QUITE A COMPETITION GOING.
CONOVER AGAIN. IS IT POSSIBLE--?!
I CAN'T BELIEVE THAT HE'D BE A HOBGOBLIN CONNECTION. THEN AGAIN, WHERE THE HOBGOBLIN'S CONCERNED...

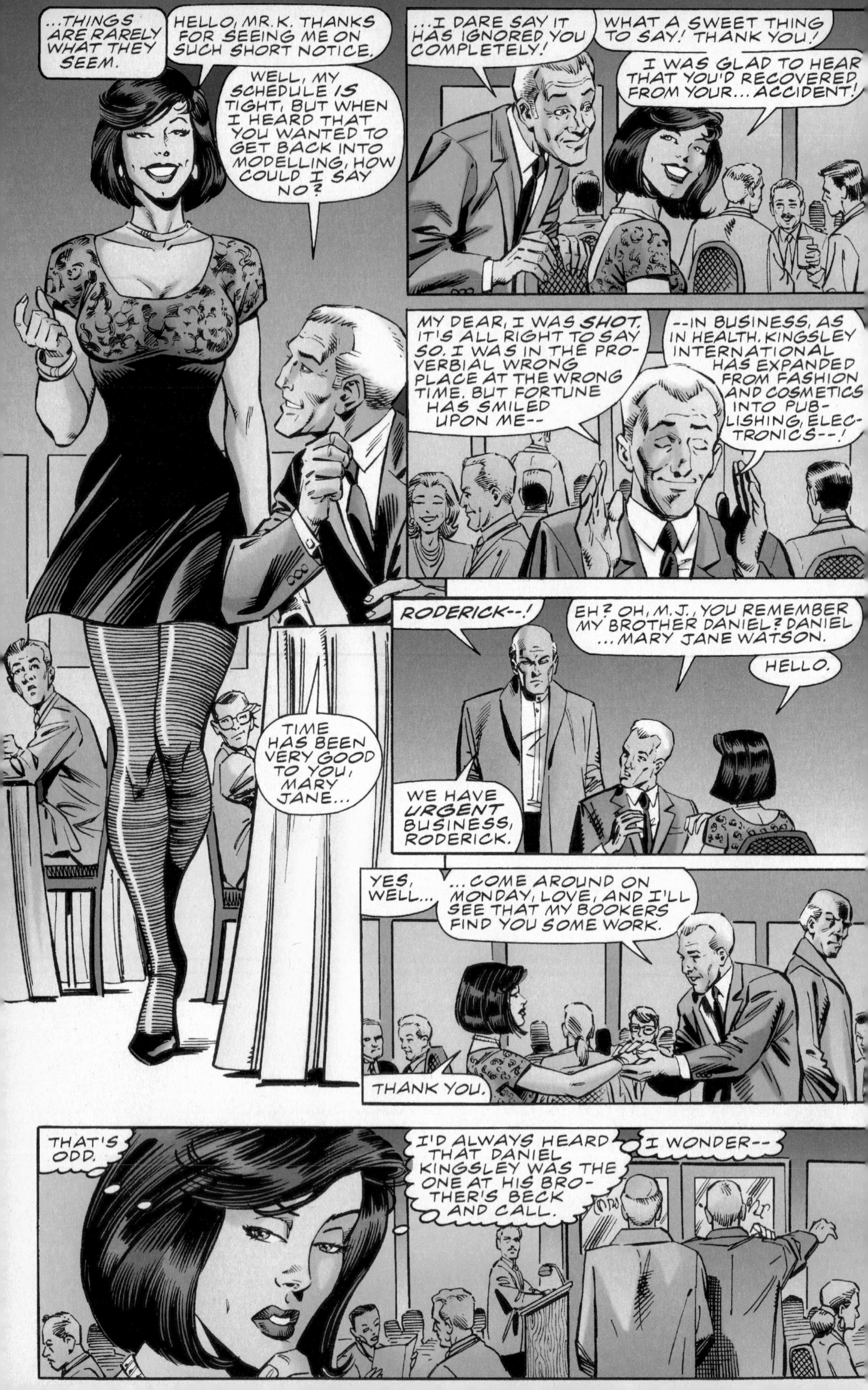
...THINGS ARE RARELY WHAT THEY SEEM.
HELLO, MR. K. THANKS FOR SEEING ME ON SUCH SHORT NOTICE.
WELL, MY SCHEDULE IS TIGHT, BUT WHEN I HEARD THAT YOU WANTED TO GET BACK INTO MODELLING, HOW COULD I SAY NO?
TIME HAS BEEN VERY GOOD TO YOU, MARY JANE...
...I DARE SAY IT HAS IGNORED YOU COMPLETELY!
WHAT A SWEET THING TO SAY! THANK YOU!
I WAS GLAD TO HEAR THAT YOU'D RECOVERED FROM YOUR... ACCIDENT!
MY DEAR, I WAS SHOT. IT'S ALL RIGHT TO SAY SO. I WAS IN THE PROVERBIAL WRONG PLACE AT THE WRONG TIME. BUT FORTUNE HAS SMILED UPON ME--
--IN BUSINESS, AS IN HEALTH. KINGSLEY INTERNATIONAL HAS EXPANDED FROM FASHION AND COSMETICS INTO PUBLISHING, ELECTRONICS--!
RODERICK--!
EH? OH, M.J., YOU REMEMBER MY BROTHER DANIEL? DANIEL ...MARY JANE WATSON.
HELLO.
WE HAVE URGENT BUSINESS, RODERICK.
YES, WELL...
...COME AROUND ON MONDAY, LOVE, AND I'LL SEE THAT MY BOOKERS FIND YOU SOME WORK.
THANK YOU.
THAT'S ODD.
I'D ALWAYS HEARD THAT DANIEL KINGSLEY WAS THE ONE AT HIS BROTHER'S BECK AND CALL.
I WONDER--

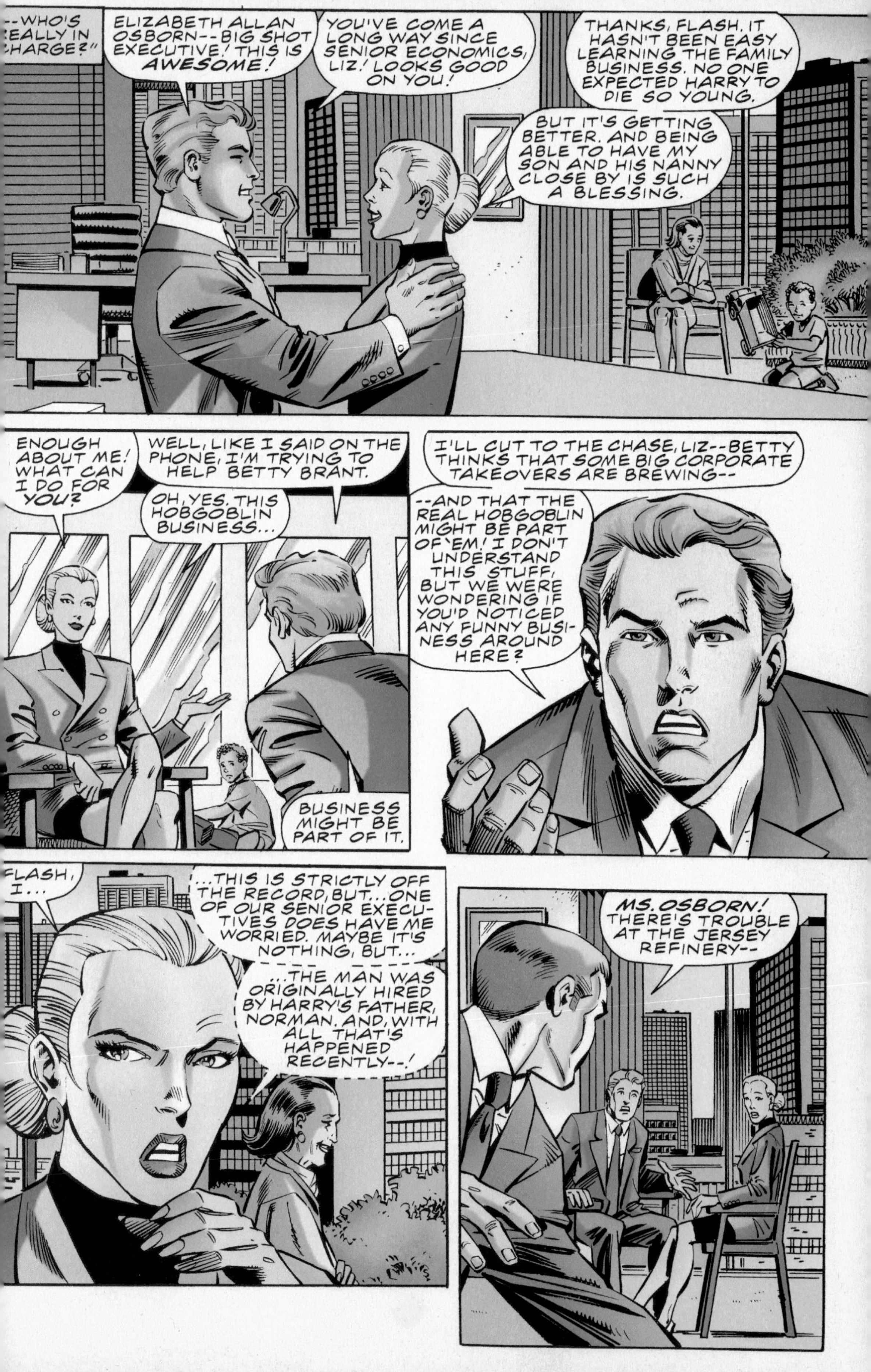

--WHO'S
EALLY IN
HARGE?"
ELIZABETH ALLAN OSBORN--BIG SHOT EXECUTIVE! THIS IS AWESOME!
YOU'VE COME A LONG WAY SINCE SENIOR ECONOMICS, LIZ! LOOKS GOOD ON YOU!
THANKS, FLASH. IT HASN'T BEEN EASY LEARNING THE FAMILY BUSINESS. NO ONE EXPECTED HARRY TO DIE SO YOUNG.
BUT IT'S GETTING BETTER. AND BEING ABLE TO HAVE MY SON AND HIS NANNY CLOSE BY IS SUCH A BLESSING.
ENOUGH ABOUT ME! WHAT CAN I DO FOR YOU?
WELL, LIKE I SAID ON THE PHONE, I'M TRYING TO HELP BETTY BRANT.
OH, YES. THIS HOBGOBLIN BUSINESS...
BUSINESS MIGHT BE PART OF IT.
I'LL CUT TO THE CHASE, LIZ--BETTY THINKS THAT SOME BIG CORPORATE TAKEOVERS ARE BREWING--
--AND THAT THE REAL HOBGOBLIN MIGHT BE PART OF 'EM! I DON'T UNDERSTAND THIS STUFF, BUT WE WERE WONDERING IF YOU'D NOTICED ANY FUNNY BUSINESS AROUND HERE?
FLASH, I...
...THIS IS STRICTLY OFF THE RECORD, BUT... ONE OF OUR SENIOR EXECUTIVES DOES HAVE ME WORRIED. MAYBE IT'S NOTHING, BUT...
...THE MAN WAS ORIGINALLY HIRED BY HARRY'S FATHER, NORMAN. AND, WITH ALL THAT'S HAPPENED RECENTLY--!
MS. OSBORN! THERE'S TROUBLE AT THE JERSEY REFINERY--

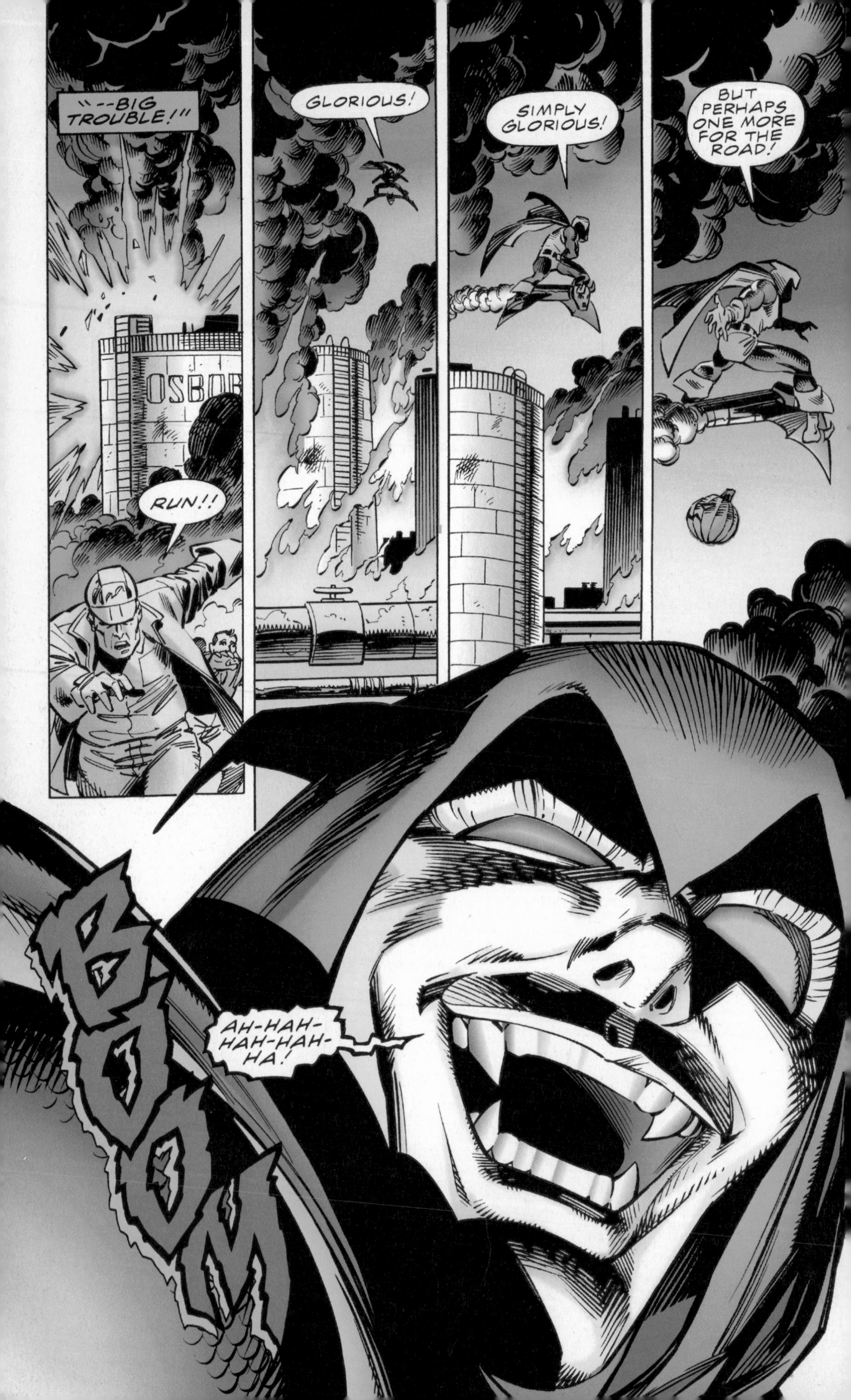
"--BIG TROUBLE!"
RUN!!
GLORIOUS!
SIMPLY GLORIOUS!
BUT PERHAPS ONE MORE FOR THE ROAD!
BOOM
AH-HAH-HAH-HAH-HAH-HA!

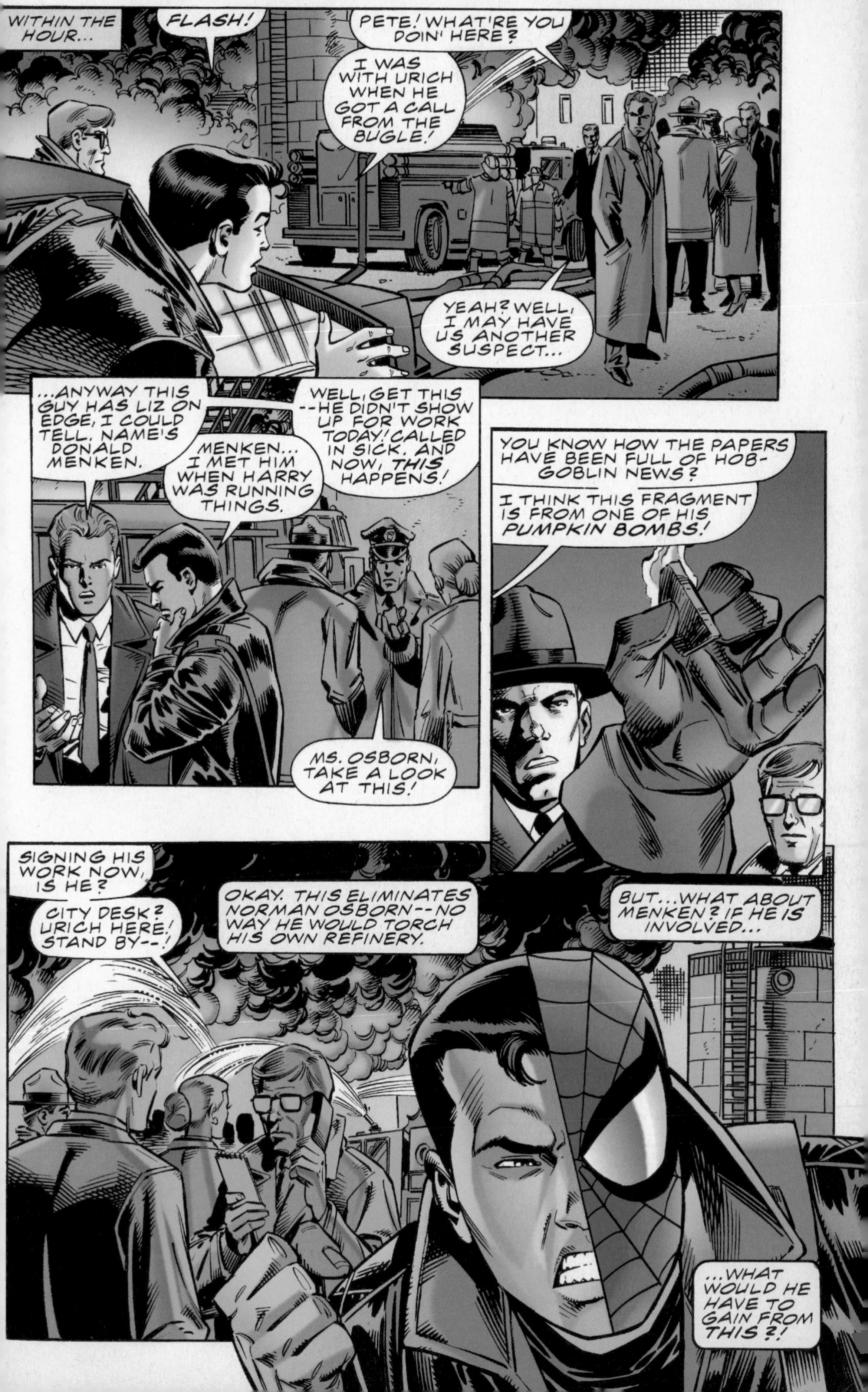

WITHIN THE HOUR...
FLASH!
PETE! WHAT'RE YOU DOIN' HERE?
I WAS WITH URICH WHEN HE GOT A CALL FROM THE BUGLE!
YEAH? WELL, I MAY HAVE US ANOTHER SUSPECT...
...ANYWAY THIS GUY HAS LIZ ON EDGE, I COULD TELL. NAME'S DONALD MENKEN.
MENKEN... I MET HIM WHEN HARRY WAS RUNNING THINGS.
WELL, GET THIS --HE DIDN'T SHOW UP FOR WORK TODAY! CALLED IN SICK. AND NOW, THIS HAPPENS!
MS. OSBORN, TAKE A LOOK AT THIS!
YOU KNOW HOW THE PAPERS HAVE BEEN FULL OF HOB-GOBLIN NEWS?
I THINK THIS FRAGMENT IS FROM ONE OF HIS PUMPKIN BOMBS!
SIGNING HIS WORK NOW, IS HE?
CITY DESK? URICH HERE! STAND BY--!
OKAY. THIS ELIMINATES NORMAN OSBORN--NO WAY HE WOULD TORCH HIS OWN REFINERY.
BUT...WHAT ABOUT MENKEN? IF HE IS INVOLVED...
...WHAT WOULD HE HAVE TO GAIN FROM THIS?!

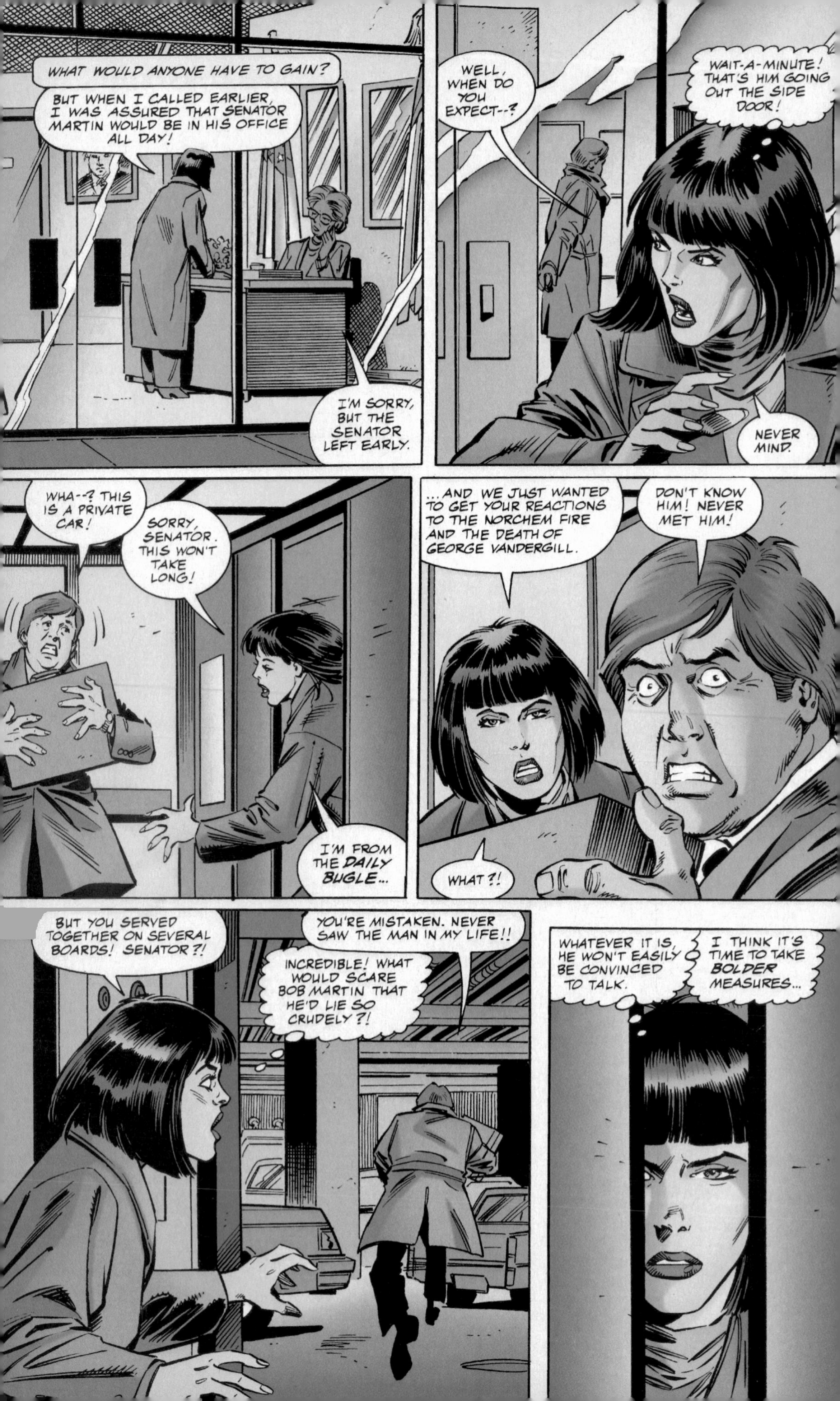
WHAT WOULD ANYONE HAVE TO GAIN?
BUT WHEN I CALLED EARLIER, I WAS ASSURED THAT SENATOR MARTIN WOULD BE IN HIS OFFICE ALL DAY!
I'M SORRY, BUT THE SENATOR LEFT EARLY.
WELL, WHEN DO YOU EXPECT--?
WAIT-A-MINUTE! THAT'S HIM GOING OUT THE SIDE DOOR!
NEVER MIND.
WHA--? THIS IS A PRIVATE CAR!
SORRY, SENATOR. THIS WON'T TAKE LONG!
I'M FROM THE DAILY BUGLE...
...AND WE JUST WANTED TO GET YOUR REACTIONS TO THE NORCHEM FIRE AND THE DEATH OF GEORGE VANDERGILL.
DON'T KNOW HIM! NEVER MET HIM!
WHAT?!
BUT YOU SERVED TOGETHER ON SEVERAL BOARDS! SENATOR?!
YOU'RE MISTAKEN. NEVER SAW THE MAN IN MY LIFE!!
INCREDIBLE! WHAT WOULD SCARE BOB MARTIN THAT HE'D LIE SO CRUDELY?!
WHATEVER IT IS, HE WON'T EASILY BE CONVINCED TO TALK.
I THINK IT'S TIME TO TAKE BOLDER MEASURES...

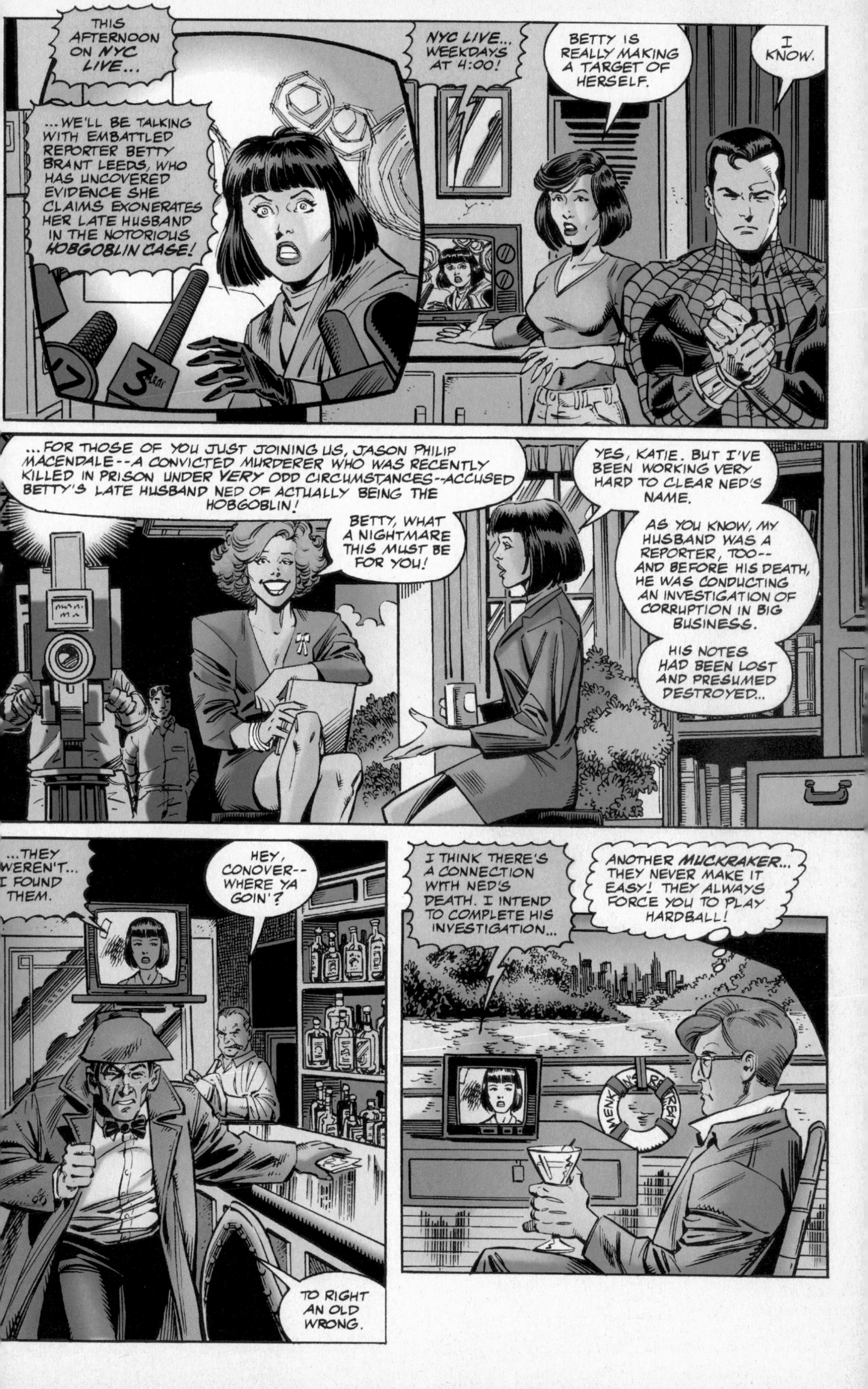
THIS AFTERNOON ON NYC LIVE...
...WE'LL BE TALKING WITH EMBATTLED REPORTER BETTY BRANT LEEDS, WHO HAS UNCOVERED EVIDENCE SHE CLAIMS EXONERATES HER LATE HUSBAND IN THE NOTORIOUS HOBGOBLIN CASE!
NYC LIVE... WEEKDAYS AT 4:00!
BETTY IS REALLY MAKING A TARGET OF HERSELF.
I KNOW.
...FOR THOSE OF YOU JUST JOINING US, JASON PHILIP MACENDALE--A CONVICTED MURDERER WHO WAS RECENTLY KILLED IN PRISON UNDER VERY ODD CIRCUMSTANCES--ACCUSED BETTY'S LATE HUSBAND NED OF ACTUALLY BEING THE HOBGOBLIN!
BETTY, WHAT A NIGHTMARE THIS MUST BE FOR YOU!
YES, KATIE. BUT I'VE BEEN WORKING VERY HARD TO CLEAR NED'S NAME.
AS YOU KNOW, MY HUSBAND WAS A REPORTER, TOO-- AND BEFORE HIS DEATH, HE WAS CONDUCTING AN INVESTIGATION OF CORRUPTION IN BIG BUSINESS.
HIS NOTES HAD BEEN LOST AND PRESUMED DESTROYED...
...THEY WEREN'T... I FOUND THEM.
HEY, CONOVER-- WHERE YA GOIN'?
TO RIGHT AN OLD WRONG.
I THINK THERE'S A CONNECTION WITH NED'S DEATH. I INTEND TO COMPLETE HIS INVESTIGATION...
ANOTHER MUCKRAKER... THEY NEVER MAKE IT EASY! THEY ALWAYS FORCE YOU TO PLAY HARDBALL!

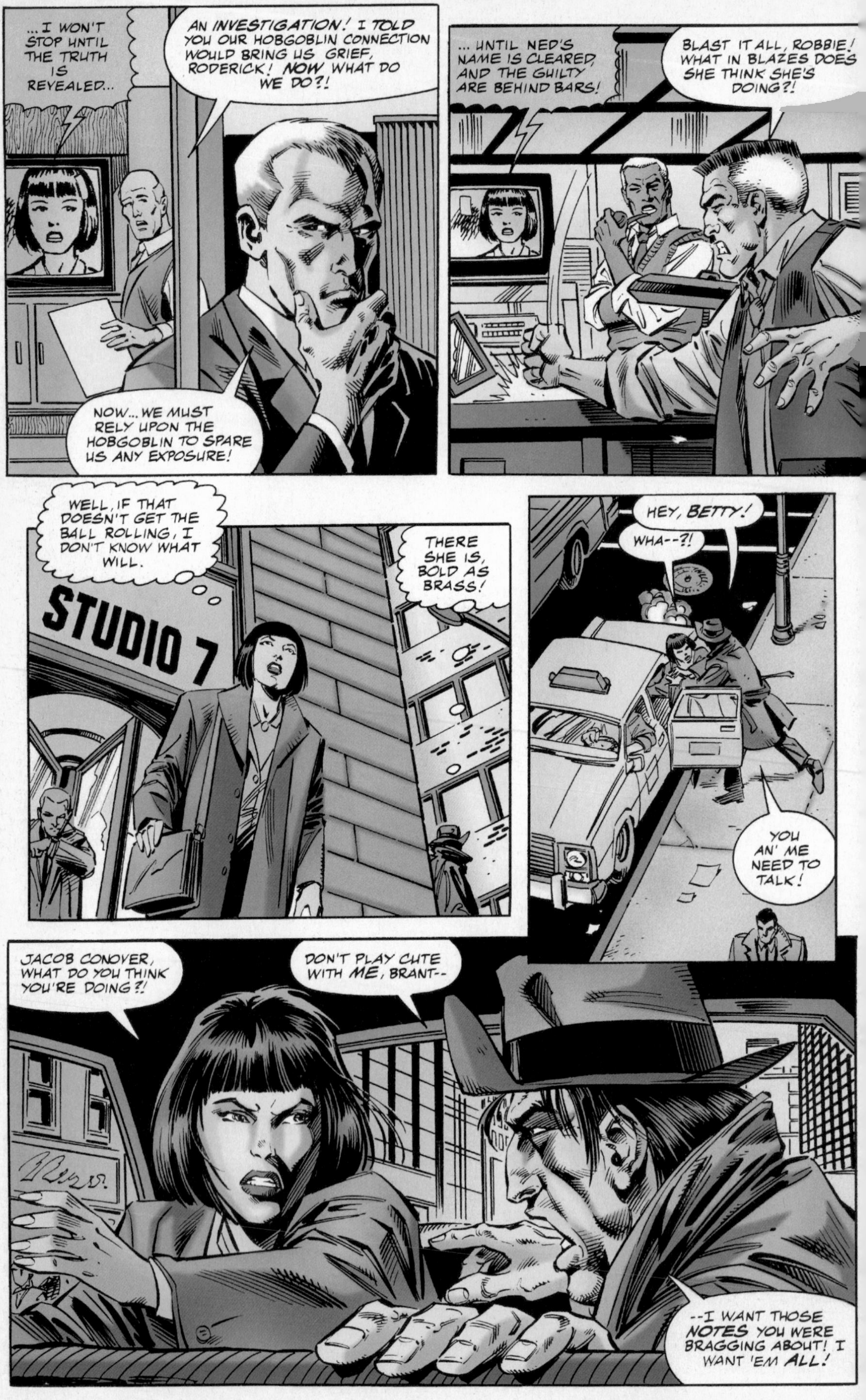
...I WON'T STOP UNTIL THE TRUTH IS REVEALED...
AN INVESTIGATION! I TOLD YOU OUR HOBGOBLIN CONNECTION WOULD BRING US GRIEF, RODERICK! NOW WHAT DO WE DO?!
NOW... WE MUST RELY UPON THE HOBGOBLIN TO SPARE US ANY EXPOSURE!
... UNTIL NED'S NAME IS CLEARED, AND THE GUILTY ARE BEHIND BARS!
BLAST IT ALL, ROBBIE! WHAT IN BLAZES DOES SHE THINK SHE'S DOING?!
WELL, IF THAT DOESN'T GET THE BALL ROLLING, I DON'T KNOW WHAT WILL.
STUDIO 7
THERE SHE IS, BOLD AS BRASS!
HEY, BETTY!
WHA--?!
YOU AN' ME NEED TO TALK!
JACOB CONOVER, WHAT DO YOU THINK YOU'RE DOING?!
DON'T PLAY CUTE WITH ME, BRANT--
--I WANT THOSE NOTES YOU WERE BRAGGING ABOUT! I WANT 'EM ALL!

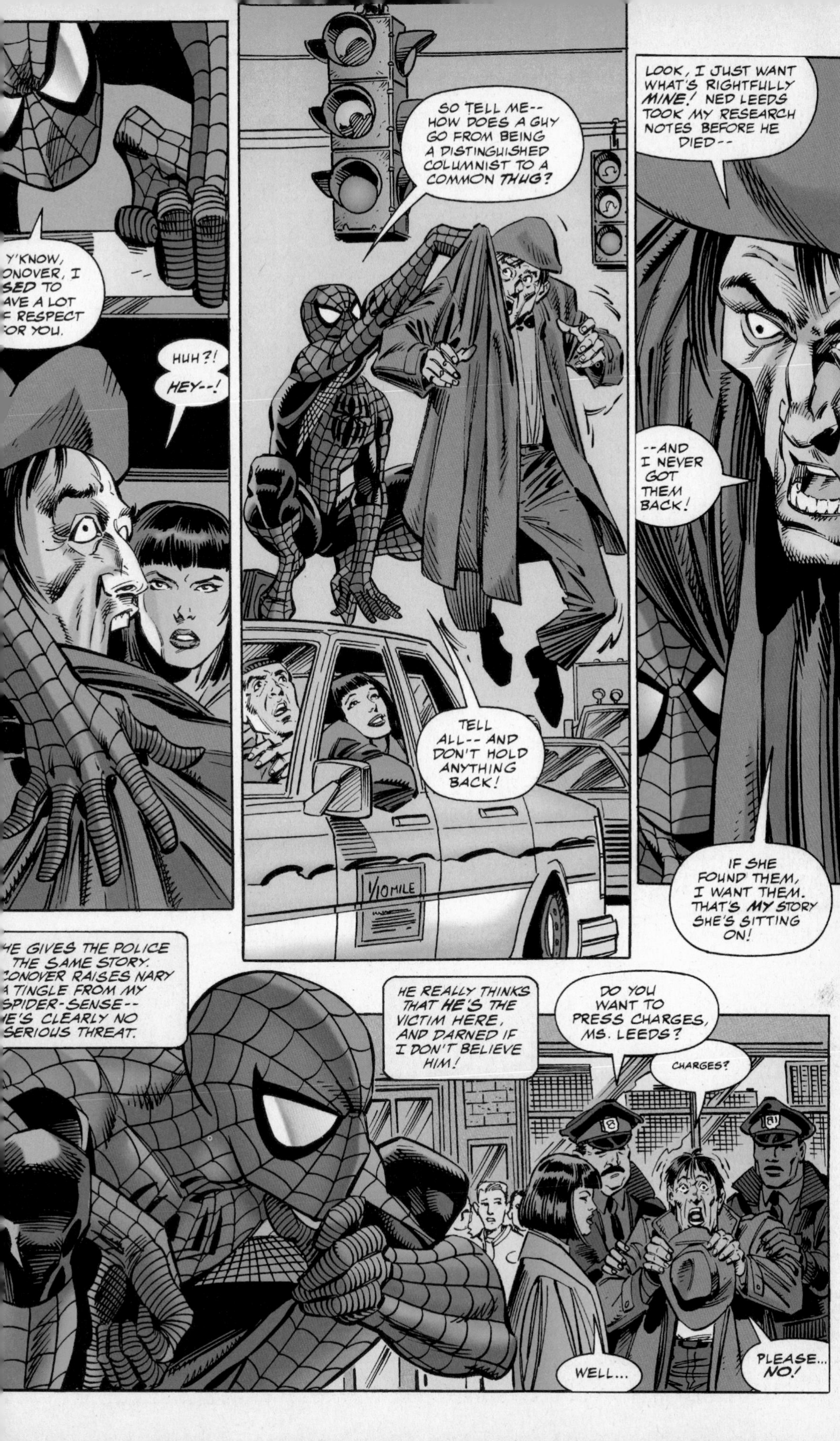

Y'KNOW, ONOVER, I SED TO AVE A LOT F RESPECT FOR YOU.
HUH?! HEY--!
SO TELL ME-- HOW DOES A GUY GO FROM BEING A DISTINGUISHED COLUMNIST TO A COMMON THUG?
TELL ALL-- AND DON'T HOLD ANYTHING BACK!
1/10 MILE
LOOK, I JUST WANT WHAT'S RIGHTFULLY MINE! NED LEEDS TOOK MY RESEARCH NOTES BEFORE HE DIED--
--AND I NEVER GOT THEM BACK!
IF SHE FOUND THEM, I WANT THEM. THAT'S MY STORY SHE'S SITTING ON!
HE GIVES THE POLICE THE SAME STORY. CONOVER RAISES NARY A TINGLE FROM MY SPIDER-SENSE-- HE'S CLEARLY NO SERIOUS THREAT.
HE REALLY THINKS THAT HE'S THE VICTIM HERE, AND DARNED IF I DON'T BELIEVE HIM!
DO YOU WANT TO PRESS CHARGES, MS. LEEDS?
CHARGES?
WELL...
PLEASE... NO!

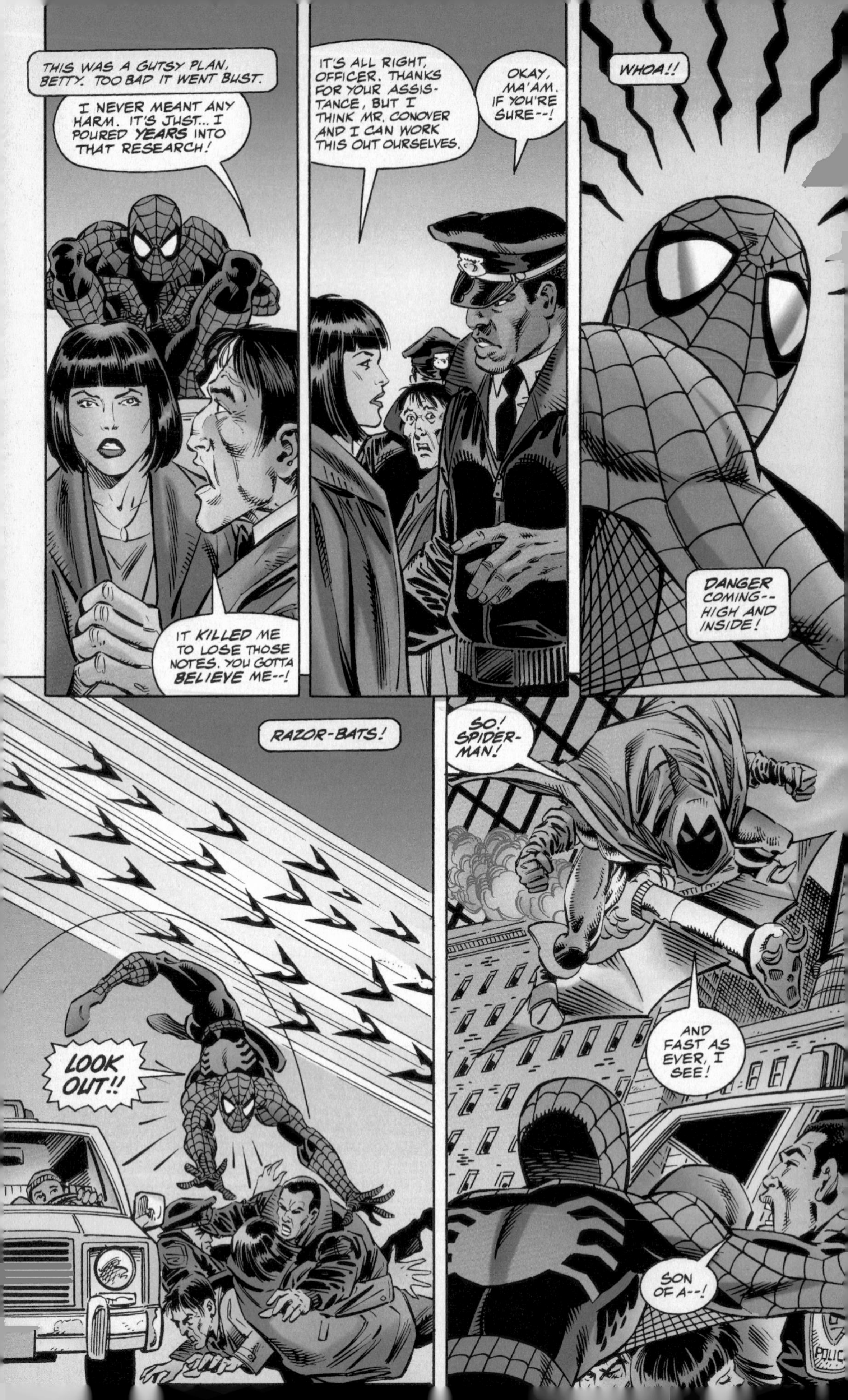

THIS WAS A GUTSY PLAN, BETTY. TOO BAD IT WENT BUST.
I NEVER MEANT ANY HARM. IT'S JUST... I POURED YEARS INTO THAT RESEARCH!
IT KILLED ME TO LOSE THOSE NOTES. YOU GOTTA BELIEVE ME--!
IT'S ALL RIGHT, OFFICER. THANKS FOR YOUR ASSIS-TANCE, BUT I THINK MR. CONOVER AND I CAN WORK THIS OUT OURSELVES.
OKAY, MA'AM. IF YOU'RE SURE--!
WHOA!!
DANGER COMING-- HIGH AND INSIDE!
RAZOR-BATS!
LOOK OUT!!
SO! SPIDER-MAN!
AND FAST AS EVER, I SEE!
SON OF A--!

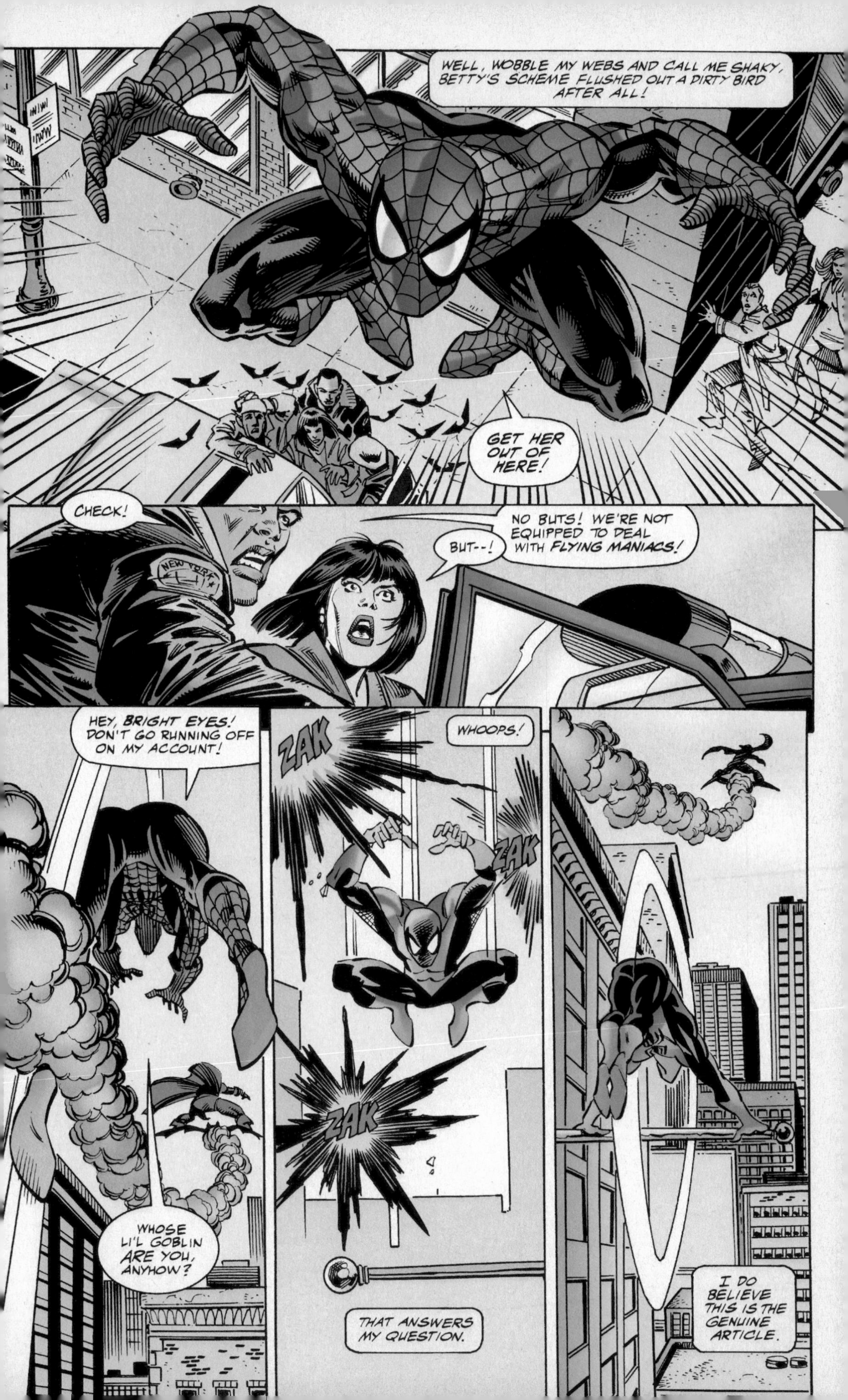
WELL, WOBBLE MY WEBS AND CALL ME SHAKY. BETTY'S SCHEME FLUSHED OUT A DIRTY BIRD AFTER ALL!
GET HER OUT OF HERE!
CHECK!
BUT--!
NO BUTS! WE'RE NOT EQUIPPED TO DEAL WITH FLYING MANIACS!
NEW YORK
HEY, BRIGHT EYES! DON'T GO RUNNING OFF ON MY ACCOUNT!
WHOSE LI'L GOBLIN ARE YOU, ANYHOW?
ZAK
WHOOPS!
ZAK
ZAK
THAT ANSWERS MY QUESTION.
I DO BELIEVE THIS IS THE GENUINE ARTICLE.

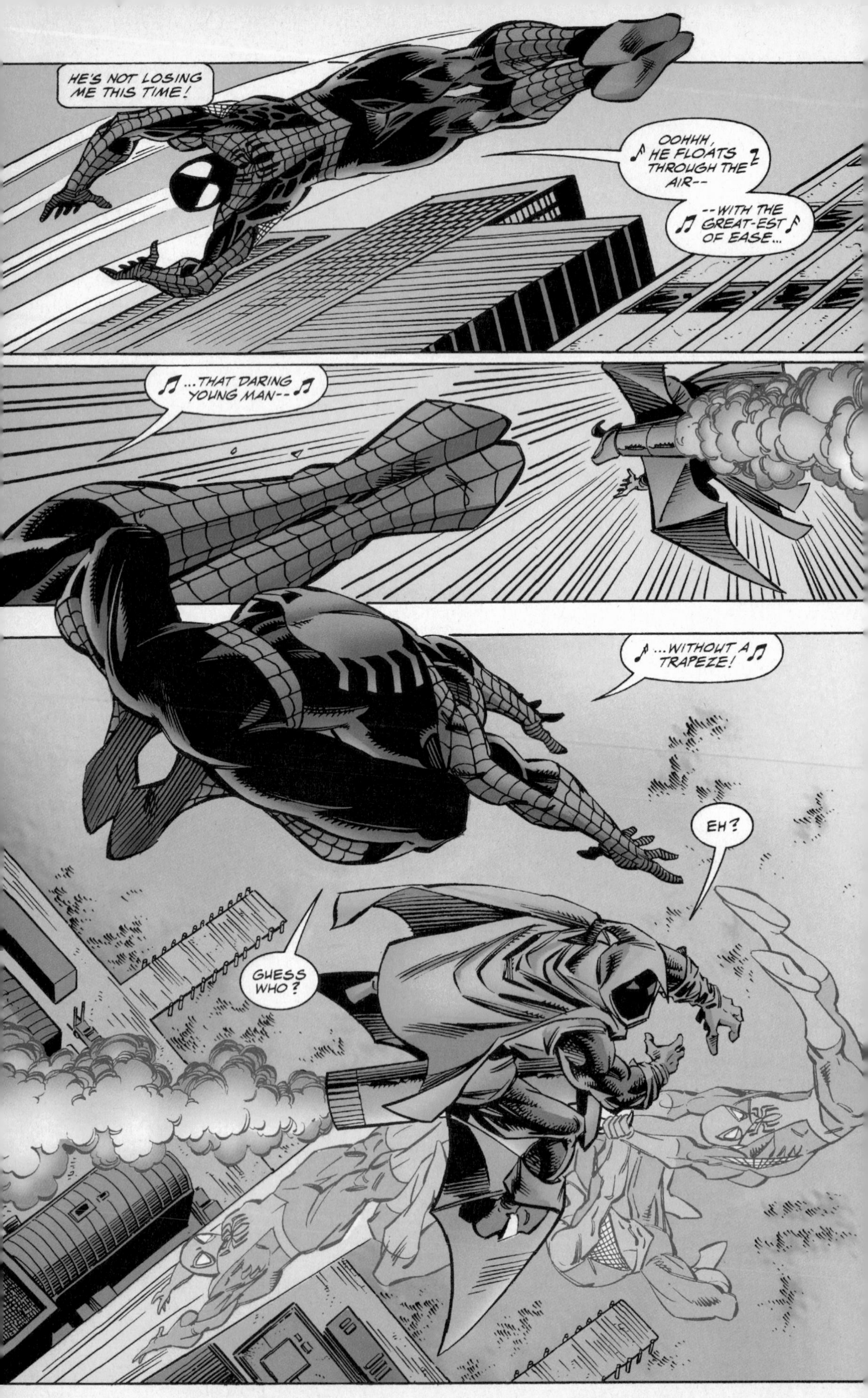
HE'S NOT LOSING ME THIS TIME!
OOHHH, HE FLOATS THROUGH THE AIR--
--WITH THE GREAT-EST OF EASE...
...THAT DARING YOUNG MAN--
...WITHOUT A TRAPEZE!
EH?
GUESS WHO?

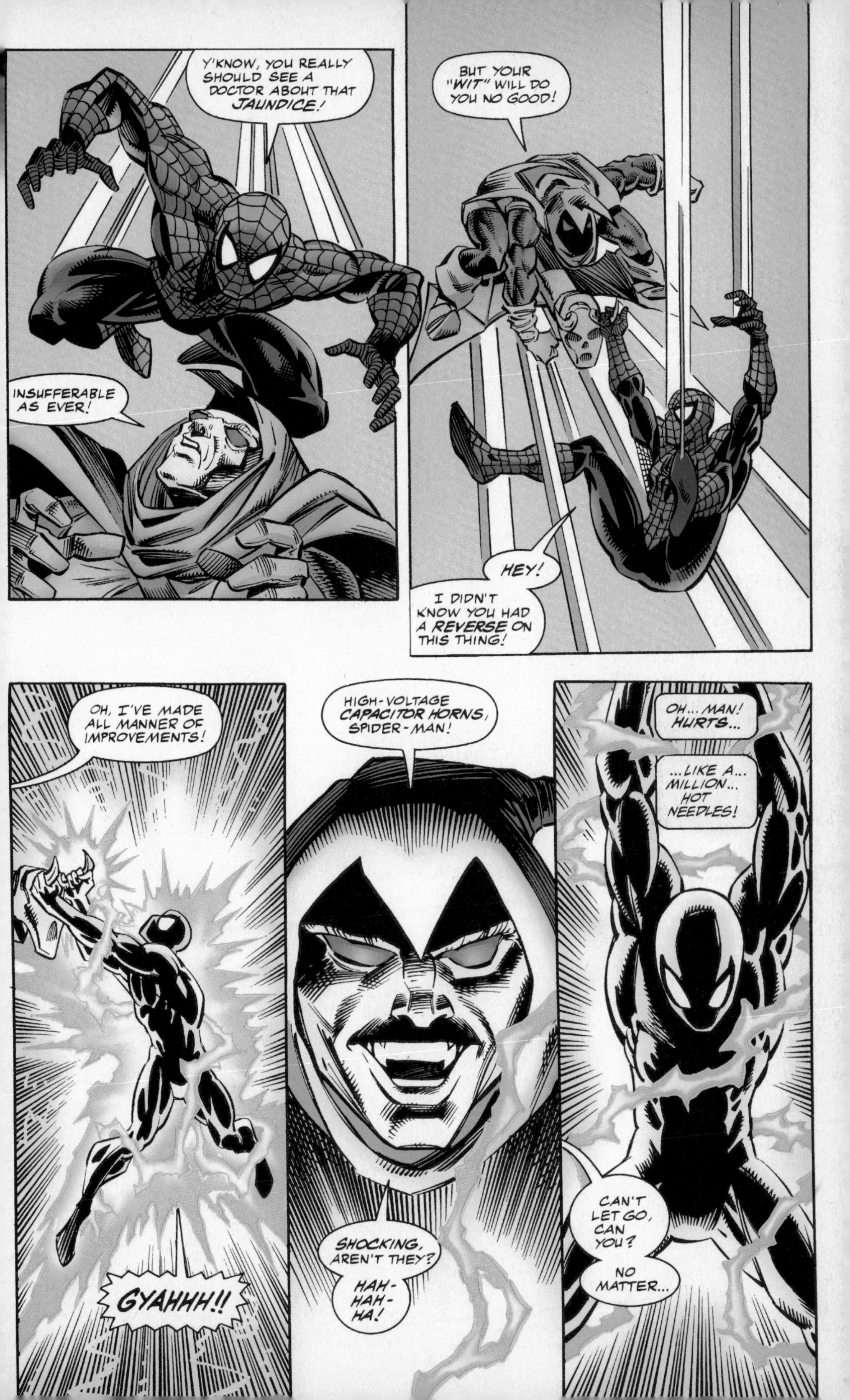
Y'KNOW, YOU REALLY SHOULD SEE A DOCTOR ABOUT THAT JAUNDICE!
INSUFFERABLE AS EVER!
BUT YOUR "WIT" WILL DO YOU NO GOOD!
HEY!
I DIDN'T KNOW YOU HAD A REVERSE ON THIS THING!
OH, I'VE MADE ALL MANNER OF IMPROVEMENTS!
GYAHHH!!
HIGH-VOLTAGE CAPACITOR HORNS, SPIDER-MAN!
SHOCKING, AREN'T THEY?
HAH-HAH-HA!
OH... MAN! HURTS...
...LIKE A... MILLION... HOT NEEDLES!
CAN'T LET GO, CAN YOU?
NO MATTER...

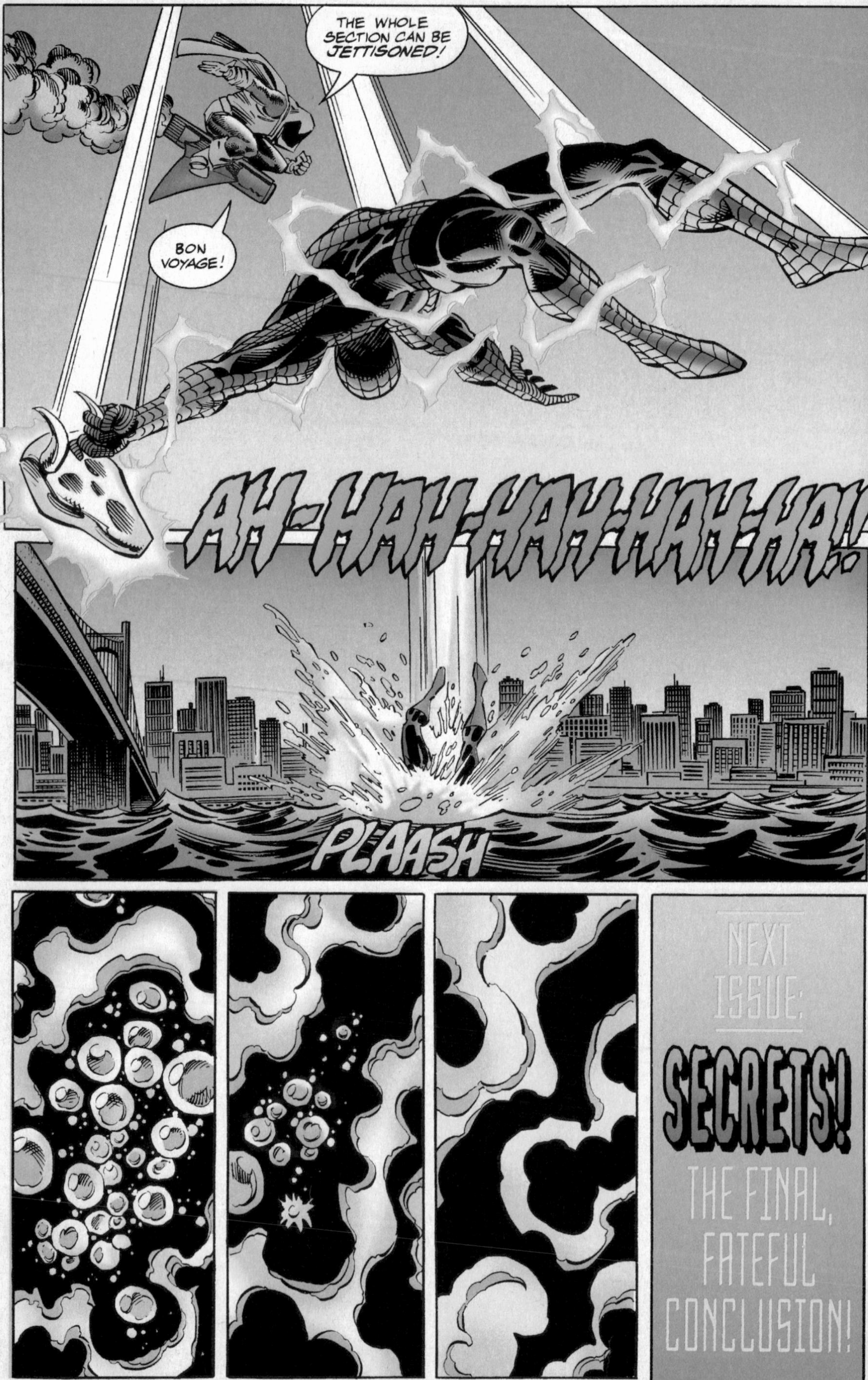

THE WHOLE SECTION CAN BE JETTISONED!
BON VOYAGE!
AH-HAH-HAH-HAH-HAH-HA!
PLAASH
NEXT ISSUE:
SECRETS!
THE FINAL, FATEFUL CONCLUSION!

HOBGOBLIN LIVES SOURCES

Page 3 Dr. Winkler's bio-electronic brainwashing device was employed by the Kingpin in AMAZING SPIDER-MAN #59-61. An earlier version was field-tested in UNTOLD TALES OF SPIDER-MAN #7

Page 4 The Hobgoblin killed Jason Macendale in our previous issue

Page 5 Jameson assigned Ned Leeds to track down the Hobgoblin shortly before he began writing his last official editorial as *Daily Bugle* editor in chief in AMAZING SPIDER-MAN #250

Page 6 The secret of Peter Parker's parents was revealed in AMAZING SPIDER-MAN ANNUAL #5

Page 10 Flash Thompson knocked Ned Leeds to the pavement with a single punch in AMAZING SPIDER-MAN #275

Page 11 George Vandergill was one of a select group of potential blackmail victims who gathered at the Century Club in AMAZING SPIDER-MAN #249

Page 15 Mary Jane and Peter lost their baby in AMAZING SPIDER-MAN #418. Spider-Man has known that Lefty Donovan was used by the Hobgoblin since AMAZING SPIDER-MAN #245

Page 16 Jacob Conover publicly questioned Macendale last issue. It was first revealed that Mary Jane was a model for the fashion division of Kingsley International in AMAZING SPIDER-MAN #271

Page 18 Though not public knowledge, it was shown that Doctor Jonas Harrow secretly works for Roxxon in SPECTACULAR SPIDER-MAN #235-236

Page 19 Leeds' investigation of the Brand Corporation ended in AMAZING SPIDER-MAN #235

Page 20 An agent of the Rose shot Kingsley in WEB OF SPIDER-MAN #29

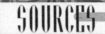

The original Hobgoblin continues his reign of terror in New York City -- and he's not letting Spider-Man get in his way!

Long believed to be Ned Leeds, the late investigative reporter for the Daily Bugle, the Hobgoblin has emerged from years of inactivity! Having murdered Jason Philip Macendale, the second Hobgoblin, and proven that Leeds was only a dupe, the Hobgoblin has attracted the attention of his old enemy, the ever-amazing Spider-Man, who is now intent on bringing the arch-villain down and learning his identity once and for all! And joining the web-slinger on this quest for the truth and justice is Leeds's wife, reporter Betty Brant, desperate to learn who set her husband up, and why!

Now, the pieces are all falling together and the identity of the Hobgoblin is about to be revealed at long last! But will Spider-Man and Betty survive long enough to discover it?

The Hobgoblin lives... and he means business!

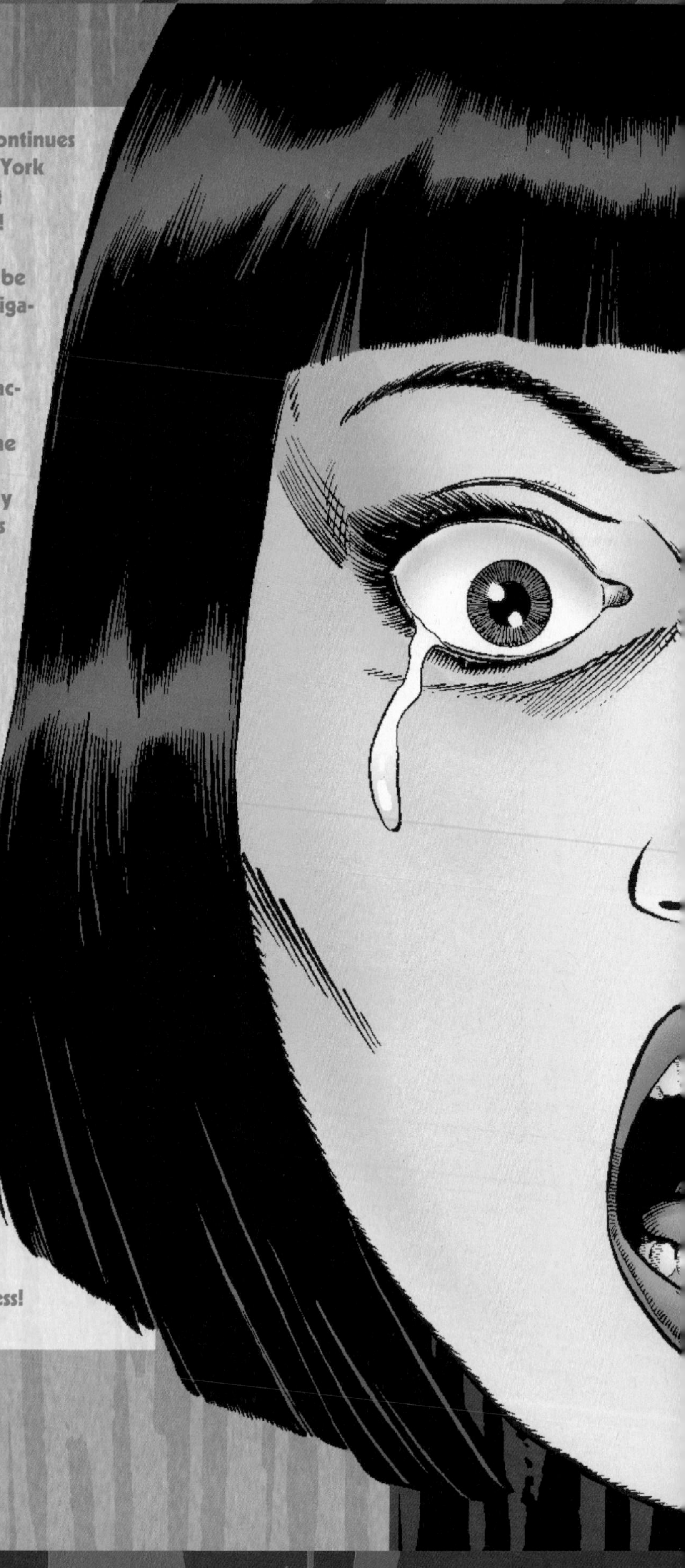

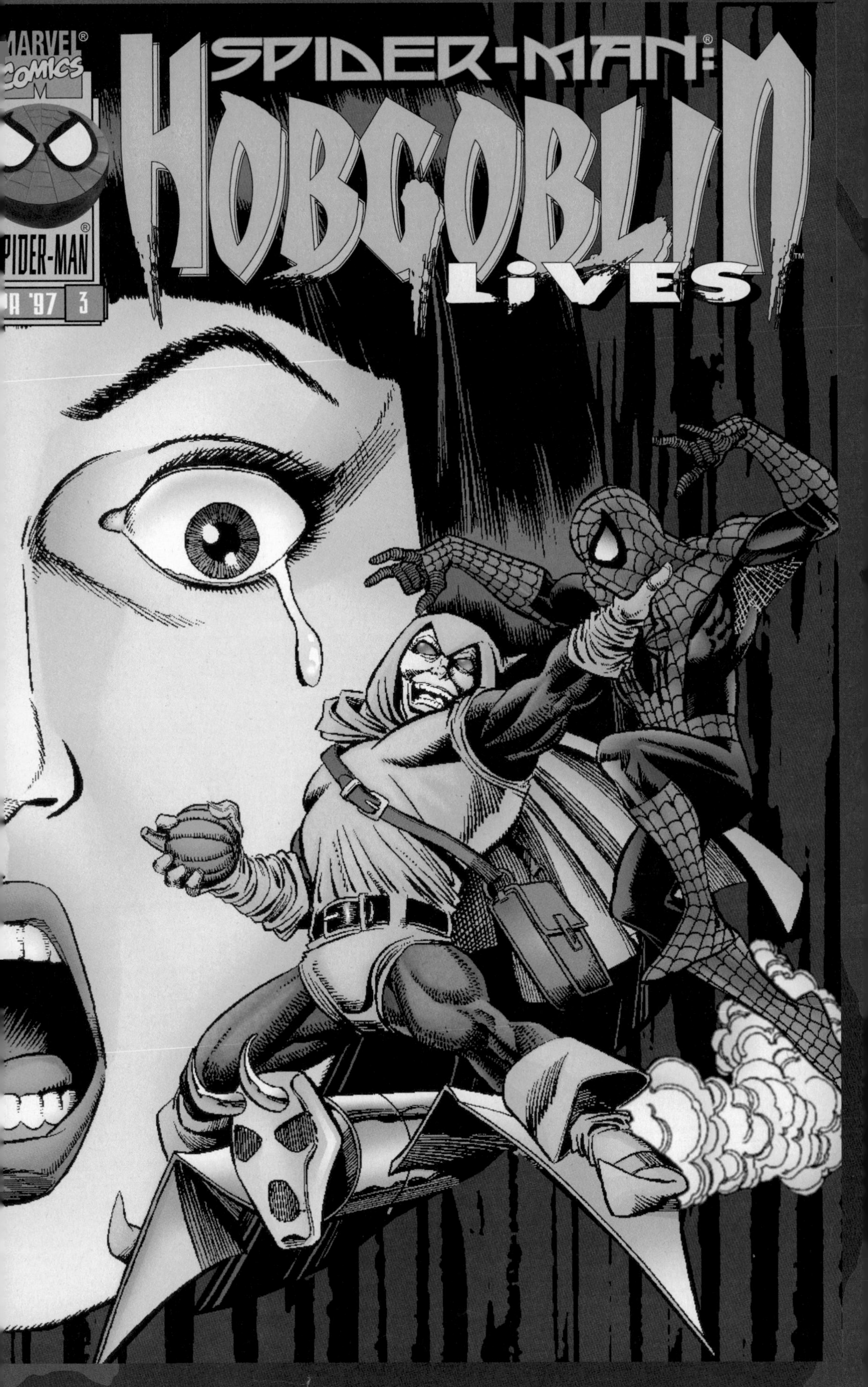
MARVEL® COMICS
SPIDER-MAN®
R '97 3
SPIDER-MAN®:
HOBGOBLIN™
LIVES

SPIDER-MAN: HOBGOBLIN LIVES

Roger Stern — WRITER

Ron Frenz & Bob McLeod — ARTISTS

Jim Novak — LETTERER

Christie Scheele — COLORIST

Glenn Greenberg & Tom Brevoort — EDITORS

Bob Harras — EDITOR IN CHIEF

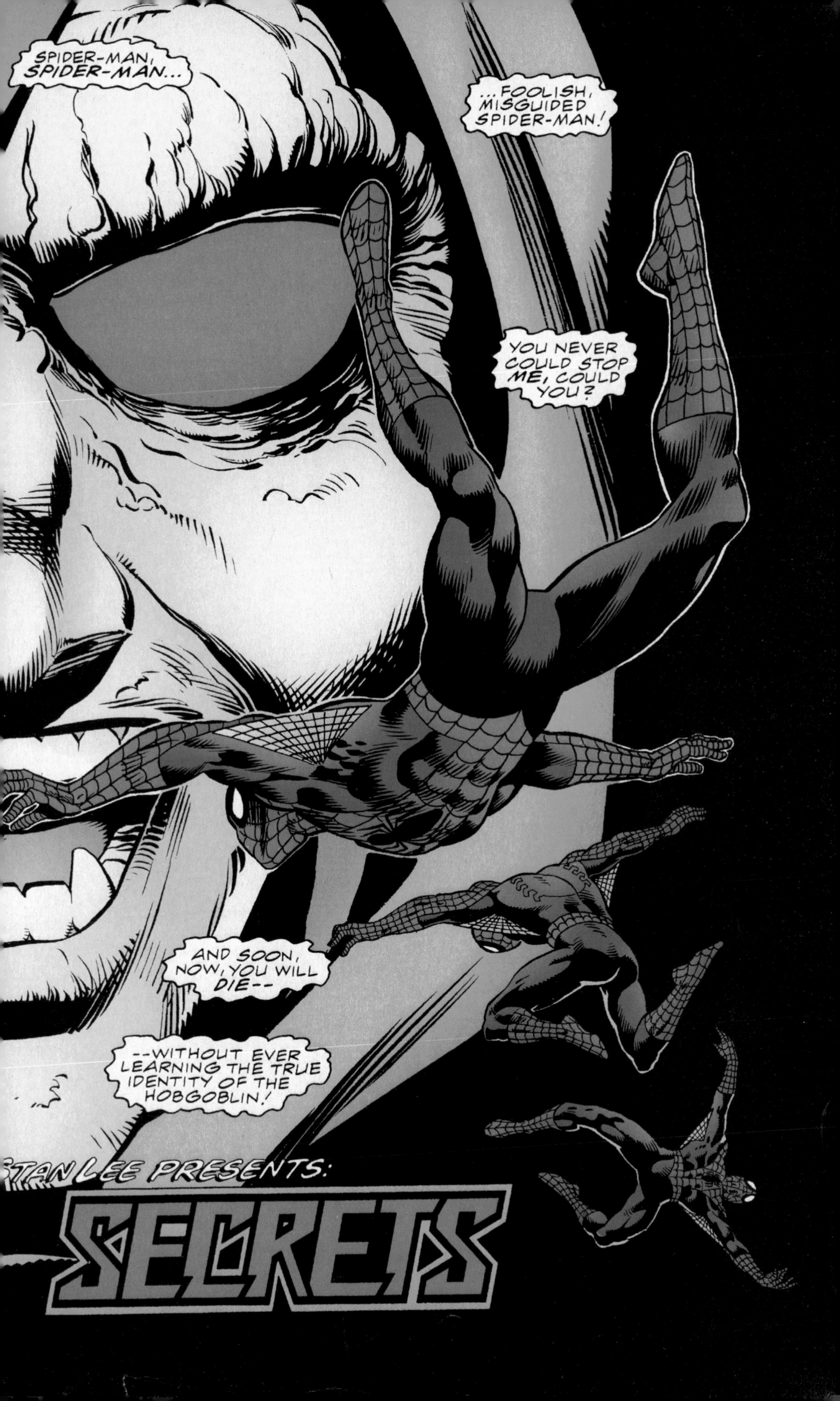
SPIDER-MAN, SPIDER-MAN...
...FOOLISH, MISGUIDED SPIDER-MAN!
YOU NEVER COULD STOP ME, COULD YOU?
AND SOON, NOW, YOU WILL DIE--
--WITHOUT EVER LEARNING THE TRUE IDENTITY OF THE HOBGOBLIN!
STAN LEE PRESENTS:
SECRETS

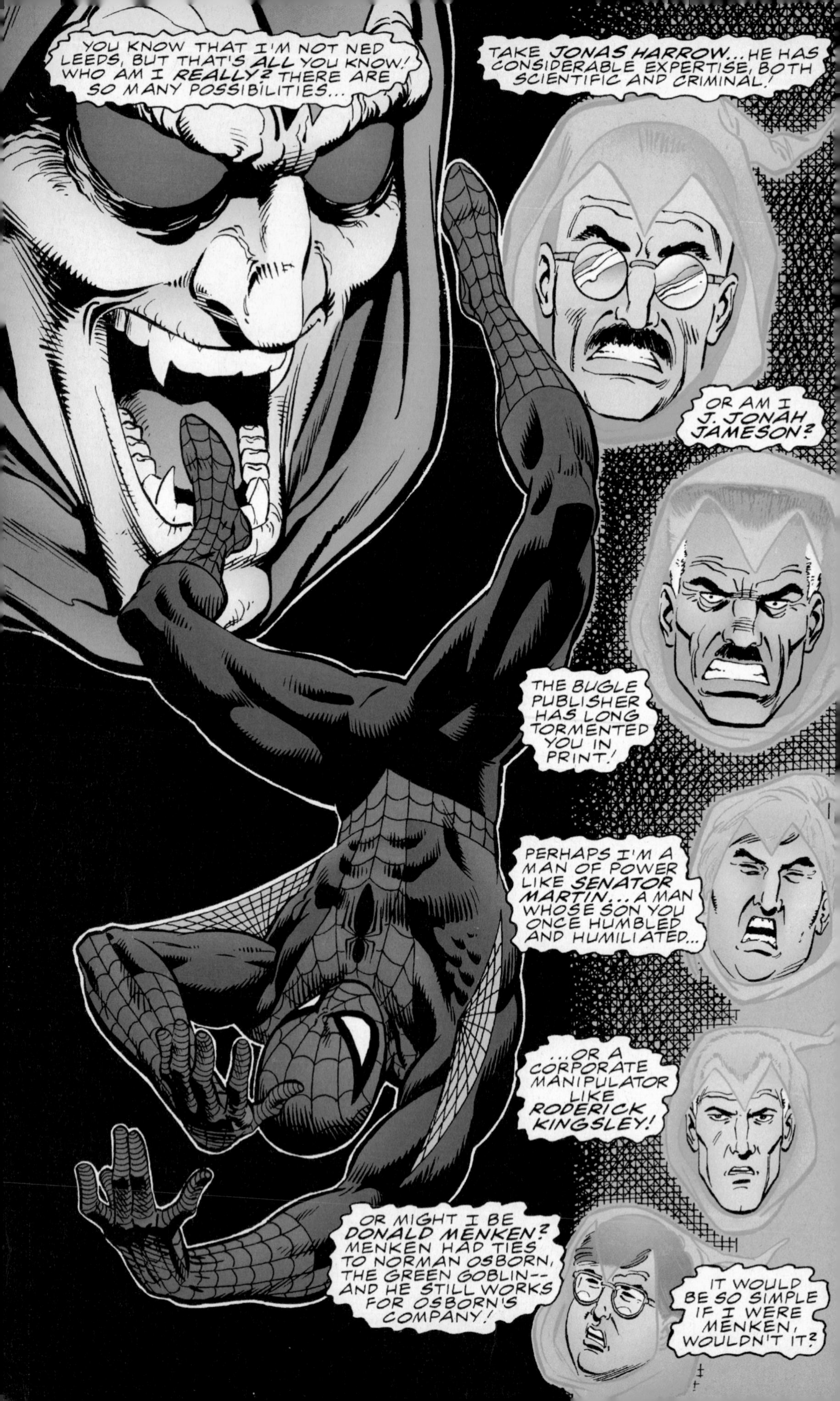
YOU KNOW THAT I'M NOT NED LEEDS, BUT THAT'S ALL YOU KNOW! WHO AM I REALLY? THERE ARE SO MANY POSSIBILITIES...
TAKE JONAS HARROW... HE HAS CONSIDERABLE EXPERTISE, BOTH SCIENTIFIC AND CRIMINAL!
OR AM I J. JONAH JAMESON?
THE BUGLE PUBLISHER HAS LONG TORMENTED YOU IN PRINT!
PERHAPS I'M A MAN OF POWER LIKE SENATOR MARTIN... A MAN WHOSE SON YOU ONCE HUMBLED AND HUMILIATED...
...OR A CORPORATE MANIPULATOR LIKE RODERICK KINGSLEY!
OR MIGHT I BE DONALD MENKEN? MENKEN HAD TIES TO NORMAN OSBORN, THE GREEN GOBLIN-- AND HE STILL WORKS FOR OSBORN'S COMPANY!
IT WOULD BE SO SIMPLE IF I WERE MENKEN, WOULDN'T IT?

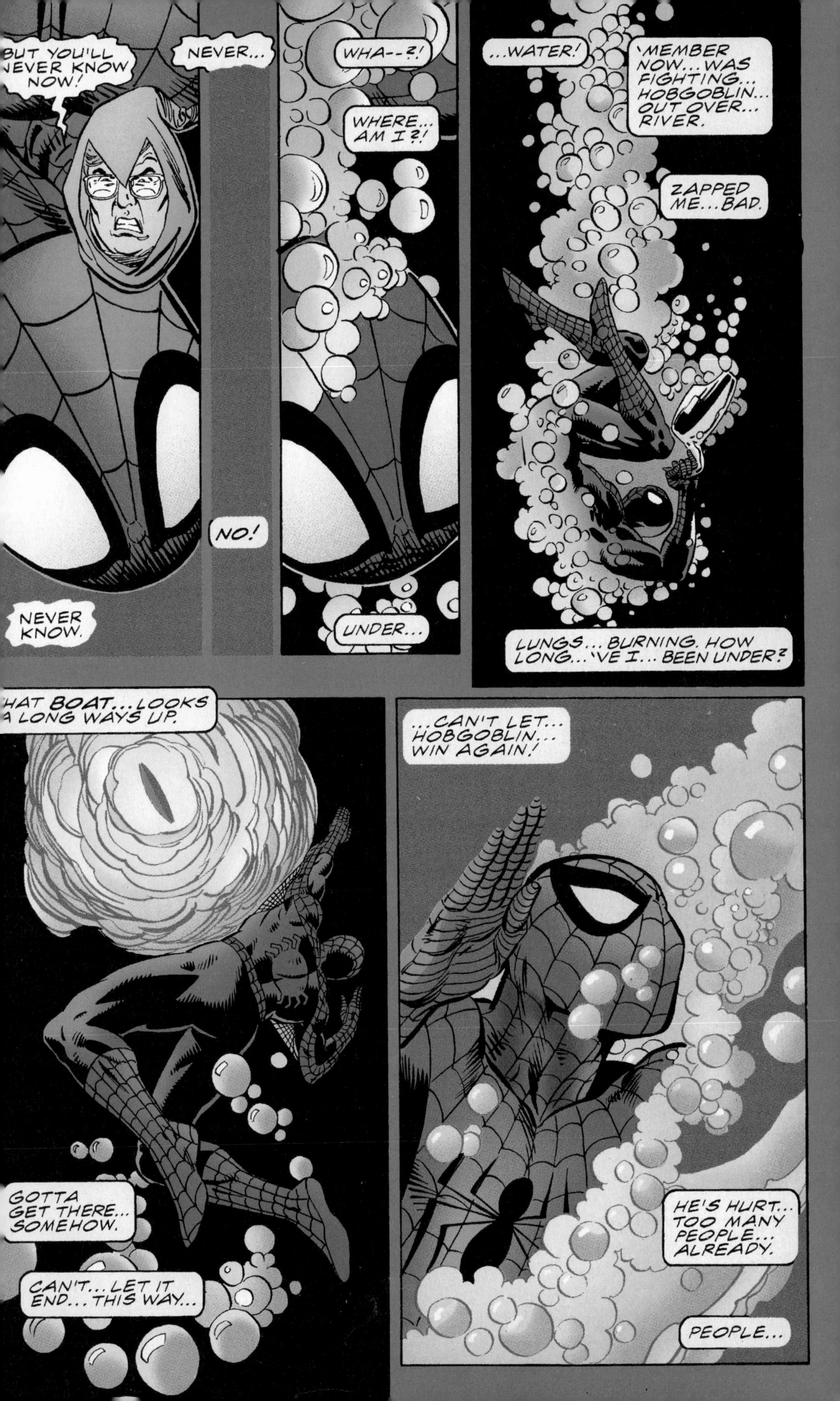
BUT YOU'LL NEVER KNOW NOW!
NEVER...
NO!
NEVER KNOW.
WHA--?!
WHERE... AM I?!
UNDER...
...WATER!
'MEMBER NOW... WAS FIGHTING... HOBGOBLIN... OUT OVER... RIVER.
ZAPPED ME... BAD.
LUNGS... BURNING. HOW LONG... 'VE I... BEEN UNDER?
HAT BOAT... LOOKS A LONG WAYS UP.
GOTTA GET THERE... SOMEHOW.
CAN'T... LET IT END... THIS WAY...
...CAN'T LET... HOBGOBLIN... WIN AGAIN!
HE'S HURT... TOO MANY PEOPLE... ALREADY.
PEOPLE...

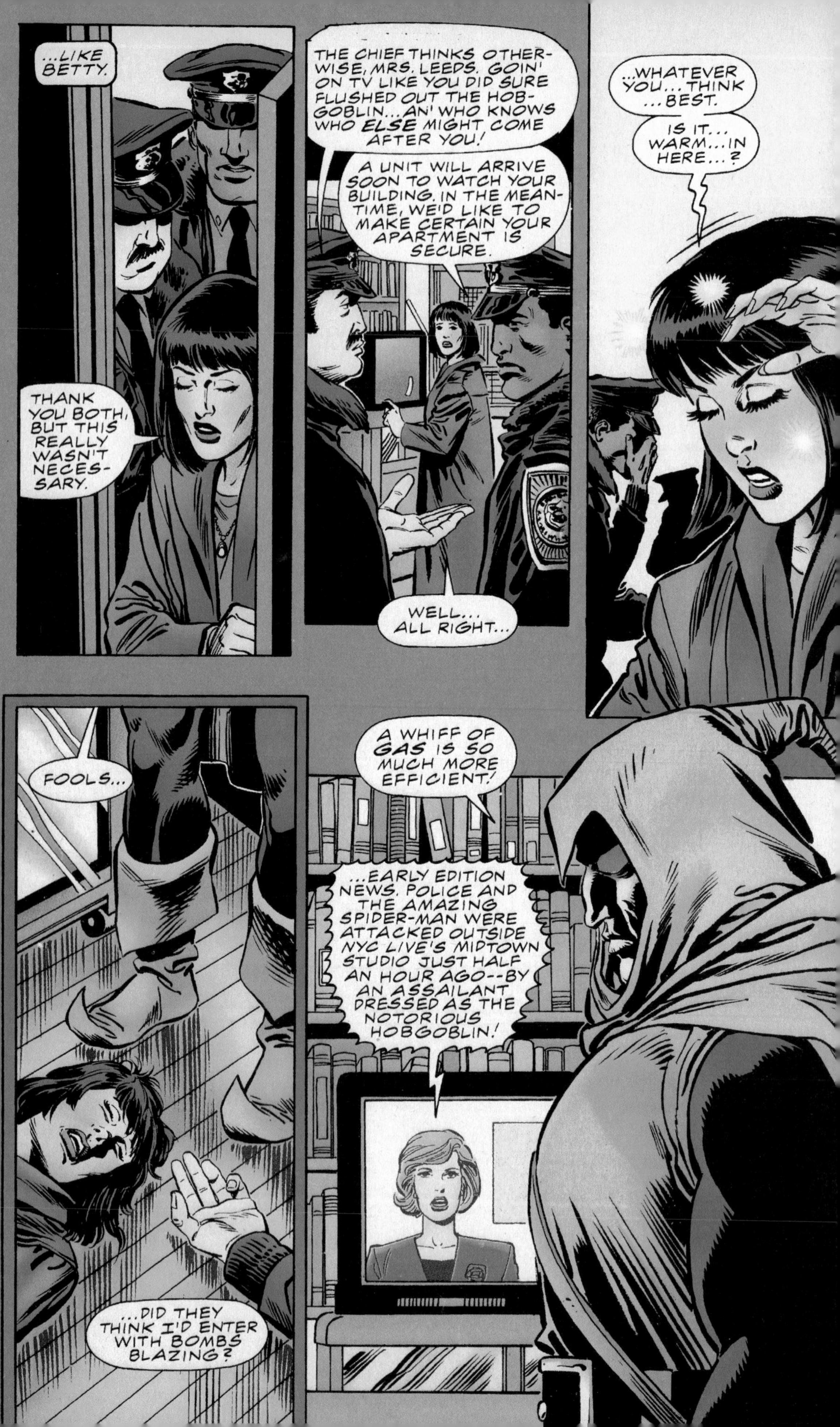
...LIKE BETTY.
THANK YOU BOTH, BUT THIS REALLY WASN'T NECES-SARY.
THE CHIEF THINKS OTHER-WISE, MRS. LEEDS. GOIN' ON TV LIKE YOU DID SURE FLUSHED OUT THE HOB-GOBLIN... AN' WHO KNOWS WHO ELSE MIGHT COME AFTER YOU!
A UNIT WILL ARRIVE SOON TO WATCH YOUR BUILDING. IN THE MEAN-TIME, WE'D LIKE TO MAKE CERTAIN YOUR APARTMENT IS SECURE.
WELL... ALL RIGHT...
...WHATEVER YOU... THINK ...BEST.
IS IT... WARM... IN HERE...?
FOOLS...
...DID THEY THINK I'D ENTER WITH BOMBS BLAZING?
A WHIFF OF GAS IS SO MUCH MORE EFFICIENT!
...EARLY EDITION NEWS. POLICE AND THE AMAZING SPIDER-MAN WERE ATTACKED OUTSIDE NYC LIVE'S MIDTOWN STUDIO JUST HALF AN HOUR AGO--BY AN ASSAILANT DRESSED AS THE NOTORIOUS HOBGOBLIN!

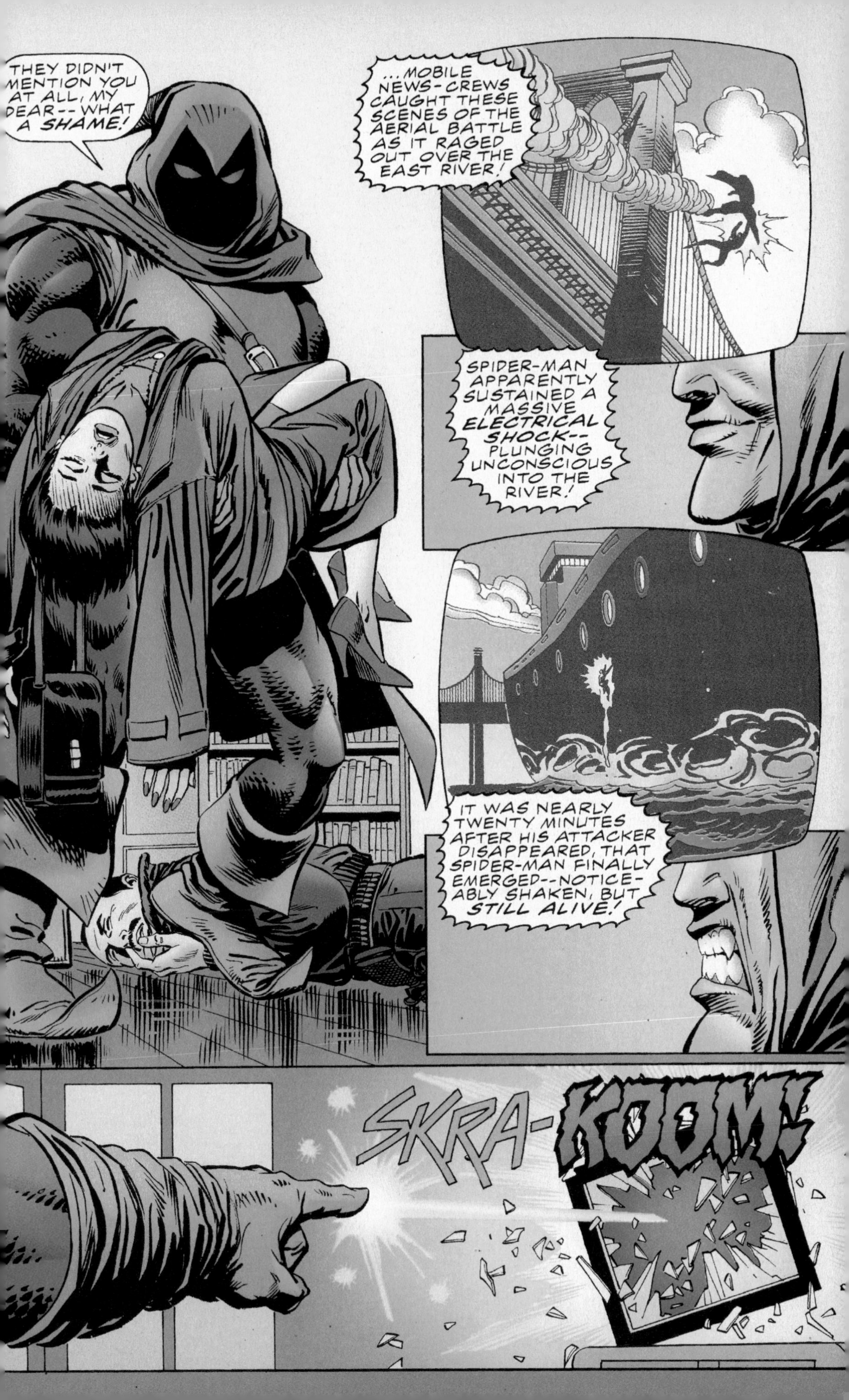
THEY DIDN'T MENTION YOU AT ALL, MY DEAR-- WHAT A SHAME!
...MOBILE NEWS-CREWS CAUGHT THESE SCENES OF THE AERIAL BATTLE AS IT RAGED OUT OVER THE EAST RIVER!
SPIDER-MAN APPARENTLY SUSTAINED A MASSIVE ELECTRICAL SHOCK-- PLUNGING UNCONSCIOUS INTO THE RIVER!
IT WAS NEARLY TWENTY MINUTES AFTER HIS ATTACKER DISAPPEARED, THAT SPIDER-MAN FINALLY EMERGED--NOTICE-ABLY SHAKEN, BUT STILL ALIVE!
SKRA-KOOM!

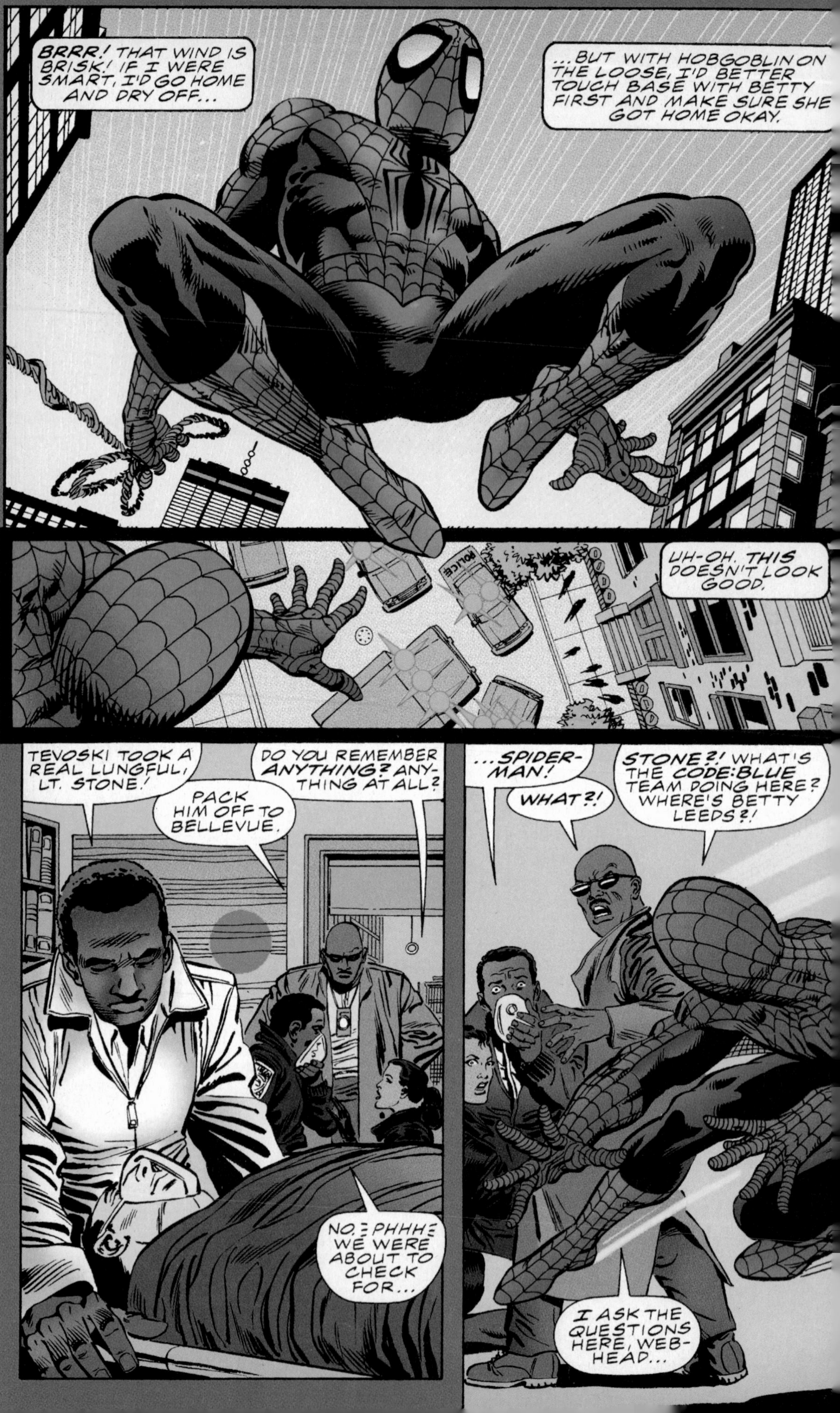
BRRR! THAT WIND IS BRISK! IF I WERE SMART, I'D GO HOME AND DRY OFF...
...BUT WITH HOBGOBLIN ON THE LOOSE, I'D BETTER TOUCH BASE WITH BETTY FIRST AND MAKE SURE SHE GOT HOME OKAY.
POLICE
UH-OH. THIS DOESN'T LOOK GOOD.
TEVOSKI TOOK A REAL LUNGFUL, LT. STONE!
PACK HIM OFF TO BELLEVUE.
DO YOU REMEMBER ANYTHING? ANYTHING AT ALL?
NO. PHHH WE WERE ABOUT TO CHECK FOR...
...SPIDER-MAN!
WHAT?!
STONE?! WHAT'S THE CODE:BLUE TEAM DOING HERE? WHERE'S BETTY LEEDS?!
I ASK THE QUESTIONS HERE, WEB-HEAD...

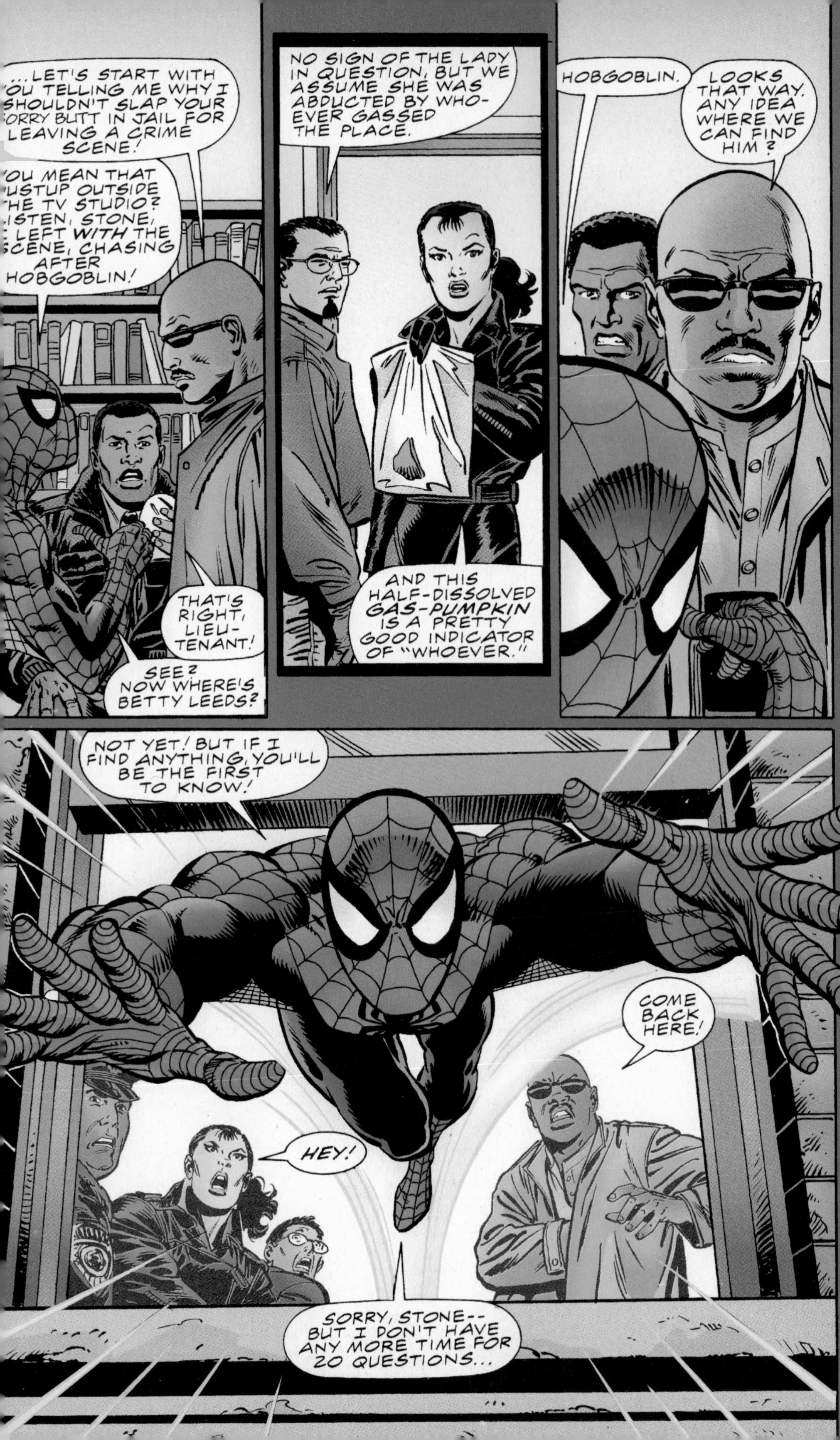
...LET'S START WITH YOU TELLING ME WHY I SHOULDN'T SLAP YOUR SORRY BUTT IN JAIL FOR LEAVING A CRIME SCENE!
YOU MEAN THAT DUSTUP OUTSIDE THE TV STUDIO? LISTEN, STONE, I LEFT WITH THE SCENE, CHASING AFTER HOBGOBLIN!
THAT'S RIGHT, LIEU-TENANT!
SEE? NOW WHERE'S BETTY LEEDS?
NO SIGN OF THE LADY IN QUESTION, BUT WE ASSUME SHE WAS ABDUCTED BY WHO-EVER GASSED THE PLACE.
AND THIS HALF-DISSOLVED GAS-PUMPKIN IS A PRETTY GOOD INDICATOR OF "WHOEVER."
HOBGOBLIN.
LOOKS THAT WAY. ANY IDEA WHERE WE CAN FIND HIM?
NOT YET! BUT IF I FIND ANYTHING, YOU'LL BE THE FIRST TO KNOW!
HEY!
COME BACK HERE!
SORRY, STONE-- BUT I DON'T HAVE ANY MORE TIME FOR 20 QUESTIONS...

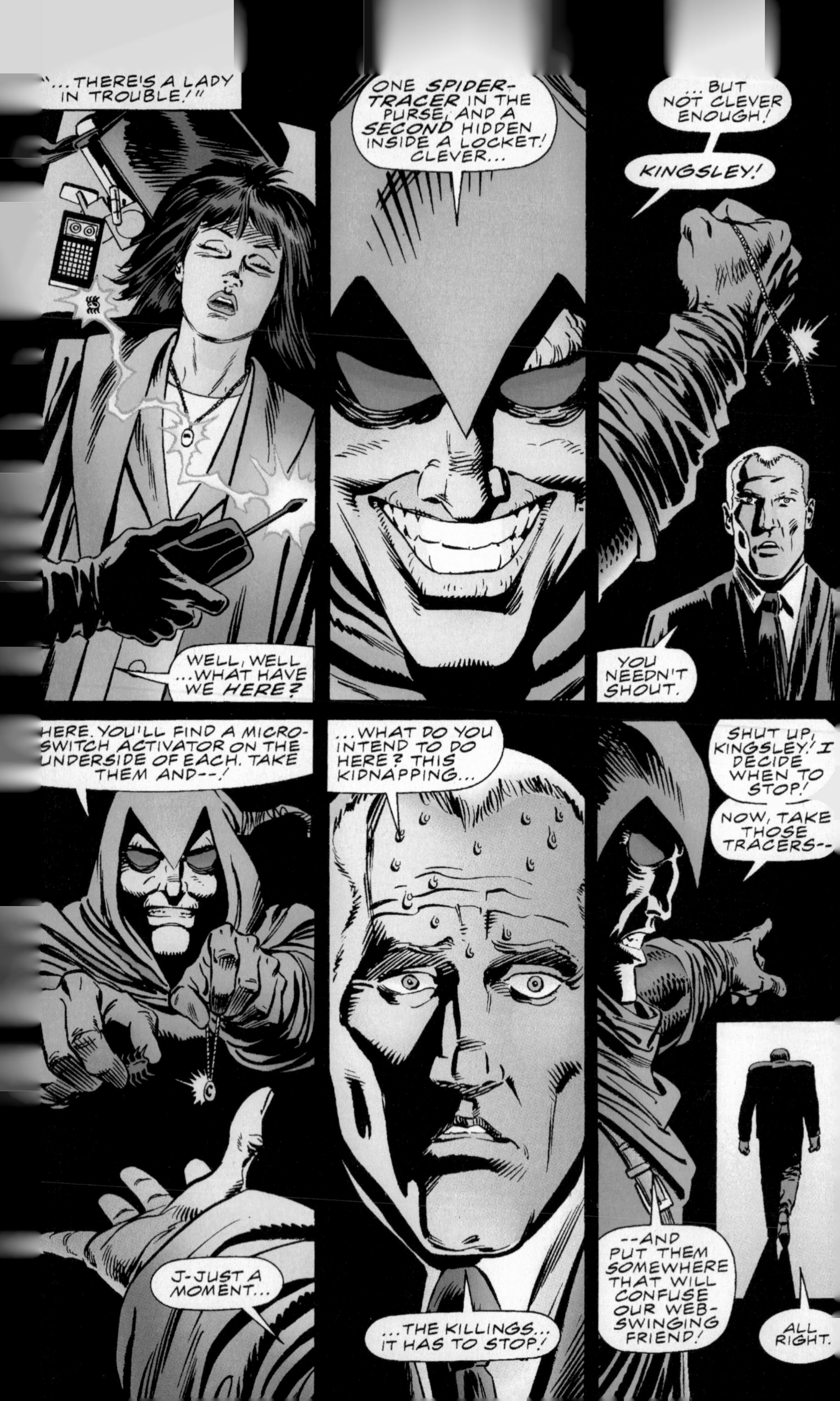
"...THERE'S A LADY IN TROUBLE!"
WELL, WELL ...WHAT HAVE WE HERE?
ONE SPIDER-TRACER IN THE PURSE, AND A SECOND HIDDEN INSIDE A LOCKET! CLEVER...
...BUT NOT CLEVER ENOUGH!
KINGSLEY!
YOU NEEDN'T SHOUT.
HERE. YOU'LL FIND A MICRO-SWITCH ACTIVATOR ON THE UNDERSIDE OF EACH. TAKE THEM AND--!
J-JUST A MOMENT...
...WHAT DO YOU INTEND TO DO HERE? THIS KIDNAPPING...
...THE KILLINGS... IT HAS TO STOP!
SHUT UP, KINGSLEY! I DECIDE WHEN TO STOP!
NOW, TAKE THOSE TRACERS--
--AND PUT THEM SOMEWHERE THAT WILL CONFUSE OUR WEB-SWINGING FRIEND!
ALL RIGHT.

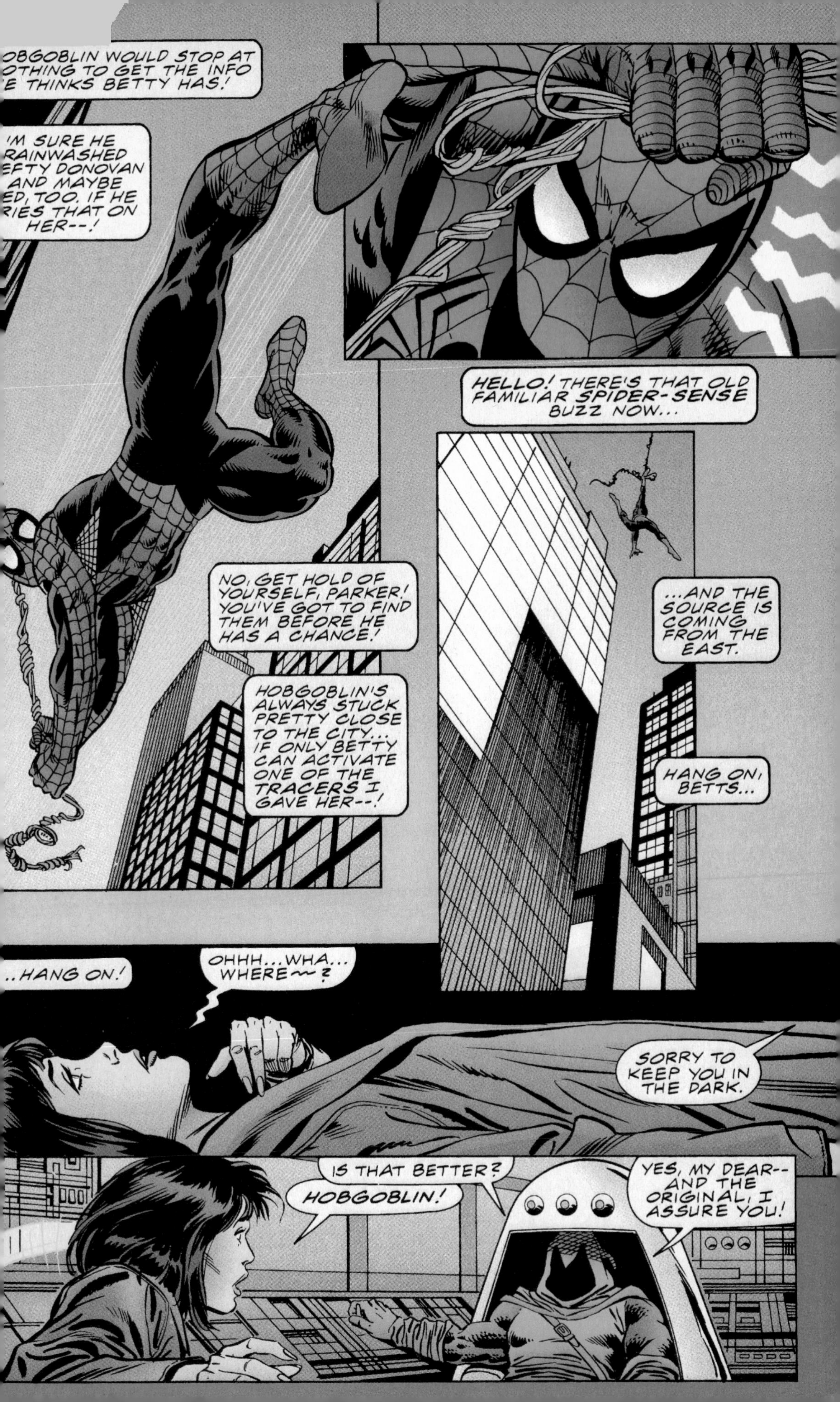

OBGOBLIN WOULD STOP AT
OTHING TO GET THE INFO
E THINKS BETTY HAS!
'M SURE HE RAINWASHED EFTY DONOVAN AND MAYBE ED, TOO. IF HE RIES THAT ON HER--!
HELLO! THERE'S THAT OLD FAMILIAR SPIDER-SENSE BUZZ NOW...
NO, GET HOLD OF YOURSELF, PARKER! YOU'VE GOT TO FIND THEM BEFORE HE HAS A CHANCE!
HOBGOBLIN'S ALWAYS STUCK PRETTY CLOSE TO THE CITY... IF ONLY BETTY CAN ACTIVATE ONE OF THE TRACERS I GAVE HER--!
...AND THE SOURCE IS COMING FROM THE EAST.
HANG ON, BETTS...
..HANG ON!
OHHH...WHA... WHERE~~?
SORRY TO KEEP YOU IN THE DARK.
IS THAT BETTER?
HOBGOBLIN!
YES, MY DEAR-- AND THE ORIGINAL, I ASSURE YOU!

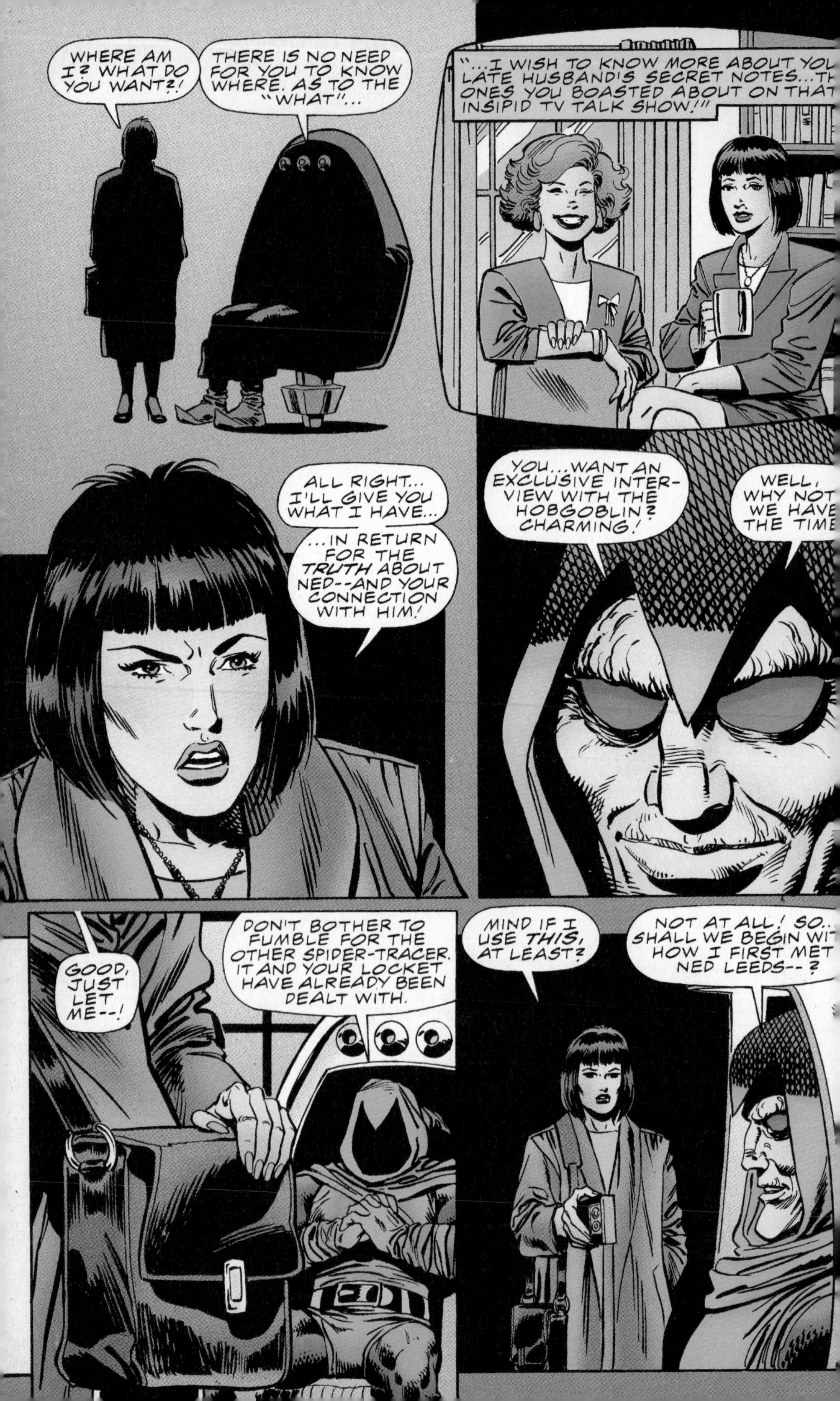

WHERE AM I? WHAT DO YOU WANT?!
THERE IS NO NEED FOR YOU TO KNOW WHERE. AS TO THE "WHAT"...
"...I WISH TO KNOW MORE ABOUT YOU LATE HUSBAND'S SECRET NOTES...TH ONES YOU BOASTED ABOUT ON THAT INSIPID TV TALK SHOW!"
ALL RIGHT... I'LL GIVE YOU WHAT I HAVE...
...IN RETURN FOR THE TRUTH ABOUT NED--AND YOUR CONNECTION WITH HIM!
YOU...WANT AN EXCLUSIVE INTER-VIEW WITH THE HOBGOBLIN? CHARMING!
WELL, WHY NOT WE HAVE THE TIME
GOOD, JUST LET ME--!
DON'T BOTHER TO FUMBLE FOR THE OTHER SPIDER-TRACER. IT AND YOUR LOCKET HAVE ALREADY BEEN DEALT WITH.
MIND IF I USE THIS, AT LEAST?
NOT AT ALL! SO... SHALL WE BEGIN WIT HOW I FIRST MET NED LEEDS--?

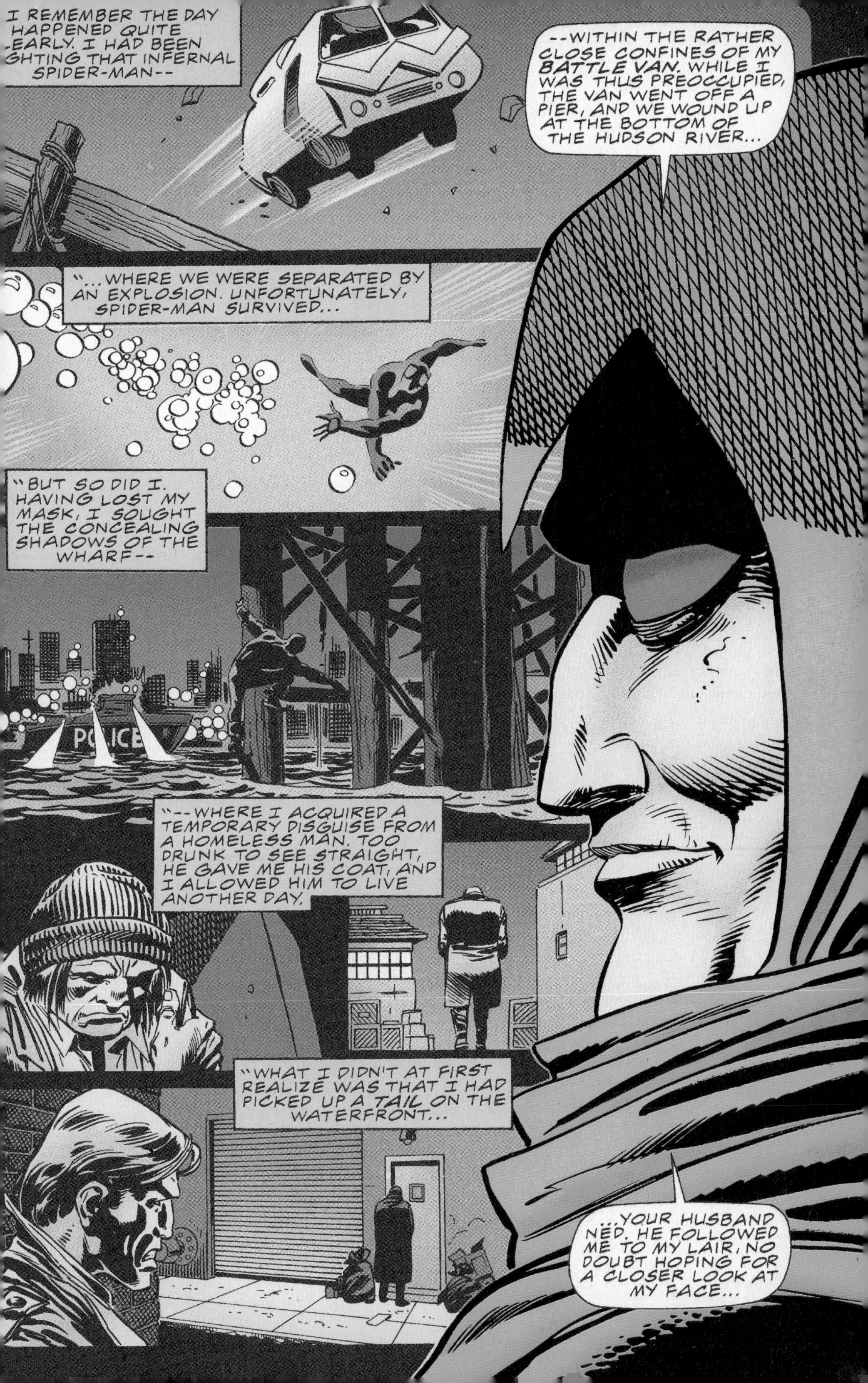
I REMEMBER THE DAY
HAPPENED QUITE
-EARLY. I HAD BEEN
GHTING THAT INFERNAL
SPIDER-MAN--
--WITHIN THE RATHER CLOSE CONFINES OF MY BATTLE VAN. WHILE I WAS THUS PREOCCUPIED, THE VAN WENT OFF A PIER, AND WE WOUND UP AT THE BOTTOM OF THE HUDSON RIVER...
"...WHERE WE WERE SEPARATED BY AN EXPLOSION. UNFORTUNATELY, SPIDER-MAN SURVIVED...
"BUT SO DID I. HAVING LOST MY MASK, I SOUGHT THE CONCEALING SHADOWS OF THE WHARF--
POLICE
"--WHERE I ACQUIRED A TEMPORARY DISGUISE FROM A HOMELESS MAN. TOO DRUNK TO SEE STRAIGHT, HE GAVE ME HIS COAT, AND I ALLOWED HIM TO LIVE ANOTHER DAY.
"WHAT I DIDN'T AT FIRST REALIZE WAS THAT I HAD PICKED UP A TAIL ON THE WATERFRONT...
...YOUR HUSBAND NED. HE FOLLOWED ME TO MY LAIR, NO DOUBT HOPING FOR A CLOSER LOOK AT MY FACE...

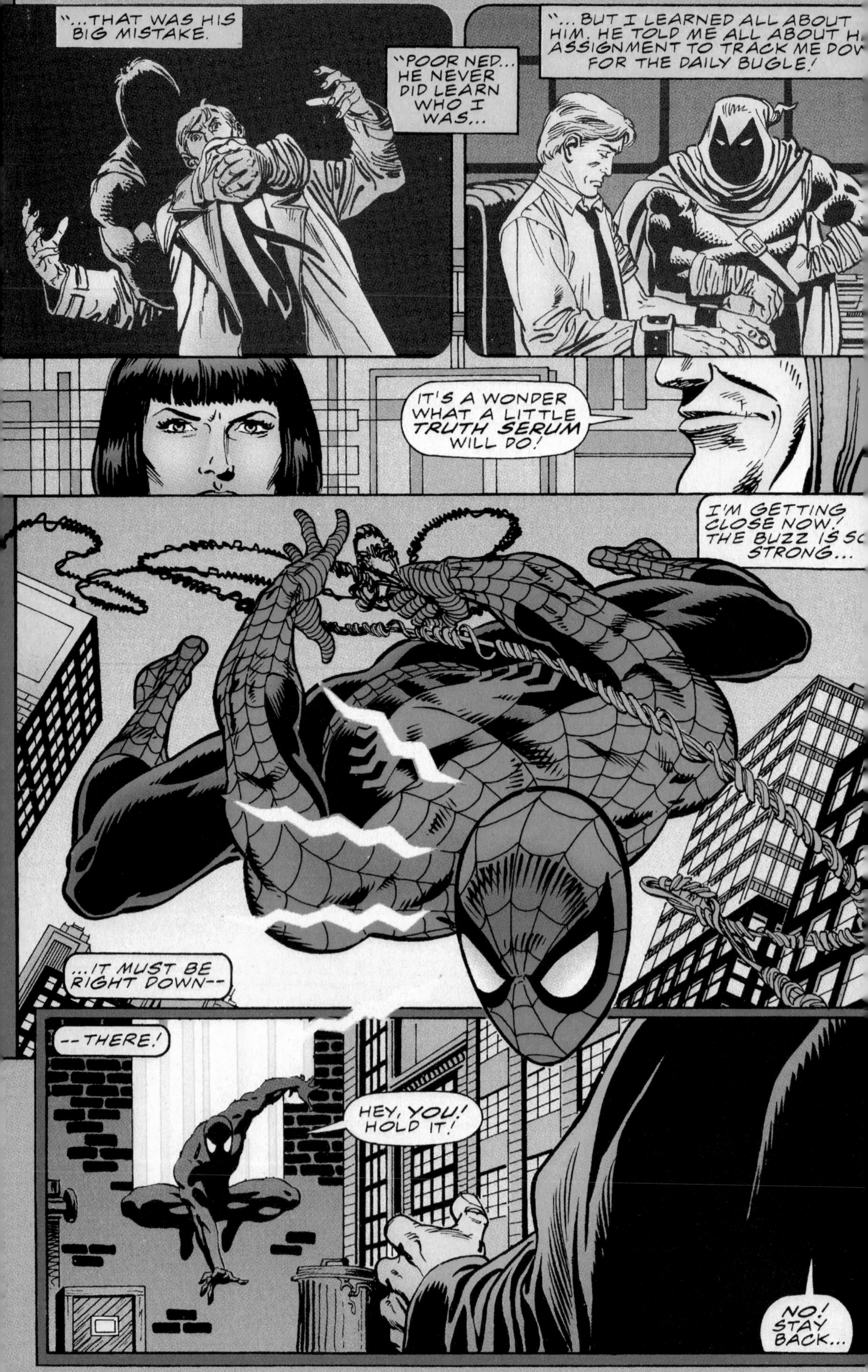
"...THAT WAS HIS BIG MISTAKE.
"POOR NED... HE NEVER DID LEARN WHO I WAS...
"...BUT I LEARNED ALL ABOUT HIM. HE TOLD ME ALL ABOUT HI ASSIGNMENT TO TRACK ME DOW FOR THE DAILY BUGLE!
IT'S A WONDER WHAT A LITTLE TRUTH SERUM WILL DO!
I'M GETTING CLOSE NOW! THE BUZZ IS SO STRONG...
...IT MUST BE RIGHT DOWN--
--THERE!
HEY, YOU! HOLD IT!
NO! STAY BACK...

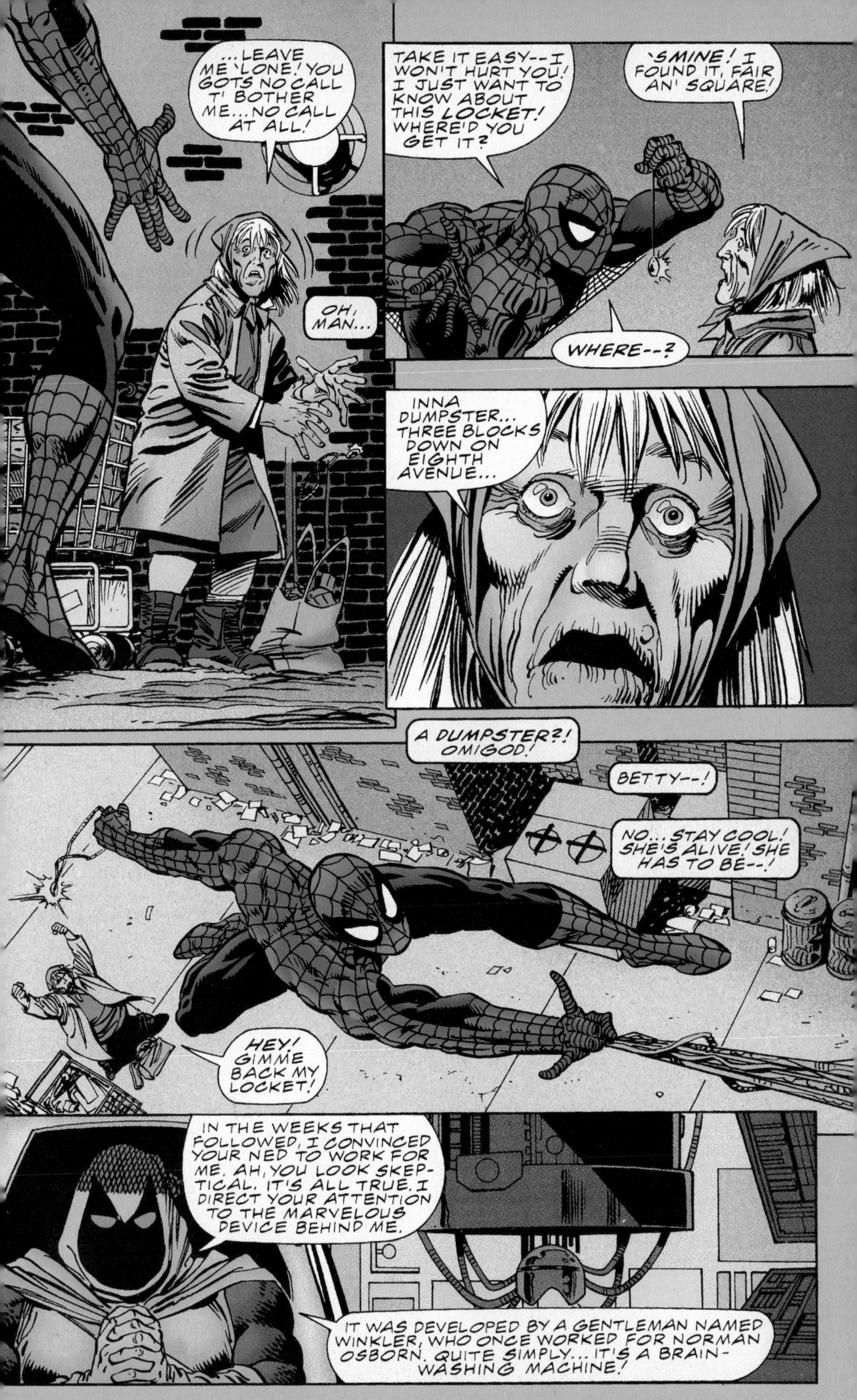
...LEAVE ME 'LONE! YOU GOTS NO CALL T' BOTHER ME...NO CALL AT ALL!
OH, MAN...
TAKE IT EASY--I WON'T HURT YOU! I JUST WANT TO KNOW ABOUT THIS LOCKET! WHERE'D YOU GET IT?
'SMINE! I FOUND IT, FAIR AN' SQUARE!
WHERE--?
INNA DUMPSTER... THREE BLOCKS DOWN ON EIGHTH AVENUE...
A DUMPSTER?! OMIGOD!
BETTY--!
NO... STAY COOL! SHE'S ALIVE! SHE HAS TO BE--!
HEY! GIMME BACK MY LOCKET!
IN THE WEEKS THAT FOLLOWED, I CONVINCED YOUR NED TO WORK FOR ME. AH, YOU LOOK SKEPTICAL. IT'S ALL TRUE. I DIRECT YOUR ATTENTION TO THE MARVELOUS DEVICE BEHIND ME.
IT WAS DEVELOPED BY A GENTLEMAN NAMED WINKLER, WHO ONCE WORKED FOR NORMAN OSBORN. QUITE SIMPLY... IT'S A BRAIN-WASHING MACHINE!

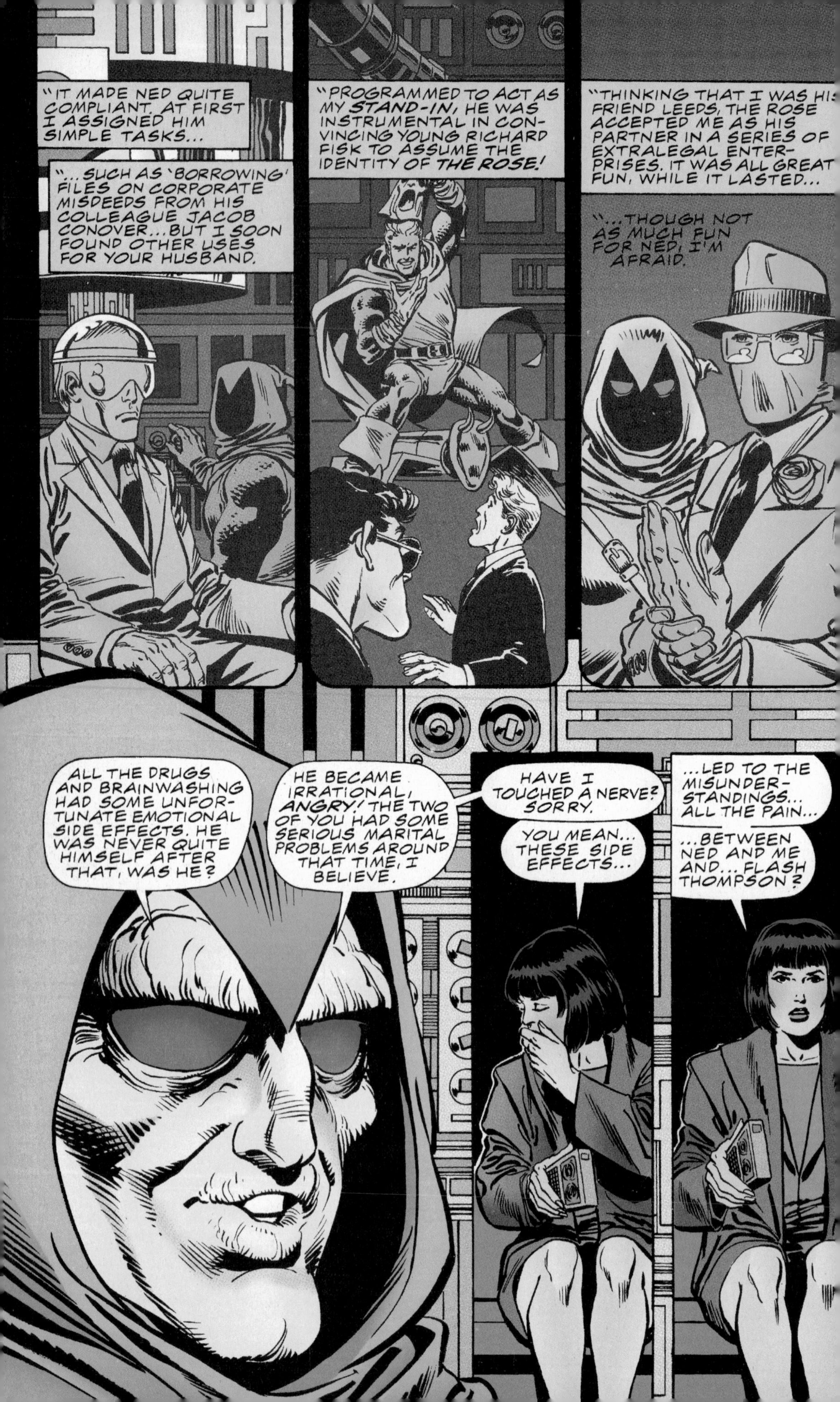

"IT MADE NED QUITE COMPLIANT. AT FIRST I ASSIGNED HIM SIMPLE TASKS...
"...SUCH AS 'BORROWING' FILES ON CORPORATE MISDEEDS FROM HIS COLLEAGUE JACOB CONOVER... BUT I SOON FOUND OTHER USES FOR YOUR HUSBAND.
"PROGRAMMED TO ACT AS MY STAND-IN, HE WAS INSTRUMENTAL IN CONVINCING YOUNG RICHARD FISK TO ASSUME THE IDENTITY OF THE ROSE!
"THINKING THAT I WAS HIS FRIEND LEEDS, THE ROSE ACCEPTED ME AS HIS PARTNER IN A SERIES OF EXTRALEGAL ENTERPRISES. IT WAS ALL GREAT FUN, WHILE IT LASTED...
"...THOUGH NOT AS MUCH FUN FOR NED, I'M AFRAID.
ALL THE DRUGS AND BRAINWASHING HAD SOME UNFORTUNATE EMOTIONAL SIDE EFFECTS. HE WAS NEVER QUITE HIMSELF AFTER THAT, WAS HE?
HE BECAME IRRATIONAL, ANGRY! THE TWO OF YOU HAD SOME SERIOUS MARITAL PROBLEMS AROUND THAT TIME, I BELIEVE.
HAVE I TOUCHED A NERVE? SORRY.
YOU MEAN... THESE SIDE EFFECTS...
...LED TO THE MISUNDERSTANDINGS... ALL THE PAIN...
...BETWEEN NED AND ME AND... FLASH THOMPSON?

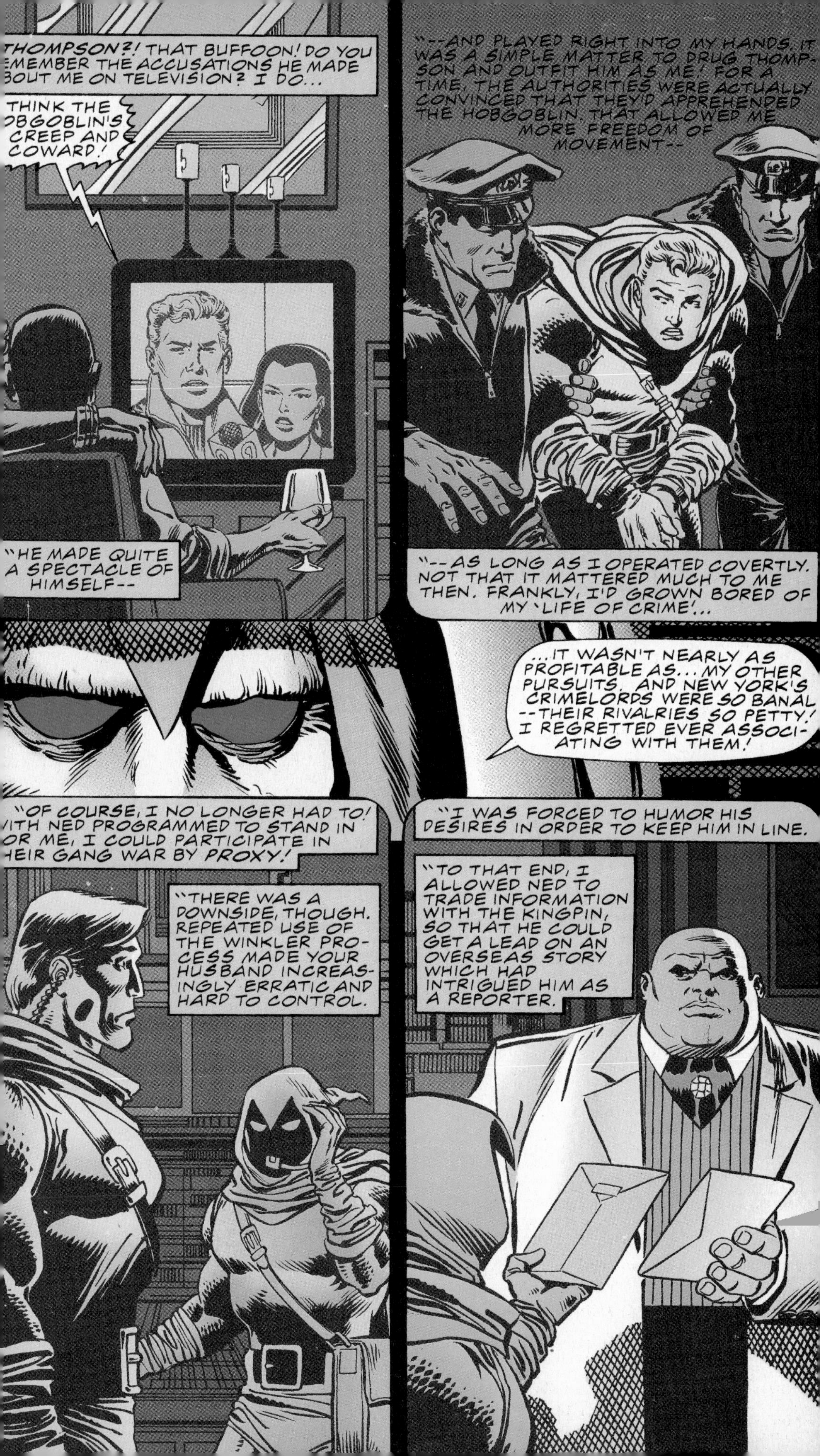

THOMPSON?! THAT BUFFOON! DO YOU REMEMBER THE ACCUSATIONS HE MADE ABOUT ME ON TELEVISION? I DO...
THINK THE HOBGOBLIN'S A CREEP AND A COWARD!
"HE MADE QUITE A SPECTACLE OF HIMSELF--
"--AND PLAYED RIGHT INTO MY HANDS. IT WAS A SIMPLE MATTER TO DRUG THOMPSON AND OUTFIT HIM AS ME! FOR A TIME, THE AUTHORITIES WERE ACTUALLY CONVINCED THAT THEY'D APPREHENDED THE HOBGOBLIN. THAT ALLOWED ME MORE FREEDOM OF MOVEMENT--
"--AS LONG AS I OPERATED COVERTLY. NOT THAT IT MATTERED MUCH TO ME THEN. FRANKLY, I'D GROWN BORED OF MY 'LIFE OF CRIME'...
...IT WASN'T NEARLY AS PROFITABLE AS... MY OTHER PURSUITS. AND NEW YORK'S CRIMELORDS WERE SO BANAL --THEIR RIVALRIES SO PETTY! I REGRETTED EVER ASSOCIATING WITH THEM!
"OF COURSE, I NO LONGER HAD TO! WITH NED PROGRAMMED TO STAND IN FOR ME, I COULD PARTICIPATE IN THEIR GANG WAR BY PROXY!
"THERE WAS A DOWNSIDE, THOUGH. REPEATED USE OF THE WINKLER PROCESS MADE YOUR HUSBAND INCREASINGLY ERRATIC AND HARD TO CONTROL.
"I WAS FORCED TO HUMOR HIS DESIRES IN ORDER TO KEEP HIM IN LINE.
"TO THAT END, I ALLOWED NED TO TRADE INFORMATION WITH THE KINGPIN, SO THAT HE COULD GET A LEAD ON AN OVERSEAS STORY WHICH HAD INTRIGUED HIM AS A REPORTER.

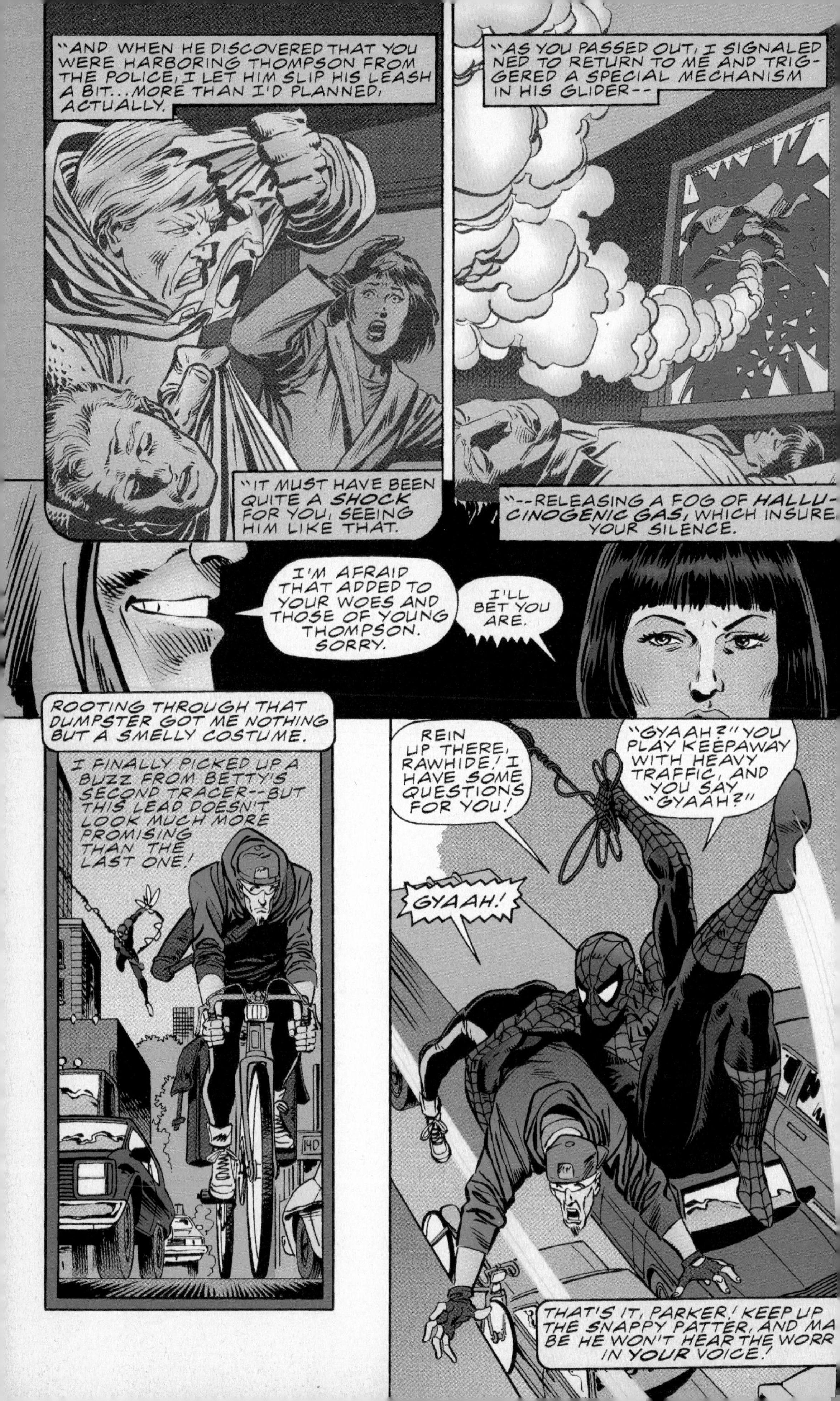
"AND WHEN HE DISCOVERED THAT YOU WERE HARBORING THOMPSON FROM THE POLICE, I LET HIM SLIP HIS LEASH A BIT... MORE THAN I'D PLANNED, ACTUALLY.
"IT MUST HAVE BEEN QUITE A SHOCK FOR YOU, SEEING HIM LIKE THAT.
"AS YOU PASSED OUT, I SIGNALED NED TO RETURN TO ME AND TRIGGERED A SPECIAL MECHANISM IN HIS GLIDER--
"--RELEASING A FOG OF HALLUCINOGENIC GAS, WHICH INSURE YOUR SILENCE.
I'M AFRAID THAT ADDED TO YOUR WOES AND THOSE OF YOUNG THOMPSON. SORRY.
I'LL BET YOU ARE.
ROOTING THROUGH THAT DUMPSTER GOT ME NOTHING BUT A SMELLY COSTUME.
I FINALLY PICKED UP A BUZZ FROM BETTY'S SECOND TRACER--BUT THIS LEAD DOESN'T LOOK MUCH MORE PROMISING THAN THE LAST ONE!
140
REIN UP THERE, RAWHIDE! I HAVE SOME QUESTIONS FOR YOU!
"GYAAH?" YOU PLAY KEEPAWAY WITH HEAVY TRAFFIC, AND YOU SAY "GYAAH?"
GYAAH!
THAT'S IT, PARKER! KEEP UP THE SNAPPY PATTER, AND MA BE HE WON'T HEAR THE WORR IN YOUR VOICE!

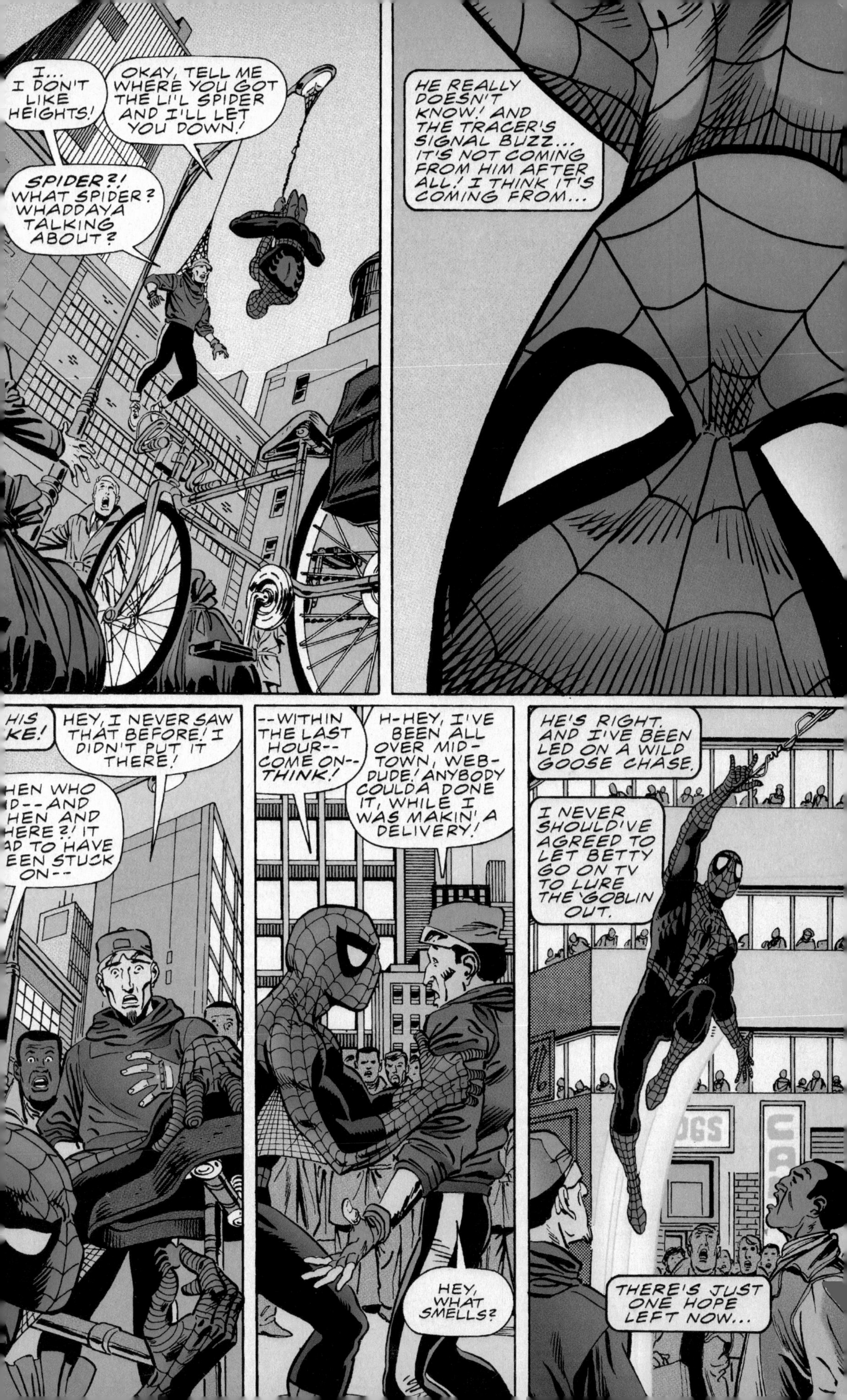
I... I DON'T LIKE HEIGHTS!
OKAY, TELL ME WHERE YOU GOT THE LI'L SPIDER AND I'LL LET YOU DOWN!
SPIDER?! WHAT SPIDER? WHADDAYA TALKING ABOUT?
HE REALLY DOESN'T KNOW! AND THE TRACER'S SIGNAL BUZZ... IT'S NOT COMING FROM HIM AFTER ALL! I THINK IT'S COMING FROM...
HIS KE!
HEY, I NEVER SAW THAT BEFORE! I DIDN'T PUT IT THERE!
HEN WHO D--AND HEN AND HERE?! IT AD TO HAVE EEN STUCK ON--
--WITHIN THE LAST HOUR--COME ON--THINK!
H-HEY, I'VE BEEN ALL OVER MID-TOWN, WEB-DUDE! ANYBODY COULDA DONE IT, WHILE I WAS MAKIN' A DELIVERY!
HEY, WHAT SMELLS?
HE'S RIGHT. AND I'VE BEEN LED ON A WILD GOOSE CHASE.
I NEVER SHOULD'VE AGREED TO LET BETTY GO ON TV TO LURE THE GOBLIN OUT.
THERE'S JUST ONE HOPE LEFT NOW...

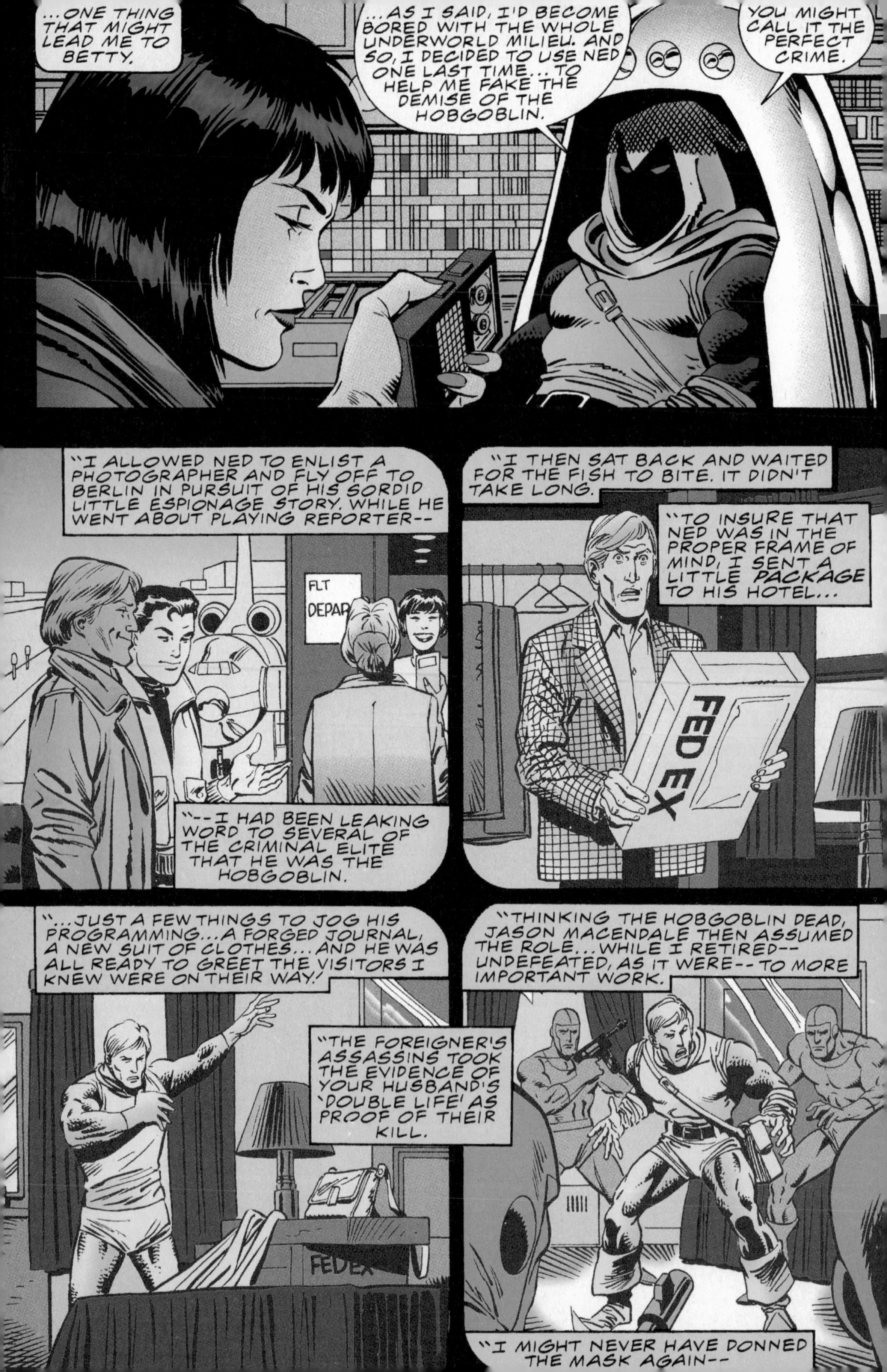
...ONE THING THAT MIGHT LEAD ME TO BETTY.
...AS I SAID, I'D BECOME BORED WITH THE WHOLE UNDERWORLD MILIEU. AND SO, I DECIDED TO USE NED ONE LAST TIME... TO HELP ME FAKE THE DEMISE OF THE HOBGOBLIN.
YOU MIGHT CALL IT THE PERFECT CRIME.
"I ALLOWED NED TO ENLIST A PHOTOGRAPHER AND FLY OFF TO BERLIN IN PURSUIT OF HIS SORDID LITTLE ESPIONAGE STORY. WHILE HE WENT ABOUT PLAYING REPORTER--
FLT
DEPAR
"--I HAD BEEN LEAKING WORD TO SEVERAL OF THE CRIMINAL ELITE THAT HE WAS THE HOBGOBLIN.
"I THEN SAT BACK AND WAITED FOR THE FISH TO BITE. IT DIDN'T TAKE LONG.
"TO INSURE THAT NED WAS IN THE PROPER FRAME OF MIND, I SENT A LITTLE PACKAGE TO HIS HOTEL...
FED EX
"...JUST A FEW THINGS TO JOG HIS PROGRAMMING... A FORGED JOURNAL, A NEW SUIT OF CLOTHES... AND HE WAS ALL READY TO GREET THE VISITORS I KNEW WERE ON THEIR WAY!
"THE FOREIGNER'S ASSASSINS TOOK THE EVIDENCE OF YOUR HUSBAND'S 'DOUBLE LIFE' AS PROOF OF THEIR KILL.
FEDEX
"THINKING THE HOBGOBLIN DEAD, JASON MACENDALE THEN ASSUMED THE ROLE... WHILE I RETIRED-- UNDEFEATED, AS IT WERE-- TO MORE IMPORTANT WORK.
"I MIGHT NEVER HAVE DONNED THE MASK AGAIN--

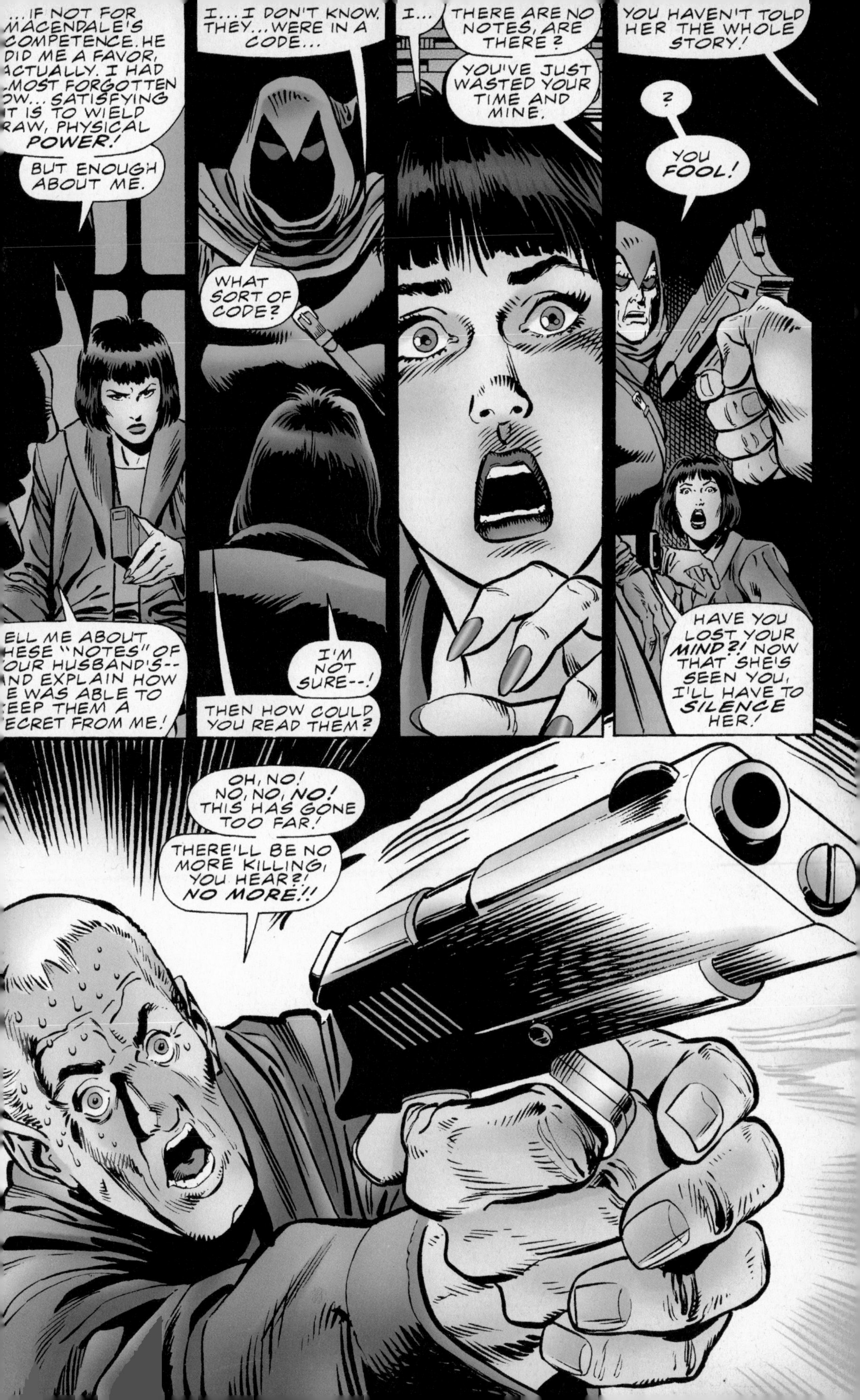
...IF NOT FOR MACENDALE'S COMPETENCE. HE DID ME A FAVOR, ACTUALLY. I HAD ALMOST FORGOTTEN HOW... SATISFYING IT IS TO WIELD RAW, PHYSICAL POWER!
BUT ENOUGH ABOUT ME.
TELL ME ABOUT THESE "NOTES" OF YOUR HUSBAND'S-- AND EXPLAIN HOW HE WAS ABLE TO KEEP THEM A SECRET FROM ME!
I... I DON'T KNOW. THEY... WERE IN A CODE...
WHAT SORT OF CODE?
I'M NOT SURE--!
THEN HOW COULD YOU READ THEM?
I...
THERE ARE NO NOTES, ARE THERE?
YOU'VE JUST WASTED YOUR TIME AND MINE.
YOU HAVEN'T TOLD HER THE WHOLE STORY!
?
YOU FOOL!
HAVE YOU LOST YOUR MIND?! NOW THAT SHE'S SEEN YOU, I'LL HAVE TO SILENCE HER!
OH, NO! NO, NO, NO! THIS HAS GONE TOO FAR!
THERE'LL BE NO MORE KILLING, YOU HEAR?! NO MORE!!

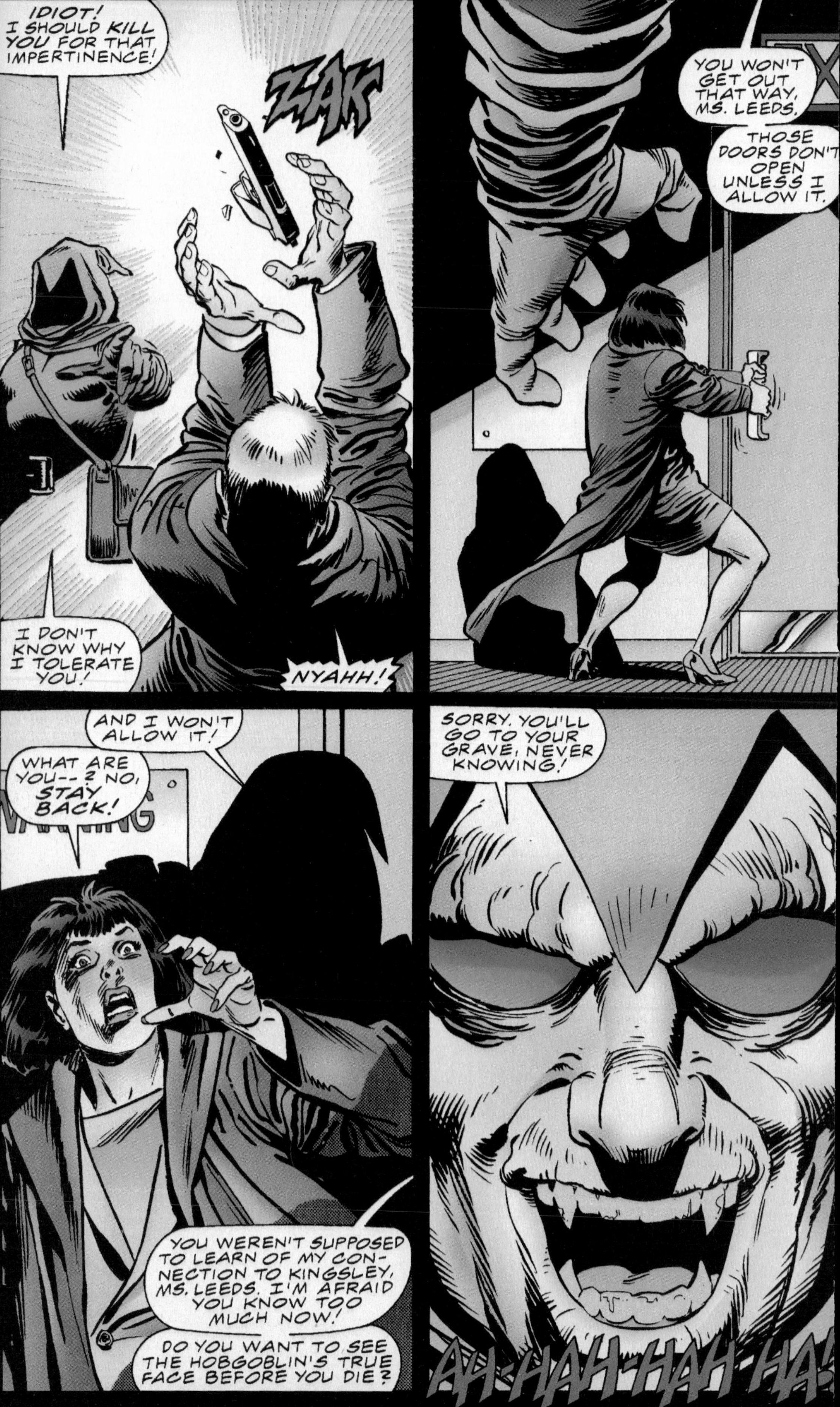
IDIOT! I SHOULD KILL YOU FOR THAT IMPERTINENCE!
ZAK
I DON'T KNOW WHY I TOLERATE YOU!
NYAHH!
YOU WON'T GET OUT THAT WAY, MS. LEEDS.
THOSE DOORS DON'T OPEN UNLESS I ALLOW IT.
AND I WON'T ALLOW IT!
WHAT ARE YOU-- ? NO, STAY BACK!
WARNING
YOU WEREN'T SUPPOSED TO LEARN OF MY CONNECTION TO KINGSLEY, MS. LEEDS. I'M AFRAID YOU KNOW TOO MUCH NOW!
DO YOU WANT TO SEE THE HOBGOBLIN'S TRUE FACE BEFORE YOU DIE?
SORRY. YOU'LL GO TO YOUR GRAVE, NEVER KNOWING!
AH-HAH-HAH-HAH HA!

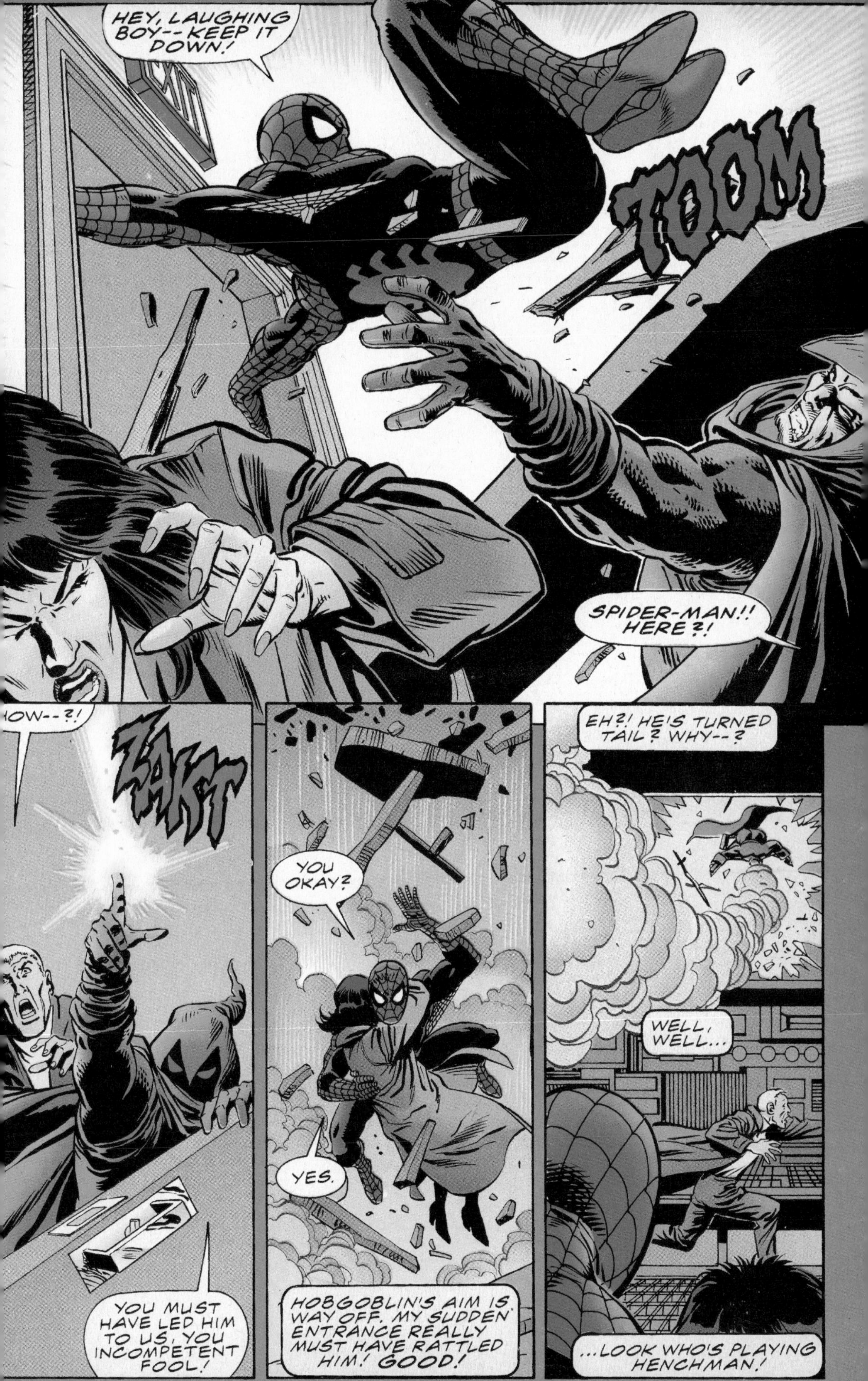

HEY, LAUGHING BOY--KEEP IT DOWN!
EXIT
TOOM
SPIDER-MAN!! HERE?!
HOW--?!
ZAKT
YOU MUST HAVE LED HIM TO US, YOU INCOMPETENT FOOL!
YOU OKAY?
YES.
HOBGOBLIN'S AIM IS WAY OFF. MY SUDDEN ENTRANCE REALLY MUST HAVE RATTLED HIM! GOOD!
EH?! HE'S TURNED TAIL? WHY--?
WELL, WELL...
...LOOK WHO'S PLAYING HENCHMAN!

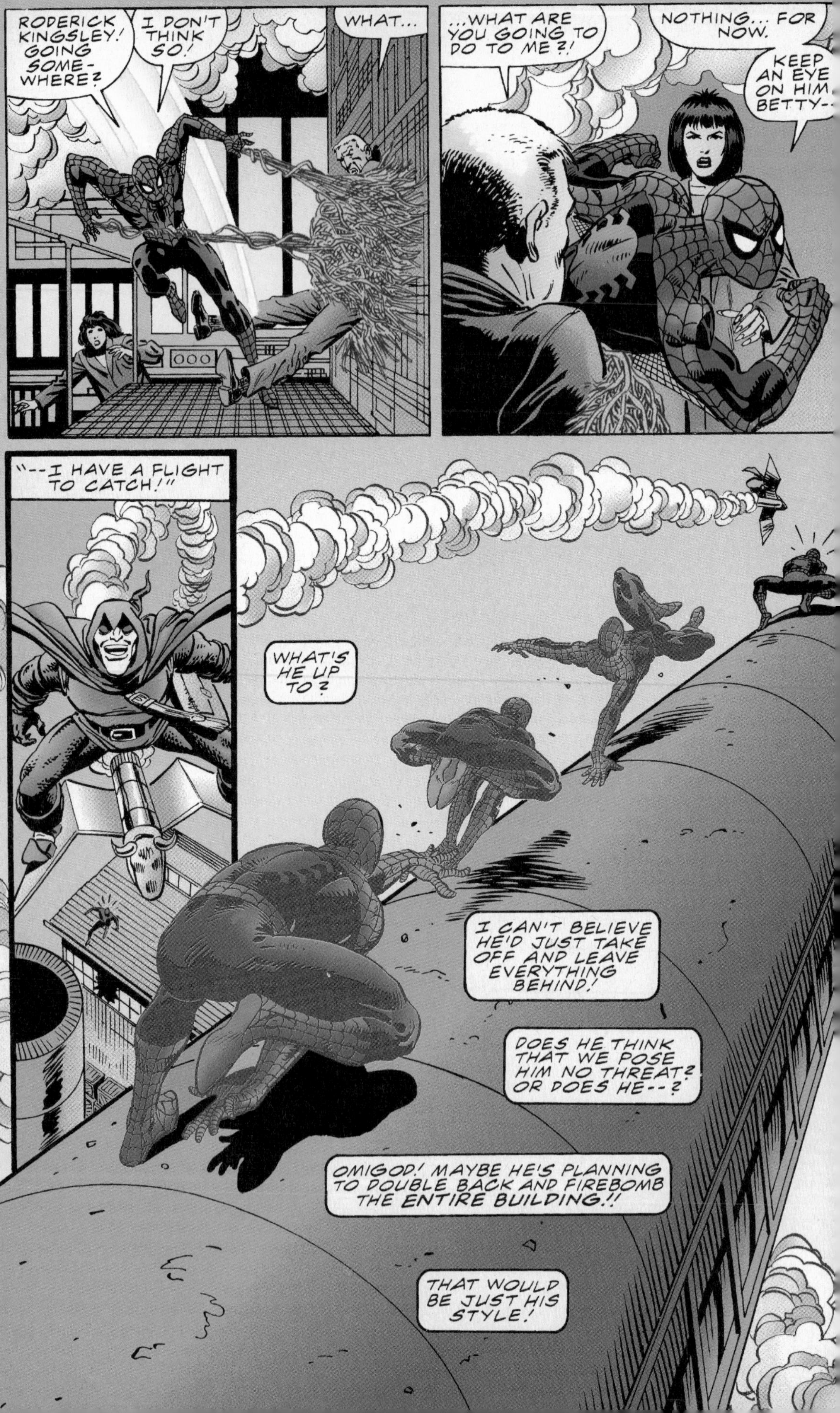
RODERICK KINGSLEY! GOING SOME-WHERE?
I DON'T THINK SO!
WHAT...
...WHAT ARE YOU GOING TO DO TO ME?!
NOTHING... FOR NOW.
KEEP AN EYE ON HIM BETTY--
"--I HAVE A FLIGHT TO CATCH!"
WHAT'S HE UP TO?
I CAN'T BELIEVE HE'D JUST TAKE OFF AND LEAVE EVERYTHING BEHIND!
DOES HE THINK THAT WE POSE HIM NO THREAT? OR DOES HE--?
OMIGOD! MAYBE HE'S PLANNING TO DOUBLE BACK AND FIREBOMB THE ENTIRE BUILDING!!
THAT WOULD BE JUST HIS STYLE!

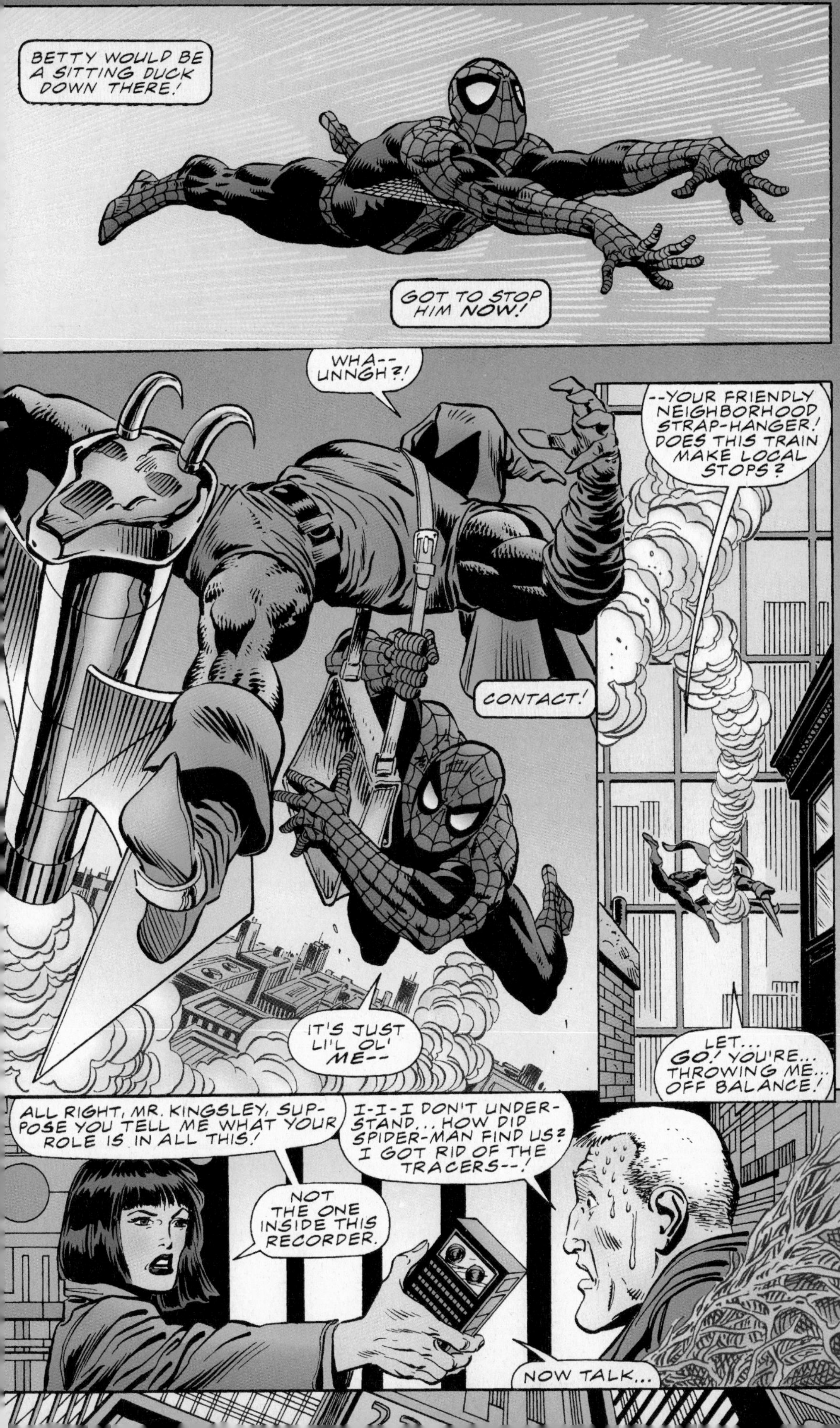
BETTY WOULD BE A SITTING DUCK DOWN THERE!
GOT TO STOP HIM NOW!
WHA-- UNNGH?!
--YOUR FRIENDLY NEIGHBORHOOD STRAP-HANGER! DOES THIS TRAIN MAKE LOCAL STOPS?
CONTACT!
IT'S JUST LI'L OL' ME--
LET... GO! YOU'RE... THROWING ME... OFF BALANCE!
ALL RIGHT, MR. KINGSLEY, SUPPOSE YOU TELL ME WHAT YOUR ROLE IS IN ALL THIS!
I-I-I DON'T UNDERSTAND... HOW DID SPIDER-MAN FIND US? I GOT RID OF THE TRACERS--!
NOT THE ONE INSIDE THIS RECORDER.
NOW TALK...

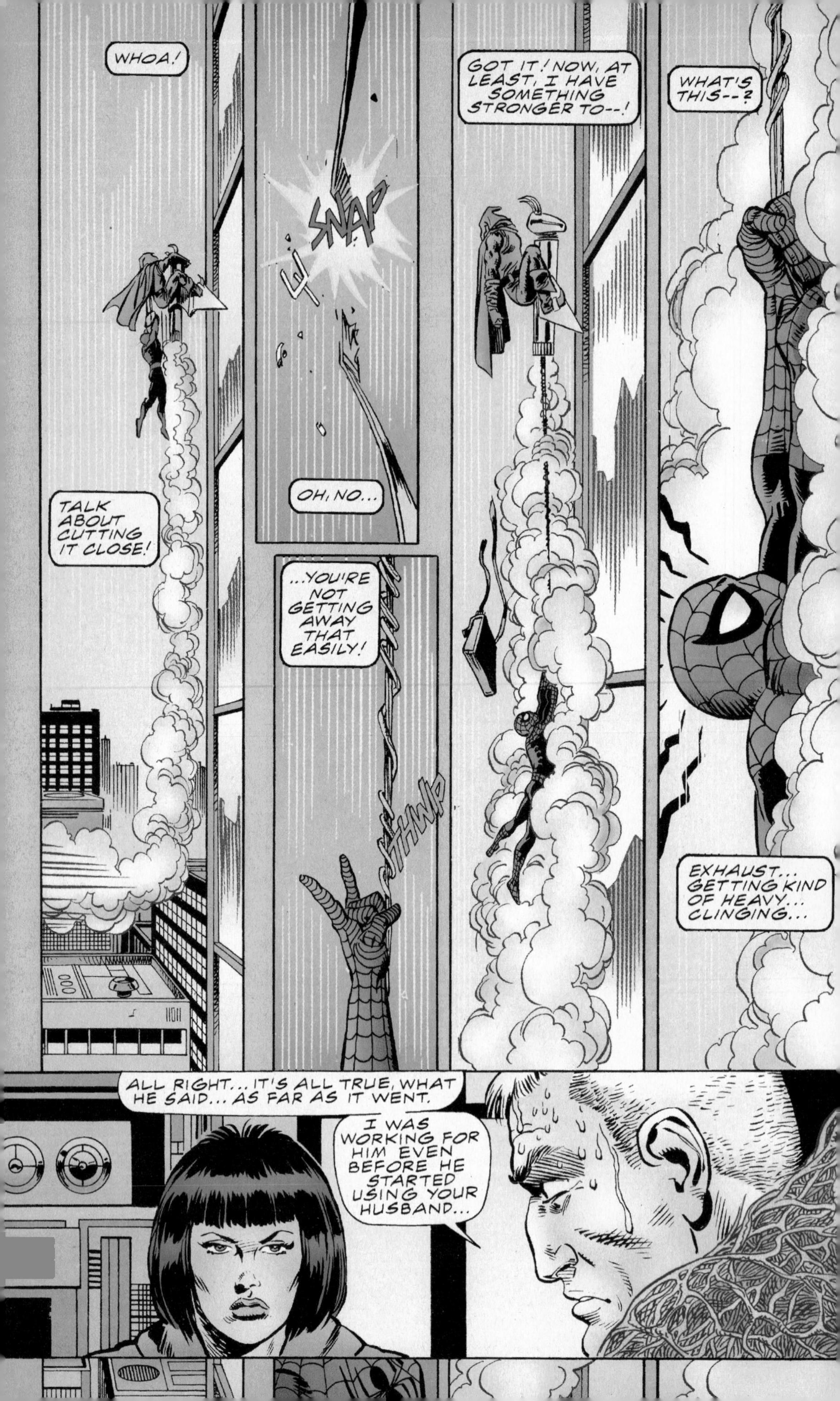
WHOA!
TALK ABOUT CUTTING IT CLOSE!
SNAP
OH, NO...
...YOU'RE NOT GETTING AWAY THAT EASILY!
THWIP
GOT IT! NOW, AT LEAST, I HAVE SOMETHING STRONGER TO--!
WHAT'S THIS--?
EXHAUST... GETTING KIND OF HEAVY... CLINGING...
ALL RIGHT... IT'S ALL TRUE, WHAT HE SAID... AS FAR AS IT WENT.
I WAS WORKING FOR HIM EVEN BEFORE HE STARTED USING YOUR HUSBAND...

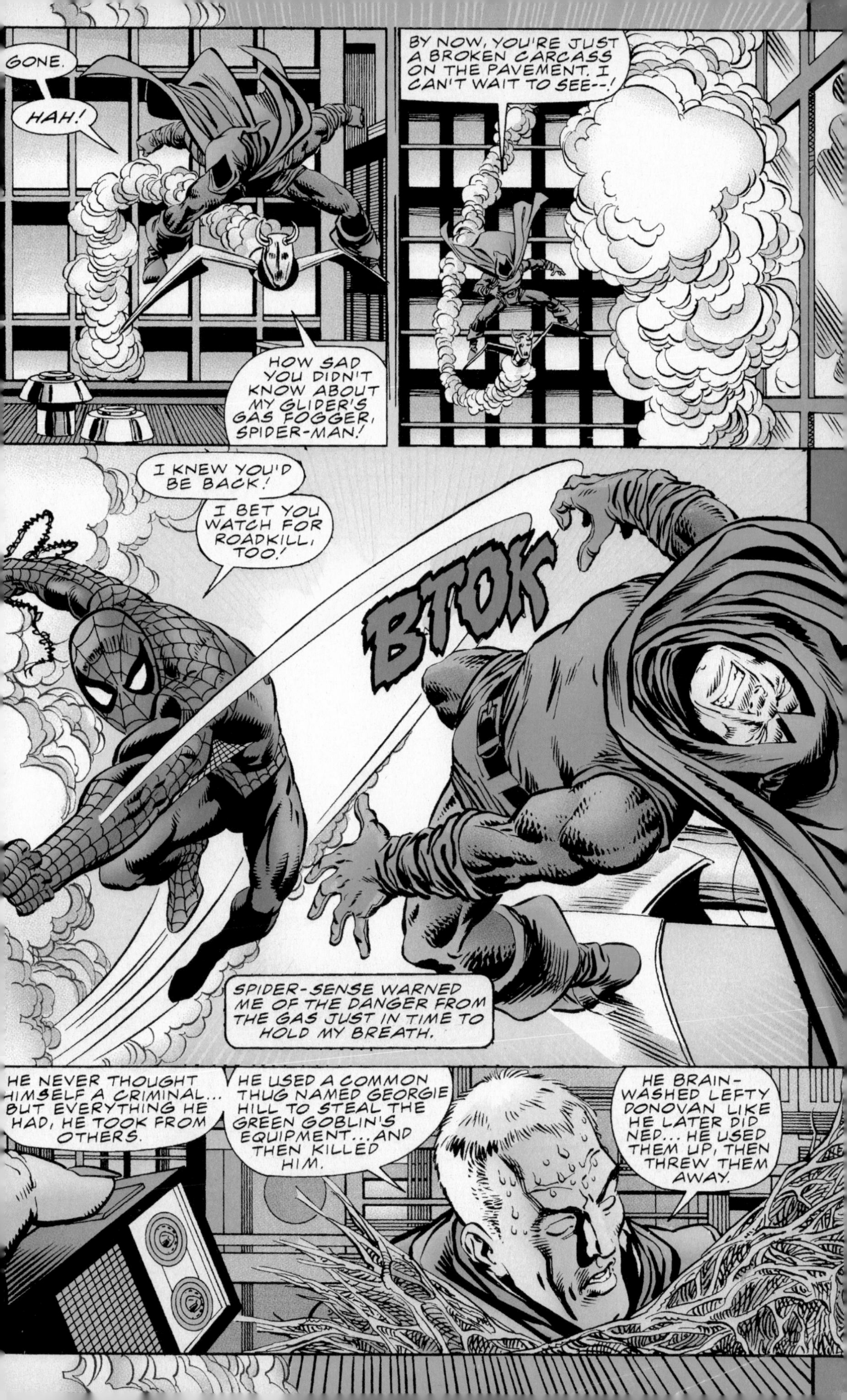
GONE.
HAH!
HOW SAD YOU DIDN'T KNOW ABOUT MY GLIDER'S GAS FOGGER, SPIDER-MAN!
BY NOW, YOU'RE JUST A BROKEN CARCASS ON THE PAVEMENT. I CAN'T WAIT TO SEE--!
I KNEW YOU'D BE BACK!
I BET YOU WATCH FOR ROADKILL, TOO!
BTOK
SPIDER-SENSE WARNED ME OF THE DANGER FROM THE GAS JUST IN TIME TO HOLD MY BREATH.
HE NEVER THOUGHT HIMSELF A CRIMINAL... BUT EVERYTHING HE HAD, HE TOOK FROM OTHERS.
HE USED A COMMON THUG NAMED GEORGIE HILL TO STEAL THE GREEN GOBLIN'S EQUIPMENT... AND THEN KILLED HIM.
HE BRAIN-WASHED LEFTY DONOVAN LIKE HE LATER DID NED... HE USED THEM UP, THEN THREW THEM AWAY.

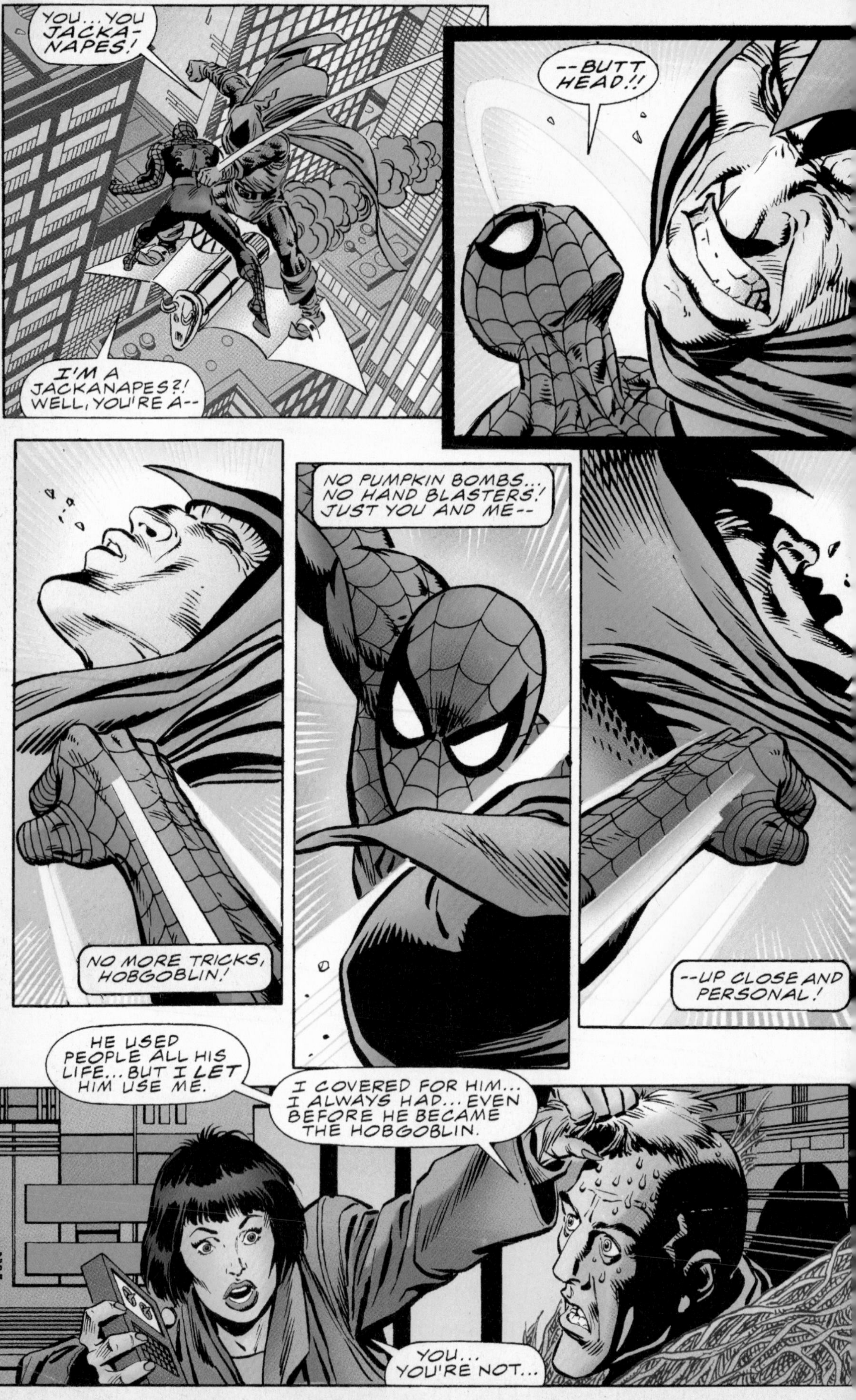
YOU...YOU JACKA-NAPES!
I'M A JACKANAPES?! WELL, YOU'RE A--
--BUTT HEAD!!
NO MORE TRICKS, HOBGOBLIN!
NO PUMPKIN BOMBS... NO HAND BLASTERS! JUST YOU AND ME--
--UP CLOSE AND PERSONAL!
HE USED PEOPLE ALL HIS LIFE... BUT I LET HIM USE ME.
I COVERED FOR HIM... I ALWAYS HAD... EVEN BEFORE HE BECAME THE HOBGOBLIN.
YOU... YOU'RE NOT...

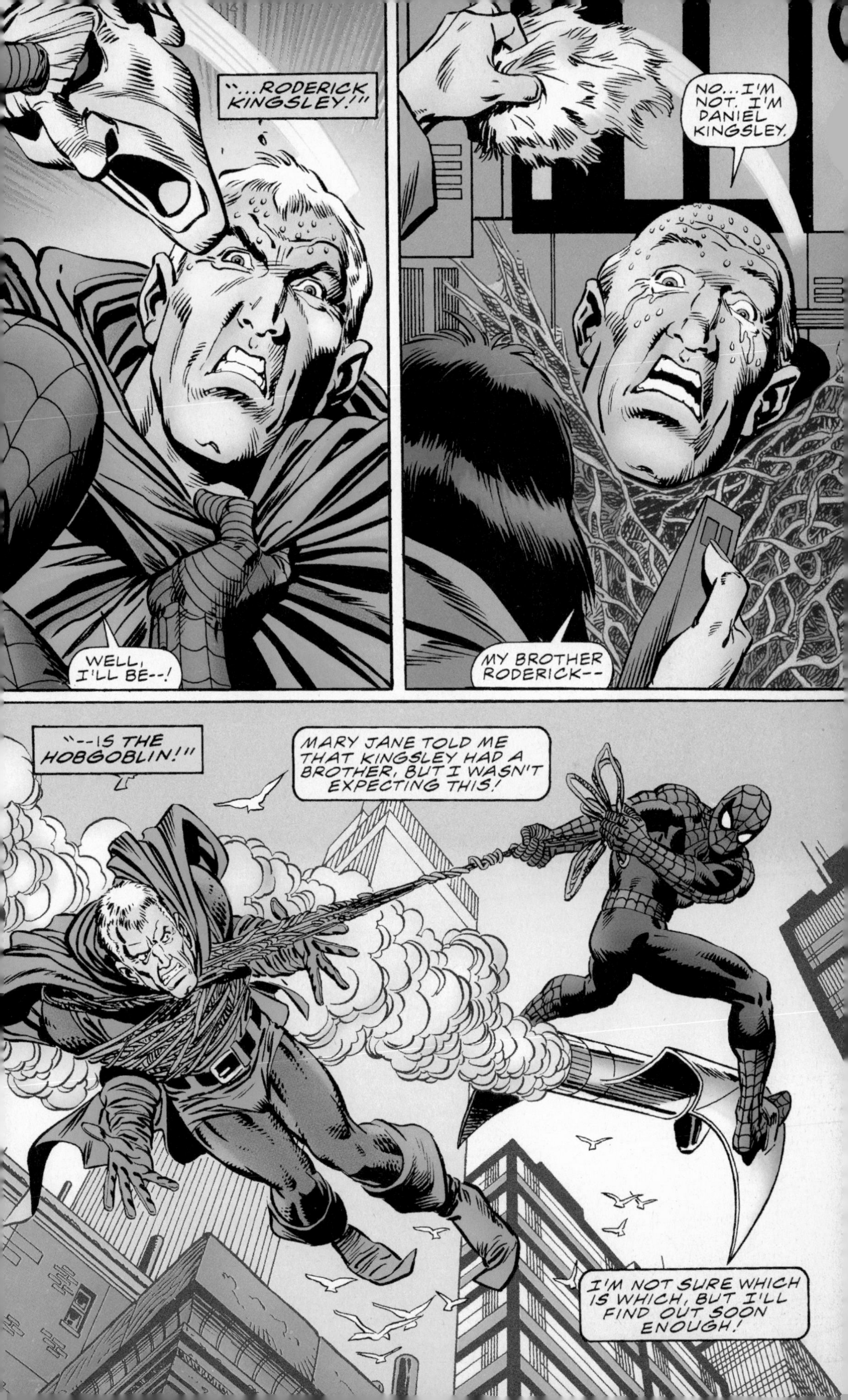
"...RODERICK KINGSLEY!"
WELL, I'LL BE--!
NO...I'M NOT. I'M DANIEL KINGSLEY.
MY BROTHER RODERICK--
"--IS THE HOBGOBLIN!"
MARY JANE TOLD ME THAT KINGSLEY HAD A BROTHER, BUT I WASN'T EXPECTING THIS!
I'M NOT SURE WHICH IS WHICH, BUT I'LL FIND OUT SOON ENOUGH!

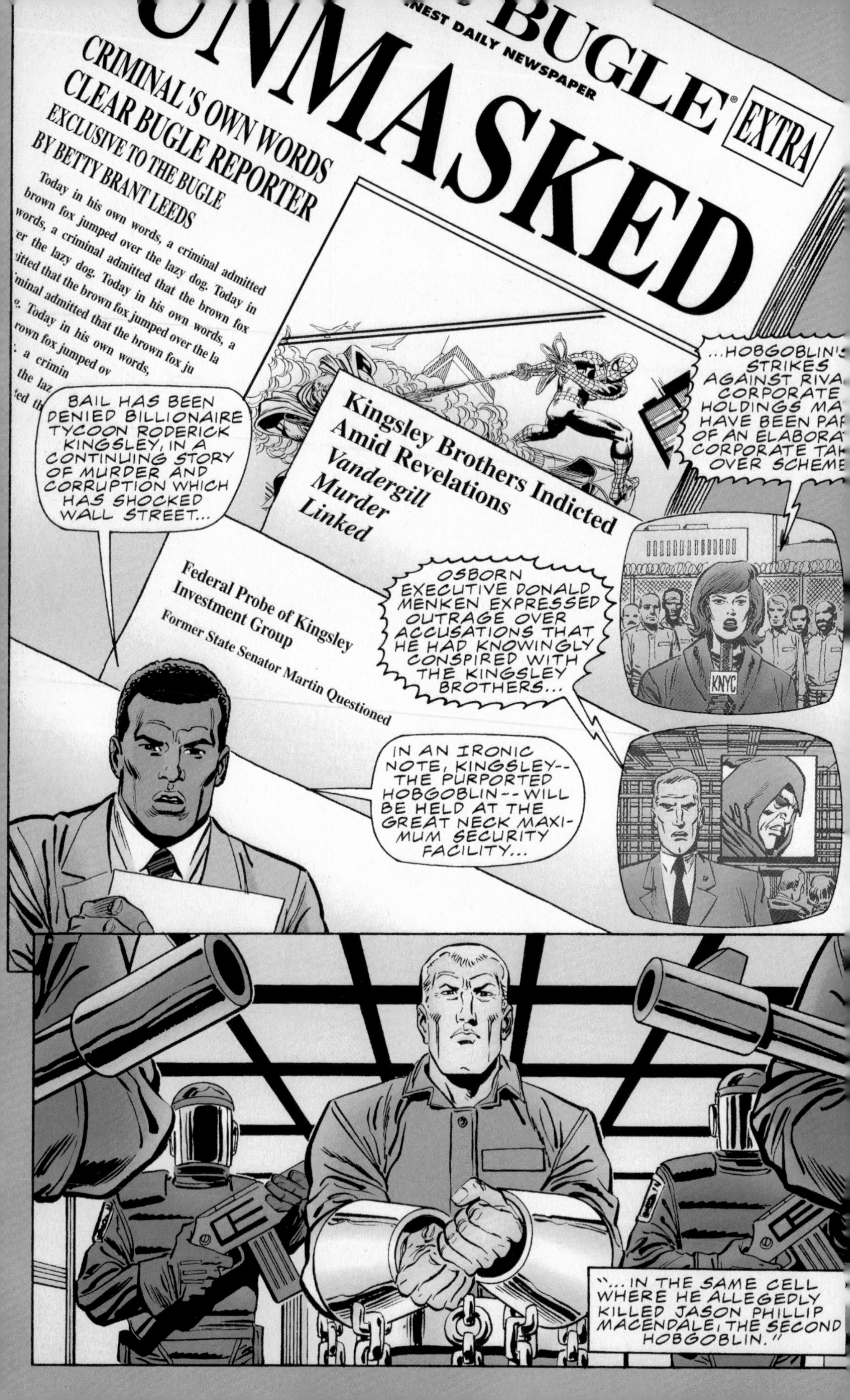

NEST DAILY NEWSPAPER
BUGLE
EXTRA
UNMASKED
CRIMINAL'S OWN WORDS CLEAR BUGLE REPORTER
EXCLUSIVE TO THE BUGLE
BY BETTY BRANT LEEDS
Today in his own words, a criminal admitted brown fox jumped over the lazy dog. Today in words, a criminal admitted that the brown fox er the lazy dog. Today in his own words, a itted that the brown fox jumped over the la iminal admitted that the brown fox ju g. Today in his own words, rown fox jumped ov
Kingsley Brothers Indicted Amid Revelations
Vandergill Murder Linked
Federal Probe of Kingsley Investment Group
Former State Senator Martin Questioned
BAIL HAS BEEN DENIED BILLIONAIRE TYCOON RODERICK KINGSLEY, IN A CONTINUING STORY OF MURDER AND CORRUPTION WHICH HAS SHOCKED WALL STREET...
...HOBGOBLIN'S STRIKES AGAINST RIVA CORPORATE HOLDINGS MA HAVE BEEN PAR OF AN ELABORA CORPORATE TAK OVER SCHEME
OSBORN EXECUTIVE DONALD MENKEN EXPRESSED OUTRAGE OVER ACCUSATIONS THAT HE HAD KNOWINGLY CONSPIRED WITH THE KINGSLEY BROTHERS...
KNYC
IN AN IRONIC NOTE, KINGSLEY-- THE PURPORTED HOBGOBLIN--WILL BE HELD AT THE GREAT NECK MAXIMUM SECURITY FACILITY...
"...IN THE SAME CELL WHERE HE ALLEGEDLY KILLED JASON PHILLIP MACENDALE, THE SECOND HOBGOBLIN."

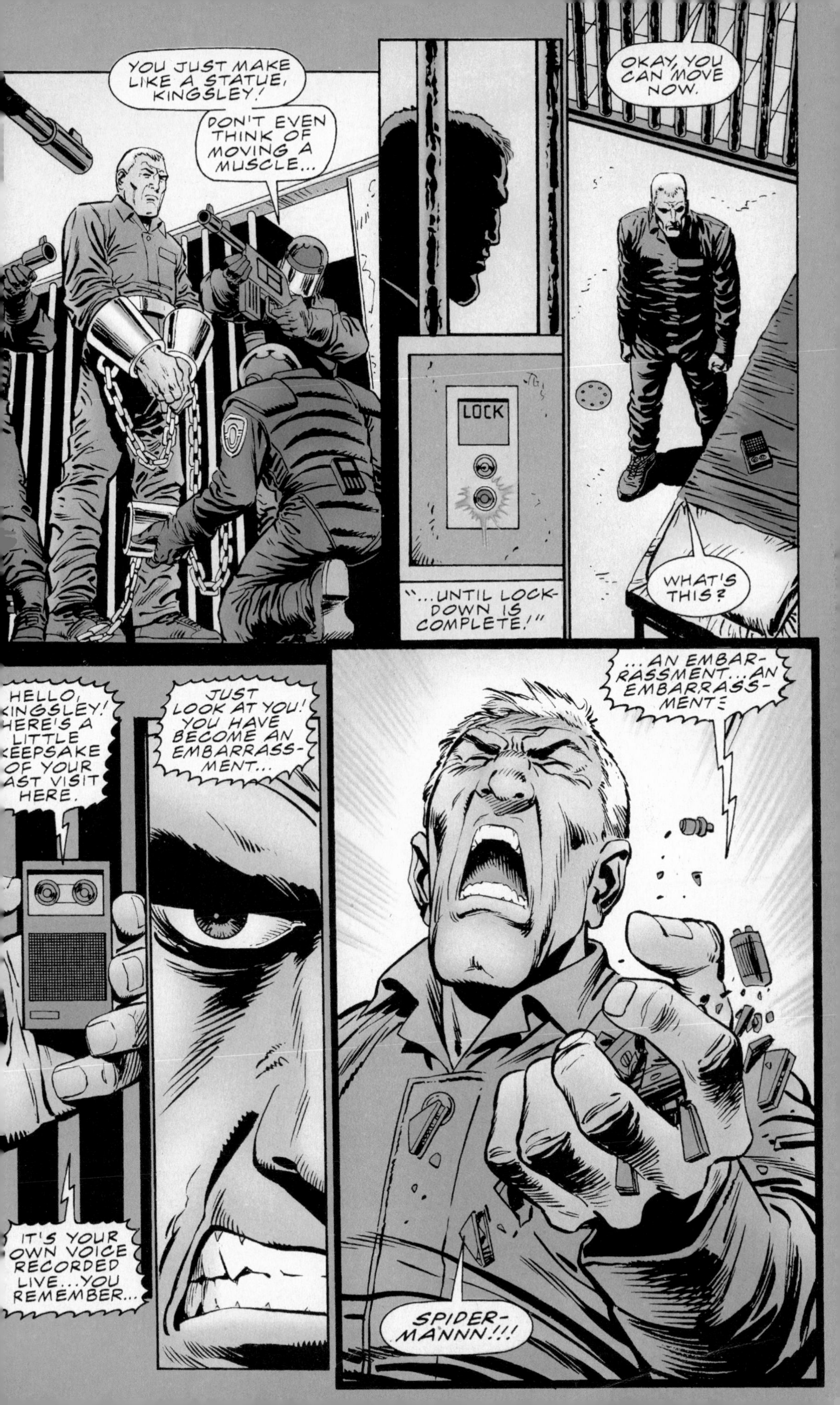
YOU JUST MAKE LIKE A STATUE, KINGSLEY!
DON'T EVEN THINK OF MOVING A MUSCLE...
LOCK
"...UNTIL LOCK-DOWN IS COMPLETE!"
OKAY, YOU CAN MOVE NOW.
WHAT'S THIS?
HELLO, KINGSLEY! HERE'S A LITTLE KEEPSAKE OF YOUR LAST VISIT HERE.
IT'S YOUR OWN VOICE RECORDED LIVE...YOU REMEMBER...
JUST LOOK AT YOU! YOU HAVE BECOME AN EMBARRASS-MENT...
...AN EMBAR-RASSMENT...AN EMBARRASS-MENT
SPIDER-MANNN!!!

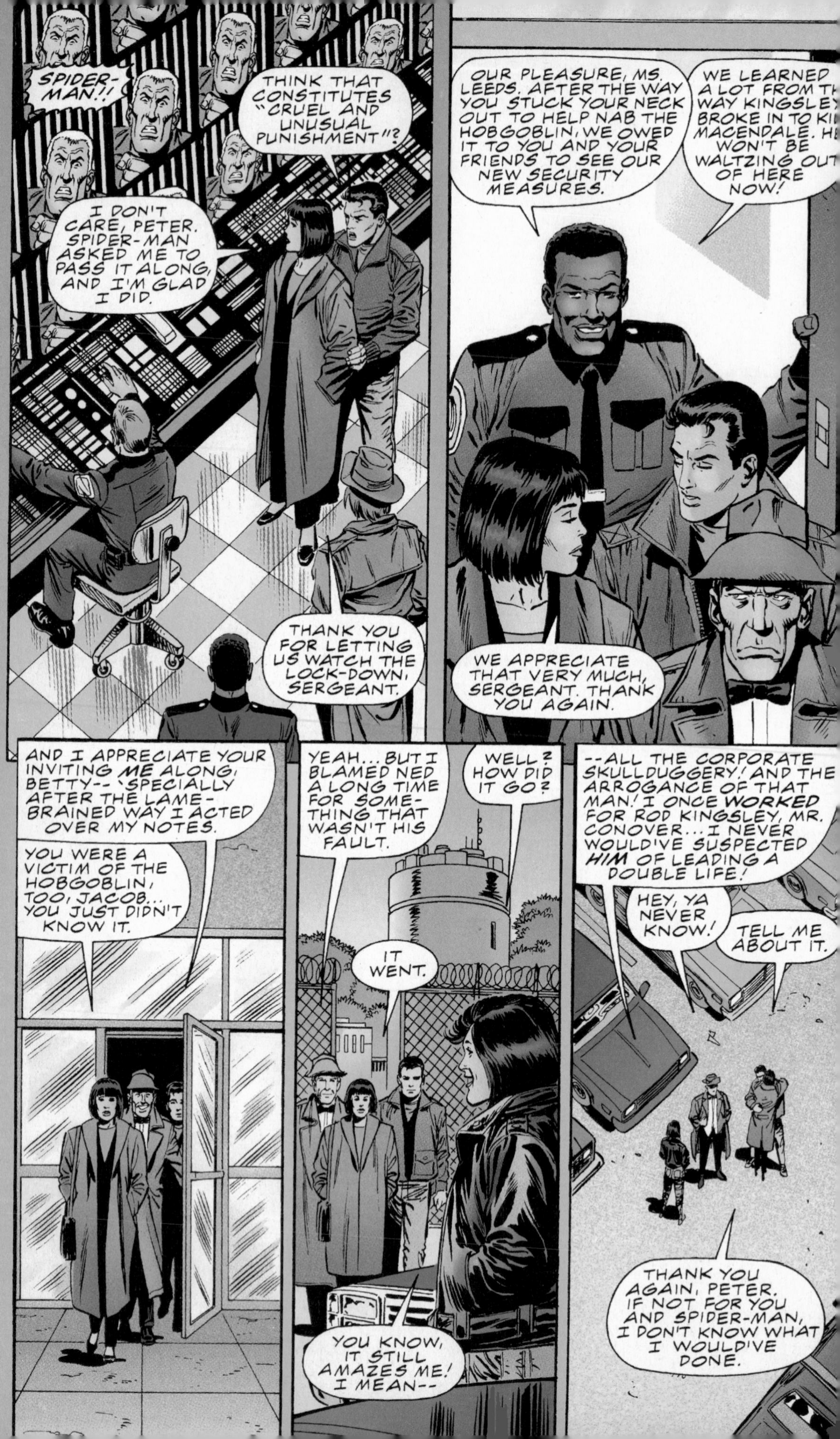
SPIDER-MAN!!
THINK THAT CONSTITUTES "CRUEL AND UNUSUAL PUNISHMENT"?
I DON'T CARE, PETER. SPIDER-MAN ASKED ME TO PASS IT ALONG, AND I'M GLAD I DID.
THANK YOU FOR LETTING US WATCH THE LOCK-DOWN, SERGEANT.
OUR PLEASURE, MS. LEEDS. AFTER THE WAY YOU STUCK YOUR NECK OUT TO HELP NAB THE HOBGOBLIN, WE OWED IT TO YOU AND YOUR FRIENDS TO SEE OUR NEW SECURITY MEASURES.
WE LEARNED A LOT FROM TH WAY KINGSLEY BROKE IN TO KI MACENDALE. HE WON'T BE WALTZING OUT OF HERE NOW!
WE APPRECIATE THAT VERY MUCH, SERGEANT. THANK YOU AGAIN.
AND I APPRECIATE YOUR INVITING ME ALONG, BETTY-- 'SPECIALLY AFTER THE LAME-BRAINED WAY I ACTED OVER MY NOTES.
YOU WERE A VICTIM OF THE HOBGOBLIN, TOO, JACOB... YOU JUST DIDN'T KNOW IT.
YEAH... BUT I BLAMED NED A LONG TIME FOR SOME-THING THAT WASN'T HIS FAULT.
WELL? HOW DID IT GO?
IT WENT.
YOU KNOW, IT STILL AMAZES ME! I MEAN--
--ALL THE CORPORATE SKULLDUGGERY! AND THE ARROGANCE OF THAT MAN! I ONCE WORKED FOR ROD KINGSLEY, MR. CONOVER... I NEVER WOULD'VE SUSPECTED HIM OF LEADING A DOUBLE LIFE!
HEY, YA NEVER KNOW!
TELL ME ABOUT IT.
THANK YOU AGAIN, PETER. IF NOT FOR YOU AND SPIDER-MAN, I DON'T KNOW WHAT I WOULD'VE DONE.

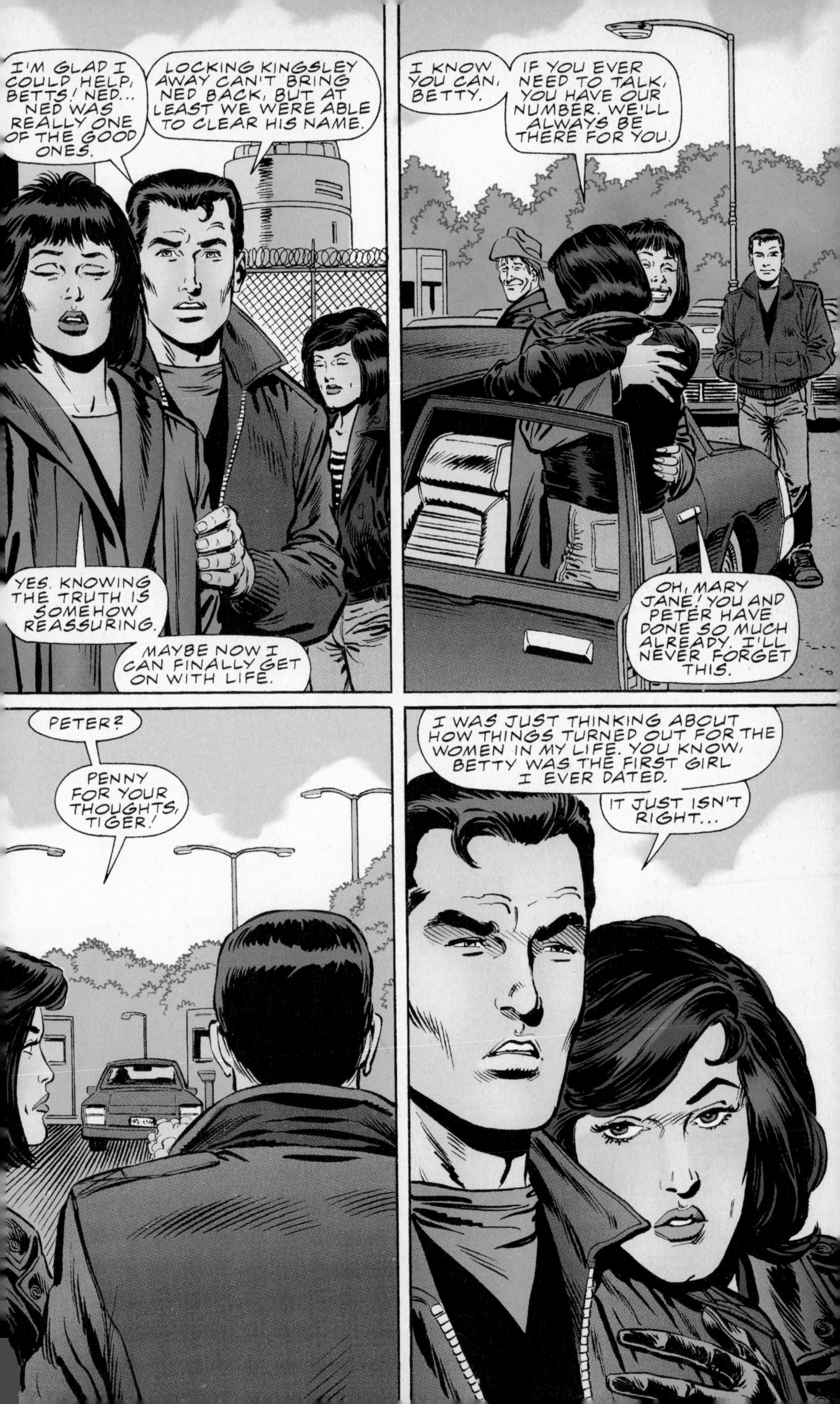
I'M GLAD I COULD HELP, BETTS! NED... NED WAS REALLY ONE OF THE GOOD ONES.
LOCKING KINGSLEY AWAY CAN'T BRING NED BACK, BUT AT LEAST WE WERE ABLE TO CLEAR HIS NAME.
YES. KNOWING THE TRUTH IS SOMEHOW REASSURING.
MAYBE NOW I CAN FINALLY GET ON WITH LIFE.
I KNOW YOU CAN, BETTY.
IF YOU EVER NEED TO TALK, YOU HAVE OUR NUMBER. WE'LL ALWAYS BE THERE FOR YOU.
OH, MARY JANE! YOU AND PETER HAVE DONE SO MUCH ALREADY. I'LL NEVER FORGET THIS.
PETER?
PENNY FOR YOUR THOUGHTS, TIGER!
I WAS JUST THINKING ABOUT HOW THINGS TURNED OUT FOR THE WOMEN IN MY LIFE. YOU KNOW, BETTY WAS THE FIRST GIRL I EVER DATED.
IT JUST ISN'T RIGHT...

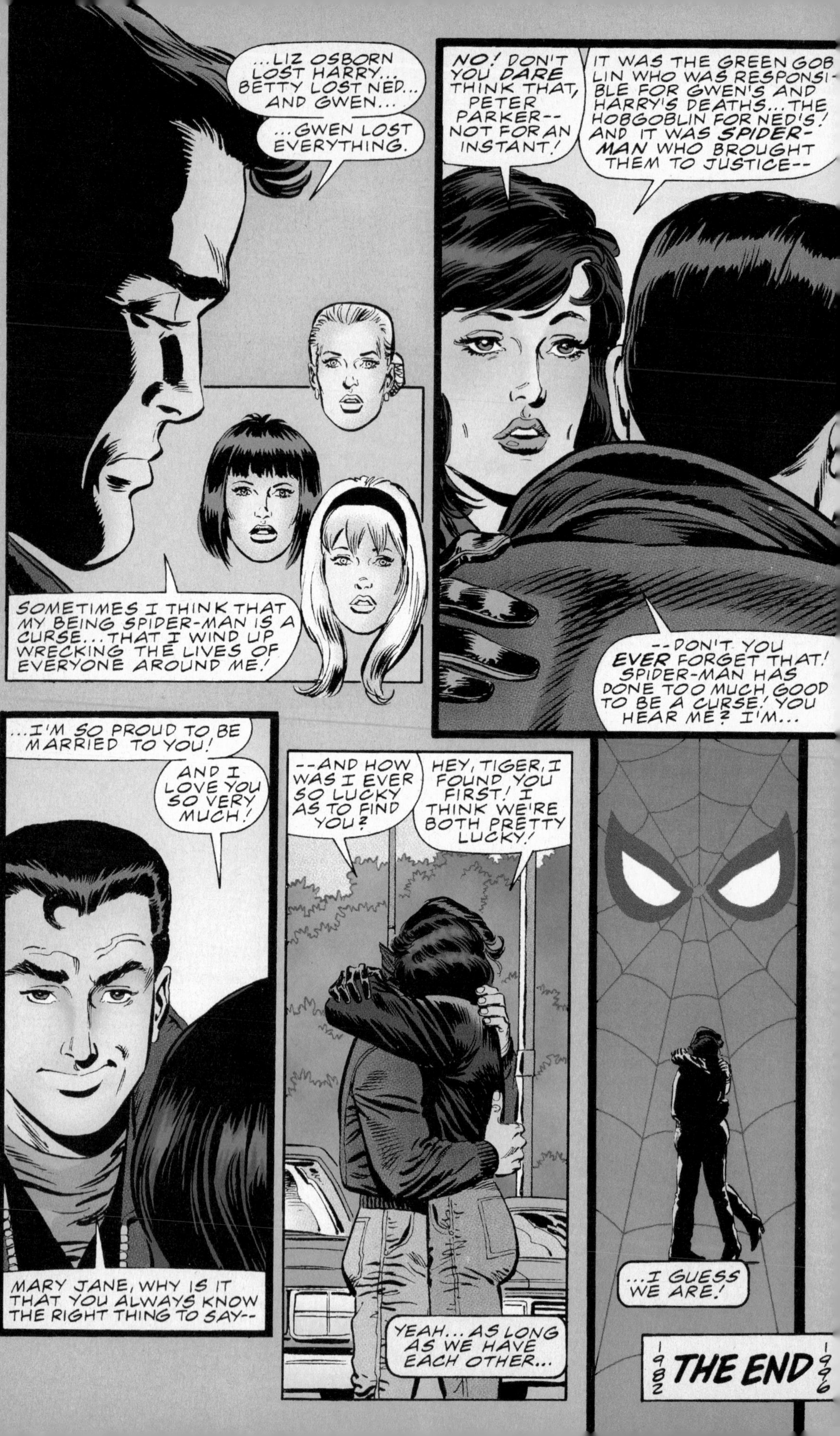
...LIZ OSBORN LOST HARRY... BETTY LOST NED... AND GWEN...
...GWEN LOST EVERYTHING.
SOMETIMES I THINK THAT MY BEING SPIDER-MAN IS A CURSE...THAT I WIND UP WRECKING THE LIVES OF EVERYONE AROUND ME!
NO! DON'T YOU DARE THINK THAT, PETER PARKER--NOT FOR AN INSTANT!
IT WAS THE GREEN GOBLIN WHO WAS RESPONSIBLE FOR GWEN'S AND HARRY'S DEATHS...THE HOBGOBLIN FOR NED'S! AND IT WAS SPIDER-MAN WHO BROUGHT THEM TO JUSTICE--
--DON'T YOU EVER FORGET THAT! SPIDER-MAN HAS DONE TOO MUCH GOOD TO BE A CURSE! YOU HEAR ME? I'M...
...I'M SO PROUD TO BE MARRIED TO YOU!
AND I LOVE YOU SO VERY MUCH!
MARY JANE, WHY IS IT THAT YOU ALWAYS KNOW THE RIGHT THING TO SAY--
--AND HOW WAS I EVER SO LUCKY AS TO FIND YOU?
HEY, TIGER, I FOUND YOU FIRST! I THINK WE'RE BOTH PRETTY LUCKY!
YEAH... AS LONG AS WE HAVE EACH OTHER...
...I GUESS WE ARE!
1982 THE END 1996

HOBGOBLIN LIVES SOURCES

Page 2 Doctor Jonas Harrow first appeared in AMAZING SPIDER-MAN #114. J. Jonah Jameson wrote his first anti-Spider-Man editorial in AMAZING SPIDER-MAN #1. Spider-Man fought Senator Martin's son in SPECTACULAR SPIDER-MAN #39. Donald Menken first appeared in AMAZING SPIDER-MAN #239.

Page 10 Betty Brant Leeds went public on television in our previous issue.

Page 11 Spider-Man's epic battle with the Hobgoblin took place in AMAZING SPIDER-MAN #251.

Page 13 Dr. Winkler had developed his bioelectric brain-washing device while in the employ of Norman Osborn prior to AMAZING SPIDER-MAN #59.

Page 14 Richard Fisk recalled his meeting with Ned Leeds in WEB OF SPIDER-MAN #30 (never realizing that Ned had been brainwashed.)

Page 15 Flash Thompson accused the Hobgoblin of cowardice, and was subsequently set up by the Hobgoblin in AMAZING SPIDER-MAN #276. "Hobgoblin" and the Kingpin traded information in AMAZING SPIDER-MAN #287.

Page 16 Betty saw the "Hobgoblin" unmask in AMAZING SPIDER-MAN #288.

Page 18 Peter Parker and Ned went to Berlin in SPIDER-MAN VS. WOLVERINE #1. Ned's attack by the Foreigner's assassins was recounted in AMAZING SPIDER-MAN #289.

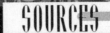

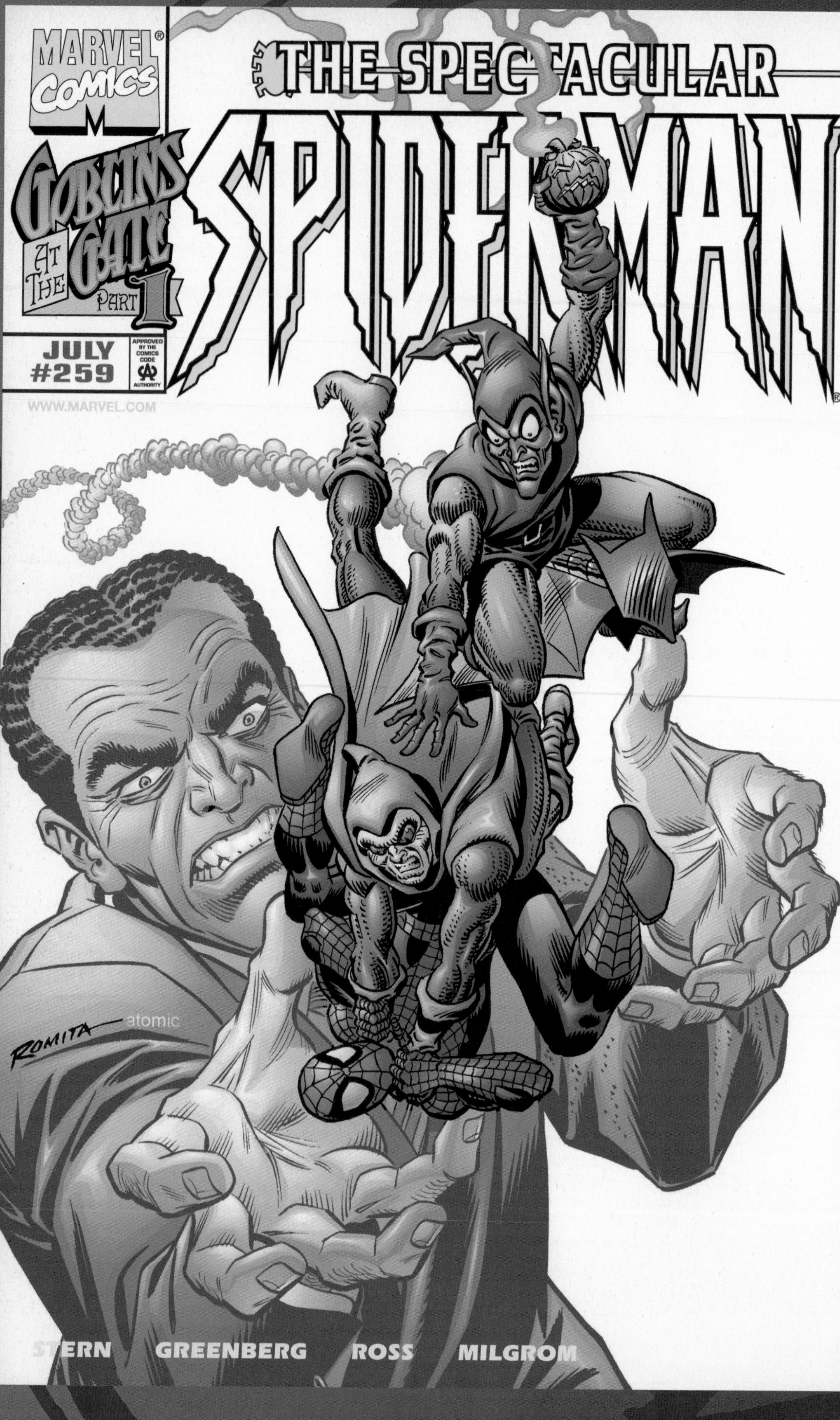

MARVEL® COMICS
THE SPECTACULAR SPIDER-MAN®
GOBLINS AT THE GATE PART 1
JULY #259
APPROVED BY THE COMICS CODE AUTHORITY
WWW.MARVEL.COM
ROMITA
atomic
STERN GREENBERG ROSS MILGROM

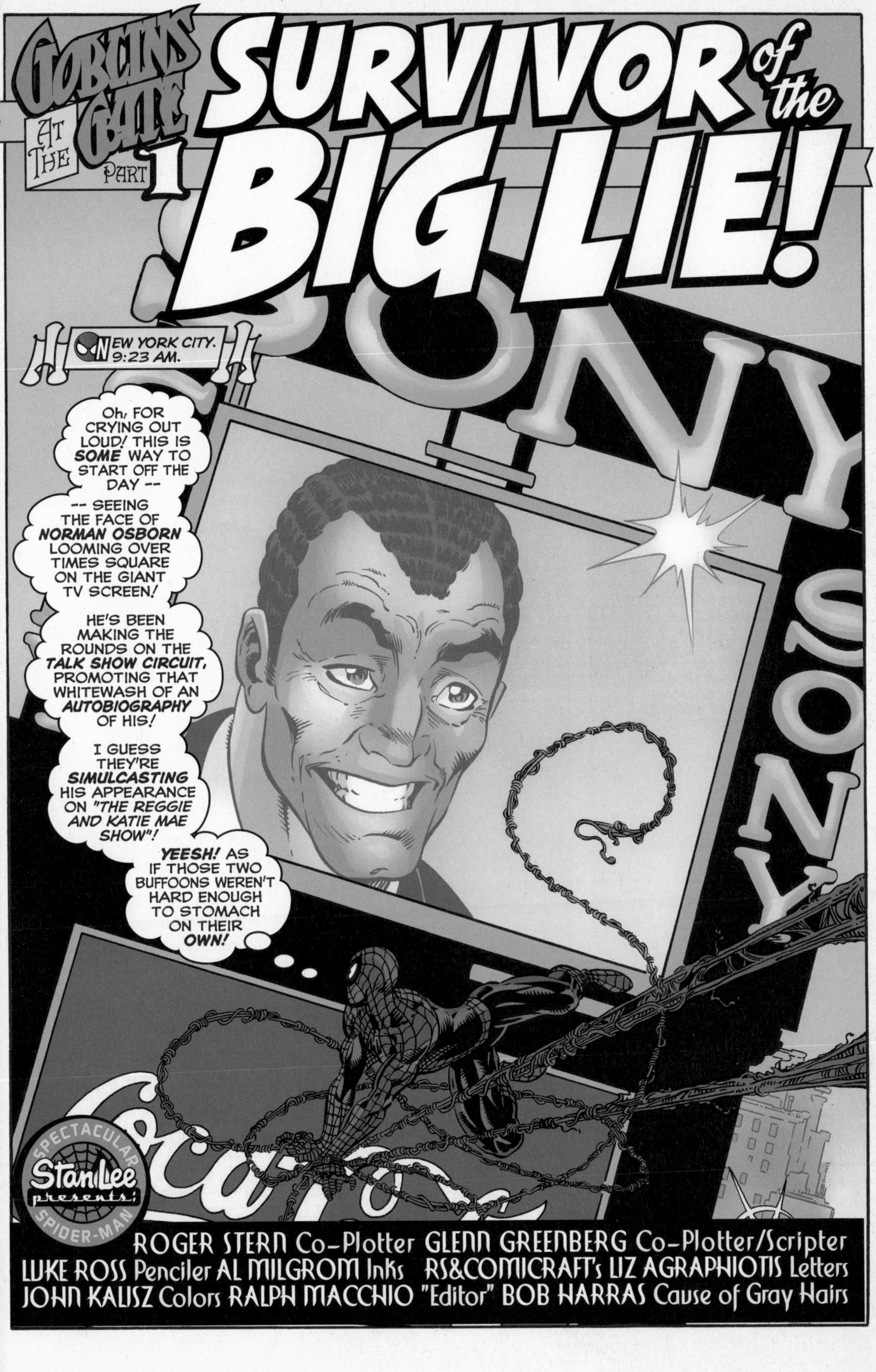
GOBLINS AT THE GATE PART 1
SURVIVOR of the BIG LIE!
NEW YORK CITY. 9:23 AM.
Oh, FOR CRYING OUT LOUD! THIS IS SOME WAY TO START OFF THE DAY --
-- SEEING THE FACE OF NORMAN OSBORN LOOMING OVER TIMES SQUARE ON THE GIANT TV SCREEN!
HE'S BEEN MAKING THE ROUNDS ON THE TALK SHOW CIRCUIT, PROMOTING THAT WHITEWASH OF AN AUTOBIOGRAPHY OF HIS!
I GUESS THEY'RE SIMULCASTING HIS APPEARANCE ON "THE REGGIE AND KATIE MAE SHOW"!
YEESH! AS IF THOSE TWO BUFFOONS WEREN'T HARD ENOUGH TO STOMACH ON THEIR OWN!
SONY
SPECTACULAR Stan Lee presents: SPIDER-MAN
ROGER STERN Co-Plotter GLENN GREENBERG Co-Plotter/Scripter
LUKE ROSS Penciler AL MILGROM Inks RS&COMICRAFT's LIZ AGRAPHIOTIS Letters
JOHN KALISZ Colors RALPH MACCHIO "Editor" BOB HARRAS Cause of Gray Hairs

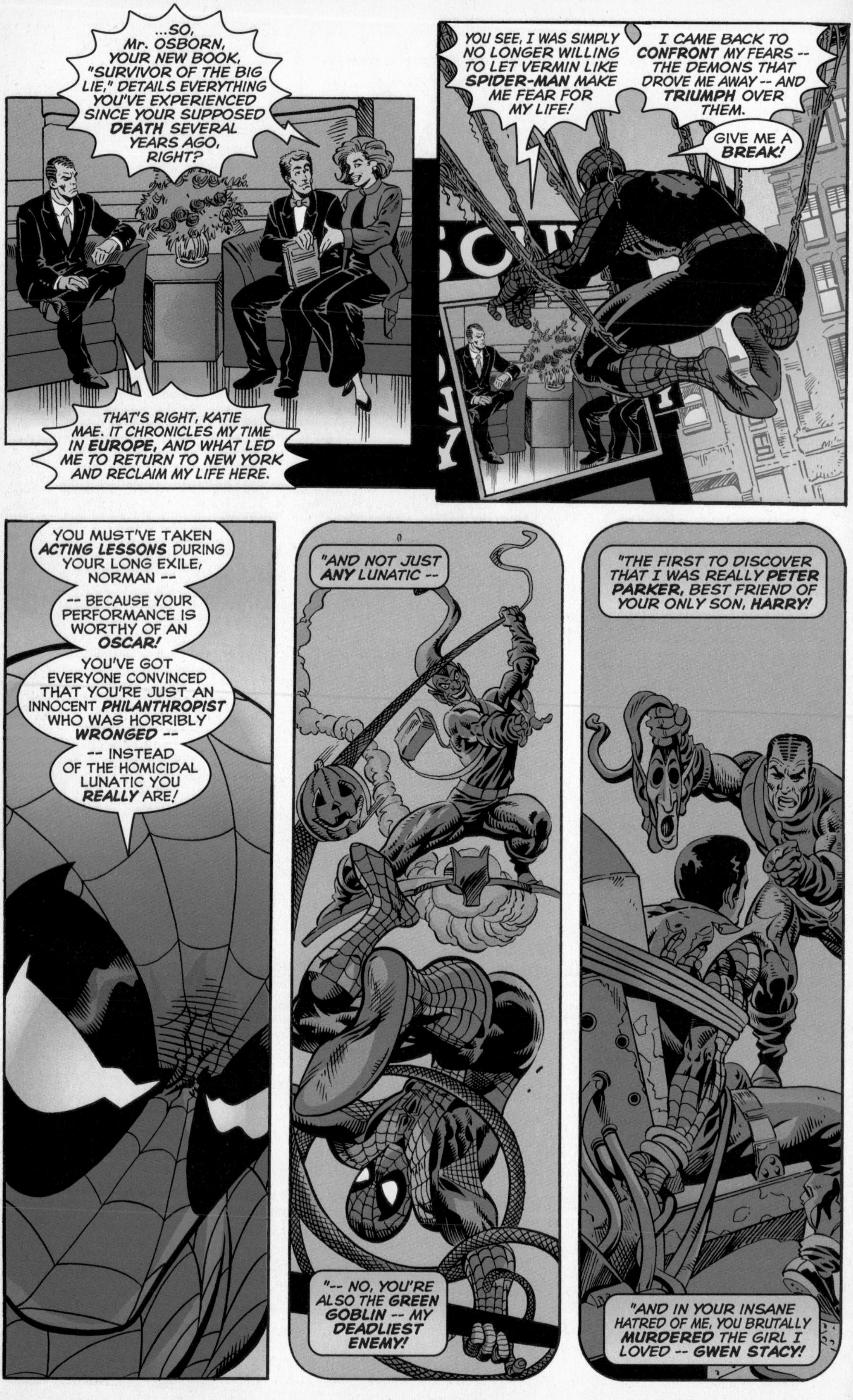
...SO, Mr. OSBORN, YOUR NEW BOOK, "SURVIVOR OF THE BIG LIE," DETAILS EVERYTHING YOU'VE EXPERIENCED SINCE YOUR SUPPOSED DEATH SEVERAL YEARS AGO, RIGHT?
THAT'S RIGHT, KATIE MAE. IT CHRONICLES MY TIME IN EUROPE, AND WHAT LED ME TO RETURN TO NEW YORK AND RECLAIM MY LIFE HERE.
YOU SEE, I WAS SIMPLY NO LONGER WILLING TO LET VERMIN LIKE SPIDER-MAN MAKE ME FEAR FOR MY LIFE!
I CAME BACK TO CONFRONT MY FEARS -- THE DEMONS THAT DROVE ME AWAY -- AND TRIUMPH OVER THEM.
GIVE ME A BREAK!
YOU MUST'VE TAKEN ACTING LESSONS DURING YOUR LONG EXILE, NORMAN --
-- BECAUSE YOUR PERFORMANCE IS WORTHY OF AN OSCAR!
YOU'VE GOT EVERYONE CONVINCED THAT YOU'RE JUST AN INNOCENT PHILANTHROPIST WHO WAS HORRIBLY WRONGED --
-- INSTEAD OF THE HOMICIDAL LUNATIC YOU REALLY ARE!
"AND NOT JUST ANY LUNATIC --
"-- NO, YOU'RE ALSO THE GREEN GOBLIN -- MY DEADLIEST ENEMY!
"THE FIRST TO DISCOVER THAT I WAS REALLY PETER PARKER, BEST FRIEND OF YOUR ONLY SON, HARRY!
"AND IN YOUR INSANE HATRED OF ME, YOU BRUTALLY MURDERED THE GIRL I LOVED -- GWEN STACY!

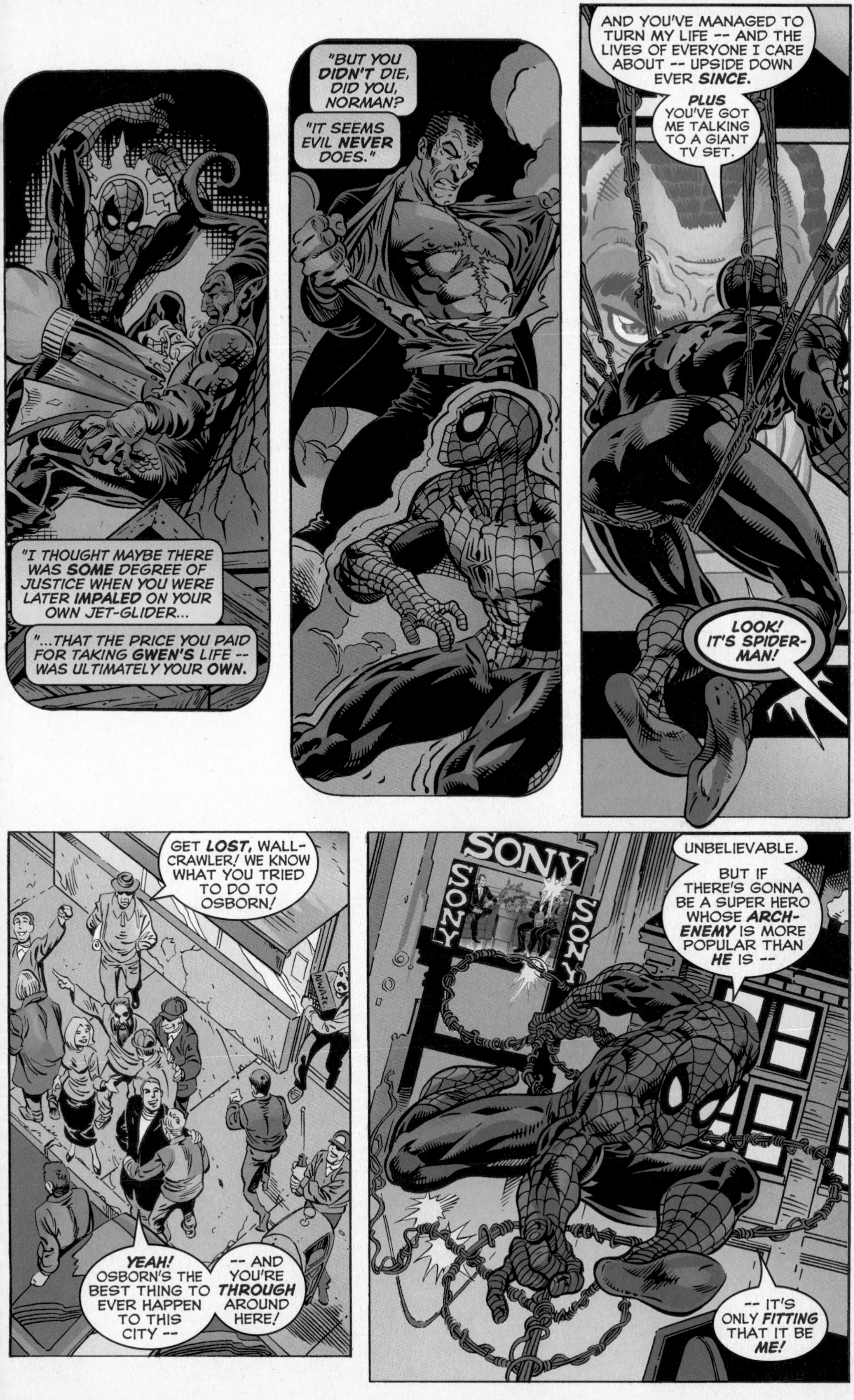

"I THOUGHT MAYBE THERE WAS SOME DEGREE OF JUSTICE WHEN YOU WERE LATER IMPALED ON YOUR OWN JET-GLIDER...
"...THAT THE PRICE YOU PAID FOR TAKING GWEN'S LIFE -- WAS ULTIMATELY YOUR OWN.
"BUT YOU DIDN'T DIE, DID YOU, NORMAN?
"IT SEEMS EVIL NEVER DOES."
AND YOU'VE MANAGED TO TURN MY LIFE -- AND THE LIVES OF EVERYONE I CARE ABOUT -- UPSIDE DOWN EVER SINCE.
PLUS YOU'VE GOT ME TALKING TO A GIANT TV SET.
LOOK! IT'S SPIDER-MAN!
GET LOST, WALL-CRAWLER! WE KNOW WHAT YOU TRIED TO DO TO OSBORN!
YEAH! OSBORN'S THE BEST THING TO EVER HAPPEN TO THIS CITY --
-- AND YOU'RE THROUGH AROUND HERE!
SONY
SONY
SONY
UNBELIEVABLE.
BUT IF THERE'S GONNA BE A SUPER HERO WHOSE ARCH-ENEMY IS MORE POPULAR THAN HE IS --
-- IT'S ONLY FITTING THAT IT BE ME!

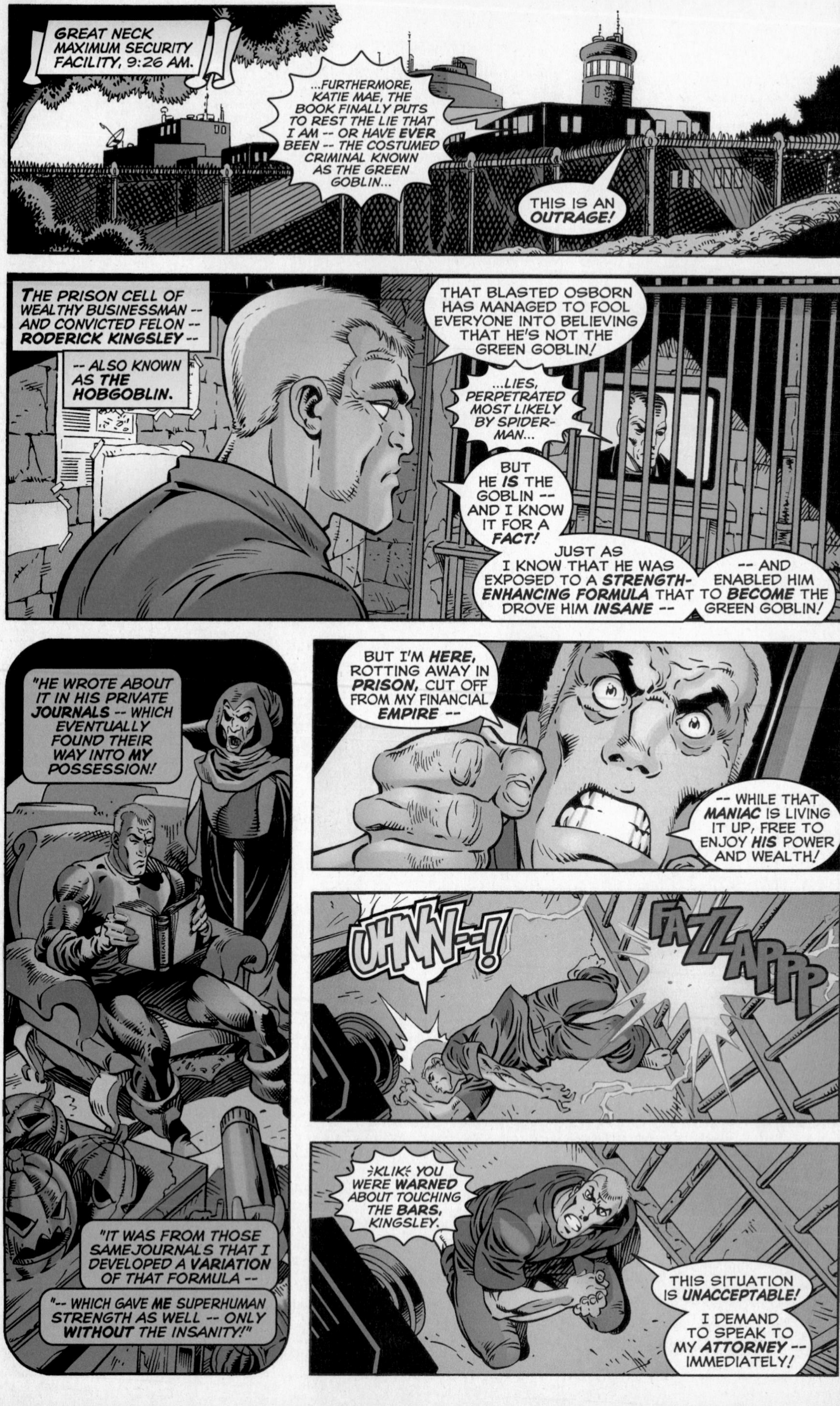

GREAT NECK MAXIMUM SECURITY FACILITY, 9:26 AM.
...FURTHERMORE, KATIE MAE, THE BOOK FINALLY PUTS TO REST THE LIE THAT I AM -- OR HAVE EVER BEEN -- THE COSTUMED CRIMINAL KNOWN AS THE GREEN GOBLIN...
THIS IS AN OUTRAGE!
THE PRISON CELL OF WEALTHY BUSINESSMAN -- AND CONVICTED FELON -- RODERICK KINGSLEY --
-- ALSO KNOWN AS THE HOBGOBLIN.
THAT BLASTED OSBORN HAS MANAGED TO FOOL EVERYONE INTO BELIEVING THAT HE'S NOT THE GREEN GOBLIN!
...LIES, PERPETRATED MOST LIKELY BY SPIDER-MAN...
BUT HE IS THE GOBLIN -- AND I KNOW IT FOR A FACT!
JUST AS I KNOW THAT HE WAS EXPOSED TO A STRENGTH-ENHANCING FORMULA THAT DROVE HIM INSANE --
-- AND ENABLED HIM TO BECOME THE GREEN GOBLIN!
"HE WROTE ABOUT IT IN HIS PRIVATE JOURNALS -- WHICH EVENTUALLY FOUND THEIR WAY INTO MY POSSESSION!
"IT WAS FROM THOSE SAMEJOURNALS THAT I DEVELOPED A VARIATION OF THAT FORMULA --
"-- WHICH GAVE ME SUPERHUMAN STRENGTH AS WELL -- ONLY WITHOUT THE INSANITY!"
BUT I'M HERE, ROTTING AWAY IN PRISON, CUT OFF FROM MY FINANCIAL EMPIRE --
-- WHILE THAT MANIAC IS LIVING IT UP, FREE TO ENJOY HIS POWER AND WEALTH!
UHNN--!
FAZZAPPP
KLIK YOU WERE WARNED ABOUT TOUCHING THE BARS, KINGSLEY.
THIS SITUATION IS UNACCEPTABLE!
I DEMAND TO SPEAK TO MY ATTORNEY -- IMMEDIATELY!

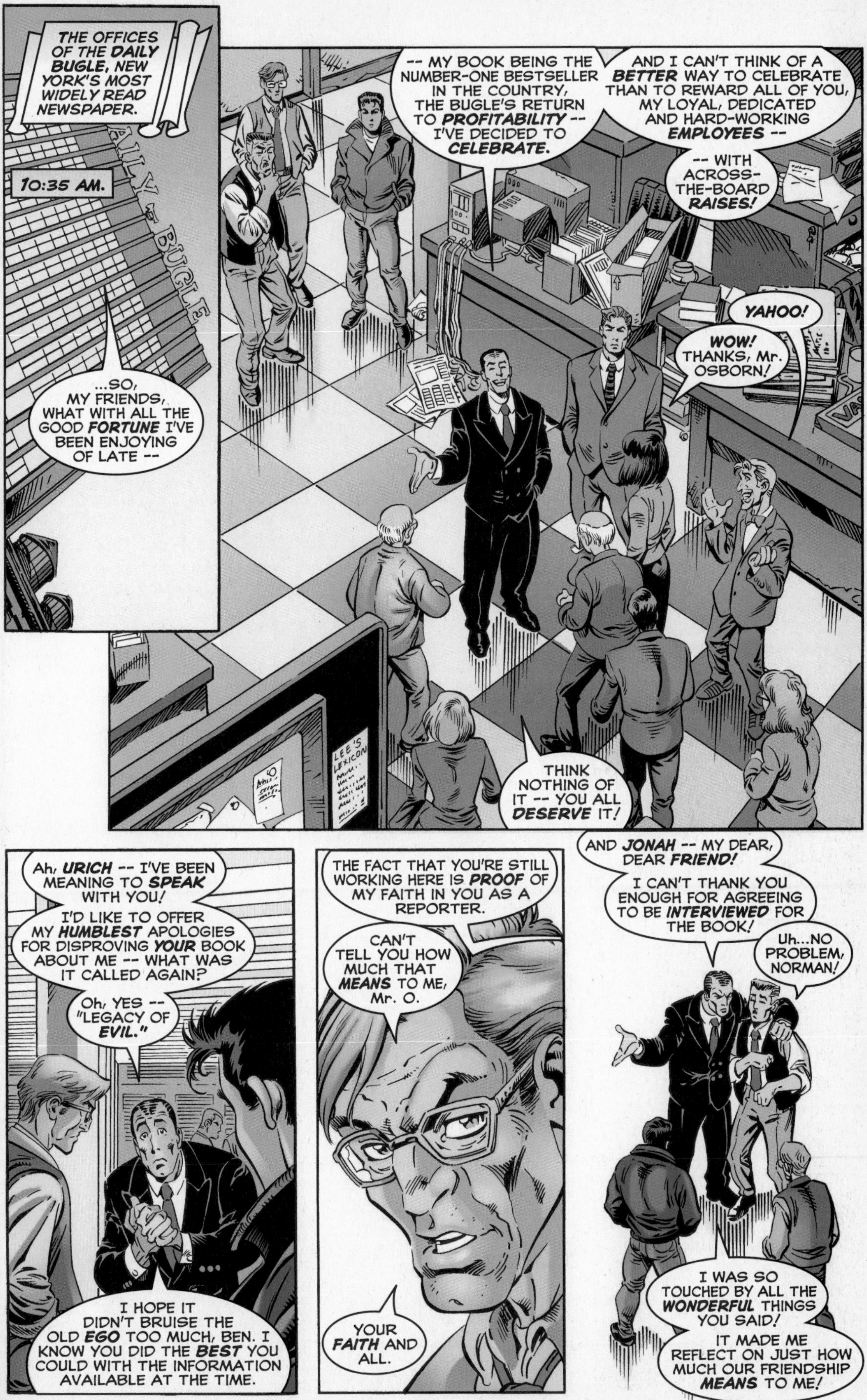
THE OFFICES OF THE DAILY BUGLE, NEW YORK'S MOST WIDELY READ NEWSPAPER.
10:35 AM.
...SO, MY FRIENDS, WHAT WITH ALL THE GOOD FORTUNE I'VE BEEN ENJOYING OF LATE --
-- MY BOOK BEING THE NUMBER-ONE BESTSELLER IN THE COUNTRY, THE BUGLE'S RETURN TO PROFITABILITY -- I'VE DECIDED TO CELEBRATE.
AND I CAN'T THINK OF A BETTER WAY TO CELEBRATE THAN TO REWARD ALL OF YOU, MY LOYAL, DEDICATED AND HARD-WORKING EMPLOYEES --
-- WITH ACROSS-THE-BOARD RAISES!
YAHOO!
WOW! THANKS, Mr. OSBORN!
THINK NOTHING OF IT -- YOU ALL DESERVE IT!
LEE'S LEXICON
Ah, URICH -- I'VE BEEN MEANING TO SPEAK WITH YOU!
I'D LIKE TO OFFER MY HUMBLEST APOLOGIES FOR DISPROVING YOUR BOOK ABOUT ME -- WHAT WAS IT CALLED AGAIN?
Oh, YES -- "LEGACY OF EVIL."
I HOPE IT DIDN'T BRUISE THE OLD EGO TOO MUCH, BEN. I KNOW YOU DID THE BEST YOU COULD WITH THE INFORMATION AVAILABLE AT THE TIME.
THE FACT THAT YOU'RE STILL WORKING HERE IS PROOF OF MY FAITH IN YOU AS A REPORTER.
CAN'T TELL YOU HOW MUCH THAT MEANS TO ME, Mr. O.
YOUR FAITH AND ALL.
AND JONAH -- MY DEAR, DEAR FRIEND!
I CAN'T THANK YOU ENOUGH FOR AGREEING TO BE INTERVIEWED FOR THE BOOK!
Uh...NO PROBLEM, NORMAN!
I WAS SO TOUCHED BY ALL THE WONDERFUL THINGS YOU SAID!
IT MADE ME REFLECT ON JUST HOW MUCH OUR FRIENDSHIP MEANS TO ME!

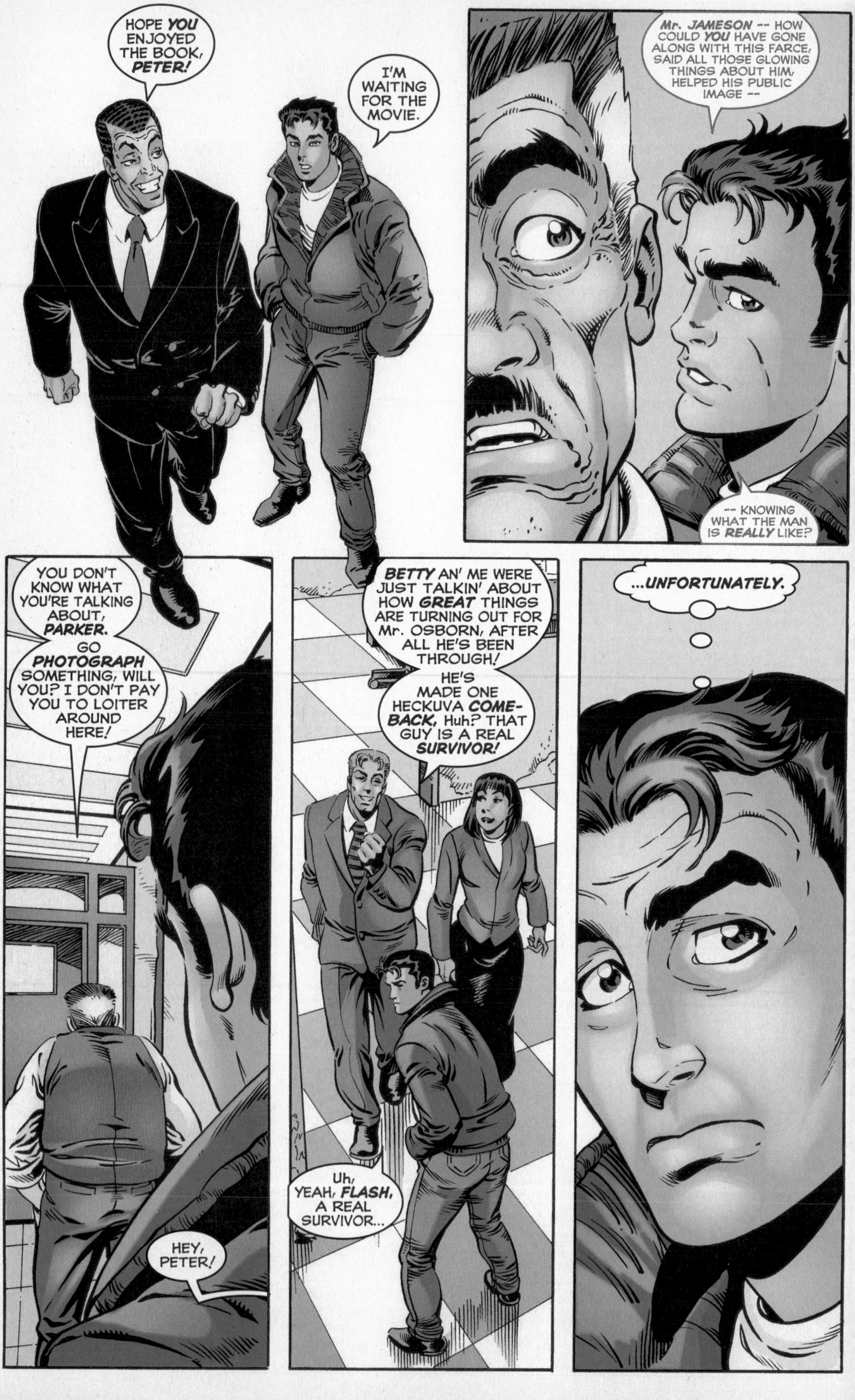
HOPE YOU ENJOYED THE BOOK, PETER!
I'M WAITING FOR THE MOVIE.
Mr. JAMESON -- HOW COULD YOU HAVE GONE ALONG WITH THIS FARCE, SAID ALL THOSE GLOWING THINGS ABOUT HIM, HELPED HIS PUBLIC IMAGE --
-- KNOWING WHAT THE MAN IS REALLY LIKE?
YOU DON'T KNOW WHAT YOU'RE TALKING ABOUT, PARKER.
GO PHOTOGRAPH SOMETHING, WILL YOU? I DON'T PAY YOU TO LOITER AROUND HERE!
HEY, PETER!
BETTY AN' ME WERE JUST TALKIN' ABOUT HOW GREAT THINGS ARE TURNING OUT FOR Mr. OSBORN, AFTER ALL HE'S BEEN THROUGH!
HE'S MADE ONE HECKUVA COME-BACK, Huh? THAT GUY IS A REAL SURVIVOR!
Uh, YEAH, FLASH, A REAL SURVIVOR...
...UNFORTUNATELY.

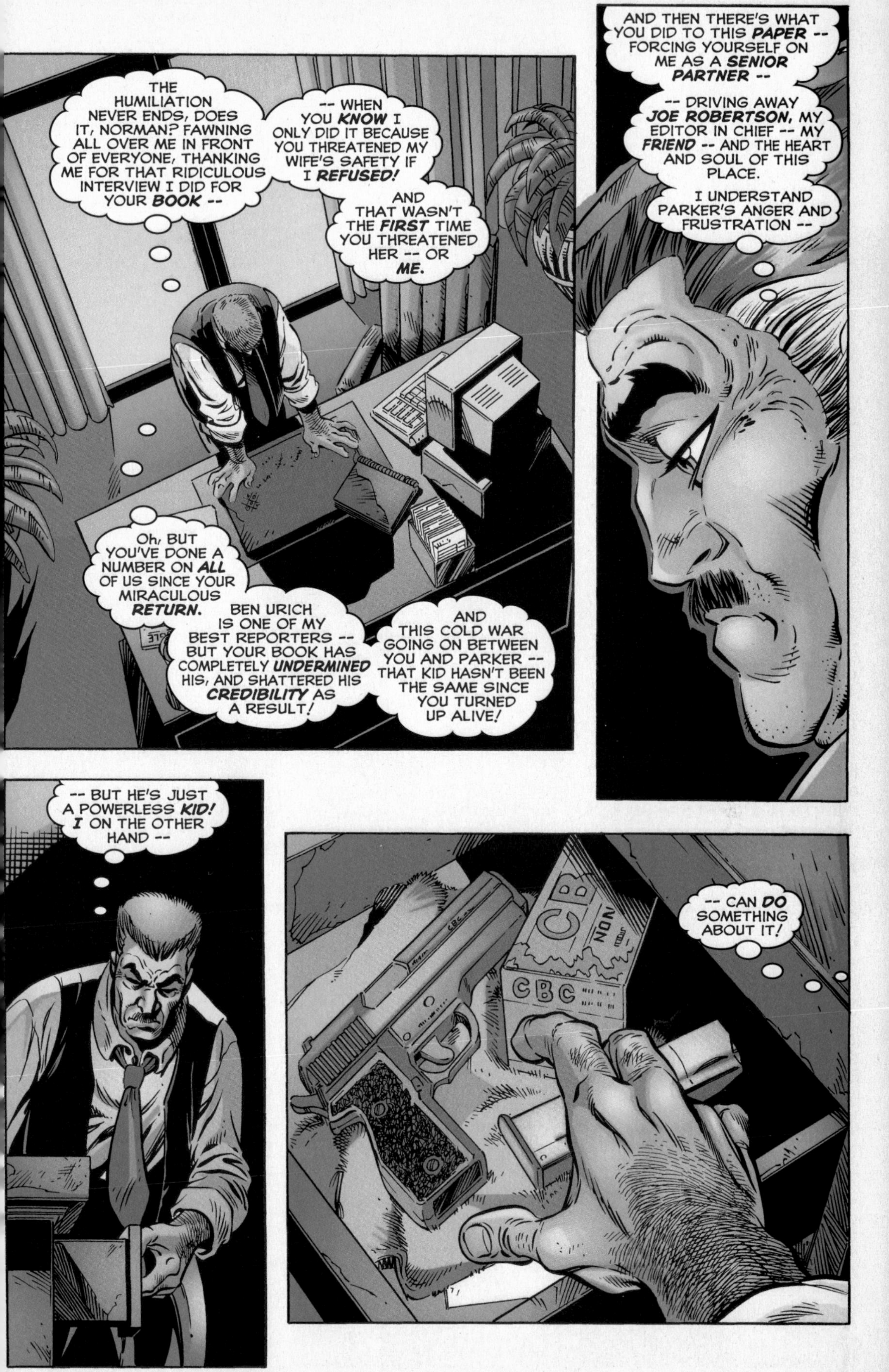
THE HUMILIATION NEVER ENDS, DOES IT, NORMAN? FAWNING ALL OVER ME IN FRONT OF EVERYONE, THANKING ME FOR THAT RIDICULOUS INTERVIEW I DID FOR YOUR BOOK --
-- WHEN YOU KNOW I ONLY DID IT BECAUSE YOU THREATENED MY WIFE'S SAFETY IF I REFUSED!
AND THAT WASN'T THE FIRST TIME YOU THREATENED HER -- OR ME.
Oh, BUT YOU'VE DONE A NUMBER ON ALL OF US SINCE YOUR MIRACULOUS RETURN.
BEN URICH IS ONE OF MY BEST REPORTERS -- BUT YOUR BOOK HAS COMPLETELY UNDERMINED HIS, AND SHATTERED HIS CREDIBILITY AS A RESULT!
AND THIS COLD WAR GOING ON BETWEEN YOU AND PARKER -- THAT KID HASN'T BEEN THE SAME SINCE YOU TURNED UP ALIVE!
AND THEN THERE'S WHAT YOU DID TO THIS PAPER -- FORCING YOURSELF ON ME AS A SENIOR PARTNER --
-- DRIVING AWAY JOE ROBERTSON, MY EDITOR IN CHIEF -- MY FRIEND -- AND THE HEART AND SOUL OF THIS PLACE.
I UNDERSTAND PARKER'S ANGER AND FRUSTRATION --
-- BUT HE'S JUST A POWERLESS KID! I ON THE OTHER HAND --
-- CAN DO SOMETHING ABOUT IT!

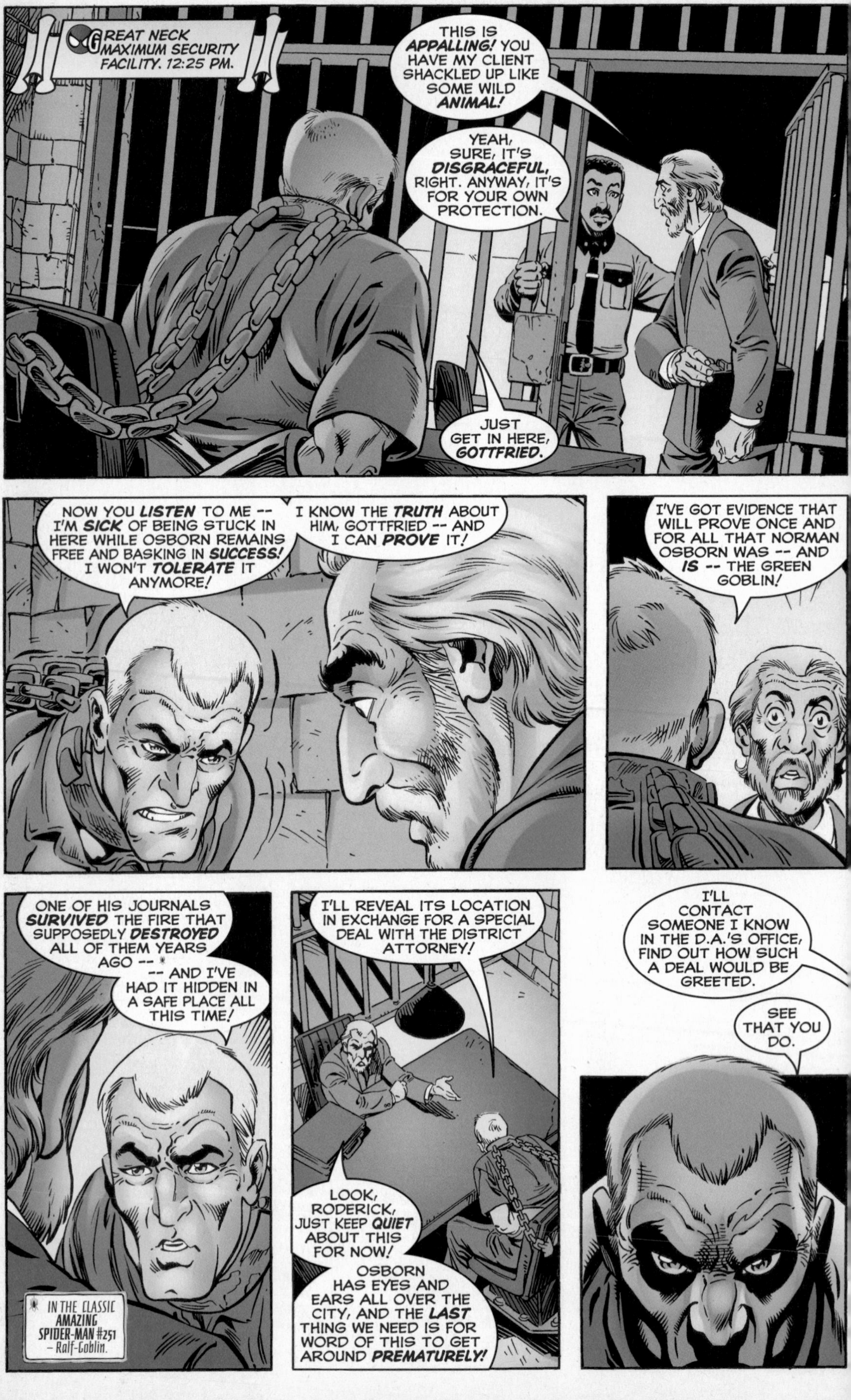
GREAT NECK MAXIMUM SECURITY FACILITY. 12:25 PM.
THIS IS APPALLING! YOU HAVE MY CLIENT SHACKLED UP LIKE SOME WILD ANIMAL!
YEAH, SURE, IT'S DISGRACEFUL, RIGHT. ANYWAY, IT'S FOR YOUR OWN PROTECTION.
JUST GET IN HERE, GOTTFRIED.
NOW YOU LISTEN TO ME -- I'M SICK OF BEING STUCK IN HERE WHILE OSBORN REMAINS FREE AND BASKING IN SUCCESS! I WON'T TOLERATE IT ANYMORE!
I KNOW THE TRUTH ABOUT HIM, GOTTFRIED -- AND I CAN PROVE IT!
I'VE GOT EVIDENCE THAT WILL PROVE ONCE AND FOR ALL THAT NORMAN OSBORN WAS -- AND IS -- THE GREEN GOBLIN!
ONE OF HIS JOURNALS SURVIVED THE FIRE THAT SUPPOSEDLY DESTROYED ALL OF THEM YEARS AGO -- *
-- AND I'VE HAD IT HIDDEN IN A SAFE PLACE ALL THIS TIME!
* IN THE CLASSIC AMAZING SPIDER-MAN #251 – Ralf-Goblin.
I'LL REVEAL ITS LOCATION IN EXCHANGE FOR A SPECIAL DEAL WITH THE DISTRICT ATTORNEY!
LOOK, RODERICK, JUST KEEP QUIET ABOUT THIS FOR NOW!
OSBORN HAS EYES AND EARS ALL OVER THE CITY, AND THE LAST THING WE NEED IS FOR WORD OF THIS TO GET AROUND PREMATURELY!
I'LL CONTACT SOMEONE I KNOW IN THE D.A.'S OFFICE, FIND OUT HOW SUCH A DEAL WOULD BE GREETED.
SEE THAT YOU DO.

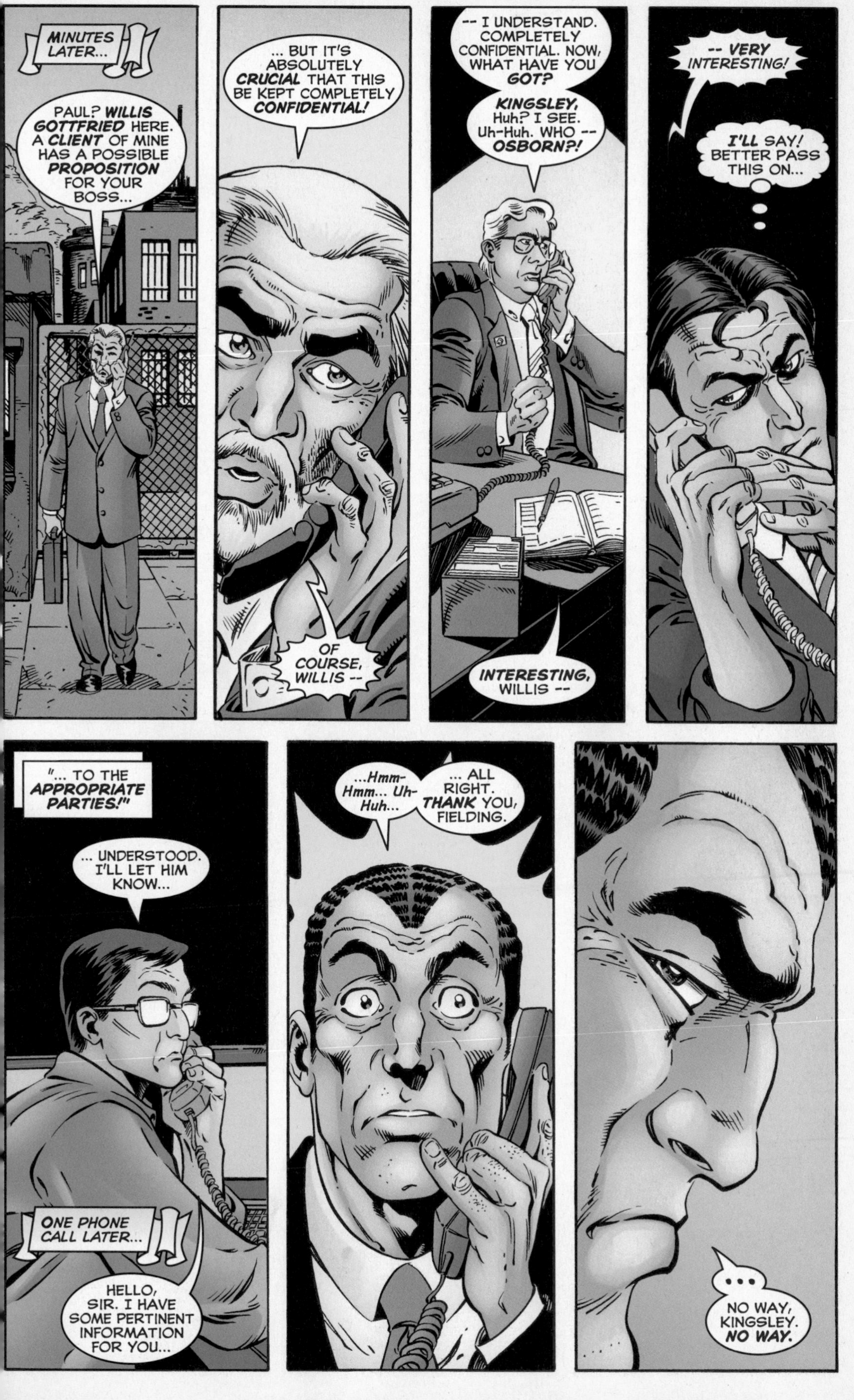

MINUTES LATER...
PAUL? WILLIS GOTTFRIED HERE. A CLIENT OF MINE HAS A POSSIBLE PROPOSITION FOR YOUR BOSS...
... BUT IT'S ABSOLUTELY CRUCIAL THAT THIS BE KEPT COMPLETELY CONFIDENTIAL!
OF COURSE, WILLIS --
-- I UNDERSTAND. COMPLETELY CONFIDENTIAL. NOW, WHAT HAVE YOU GOT?
KINGSLEY, Huh? I SEE. Uh-Huh. WHO -- OSBORN?!
INTERESTING, WILLIS --
-- VERY INTERESTING!
I'LL SAY! BETTER PASS THIS ON...
"... TO THE APPROPRIATE PARTIES!"
... UNDERSTOOD. I'LL LET HIM KNOW...
ONE PHONE CALL LATER...
HELLO, SIR. I HAVE SOME PERTINENT INFORMATION FOR YOU...
...Hmm-Hmm... Uh-Huh...
... ALL RIGHT. THANK YOU, FIELDING.
...
NO WAY, KINGSLEY. NO WAY.

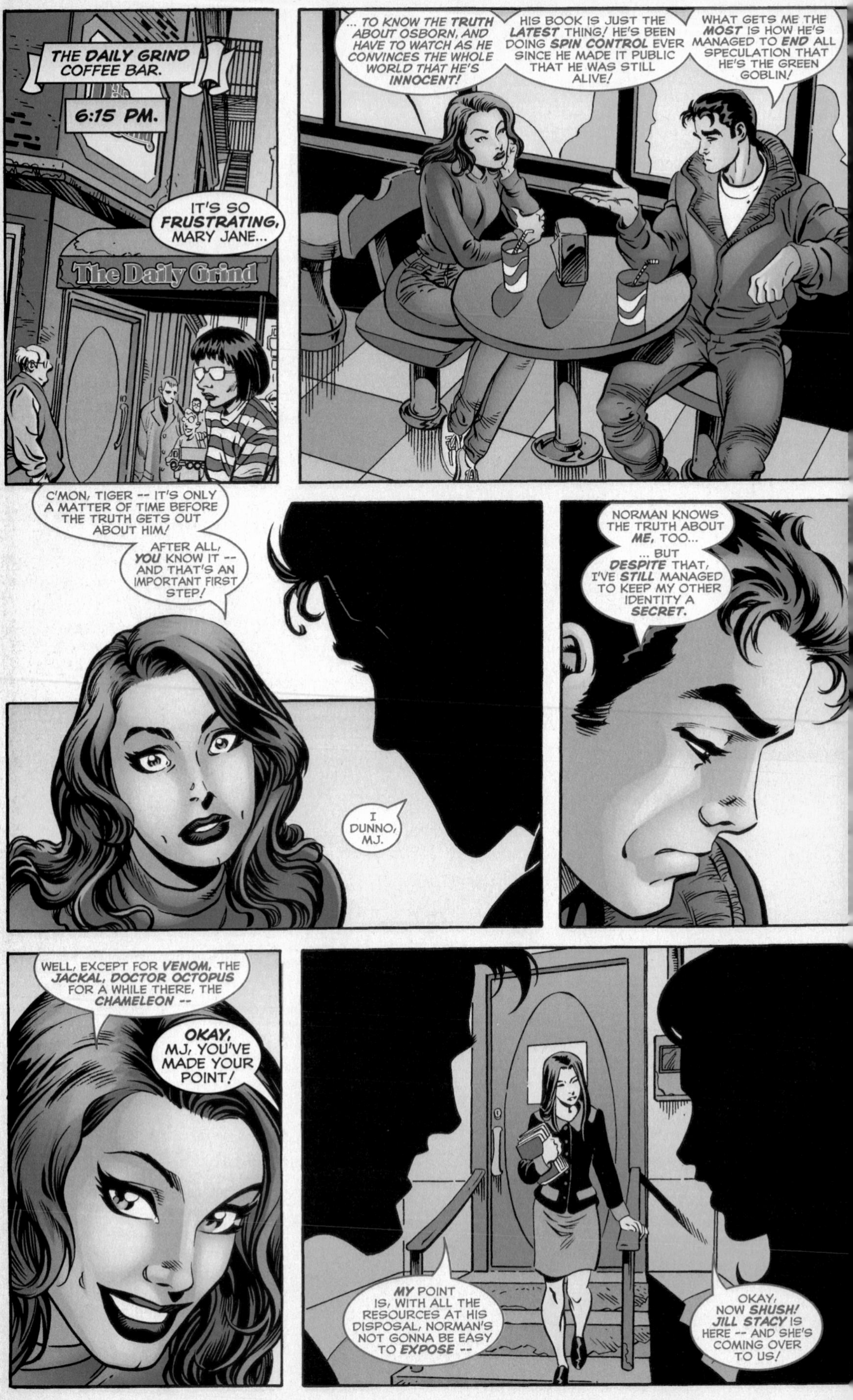
THE DAILY GRIND COFFEE BAR.
6:15 PM.
IT'S SO FRUSTRATING, MARY JANE...
The Daily Grind
... TO KNOW THE TRUTH ABOUT OSBORN, AND HAVE TO WATCH AS HE CONVINCES THE WHOLE WORLD THAT HE'S INNOCENT!
HIS BOOK IS JUST THE LATEST THING! HE'S BEEN DOING SPIN CONTROL EVER SINCE HE MADE IT PUBLIC THAT HE WAS STILL ALIVE!
WHAT GETS ME THE MOST IS HOW HE'S MANAGED TO END ALL SPECULATION THAT HE'S THE GREEN GOBLIN!
C'MON, TIGER -- IT'S ONLY A MATTER OF TIME BEFORE THE TRUTH GETS OUT ABOUT HIM!
AFTER ALL, YOU KNOW IT -- AND THAT'S AN IMPORTANT FIRST STEP!
I DUNNO, MJ.
NORMAN KNOWS THE TRUTH ABOUT ME, TOO...
... BUT DESPITE THAT, I'VE STILL MANAGED TO KEEP MY OTHER IDENTITY A SECRET.
WELL, EXCEPT FOR VENOM, THE JACKAL, DOCTOR OCTOPUS FOR A WHILE THERE, THE CHAMELEON --
OKAY, MJ, YOU'VE MADE YOUR POINT!
MY POINT IS, WITH ALL THE RESOURCES AT HIS DISPOSAL, NORMAN'S NOT GONNA BE EASY TO EXPOSE --
OKAY, NOW SHUSH! JILL STACY IS HERE -- AND SHE'S COMING OVER TO US!

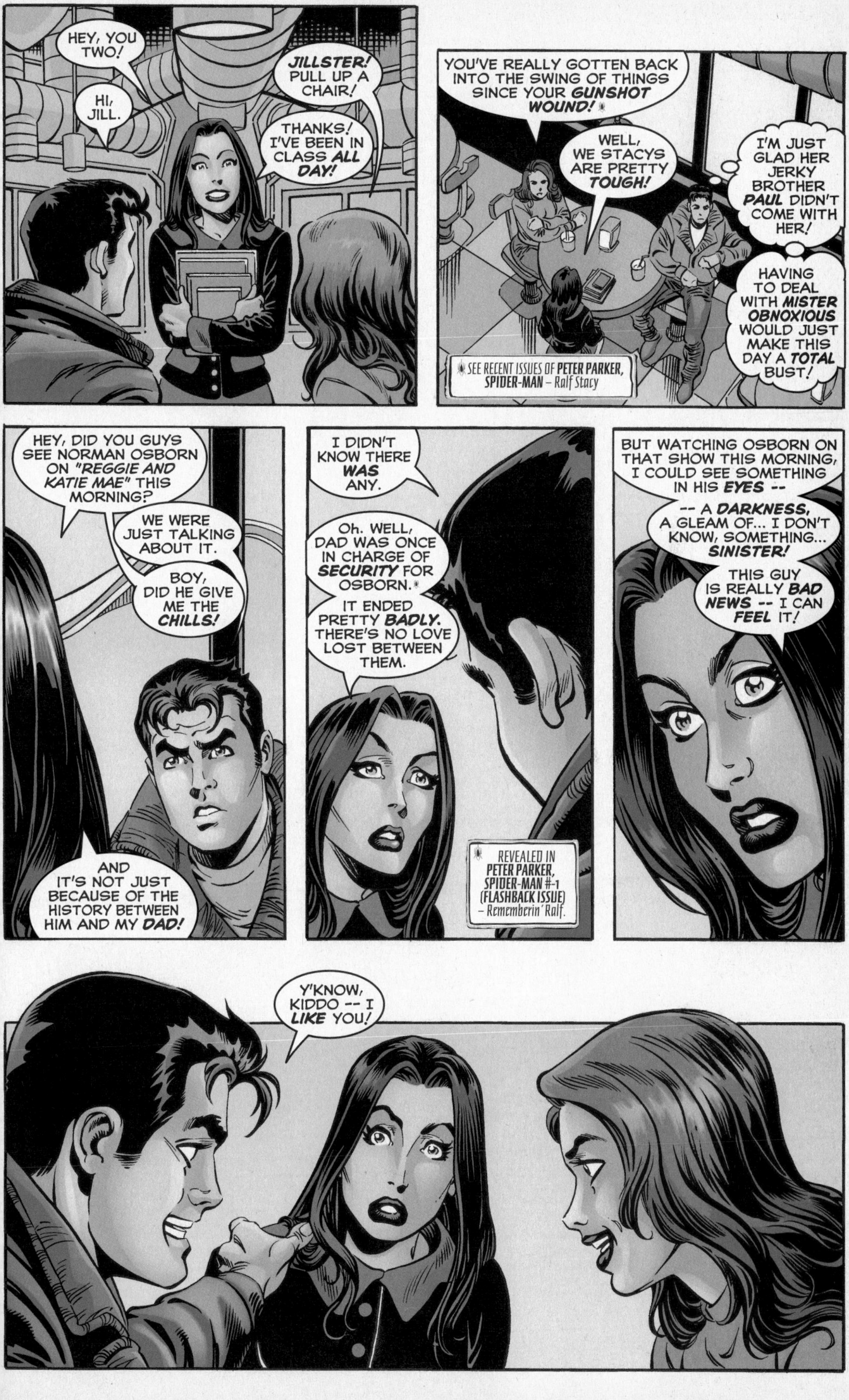
HEY, YOU TWO!
HI, JILL.
JILLSTER! PULL UP A CHAIR!
THANKS! I'VE BEEN IN CLASS ALL DAY!
YOU'VE REALLY GOTTEN BACK INTO THE SWING OF THINGS SINCE YOUR GUNSHOT WOUND!
WELL, WE STACYS ARE PRETTY TOUGH!
I'M JUST GLAD HER JERKY BROTHER PAUL DIDN'T COME WITH HER!
HAVING TO DEAL WITH MISTER OBNOXIOUS WOULD JUST MAKE THIS DAY A TOTAL BUST!
SEE RECENT ISSUES OF PETER PARKER, SPIDER-MAN – Ralf Stacy
HEY, DID YOU GUYS SEE NORMAN OSBORN ON "REGGIE AND KATIE MAE" THIS MORNING?
WE WERE JUST TALKING ABOUT IT.
BOY, DID HE GIVE ME THE CHILLS!
AND IT'S NOT JUST BECAUSE OF THE HISTORY BETWEEN HIM AND MY DAD!
I DIDN'T KNOW THERE WAS ANY.
Oh. WELL, DAD WAS ONCE IN CHARGE OF SECURITY FOR OSBORN.
IT ENDED PRETTY BADLY. THERE'S NO LOVE LOST BETWEEN THEM.
REVEALED IN PETER PARKER, SPIDER-MAN #-1 (FLASHBACK ISSUE) – Rememberin' Ralf.
BUT WATCHING OSBORN ON THAT SHOW THIS MORNING, I COULD SEE SOMETHING IN HIS EYES --
-- A DARKNESS, A GLEAM OF... I DON'T KNOW, SOMETHING... SINISTER!
THIS GUY IS REALLY BAD NEWS -- I CAN FEEL IT!
Y'KNOW, KIDDO -- I LIKE YOU!

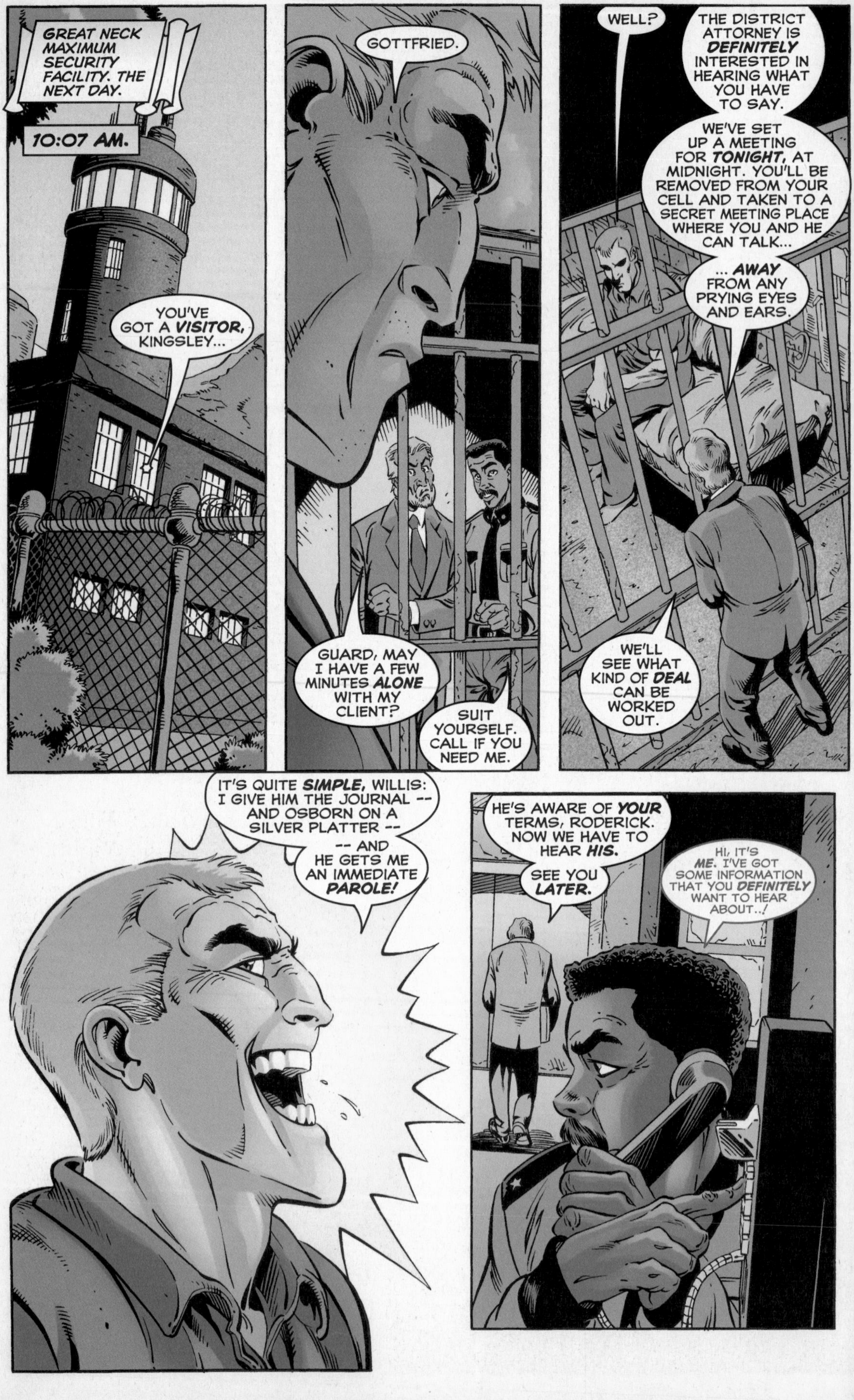
GREAT NECK MAXIMUM SECURITY FACILITY. THE NEXT DAY.
10:07 AM.
YOU'VE GOT A VISITOR, KINGSLEY...
GOTTFRIED.
GUARD, MAY I HAVE A FEW MINUTES ALONE WITH MY CLIENT?
SUIT YOURSELF. CALL IF YOU NEED ME.
WELL?
THE DISTRICT ATTORNEY IS DEFINITELY INTERESTED IN HEARING WHAT YOU HAVE TO SAY.
WE'VE SET UP A MEETING FOR TONIGHT, AT MIDNIGHT. YOU'LL BE REMOVED FROM YOUR CELL AND TAKEN TO A SECRET MEETING PLACE WHERE YOU AND HE CAN TALK...
... AWAY FROM ANY PRYING EYES AND EARS.
WE'LL SEE WHAT KIND OF DEAL CAN BE WORKED OUT.
IT'S QUITE SIMPLE, WILLIS: I GIVE HIM THE JOURNAL -- AND OSBORN ON A SILVER PLATTER --
-- AND HE GETS ME AN IMMEDIATE PAROLE!
HE'S AWARE OF YOUR TERMS, RODERICK. NOW WE HAVE TO HEAR HIS.
SEE YOU LATER.
HI, IT'S ME. I'VE GOT SOME INFORMATION THAT YOU DEFINITELY WANT TO HEAR ABOUT...!

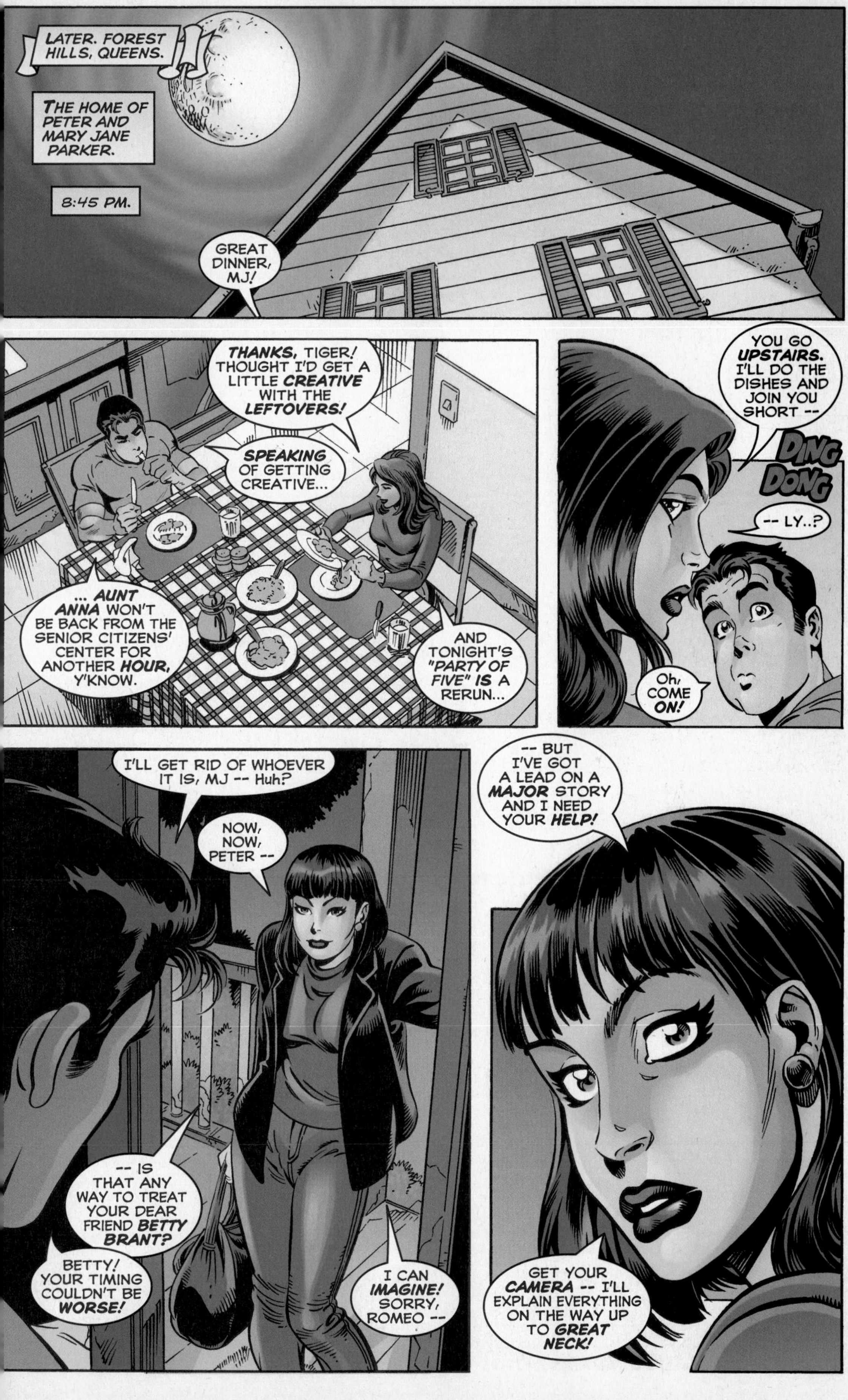
LATER. FOREST HILLS, QUEENS.
THE HOME OF PETER AND MARY JANE PARKER.
8:45 PM.
GREAT DINNER, MJ!
THANKS, TIGER! THOUGHT I'D GET A LITTLE CREATIVE WITH THE LEFTOVERS!
SPEAKING OF GETTING CREATIVE...
... AUNT ANNA WON'T BE BACK FROM THE SENIOR CITIZENS' CENTER FOR ANOTHER HOUR, Y'KNOW.
AND TONIGHT'S "PARTY OF FIVE" IS A RERUN...
YOU GO UPSTAIRS. I'LL DO THE DISHES AND JOIN YOU SHORT --
DING DONG
-- LY..?
Oh, COME ON!
I'LL GET RID OF WHOEVER IT IS, MJ -- Huh?
NOW, NOW, PETER --
-- IS THAT ANY WAY TO TREAT YOUR DEAR FRIEND BETTY BRANT?
BETTY! YOUR TIMING COULDN'T BE WORSE!
I CAN IMAGINE! SORRY, ROMEO --
-- BUT I'VE GOT A LEAD ON A MAJOR STORY AND I NEED YOUR HELP!
GET YOUR CAMERA -- I'LL EXPLAIN EVERYTHING ON THE WAY UP TO GREAT NECK!

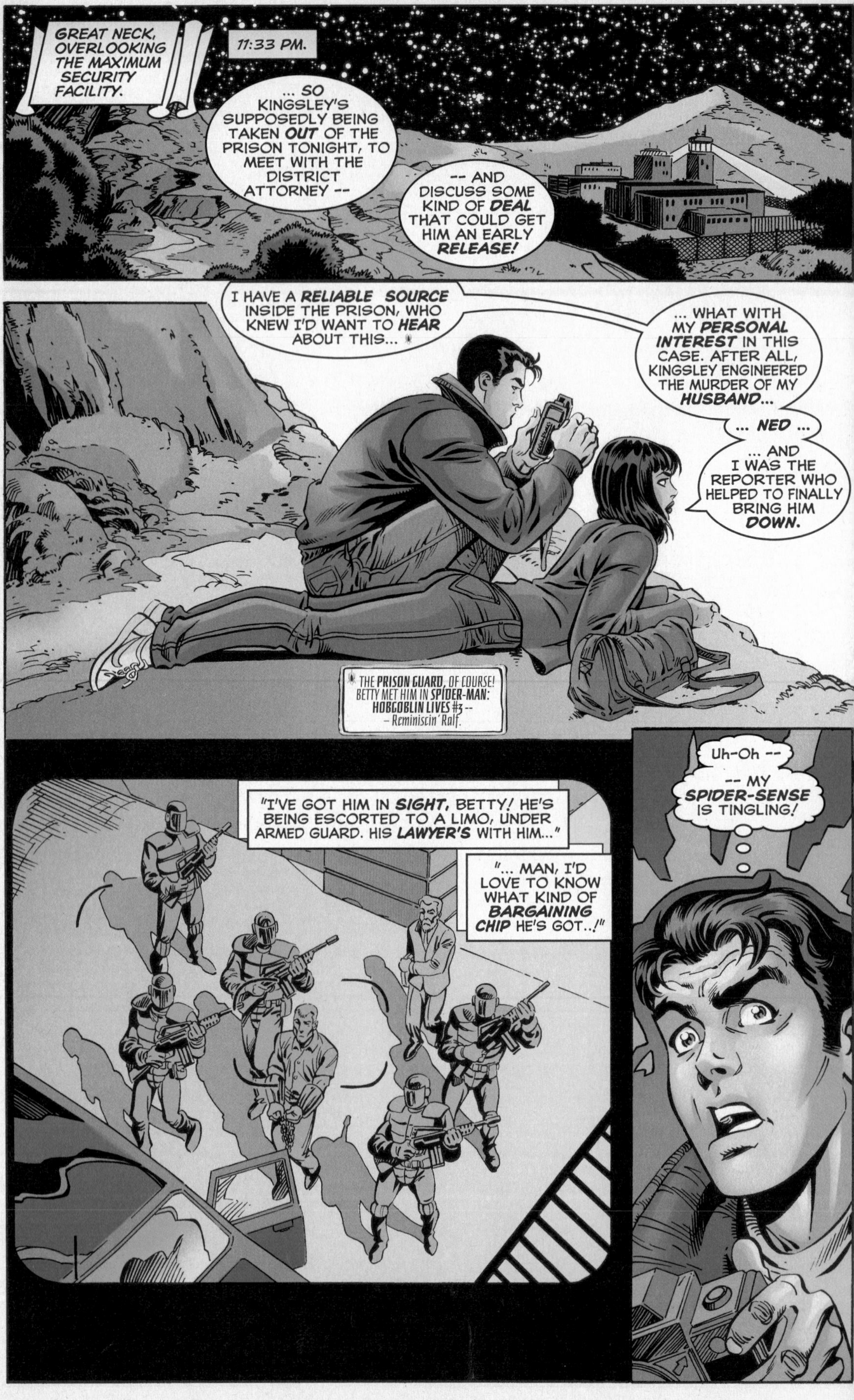
GREAT NECK, OVERLOOKING THE MAXIMUM SECURITY FACILITY.
11:33 PM.
... SO KINGSLEY'S SUPPOSEDLY BEING TAKEN OUT OF THE PRISON TONIGHT, TO MEET WITH THE DISTRICT ATTORNEY --
-- AND DISCUSS SOME KIND OF DEAL THAT COULD GET HIM AN EARLY RELEASE!
I HAVE A RELIABLE SOURCE INSIDE THE PRISON, WHO KNEW I'D WANT TO HEAR ABOUT THIS...
... WHAT WITH MY PERSONAL INTEREST IN THIS CASE. AFTER ALL, KINGSLEY ENGINEERED THE MURDER OF MY HUSBAND...
... NED ...
... AND I WAS THE REPORTER WHO HELPED TO FINALLY BRING HIM DOWN.
THE PRISON GUARD, OF COURSE! BETTY MET HIM IN SPIDER-MAN: HOBGOBLIN LIVES #3 -- – Reminiscin' Ralf.
"I'VE GOT HIM IN SIGHT, BETTY! HE'S BEING ESCORTED TO A LIMO, UNDER ARMED GUARD. HIS LAWYER'S WITH HIM..."
"... MAN, I'D LOVE TO KNOW WHAT KIND OF BARGAINING CHIP HE'S GOT..!"
Uh-Oh --
-- MY SPIDER-SENSE IS TINGLING!

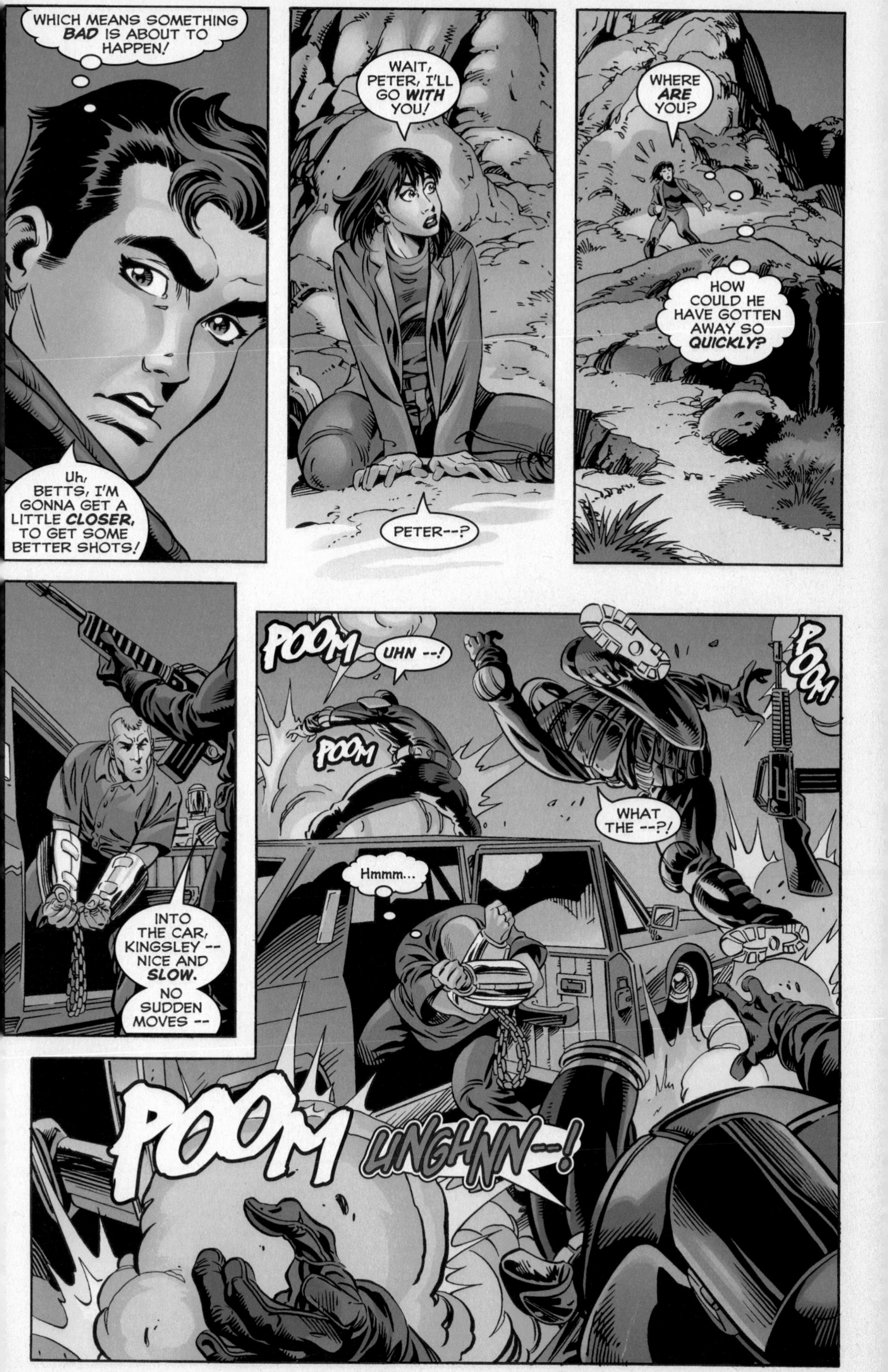
WHICH MEANS SOMETHING BAD IS ABOUT TO HAPPEN!
Uh, BETTS, I'M GONNA GET A LITTLE CLOSER, TO GET SOME BETTER SHOTS!
WAIT, PETER, I'LL GO WITH YOU!
PETER--?
WHERE ARE YOU?
HOW COULD HE HAVE GOTTEN AWAY SO QUICKLY?
INTO THE CAR, KINGSLEY -- NICE AND SLOW. NO SUDDEN MOVES --
POOM
UHN --!
POOM
POOM
WHAT THE --?!
Hmmm...
POOM
UNGHNN--!

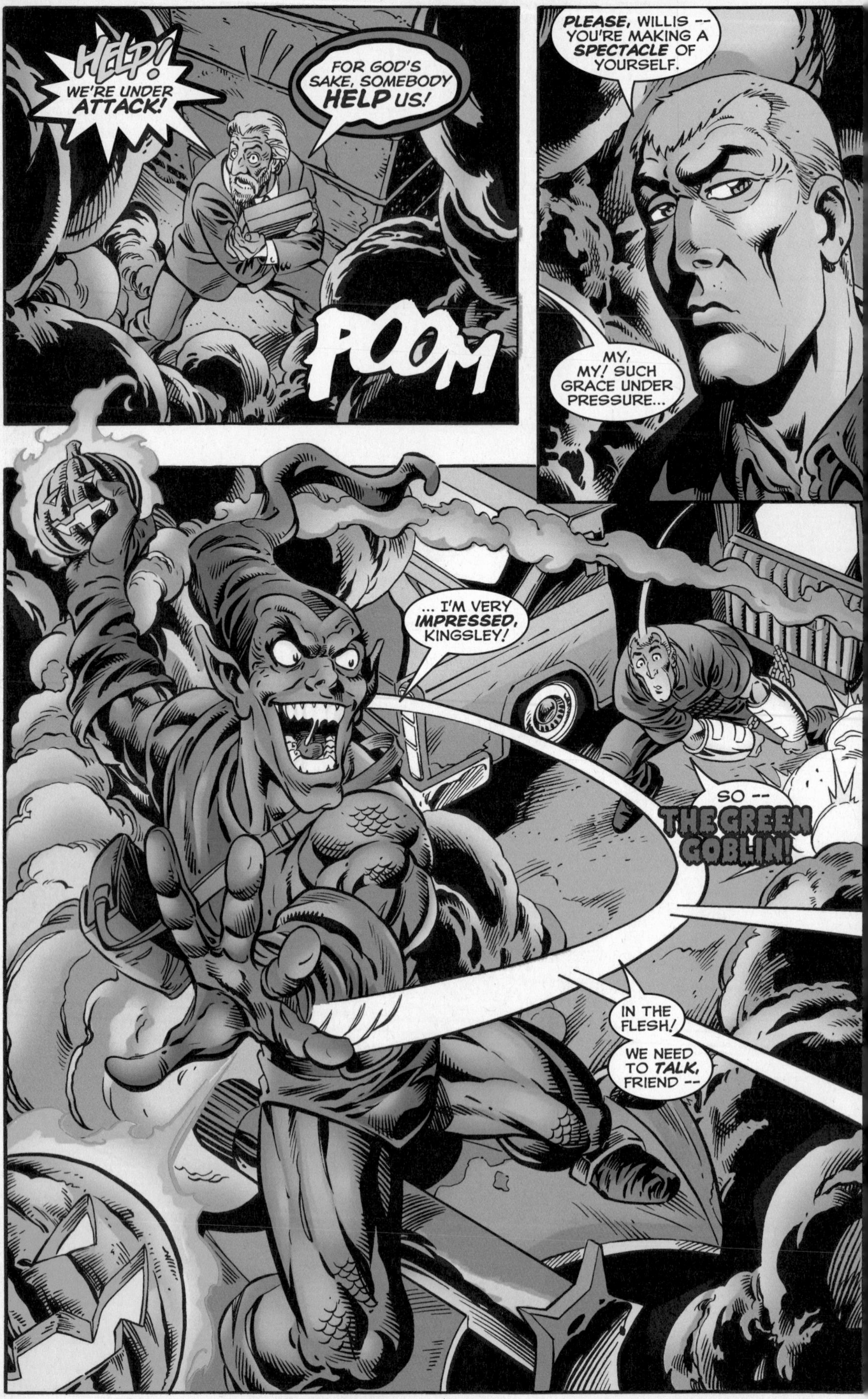
HELP! WE'RE UNDER ATTACK!
FOR GOD'S SAKE, SOMEBODY HELP US!
POOM
PLEASE, WILLIS -- YOU'RE MAKING A SPECTACLE OF YOURSELF.
MY, MY! SUCH GRACE UNDER PRESSURE...
... I'M VERY IMPRESSED, KINGSLEY!
SO -- THE GREEN GOBLIN!
IN THE FLESH!
WE NEED TO TALK, FRIEND --

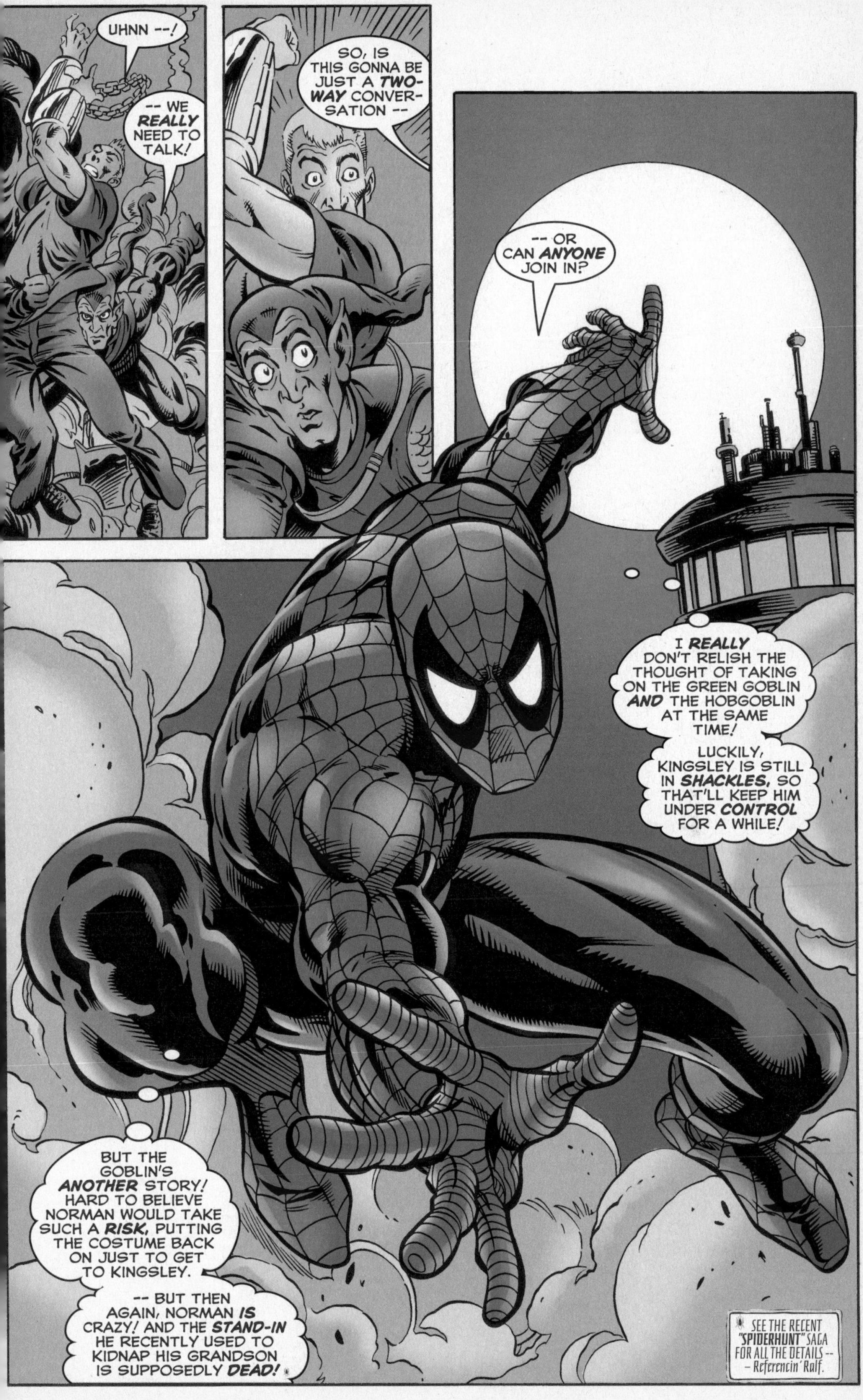
UHNN --!
-- WE REALLY NEED TO TALK!
SO, IS THIS GONNA BE JUST A TWO-WAY CONVERSATION --
-- OR CAN ANYONE JOIN IN?
I REALLY DON'T RELISH THE THOUGHT OF TAKING ON THE GREEN GOBLIN AND THE HOBGOBLIN AT THE SAME TIME!
LUCKILY, KINGSLEY IS STILL IN SHACKLES, SO THAT'LL KEEP HIM UNDER CONTROL FOR A WHILE!
BUT THE GOBLIN'S ANOTHER STORY! HARD TO BELIEVE NORMAN WOULD TAKE SUCH A RISK, PUTTING THE COSTUME BACK ON JUST TO GET TO KINGSLEY.
-- BUT THEN AGAIN, NORMAN IS CRAZY! AND THE STAND-IN HE RECENTLY USED TO KIDNAP HIS GRANDSON IS SUPPOSEDLY DEAD!*
*SEE THE RECENT "SPIDERHUNT" SAGA FOR ALL THE DETAILS -- - Referencin' Ralf.

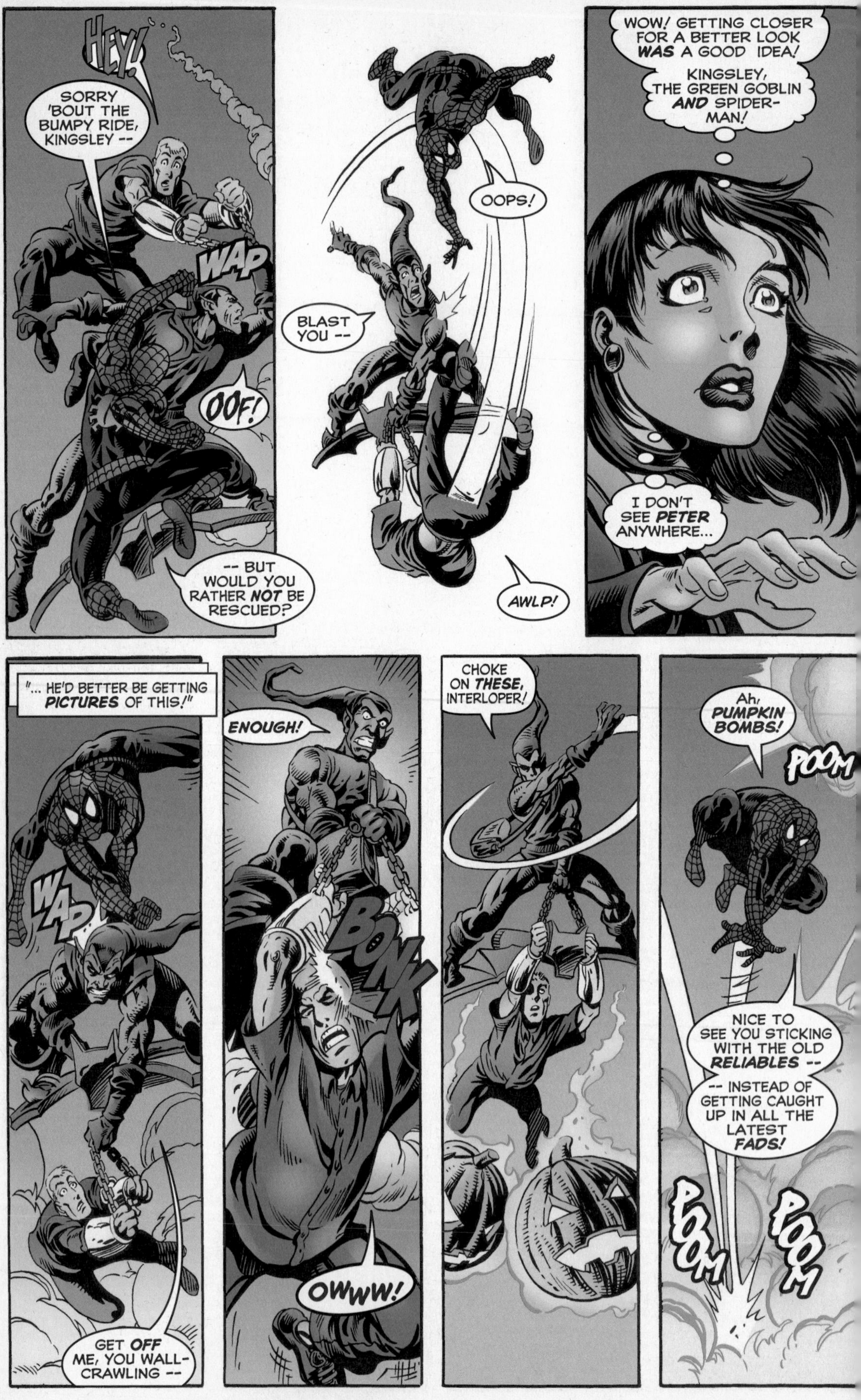

HEY!
SORRY 'BOUT THE BUMPY RIDE, KINGSLEY --
WAP
OOF!
-- BUT WOULD YOU RATHER NOT BE RESCUED?
OOPS!
BLAST YOU --
AWLP!
WOW! GETTING CLOSER FOR A BETTER LOOK WAS A GOOD IDEA!
KINGSLEY, THE GREEN GOBLIN AND SPIDER-MAN!
I DON'T SEE PETER ANYWHERE...
"... HE'D BETTER BE GETTING PICTURES OF THIS!"
WAP
GET OFF ME, YOU WALL-CRAWLING --
ENOUGH!
BONK
OWWW!
CHOKE ON THESE, INTERLOPER!
Ah, PUMPKIN BOMBS!
POOM
NICE TO SEE YOU STICKING WITH THE OLD RELIABLES --
-- INSTEAD OF GETTING CAUGHT UP IN ALL THE LATEST FADS!
POOM
POOM

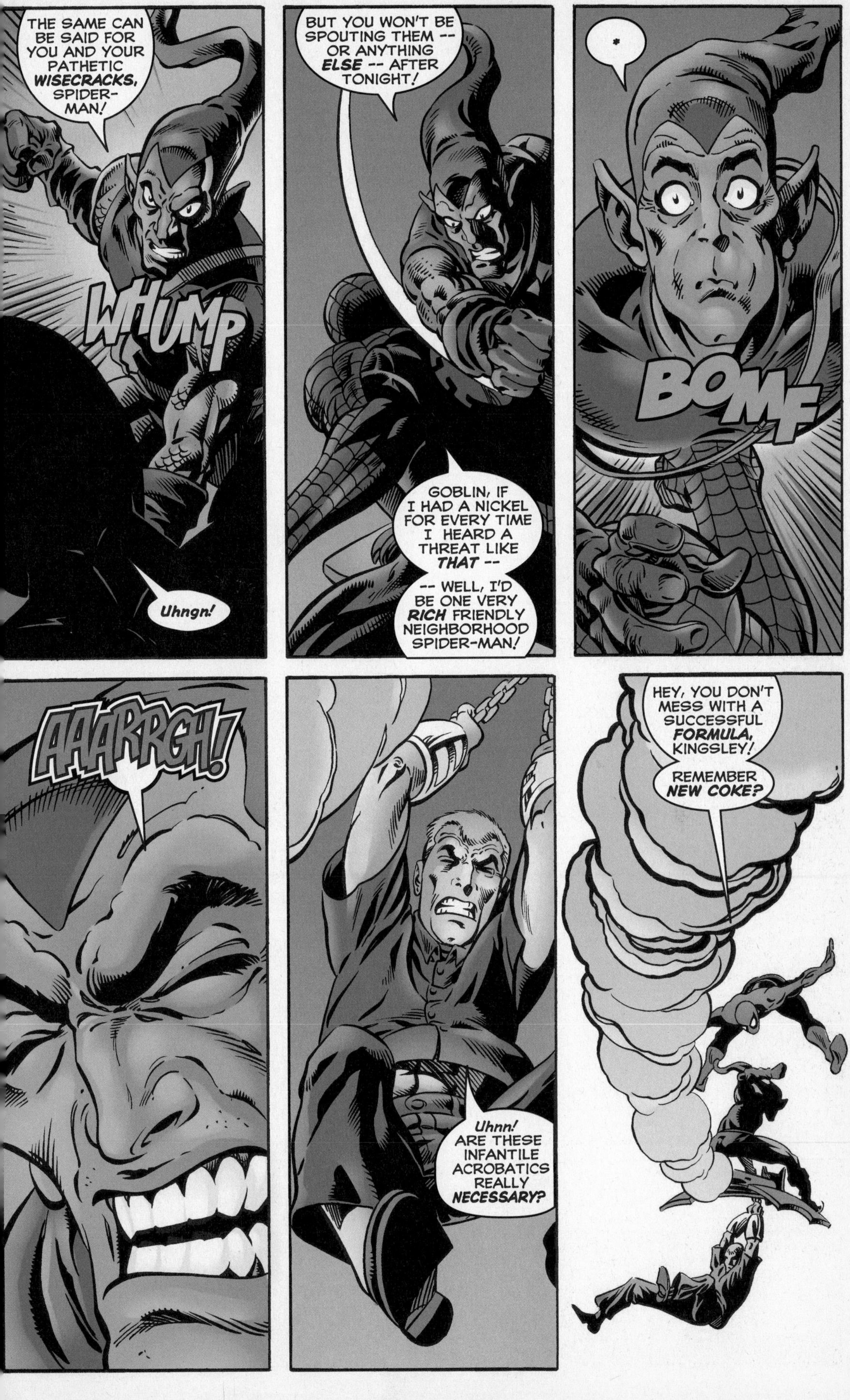
THE SAME CAN BE SAID FOR YOU AND YOUR PATHETIC WISECRACKS, SPIDER-MAN!
WHUMP
Uhngn!
BUT YOU WON'T BE SPOUTING THEM -- OR ANYTHING ELSE -- AFTER TONIGHT!
GOBLIN, IF I HAD A NICKEL FOR EVERY TIME I HEARD A THREAT LIKE THAT --
-- WELL, I'D BE ONE VERY RICH FRIENDLY NEIGHBORHOOD SPIDER-MAN!
*
BOMF
AAARRGH!
Uhnn! ARE THESE INFANTILE ACROBATICS REALLY NECESSARY?
HEY, YOU DON'T MESS WITH A SUCCESSFUL FORMULA, KINGSLEY!
REMEMBER NEW COKE?

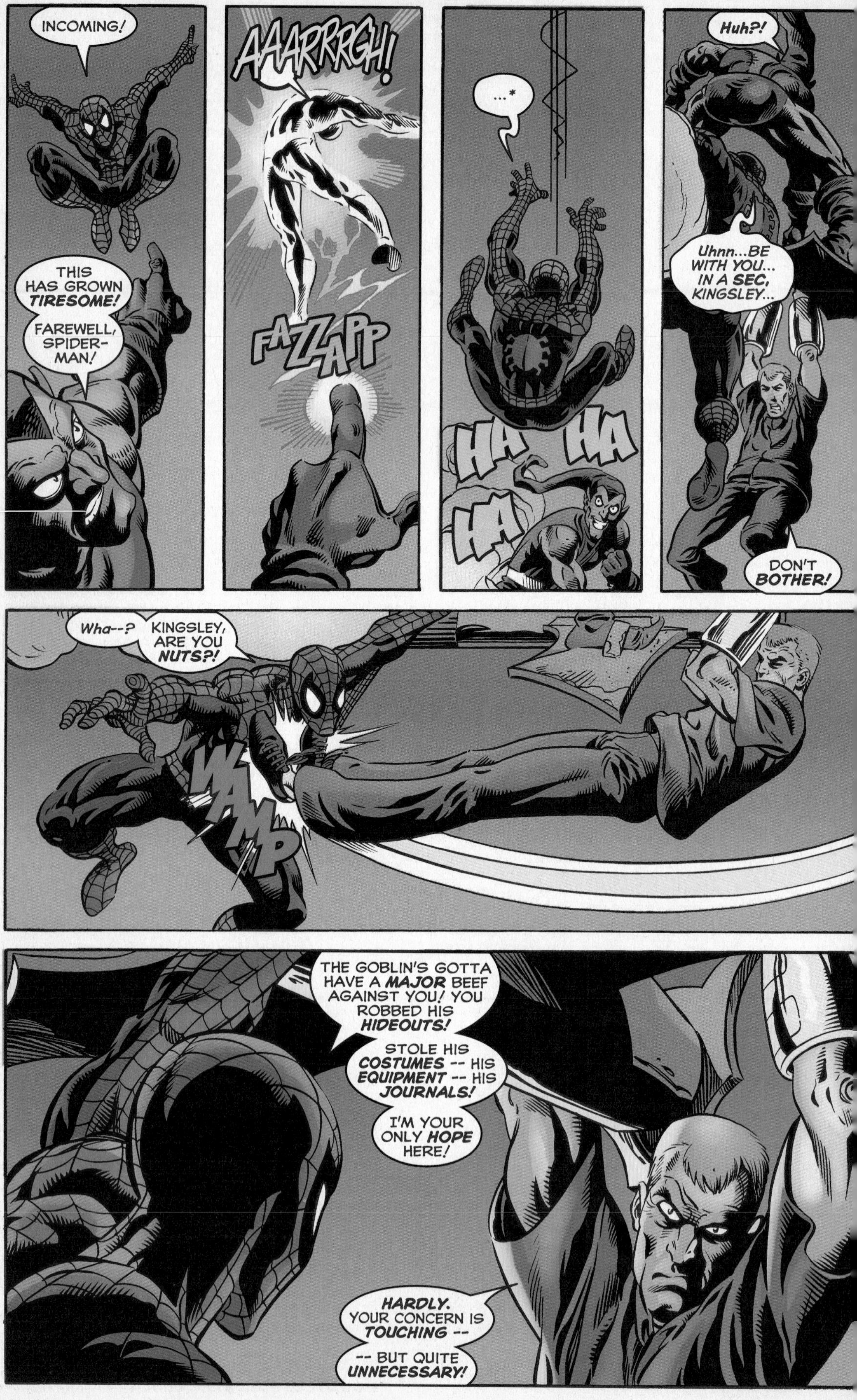

INCOMING!
THIS HAS GROWN TIRESOME!
FAREWELL, SPIDER-MAN!
AAARRRGH!
FAZZAPP
...*
HA HA HA
Huh?!
Uhnn...BE WITH YOU... IN A SEC, KINGSLEY...
DON'T BOTHER!
Wha--?
KINGSLEY, ARE YOU NUTS?!
WAMP
THE GOBLIN'S GOTTA HAVE A MAJOR BEEF AGAINST YOU! YOU ROBBED HIS HIDEOUTS!
STOLE HIS COSTUMES -- HIS EQUIPMENT -- HIS JOURNALS!
I'M YOUR ONLY HOPE HERE!
HARDLY. YOUR CONCERN IS TOUCHING --
-- BUT QUITE UNNECESSARY!

POKK

-AACK--!~

-Oof!~

WHUMP

AND AWAY THEY GO.

BLAST. DIDN'T EVEN GET A CHANCE TO SLAP A SPIDER-TRACER ON THEM.

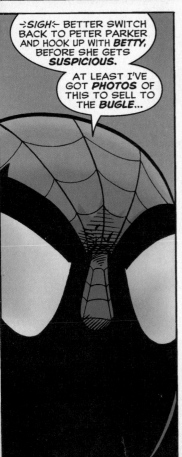

-SIGH- BETTER SWITCH BACK TO PETER PARKER AND HOOK UP WITH BETTY, BEFORE SHE GETS SUSPICIOUS.

AT LEAST I'VE GOT PHOTOS OF THIS TO SELL TO THE BUGLE...

THIS IS A NIGHTMARE!

NOW TWO OF MY ALL-TIME DEADLIEST ENEMIES ARE AT LARGE --

-- AND IN EACH OTHER'S COMPANY!

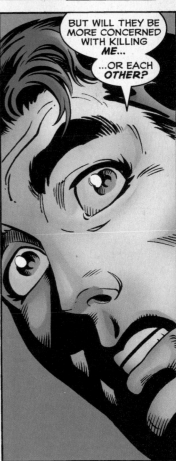

BUT WILL THEY BE MORE CONCERNED WITH KILLING ME...

...OR EACH OTHER?

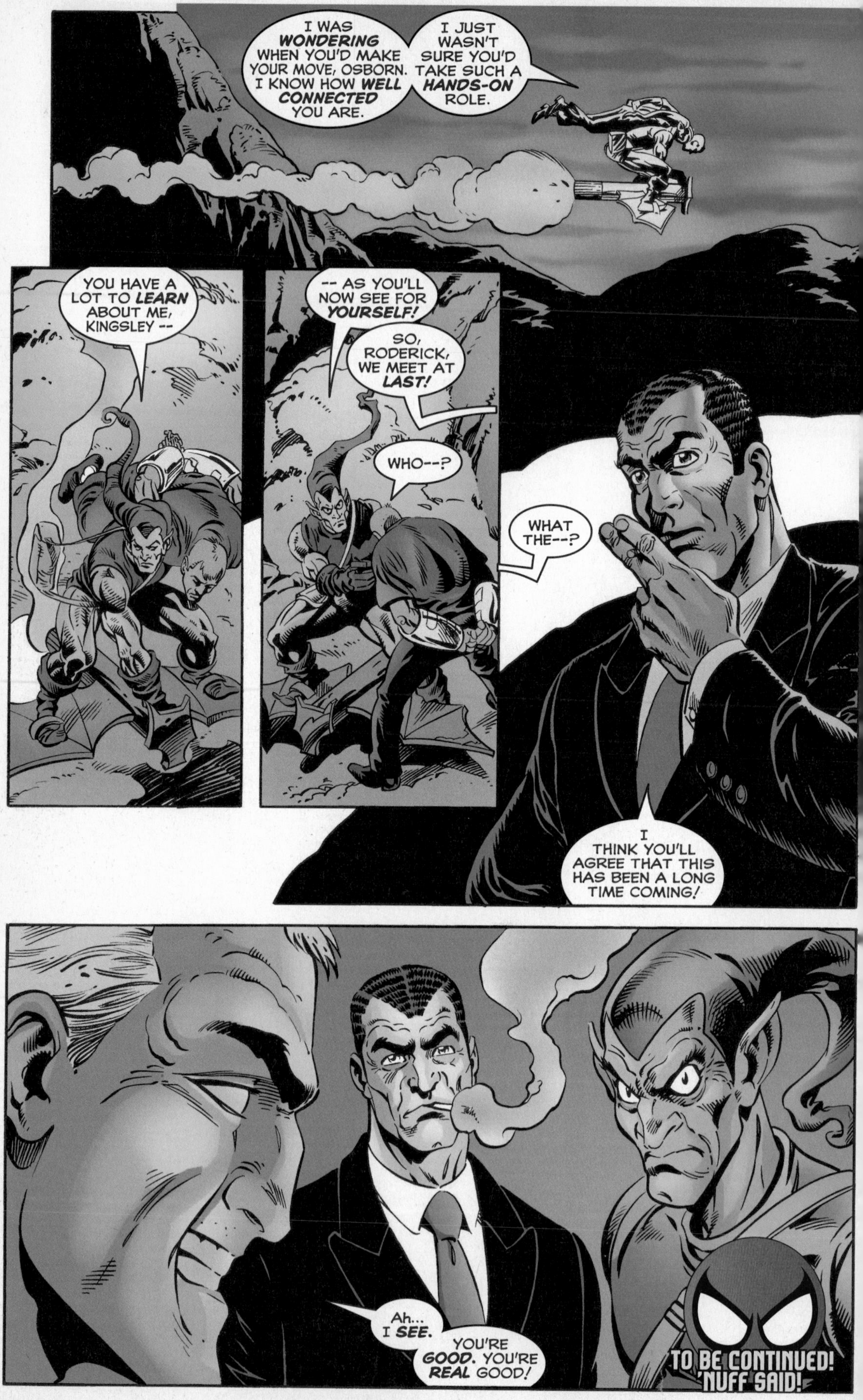
I WAS WONDERING WHEN YOU'D MAKE YOUR MOVE, OSBORN. I KNOW HOW WELL CONNECTED YOU ARE.
I JUST WASN'T SURE YOU'D TAKE SUCH A HANDS-ON ROLE.
YOU HAVE A LOT TO LEARN ABOUT ME, KINGSLEY --
-- AS YOU'LL NOW SEE FOR YOURSELF!
SO, RODERICK, WE MEET AT LAST!
WHO--?
WHAT THE--?
I THINK YOU'LL AGREE THAT THIS HAS BEEN A LONG TIME COMING!
Ah... I SEE.
YOU'RE GOOD. YOU'RE REAL GOOD!
TO BE CONTINUED! 'NUFF SAID!

MARVEL COMICS
THE SPECTACULAR
SPIDER-MAN
GOBLINS AT THE GATE PART 2
AUG #260
APPROVED BY THE COMICS CODE AUTHORITY
WWW.MARVEL.COM

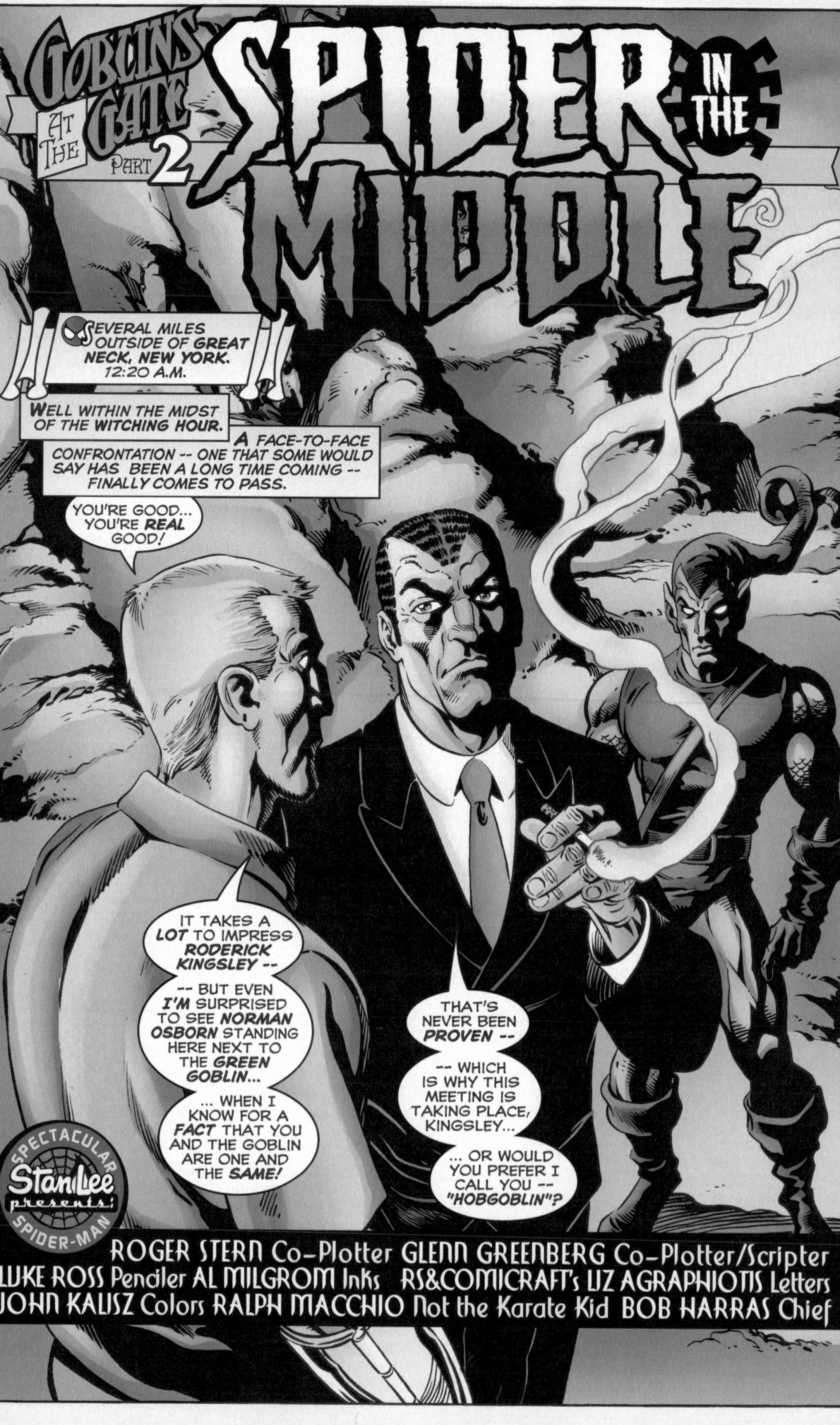
GOBLINS AT THE GATE PART 2
SPIDER IN THE MIDDLE
SEVERAL MILES OUTSIDE OF GREAT NECK, NEW YORK. 12:20 A.M.
WELL WITHIN THE MIDST OF THE WITCHING HOUR.
A FACE-TO-FACE CONFRONTATION -- ONE THAT SOME WOULD SAY HAS BEEN A LONG TIME COMING -- FINALLY COMES TO PASS.
YOU'RE GOOD... YOU'RE REAL GOOD!
IT TAKES A LOT TO IMPRESS RODERICK KINGSLEY --
-- BUT EVEN I'M SURPRISED TO SEE NORMAN OSBORN STANDING HERE NEXT TO THE GREEN GOBLIN...
... WHEN I KNOW FOR A FACT THAT YOU AND THE GOBLIN ARE ONE AND THE SAME!
THAT'S NEVER BEEN PROVEN --
-- WHICH IS WHY THIS MEETING IS TAKING PLACE, KINGSLEY...
... OR WOULD YOU PREFER I CALL YOU -- "HOBGOBLIN"?
SPECTACULAR Stan Lee presents: SPIDER-MAN
ROGER STERN Co-Plotter GLENN GREENBERG Co-Plotter/Scripter
LUKE ROSS Penciler AL MILGROM Inks RS&COMICRAFT's LIZ AGRAPHIOTIS Letters
JOHN KALISZ Colors RALPH MACCHIO Not the Karate Kid BOB HARRAS Chief

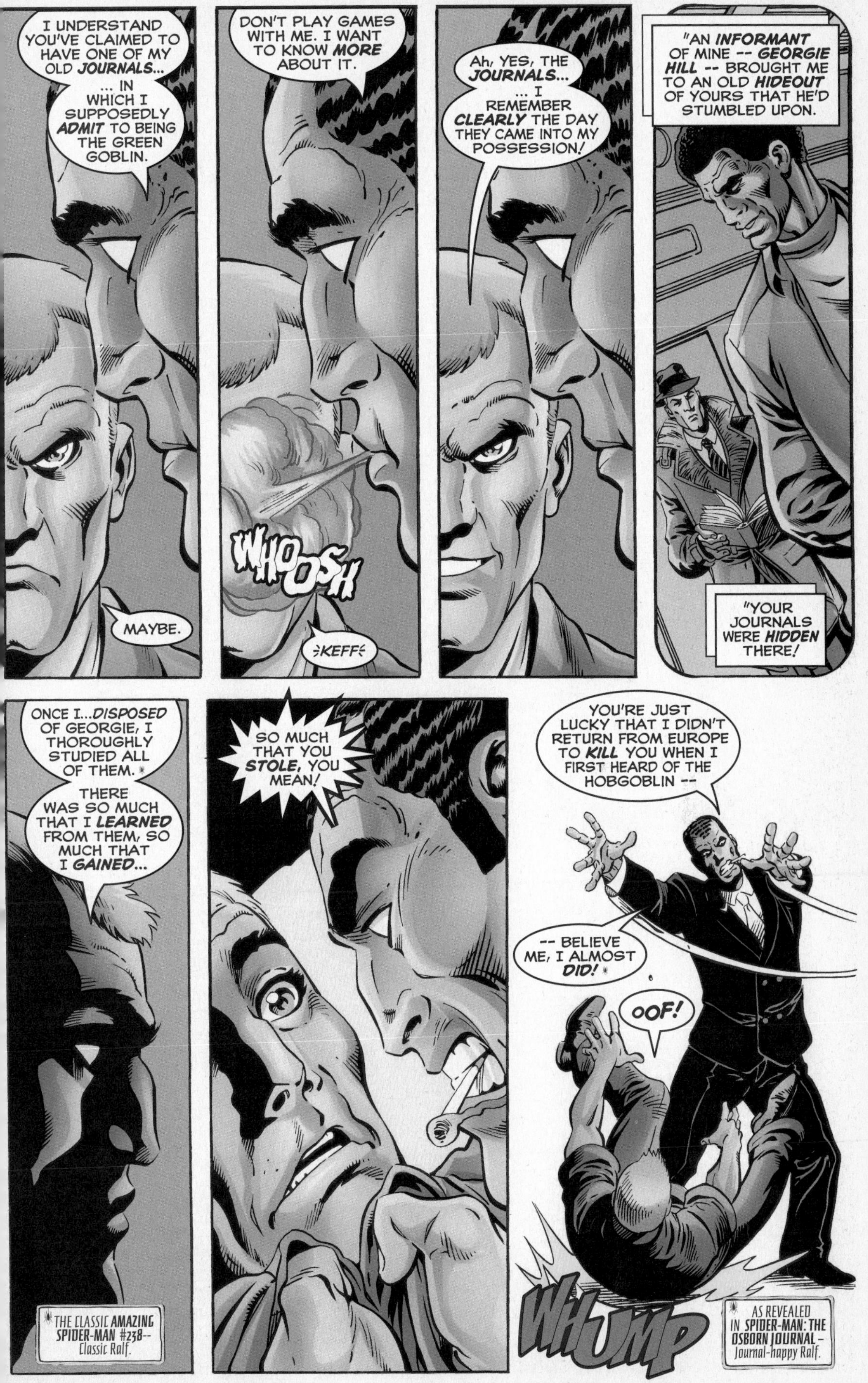
I UNDERSTAND YOU'VE CLAIMED TO HAVE ONE OF MY OLD JOURNALS...
... IN WHICH I SUPPOSEDLY ADMIT TO BEING THE GREEN GOBLIN.
MAYBE.
DON'T PLAY GAMES WITH ME. I WANT TO KNOW MORE ABOUT IT.
WHOOSH
KEFF
Ah, YES, THE JOURNALS...
... I REMEMBER CLEARLY THE DAY THEY CAME INTO MY POSSESSION!
"AN INFORMANT OF MINE -- GEORGIE HILL -- BROUGHT ME TO AN OLD HIDEOUT OF YOURS THAT HE'D STUMBLED UPON.
"YOUR JOURNALS WERE HIDDEN THERE!
ONCE I...DISPOSED OF GEORGIE, I THOROUGHLY STUDIED ALL OF THEM.
THERE WAS SO MUCH THAT I LEARNED FROM THEM, SO MUCH THAT I GAINED...
THE CLASSIC AMAZING SPIDER-MAN #238-- Classic Ralf.
SO MUCH THAT YOU STOLE, YOU MEAN!
YOU'RE JUST LUCKY THAT I DIDN'T RETURN FROM EUROPE TO KILL YOU WHEN I FIRST HEARD OF THE HOBGOBLIN --
-- BELIEVE ME, I ALMOST DID!
OOF!
WHUMP
AS REVEALED IN SPIDER-MAN: THE OSBORN JOURNAL -- Journal-happy Ralf.

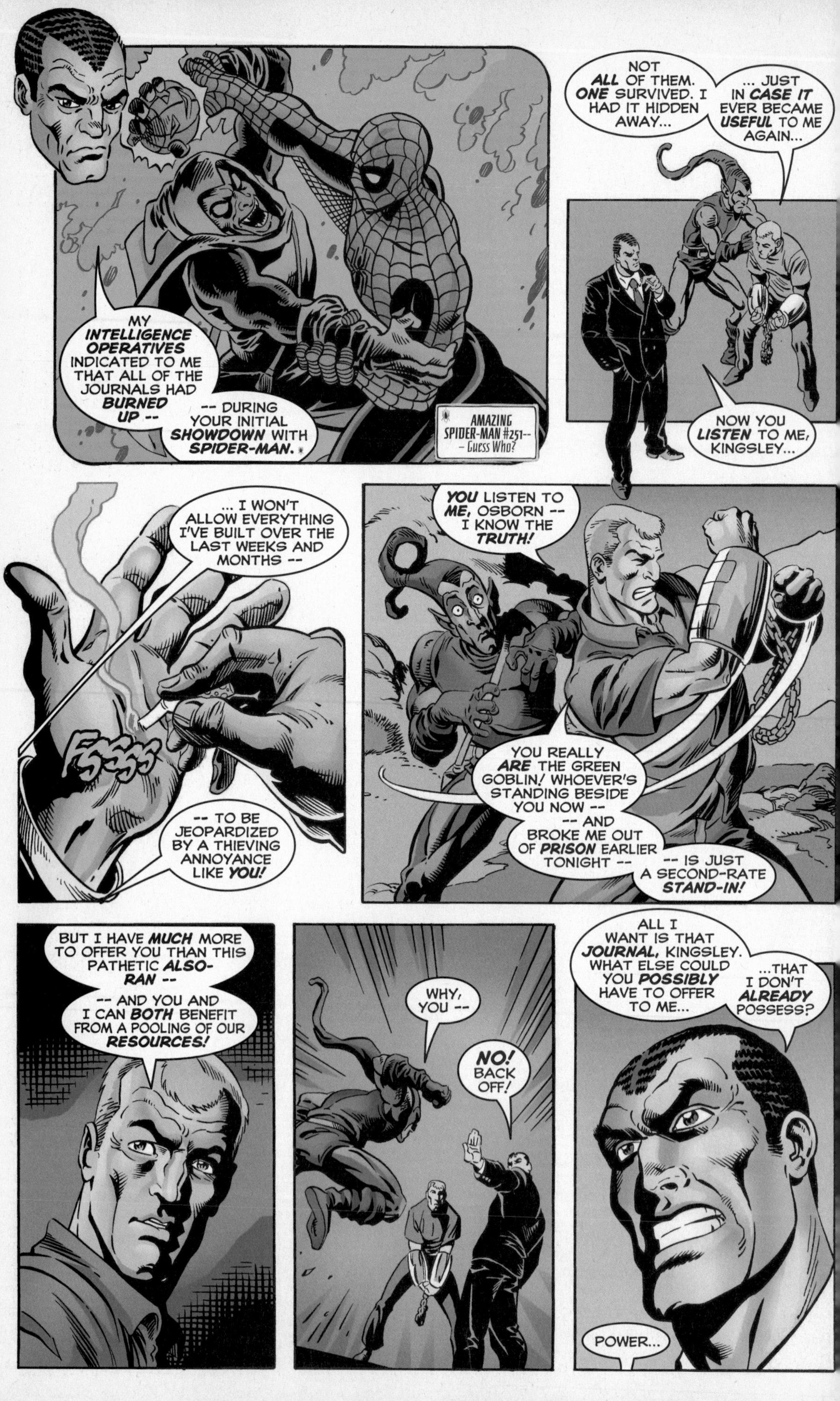
MY INTELLIGENCE OPERATIVES INDICATED TO ME THAT ALL OF THE JOURNALS HAD BURNED UP --
-- DURING YOUR INITIAL SHOWDOWN WITH SPIDER-MAN.*
*AMAZING SPIDER-MAN #251-- – Guess Who?
NOT ALL OF THEM. ONE SURVIVED. I HAD IT HIDDEN AWAY...
... JUST IN CASE IT EVER BECAME USEFUL TO ME AGAIN...
NOW YOU LISTEN TO ME, KINGSLEY...
... I WON'T ALLOW EVERYTHING I'VE BUILT OVER THE LAST WEEKS AND MONTHS --
FSSSS
-- TO BE JEOPARDIZED BY A THIEVING ANNOYANCE LIKE YOU!
YOU LISTEN TO ME, OSBORN -- I KNOW THE TRUTH!
YOU REALLY ARE THE GREEN GOBLIN! WHOEVER'S STANDING BESIDE YOU NOW --
-- AND BROKE ME OUT OF PRISON EARLIER TONIGHT --
-- IS JUST A SECOND-RATE STAND-IN!
BUT I HAVE MUCH MORE TO OFFER YOU THAN THIS PATHETIC ALSO-RAN --
-- AND YOU AND I CAN BOTH BENEFIT FROM A POOLING OF OUR RESOURCES!
WHY, YOU --
NO! BACK OFF!
ALL I WANT IS THAT JOURNAL, KINGSLEY. WHAT ELSE COULD YOU POSSIBLY HAVE TO OFFER TO ME...
...THAT I DON'T ALREADY POSSESS?
POWER...

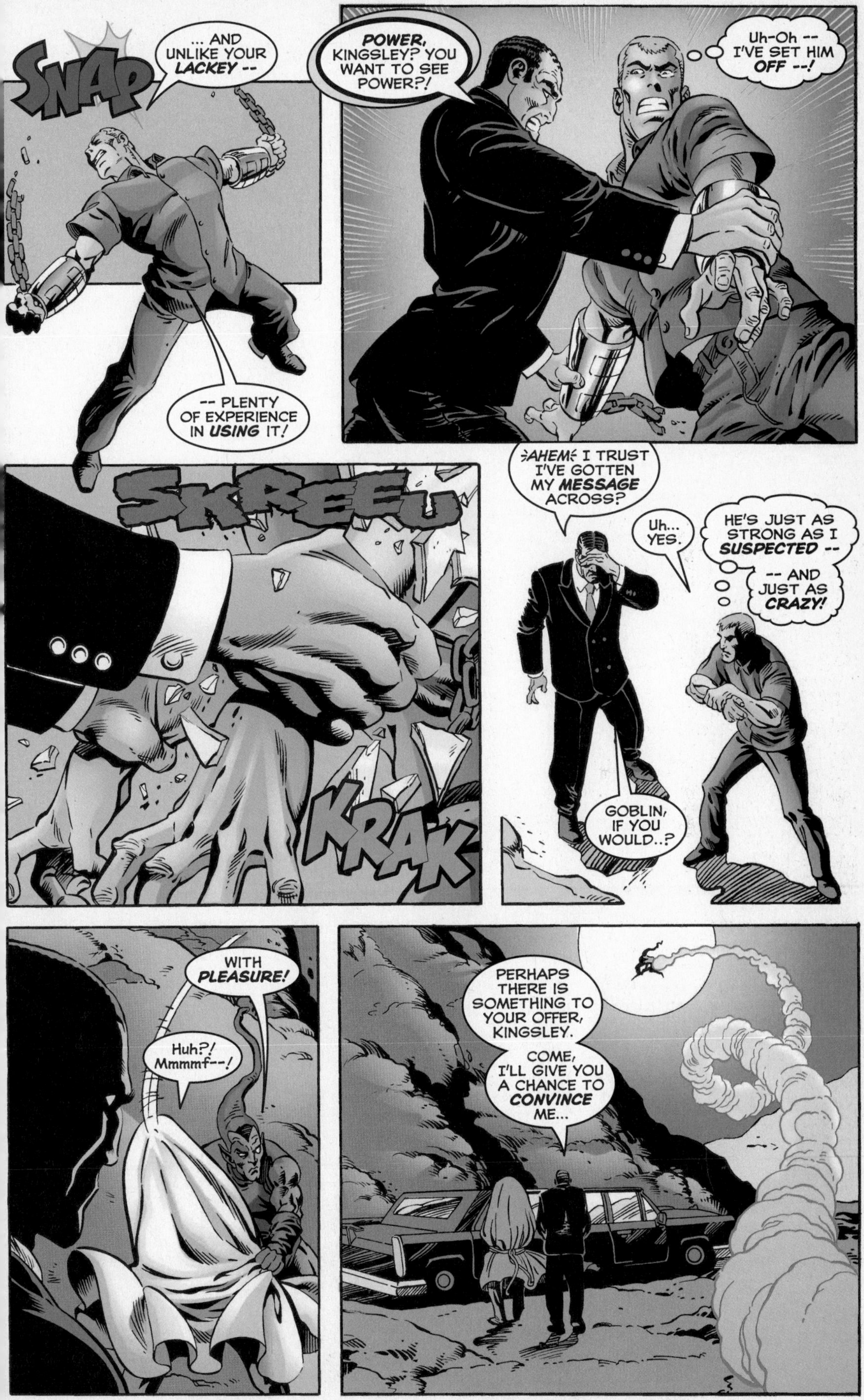
SNAP
... AND UNLIKE YOUR LACKEY --
-- PLENTY OF EXPERIENCE IN USING IT!
POWER, KINGSLEY? YOU WANT TO SEE POWER?!
Uh-Oh -- I'VE SET HIM OFF --!
SKREEU
KRAK
AHEM I TRUST I'VE GOTTEN MY MESSAGE ACROSS?
Uh... YES.
HE'S JUST AS STRONG AS I SUSPECTED --
-- AND JUST AS CRAZY!
GOBLIN, IF YOU WOULD..?
WITH PLEASURE!
Huh?! Mmmmf--!
PERHAPS THERE IS SOMETHING TO YOUR OFFER, KINGSLEY.
COME, I'LL GIVE YOU A CHANCE TO CONVINCE ME...

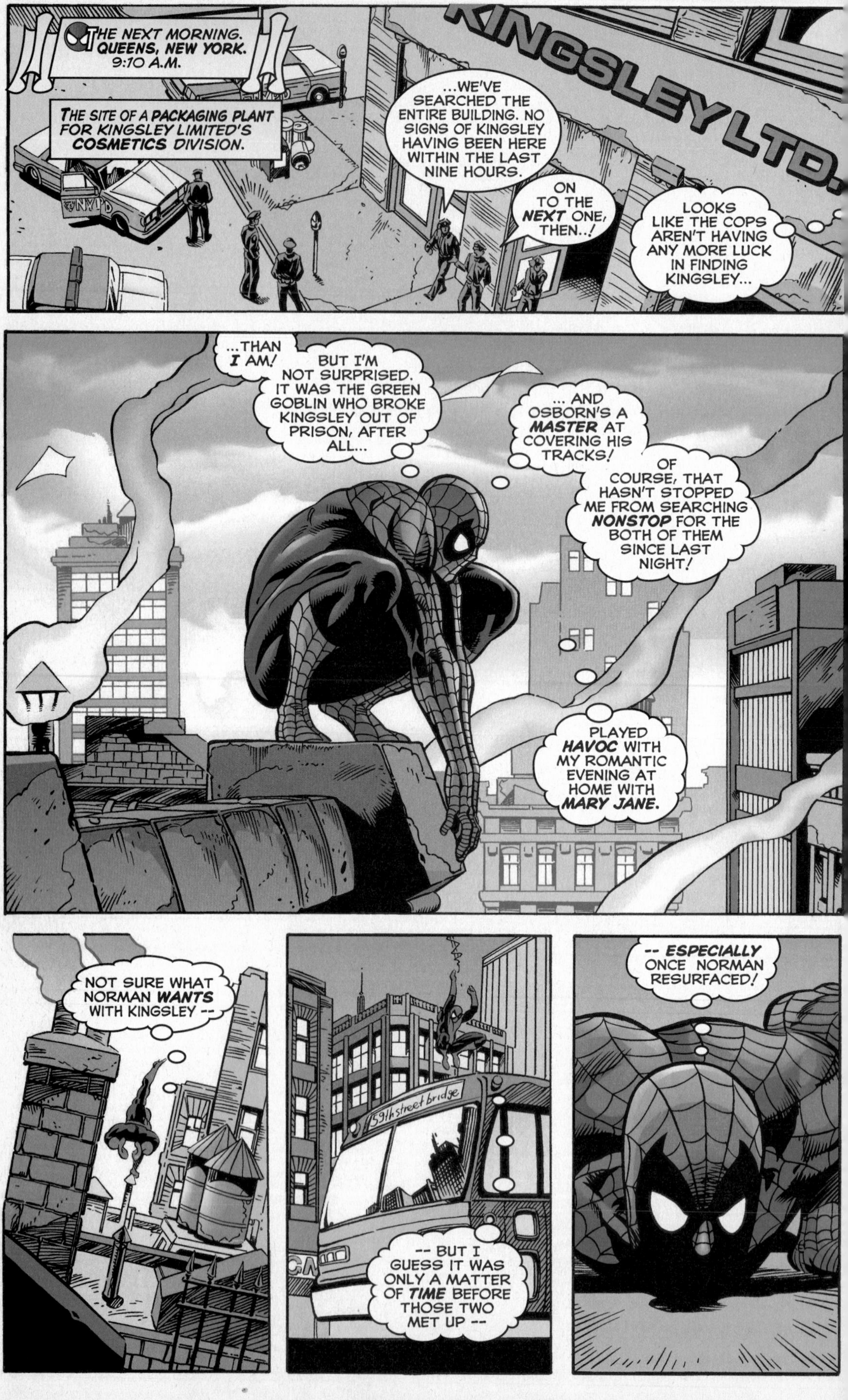
THE NEXT MORNING. QUEENS, NEW YORK. 9:10 A.M.
THE SITE OF A PACKAGING PLANT FOR KINGSLEY LIMITED'S COSMETICS DIVISION.
KINGSLEY LTD.
...WE'VE SEARCHED THE ENTIRE BUILDING. NO SIGNS OF KINGSLEY HAVING BEEN HERE WITHIN THE LAST NINE HOURS.
ON TO THE NEXT ONE, THEN...!
LOOKS LIKE THE COPS AREN'T HAVING ANY MORE LUCK IN FINDING KINGSLEY...
...THAN I AM!
BUT I'M NOT SURPRISED. IT WAS THE GREEN GOBLIN WHO BROKE KINGSLEY OUT OF PRISON, AFTER ALL...
... AND OSBORN'S A MASTER AT COVERING HIS TRACKS!
OF COURSE, THAT HASN'T STOPPED ME FROM SEARCHING NONSTOP FOR THE BOTH OF THEM SINCE LAST NIGHT!
PLAYED HAVOC WITH MY ROMANTIC EVENING AT HOME WITH MARY JANE.
NOT SURE WHAT NORMAN WANTS WITH KINGSLEY --
59th street bridge
-- BUT I GUESS IT WAS ONLY A MATTER OF TIME BEFORE THOSE TWO MET UP --
-- ESPECIALLY ONCE NORMAN RESURFACED!

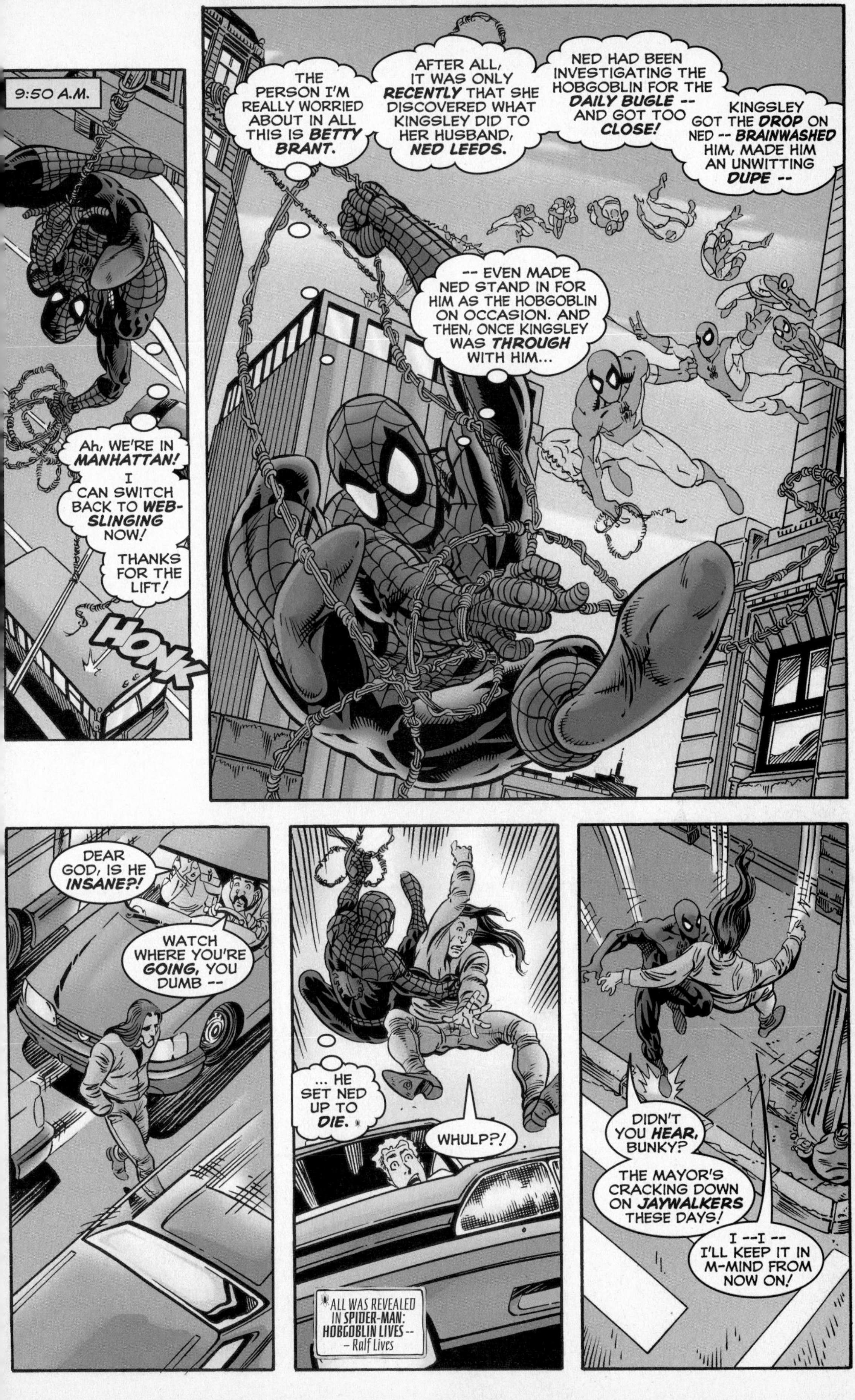
9:50 A.M.
Ah, WE'RE IN MANHATTAN!
I CAN SWITCH BACK TO WEB-SLINGING NOW!
THANKS FOR THE LIFT!
HONK
THE PERSON I'M REALLY WORRIED ABOUT IN ALL THIS IS BETTY BRANT.
AFTER ALL, IT WAS ONLY RECENTLY THAT SHE DISCOVERED WHAT KINGSLEY DID TO HER HUSBAND, NED LEEDS.
NED HAD BEEN INVESTIGATING THE HOBGOBLIN FOR THE DAILY BUGLE -- AND GOT TOO CLOSE!
KINGSLEY GOT THE DROP ON NED -- BRAINWASHED HIM, MADE HIM AN UNWITTING DUPE --
-- EVEN MADE NED STAND IN FOR HIM AS THE HOBGOBLIN ON OCCASION. AND THEN, ONCE KINGSLEY WAS THROUGH WITH HIM...
DEAR GOD, IS HE INSANE?!
WATCH WHERE YOU'RE GOING, YOU DUMB --
... HE SET NED UP TO DIE.
WHULP?!
ALL WAS REVEALED IN SPIDER-MAN: HOBGOBLIN LIVES -- – Ralf Lives
DIDN'T YOU HEAR, BUNKY?
THE MAYOR'S CRACKING DOWN ON JAYWALKERS THESE DAYS!
I --I -- I'LL KEEP IT IN M-MIND FROM NOW ON!

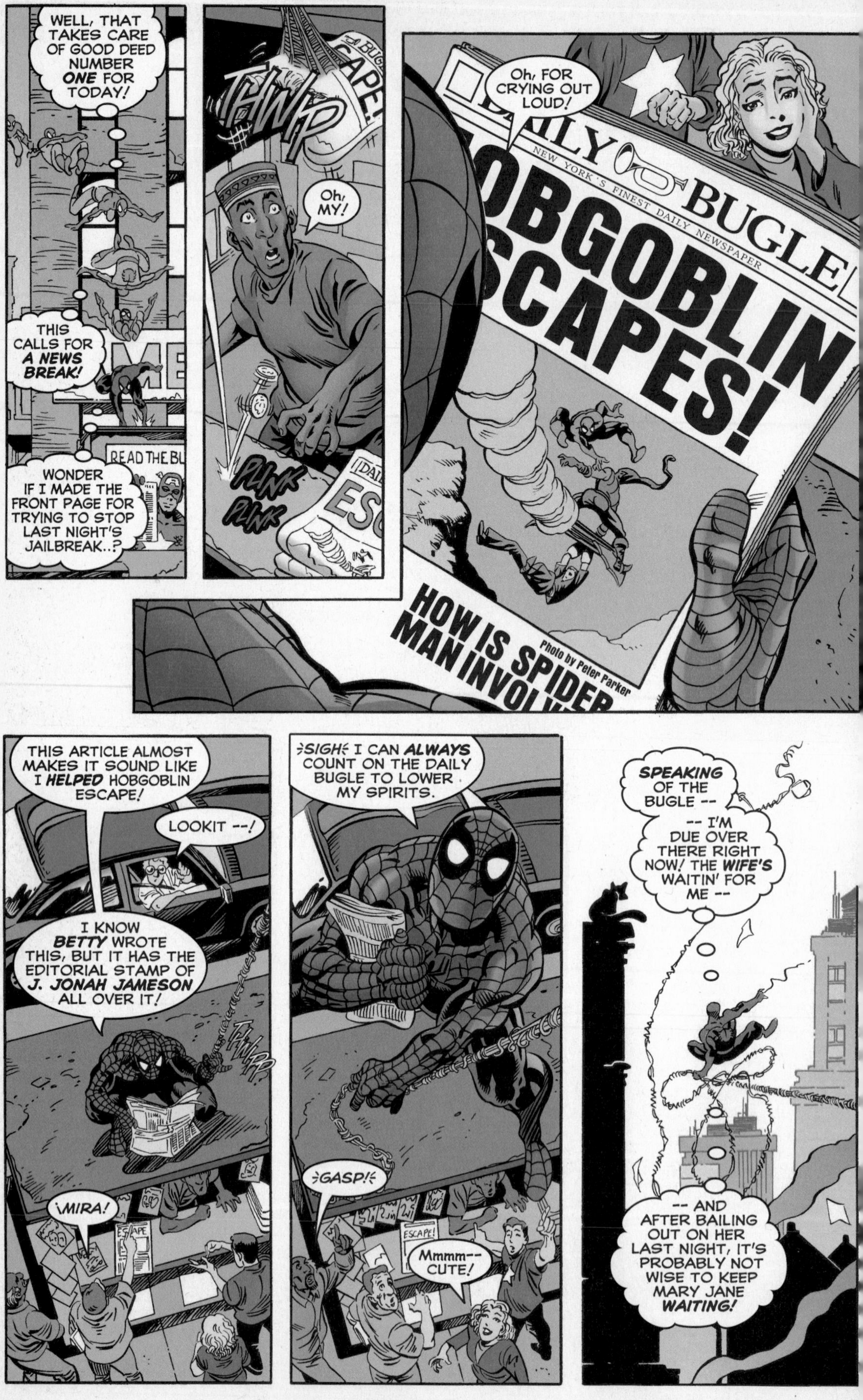

WELL, THAT TAKES CARE OF GOOD DEED NUMBER ONE FOR TODAY!
THIS CALLS FOR A NEWS BREAK!
WONDER IF I MADE THE FRONT PAGE FOR TRYING TO STOP LAST NIGHT'S JAILBREAK..?
READ THE BU
THWP
Oh, MY!
PLINK
PLINK
Oh, FOR CRYING OUT LOUD!
DAILY BUGLE
NEW YORK'S FINEST DAILY NEWSPAPER
HOBGOBLIN ESCAPES!
Photo by Peter Parker
HOW IS SPIDER MAN INVOLV
THIS ARTICLE ALMOST MAKES IT SOUND LIKE I HELPED HOBGOBLIN ESCAPE!
LOOKIT --!
I KNOW BETTY WROTE THIS, BUT IT HAS THE EDITORIAL STAMP OF J. JONAH JAMESON ALL OVER IT!
THWIP
¡MIRA!
SIGH I CAN ALWAYS COUNT ON THE DAILY BUGLE TO LOWER MY SPIRITS.
GASP!
ESCAPE!
Mmmm-- CUTE!
SPEAKING OF THE BUGLE --
-- I'M DUE OVER THERE RIGHT NOW! THE WIFE'S WAITIN' FOR ME --
-- AND AFTER BAILING OUT ON HER LAST NIGHT, IT'S PROBABLY NOT WISE TO KEEP MARY JANE WAITING!

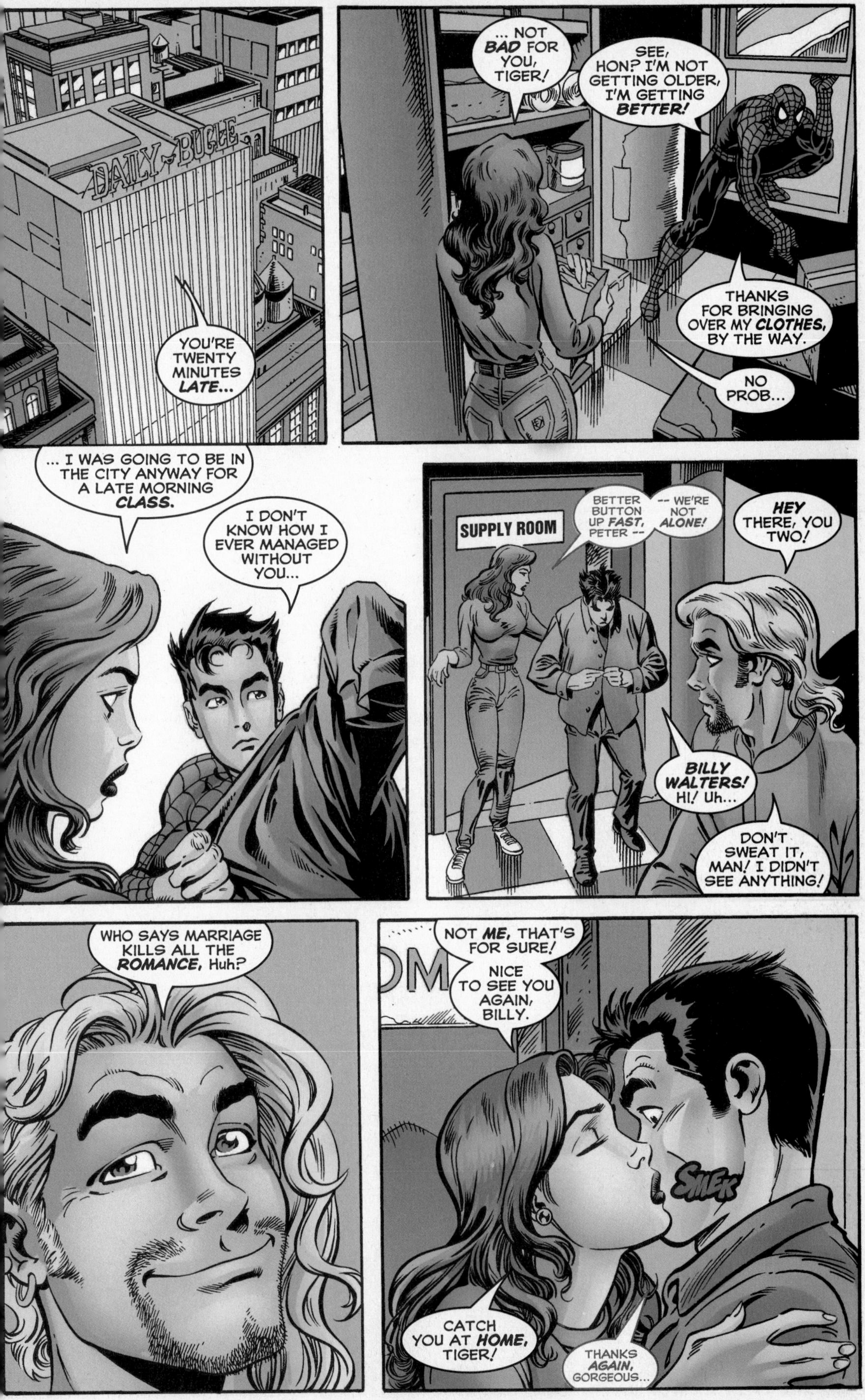

YOU'RE TWENTY MINUTES LATE...
... NOT BAD FOR YOU, TIGER!
SEE, HON? I'M NOT GETTING OLDER, I'M GETTING BETTER!
THANKS FOR BRINGING OVER MY CLOTHES, BY THE WAY.
NO PROB...
... I WAS GOING TO BE IN THE CITY ANYWAY FOR A LATE MORNING CLASS.
I DON'T KNOW HOW I EVER MANAGED WITHOUT YOU...
SUPPLY ROOM
BETTER BUTTON UP FAST, PETER --
-- WE'RE NOT ALONE!
HEY THERE, YOU TWO!
BILLY WALTERS! HI! Uh...
DON'T SWEAT IT, MAN! I DIDN'T SEE ANYTHING!
WHO SAYS MARRIAGE KILLS ALL THE ROMANCE, Huh?
NOT ME, THAT'S FOR SURE!
NICE TO SEE YOU AGAIN, BILLY.
SMEK
CATCH YOU AT HOME, TIGER!
THANKS AGAIN, GORGEOUS...

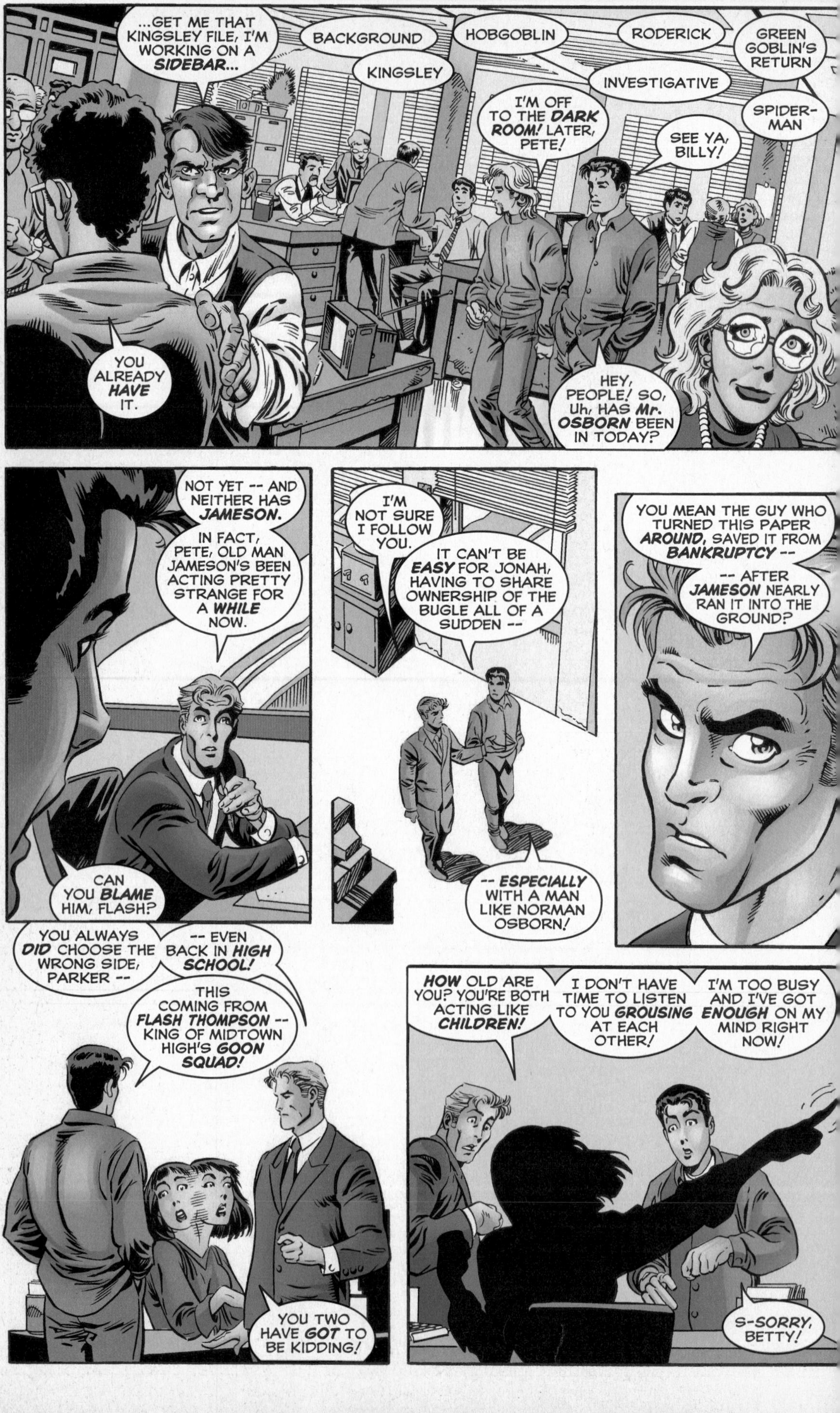
...GET ME THAT KINGSLEY FILE, I'M WORKING ON A SIDEBAR...
BACKGROUND
KINGSLEY
HOBGOBLIN
RODERICK
INVESTIGATIVE
GREEN GOBLIN'S RETURN
SPIDER-MAN
I'M OFF TO THE DARK ROOM! LATER, PETE!
SEE YA, BILLY!
YOU ALREADY HAVE IT.
HEY, PEOPLE! SO, Uh, HAS Mr. OSBORN BEEN IN TODAY?
NOT YET -- AND NEITHER HAS JAMESON.
IN FACT, PETE, OLD MAN JAMESON'S BEEN ACTING PRETTY STRANGE FOR A WHILE NOW.
CAN YOU BLAME HIM, FLASH?
I'M NOT SURE I FOLLOW YOU.
IT CAN'T BE EASY FOR JONAH, HAVING TO SHARE OWNERSHIP OF THE BUGLE ALL OF A SUDDEN --
-- ESPECIALLY WITH A MAN LIKE NORMAN OSBORN!
YOU MEAN THE GUY WHO TURNED THIS PAPER AROUND, SAVED IT FROM BANKRUPTCY --
-- AFTER JAMESON NEARLY RAN IT INTO THE GROUND?
YOU ALWAYS DID CHOOSE THE WRONG SIDE, PARKER --
-- EVEN BACK IN HIGH SCHOOL!
THIS COMING FROM FLASH THOMPSON -- KING OF MIDTOWN HIGH'S GOON SQUAD!
YOU TWO HAVE GOT TO BE KIDDING!
HOW OLD ARE YOU? YOU'RE BOTH ACTING LIKE CHILDREN!
I DON'T HAVE TIME TO LISTEN TO YOU GROUSING AT EACH OTHER!
I'M TOO BUSY AND I'VE GOT ENOUGH ON MY MIND RIGHT NOW!
S-SORRY, BETTY!

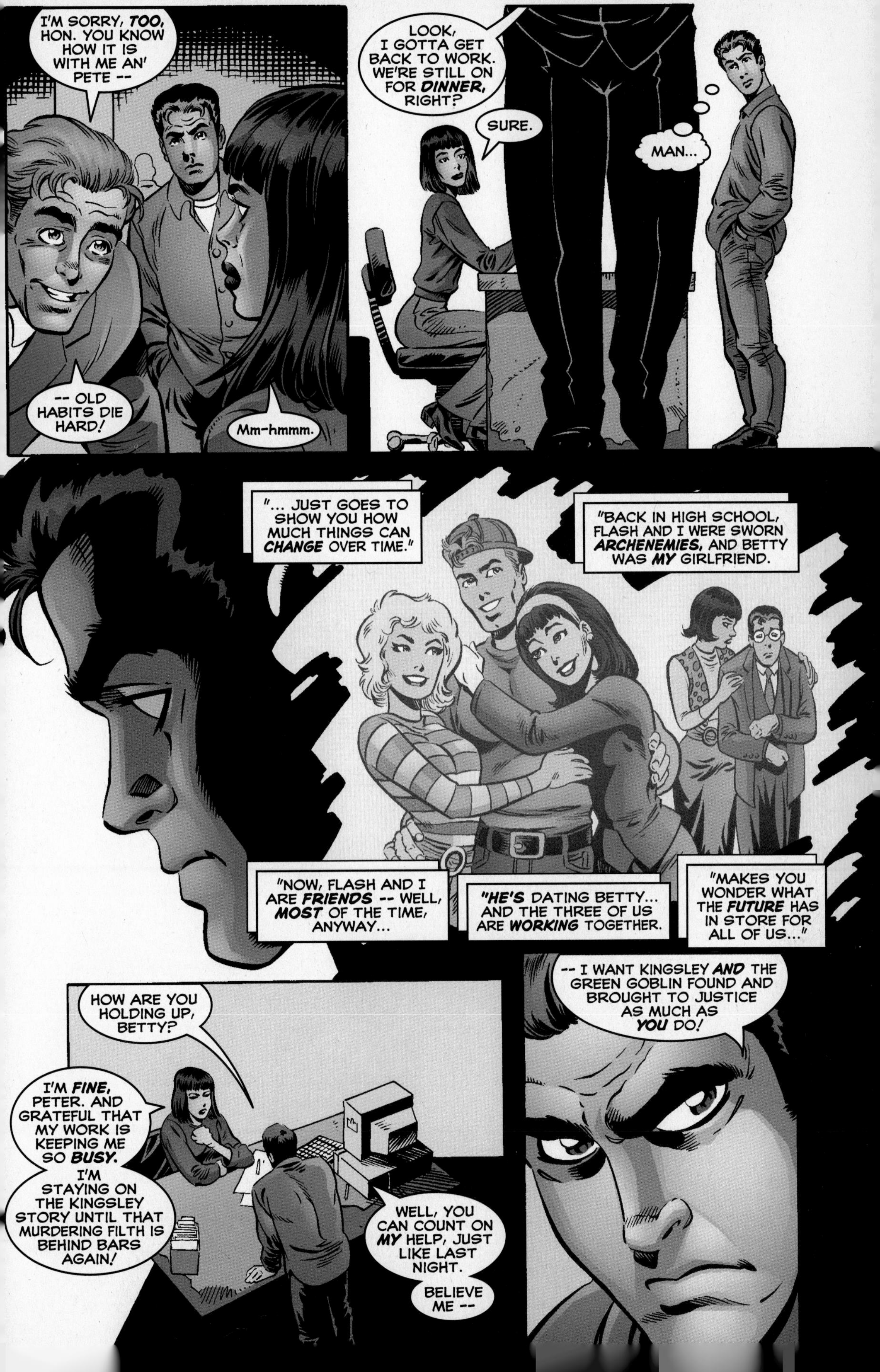

I'M SORRY, TOO, HON. YOU KNOW HOW IT IS WITH ME AN' PETE --
-- OLD HABITS DIE HARD!
Mm-hmmm.
LOOK, I GOTTA GET BACK TO WORK. WE'RE STILL ON FOR DINNER, RIGHT?
SURE.
MAN...
"... JUST GOES TO SHOW YOU HOW MUCH THINGS CAN CHANGE OVER TIME."
"BACK IN HIGH SCHOOL, FLASH AND I WERE SWORN ARCHENEMIES, AND BETTY WAS MY GIRLFRIEND.
"NOW, FLASH AND I ARE FRIENDS -- WELL, MOST OF THE TIME, ANYWAY...
"HE'S DATING BETTY... AND THE THREE OF US ARE WORKING TOGETHER.
"MAKES YOU WONDER WHAT THE FUTURE HAS IN STORE FOR ALL OF US..."
HOW ARE YOU HOLDING UP, BETTY?
I'M FINE, PETER. AND GRATEFUL THAT MY WORK IS KEEPING ME SO BUSY.
I'M STAYING ON THE KINGSLEY STORY UNTIL THAT MURDERING FILTH IS BEHIND BARS AGAIN!
WELL, YOU CAN COUNT ON MY HELP, JUST LIKE LAST NIGHT.
BELIEVE ME --
-- I WANT KINGSLEY AND THE GREEN GOBLIN FOUND AND BROUGHT TO JUSTICE AS MUCH AS YOU DO!

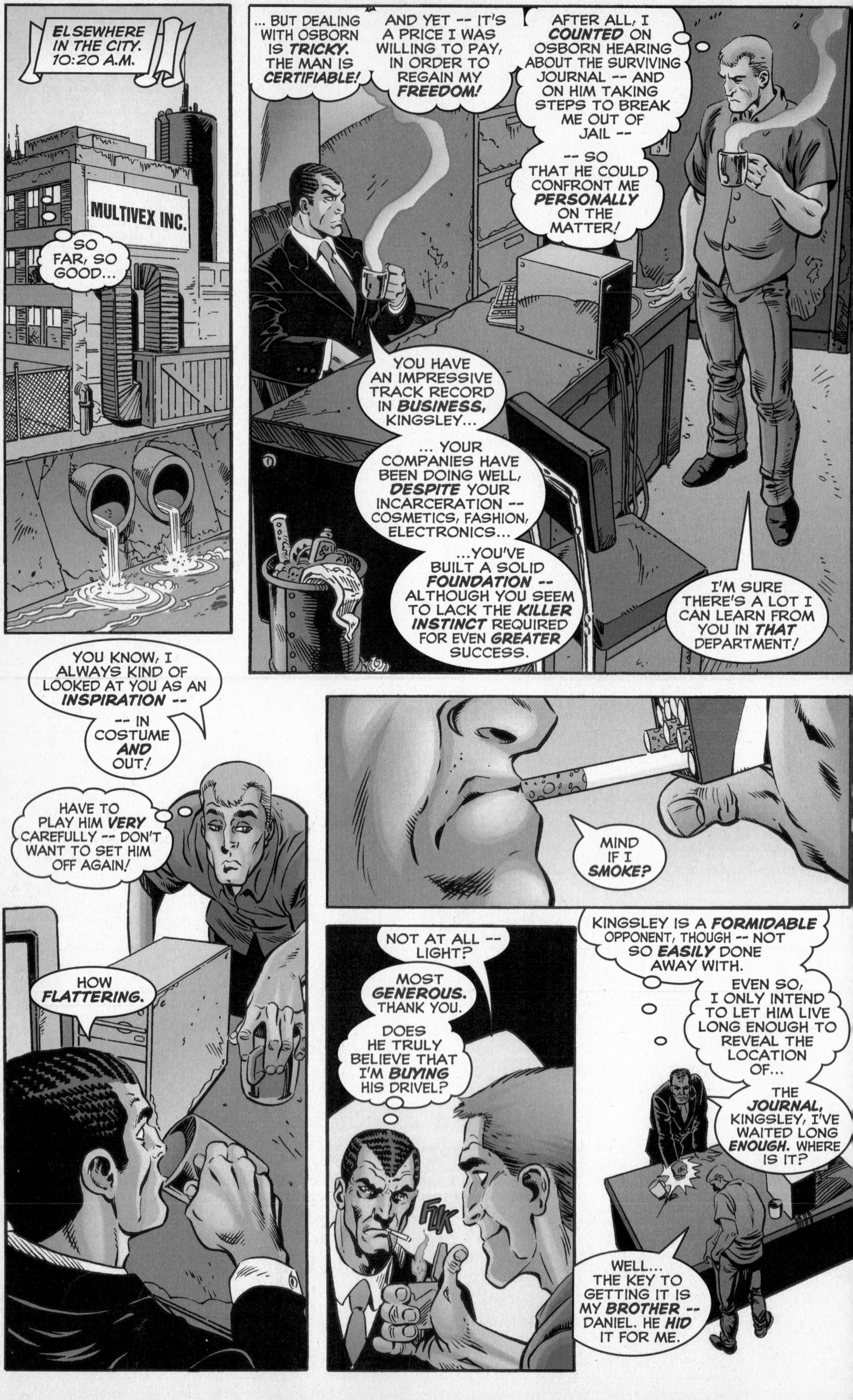
ELSEWHERE IN THE CITY. 10:20 A.M.
MULTIVEX INC.
SO FAR, SO GOOD...
... BUT DEALING WITH OSBORN IS TRICKY. THE MAN IS CERTIFIABLE!
AND YET -- IT'S A PRICE I WAS WILLING TO PAY, IN ORDER TO REGAIN MY FREEDOM!
AFTER ALL, I COUNTED ON OSBORN HEARING ABOUT THE SURVIVING JOURNAL -- AND ON HIM TAKING STEPS TO BREAK ME OUT OF JAIL --
-- SO THAT HE COULD CONFRONT ME PERSONALLY ON THE MATTER!
YOU HAVE AN IMPRESSIVE TRACK RECORD IN BUSINESS, KINGSLEY...
... YOUR COMPANIES HAVE BEEN DOING WELL, DESPITE YOUR INCARCERATION -- COSMETICS, FASHION, ELECTRONICS...
...YOU'VE BUILT A SOLID FOUNDATION -- ALTHOUGH YOU SEEM TO LACK THE KILLER INSTINCT REQUIRED FOR EVEN GREATER SUCCESS.
I'M SURE THERE'S A LOT I CAN LEARN FROM YOU IN THAT DEPARTMENT!
YOU KNOW, I ALWAYS KIND OF LOOKED AT YOU AS AN INSPIRATION --
-- IN COSTUME AND OUT!
HAVE TO PLAY HIM VERY CAREFULLY -- DON'T WANT TO SET HIM OFF AGAIN!
HOW FLATTERING.
MIND IF I SMOKE?
NOT AT ALL -- LIGHT?
MOST GENEROUS. THANK YOU.
DOES HE TRULY BELIEVE THAT I'M BUYING HIS DRIVEL?
FLIK
KINGSLEY IS A FORMIDABLE OPPONENT, THOUGH -- NOT SO EASILY DONE AWAY WITH.
EVEN SO, I ONLY INTEND TO LET HIM LIVE LONG ENOUGH TO REVEAL THE LOCATION OF...
THE JOURNAL, KINGSLEY, I'VE WAITED LONG ENOUGH. WHERE IS IT?
WELL... THE KEY TO GETTING IT IS MY BROTHER -- DANIEL. HE HID IT FOR ME.

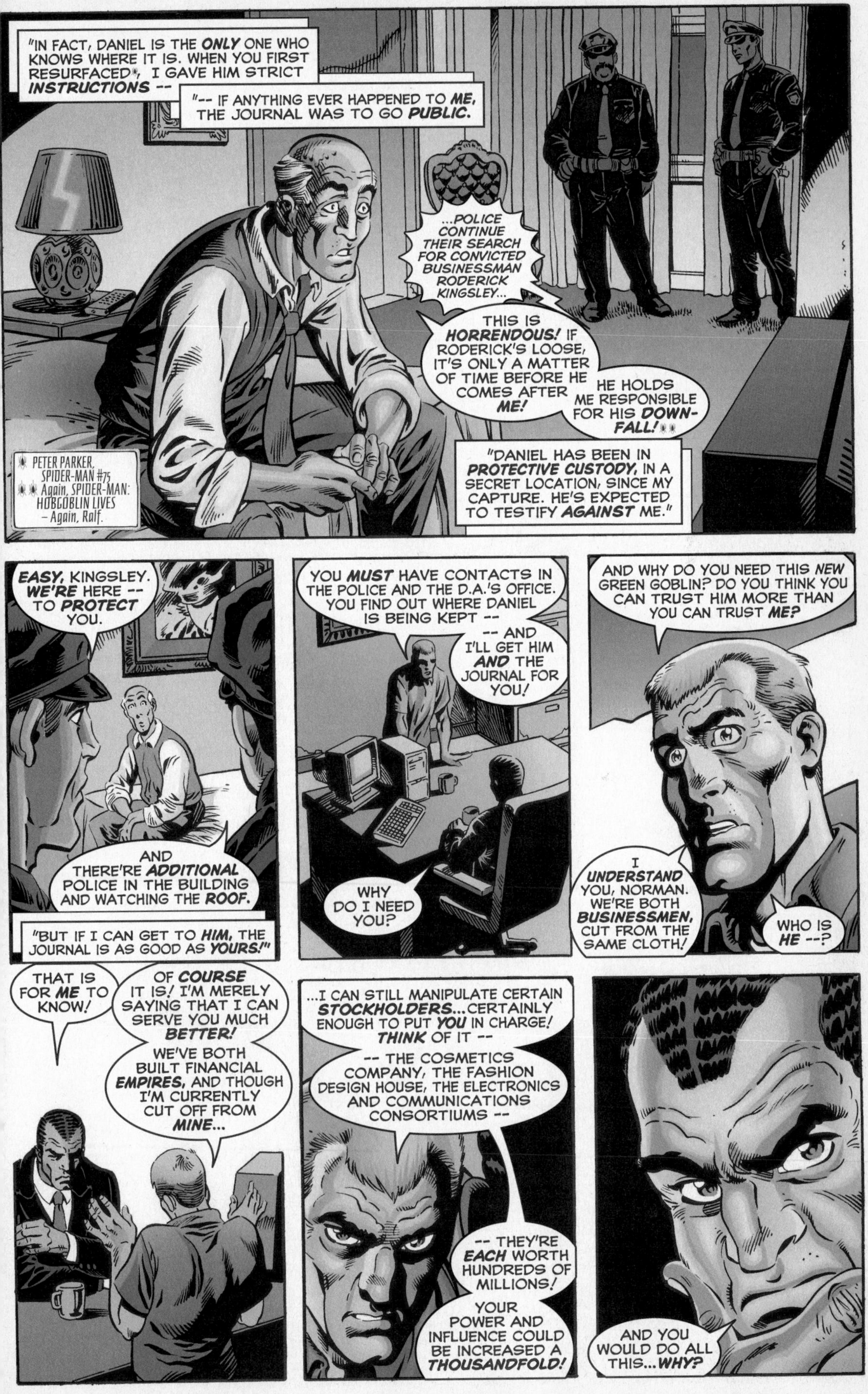
"IN FACT, DANIEL IS THE ONLY ONE WHO KNOWS WHERE IT IS. WHEN YOU FIRST RESURFACED*, I GAVE HIM STRICT INSTRUCTIONS --
"-- IF ANYTHING EVER HAPPENED TO ME, THE JOURNAL WAS TO GO PUBLIC.
...POLICE CONTINUE THEIR SEARCH FOR CONVICTED BUSINESSMAN RODERICK KINGSLEY...
THIS IS HORRENDOUS! IF RODERICK'S LOOSE, IT'S ONLY A MATTER OF TIME BEFORE HE COMES AFTER ME!
HE HOLDS ME RESPONSIBLE FOR HIS DOWNFALL!**
*PETER PARKER, SPIDER-MAN #75
**Again, SPIDER-MAN: HOBGOBLIN LIVES – Again, Ralf.
"DANIEL HAS BEEN IN PROTECTIVE CUSTODY, IN A SECRET LOCATION, SINCE MY CAPTURE. HE'S EXPECTED TO TESTIFY AGAINST ME."
EASY, KINGSLEY. WE'RE HERE -- TO PROTECT YOU.
AND THERE'RE ADDITIONAL POLICE IN THE BUILDING AND WATCHING THE ROOF.
"BUT IF I CAN GET TO HIM, THE JOURNAL IS AS GOOD AS YOURS!"
YOU MUST HAVE CONTACTS IN THE POLICE AND THE D.A.'S OFFICE. YOU FIND OUT WHERE DANIEL IS BEING KEPT --
-- AND I'LL GET HIM AND THE JOURNAL FOR YOU!
WHY DO I NEED YOU?
AND WHY DO YOU NEED THIS NEW GREEN GOBLIN? DO YOU THINK YOU CAN TRUST HIM MORE THAN YOU CAN TRUST ME?
I UNDERSTAND YOU, NORMAN. WE'RE BOTH BUSINESSMEN, CUT FROM THE SAME CLOTH!
WHO IS HE --?
THAT IS FOR ME TO KNOW!
OF COURSE IT IS! I'M MERELY SAYING THAT I CAN SERVE YOU MUCH BETTER!
WE'VE BOTH BUILT FINANCIAL EMPIRES, AND THOUGH I'M CURRENTLY CUT OFF FROM MINE...
...I CAN STILL MANIPULATE CERTAIN STOCKHOLDERS...CERTAINLY ENOUGH TO PUT YOU IN CHARGE! THINK OF IT --
-- THE COSMETICS COMPANY, THE FASHION DESIGN HOUSE, THE ELECTRONICS AND COMMUNICATIONS CONSORTIUMS --
-- THEY'RE EACH WORTH HUNDREDS OF MILLIONS!
YOUR POWER AND INFLUENCE COULD BE INCREASED A THOUSANDFOLD!
AND YOU WOULD DO ALL THIS...WHY?

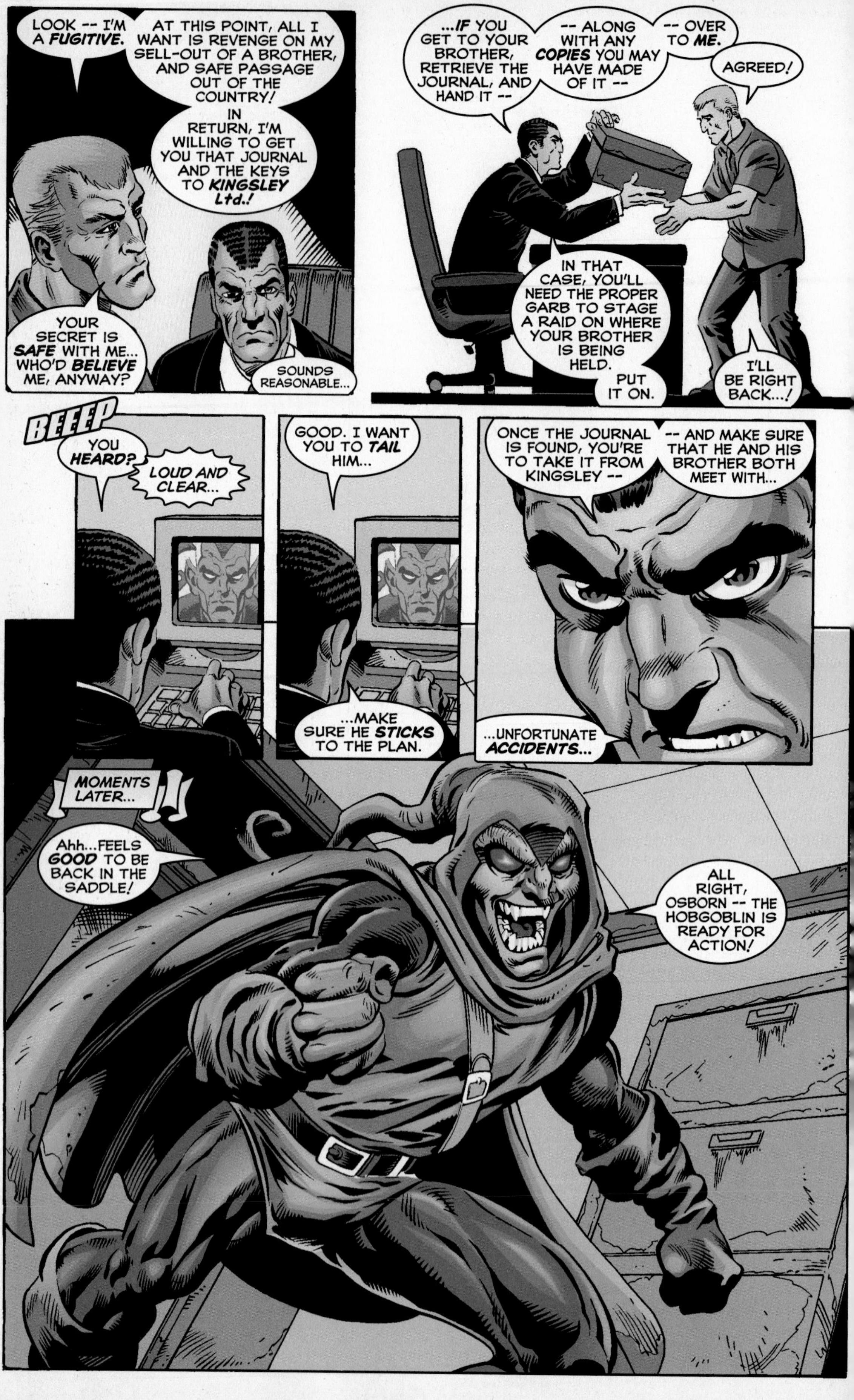

LOOK -- I'M A FUGITIVE.
AT THIS POINT, ALL I WANT IS REVENGE ON MY SELL-OUT OF A BROTHER, AND SAFE PASSAGE OUT OF THE COUNTRY!
IN RETURN, I'M WILLING TO GET YOU THAT JOURNAL AND THE KEYS TO KINGSLEY Ltd.!
YOUR SECRET IS SAFE WITH ME... WHO'D BELIEVE ME, ANYWAY?
SOUNDS REASONABLE...
...IF YOU GET TO YOUR BROTHER, RETRIEVE THE JOURNAL, AND HAND IT --
-- ALONG WITH ANY COPIES YOU MAY HAVE MADE OF IT --
-- OVER TO ME.
AGREED!
IN THAT CASE, YOU'LL NEED THE PROPER GARB TO STAGE A RAID ON WHERE YOUR BROTHER IS BEING HELD.
PUT IT ON.
I'LL BE RIGHT BACK...!
BEEEP
YOU HEARD?
LOUD AND CLEAR...
GOOD. I WANT YOU TO TAIL HIM...
...MAKE SURE HE STICKS TO THE PLAN.
ONCE THE JOURNAL IS FOUND, YOU'RE TO TAKE IT FROM KINGSLEY --
-- AND MAKE SURE THAT HE AND HIS BROTHER BOTH MEET WITH...
...UNFORTUNATE ACCIDENTS...
MOMENTS LATER...
Ahh...FEELS GOOD TO BE BACK IN THE SADDLE!
ALL RIGHT, OSBORN -- THE HOBGOBLIN IS READY FOR ACTION!

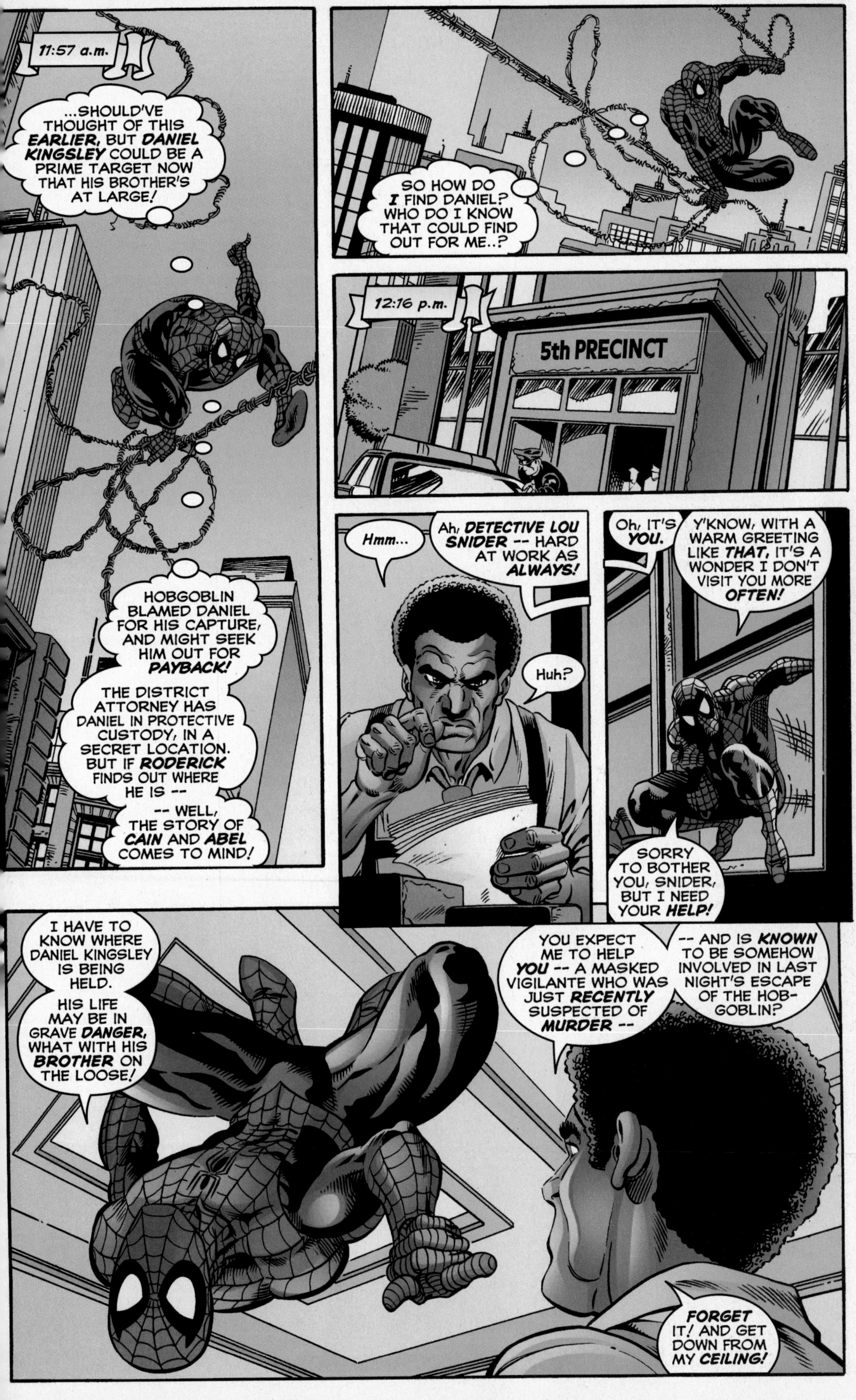
11:57 a.m.
...SHOULD'VE THOUGHT OF THIS EARLIER, BUT DANIEL KINGSLEY COULD BE A PRIME TARGET NOW THAT HIS BROTHER'S AT LARGE!
SO HOW DO I FIND DANIEL? WHO DO I KNOW THAT COULD FIND OUT FOR ME..?
HOBGOBLIN BLAMED DANIEL FOR HIS CAPTURE, AND MIGHT SEEK HIM OUT FOR PAYBACK!
THE DISTRICT ATTORNEY HAS DANIEL IN PROTECTIVE CUSTODY, IN A SECRET LOCATION. BUT IF RODERICK FINDS OUT WHERE HE IS --
-- WELL, THE STORY OF CAIN AND ABEL COMES TO MIND!
12:16 p.m.
5th PRECINCT
Hmm...
Ah, DETECTIVE LOU SNIDER -- HARD AT WORK AS ALWAYS!
Huh?
Oh, IT'S YOU.
Y'KNOW, WITH A WARM GREETING LIKE THAT, IT'S A WONDER I DON'T VISIT YOU MORE OFTEN!
SORRY TO BOTHER YOU, SNIDER, BUT I NEED YOUR HELP!
I HAVE TO KNOW WHERE DANIEL KINGSLEY IS BEING HELD.
HIS LIFE MAY BE IN GRAVE DANGER, WHAT WITH HIS BROTHER ON THE LOOSE!
YOU EXPECT ME TO HELP YOU -- A MASKED VIGILANTE WHO WAS JUST RECENTLY SUSPECTED OF MURDER --
-- AND IS KNOWN TO BE SOMEHOW INVOLVED IN LAST NIGHT'S ESCAPE OF THE HOB-GOBLIN?
FORGET IT! AND GET DOWN FROM MY CEILING!

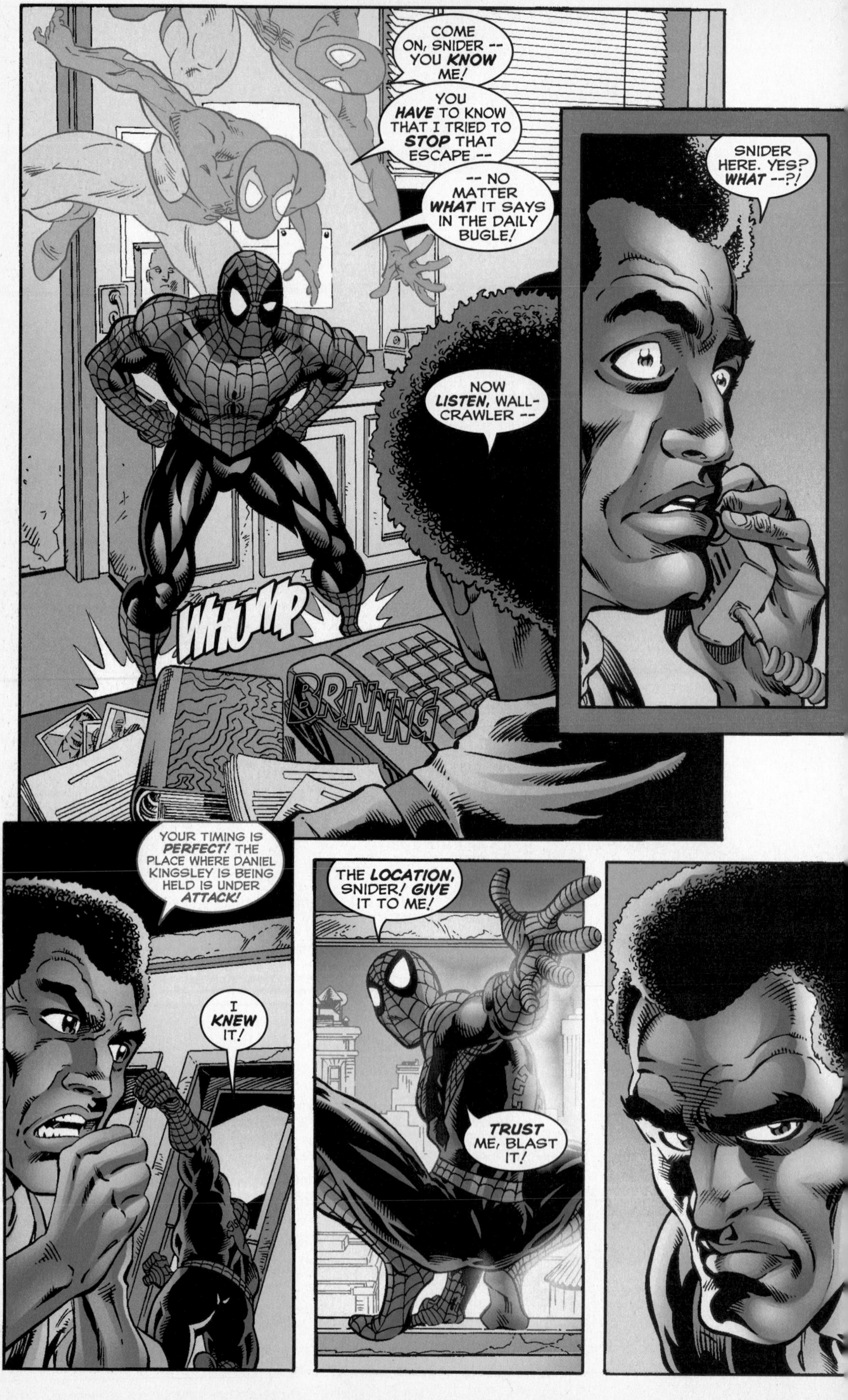
COME ON, SNIDER -- YOU KNOW ME!
YOU HAVE TO KNOW THAT I TRIED TO STOP THAT ESCAPE --
-- NO MATTER WHAT IT SAYS IN THE DAILY BUGLE!
NOW LISTEN, WALL-CRAWLER --
WHUMP
BRINNNG
SNIDER HERE. YES? WHAT --?!
YOUR TIMING IS PERFECT! THE PLACE WHERE DANIEL KINGSLEY IS BEING HELD IS UNDER ATTACK!
I KNEW IT!
THE LOCATION, SNIDER! GIVE IT TO ME!
TRUST ME, BLAST IT!

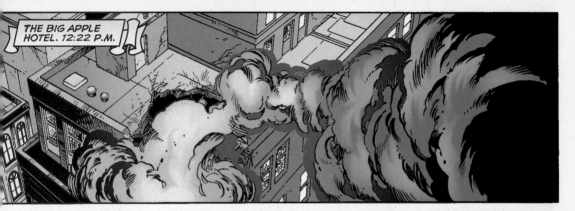

HA HA HA HA

HA HA

... I *KNEW* THIS WOULD HAPPEN! I *KNEW* IT!

I'VE *COME* FOR YOU, *DANIEL!*

BLAM BLAM

GOTTA -- CALL IN -- FOR MORE -- *BACK* UP..!

UNGHN!

AWLP!

PO OO M

AAAAAAH!

GOTTA GET OUT -- GOTTA GET *OUT!*

HUFF! HUFF!

AAACK!

I DON'T *THINK* SO, BROTHER-MINE!

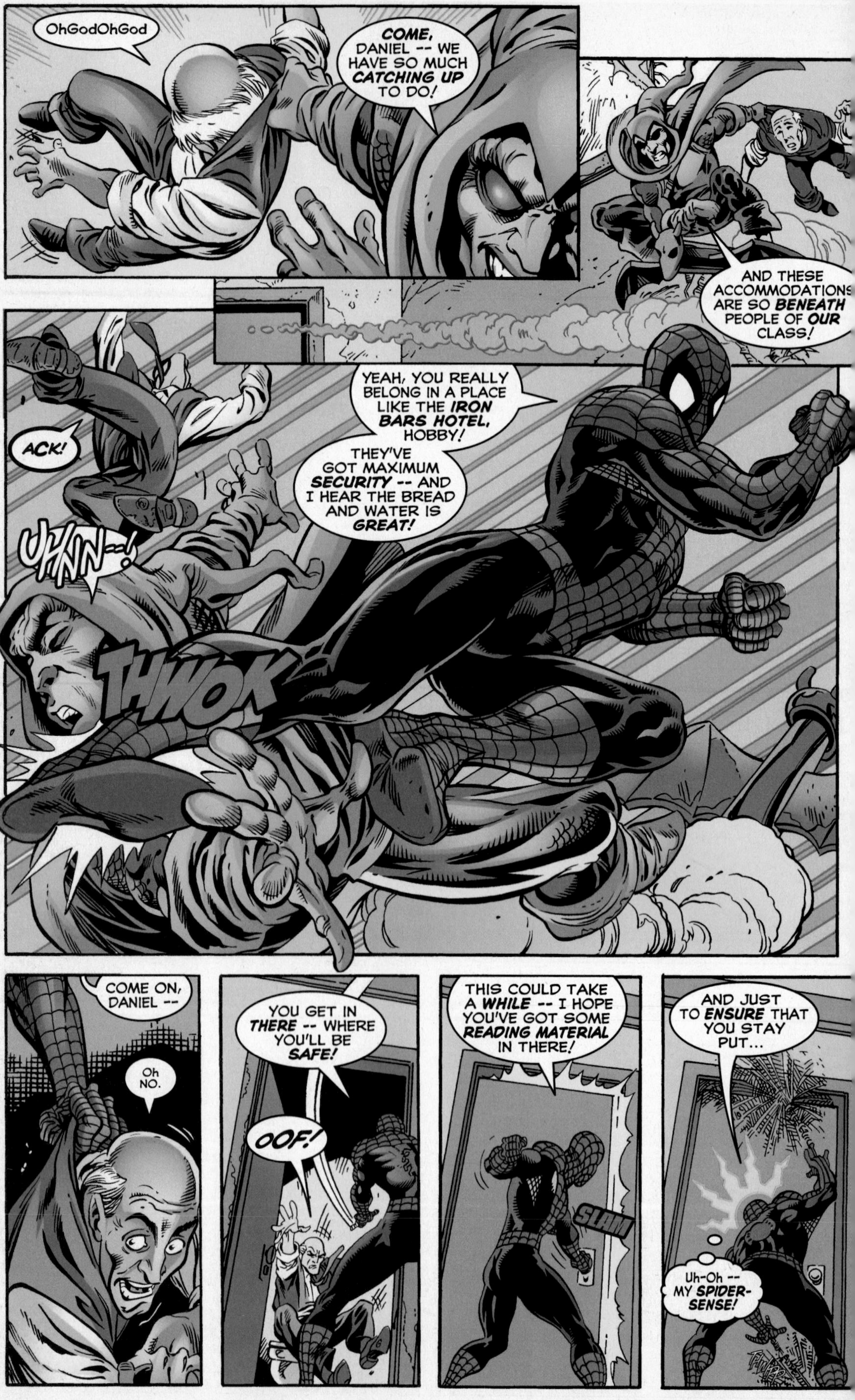
OhGodOhGod
COME, DANIEL -- WE HAVE SO MUCH CATCHING UP TO DO!
AND THESE ACCOMMODATIONS ARE SO BENEATH PEOPLE OF OUR CLASS!
YEAH, YOU REALLY BELONG IN A PLACE LIKE THE IRON BARS HOTEL, HOBBY!
THEY'VE GOT MAXIMUM SECURITY -- AND I HEAR THE BREAD AND WATER IS GREAT!
ACK!
UHNN--!
THWOK
COME ON, DANIEL --
Oh NO.
YOU GET IN THERE -- WHERE YOU'LL BE SAFE!
OOF!
THIS COULD TAKE A WHILE -- I HOPE YOU'VE GOT SOME READING MATERIAL IN THERE!
SLAM
AND JUST TO ENSURE THAT YOU STAY PUT...
Uh-Oh -- MY SPIDER-SENSE!

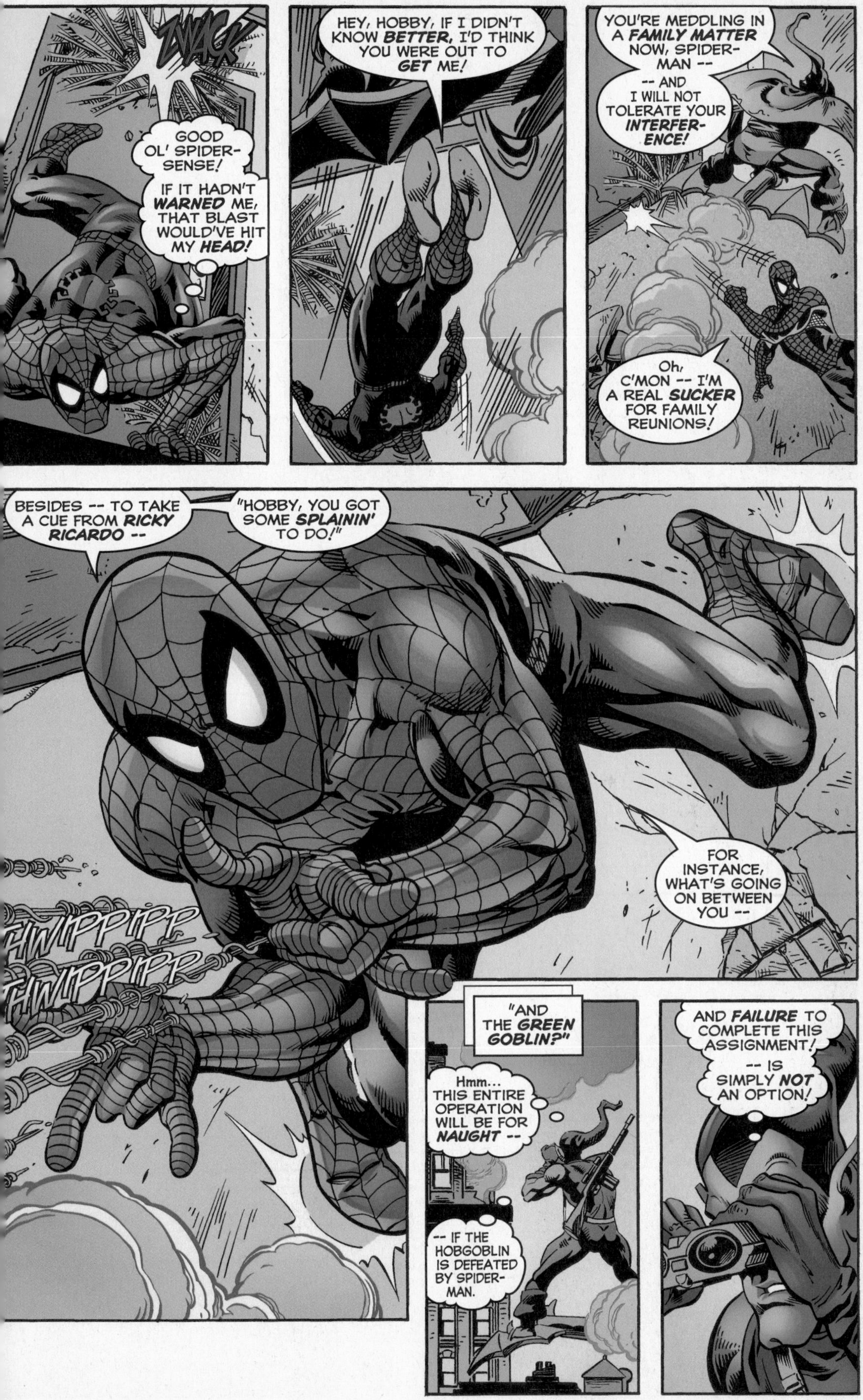

ZWACK
GOOD OL' SPIDER-SENSE!
IF IT HADN'T WARNED ME, THAT BLAST WOULD'VE HIT MY HEAD!
HEY, HOBBY, IF I DIDN'T KNOW BETTER, I'D THINK YOU WERE OUT TO GET ME!
YOU'RE MEDDLING IN A FAMILY MATTER NOW, SPIDER-MAN --
-- AND I WILL NOT TOLERATE YOUR INTERFERENCE!
Oh, C'MON -- I'M A REAL SUCKER FOR FAMILY REUNIONS!
BESIDES -- TO TAKE A CUE FROM RICKY RICARDO --
"HOBBY, YOU GOT SOME SPLAININ' TO DO!"
FOR INSTANCE, WHAT'S GOING ON BETWEEN YOU --
THWIPPIPP
THWIPPIPP
"AND THE GREEN GOBLIN?"
Hmm... THIS ENTIRE OPERATION WILL BE FOR NAUGHT --
-- IF THE HOBGOBLIN IS DEFEATED BY SPIDER-MAN.
AND FAILURE TO COMPLETE THIS ASSIGNMENT!
-- IS SIMPLY NOT AN OPTION!

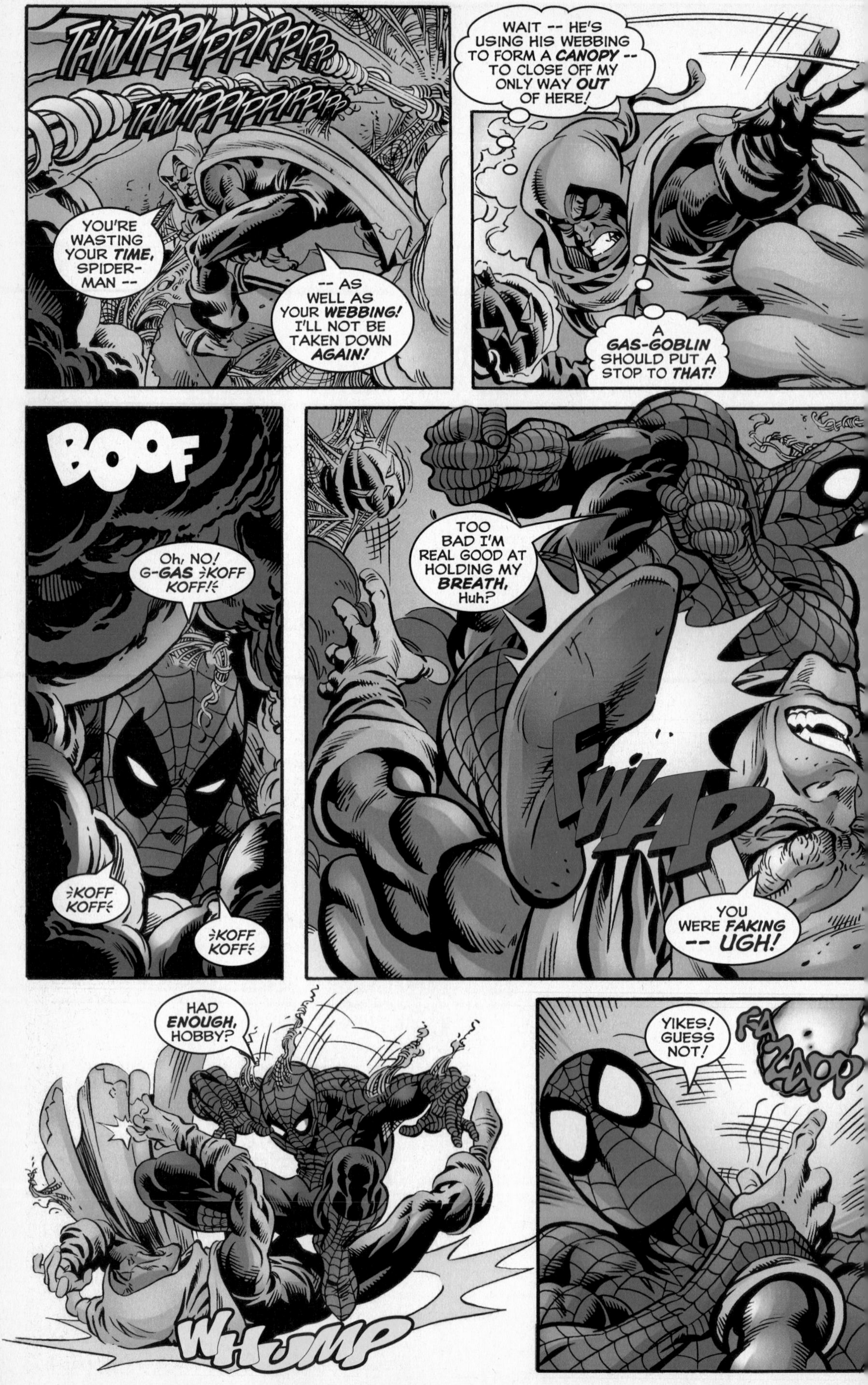
THWIPPPPPPPP
THWIPPPPPPPP
YOU'RE WASTING YOUR TIME, SPIDER-MAN --
-- AS WELL AS YOUR WEBBING! I'LL NOT BE TAKEN DOWN AGAIN!
WAIT -- HE'S USING HIS WEBBING TO FORM A CANOPY -- TO CLOSE OFF MY ONLY WAY OUT OF HERE!
A GAS-GOBLIN SHOULD PUT A STOP TO THAT!
BOOF
Oh, NO! G-GAS KOFF KOFF!
KOFF KOFF
KOFF KOFF
TOO BAD I'M REAL GOOD AT HOLDING MY BREATH, Huh?
FWAP
YOU WERE FAKING -- UGH!
HAD ENOUGH, HOBBY?
WHUMP
YIKES! GUESS NOT!

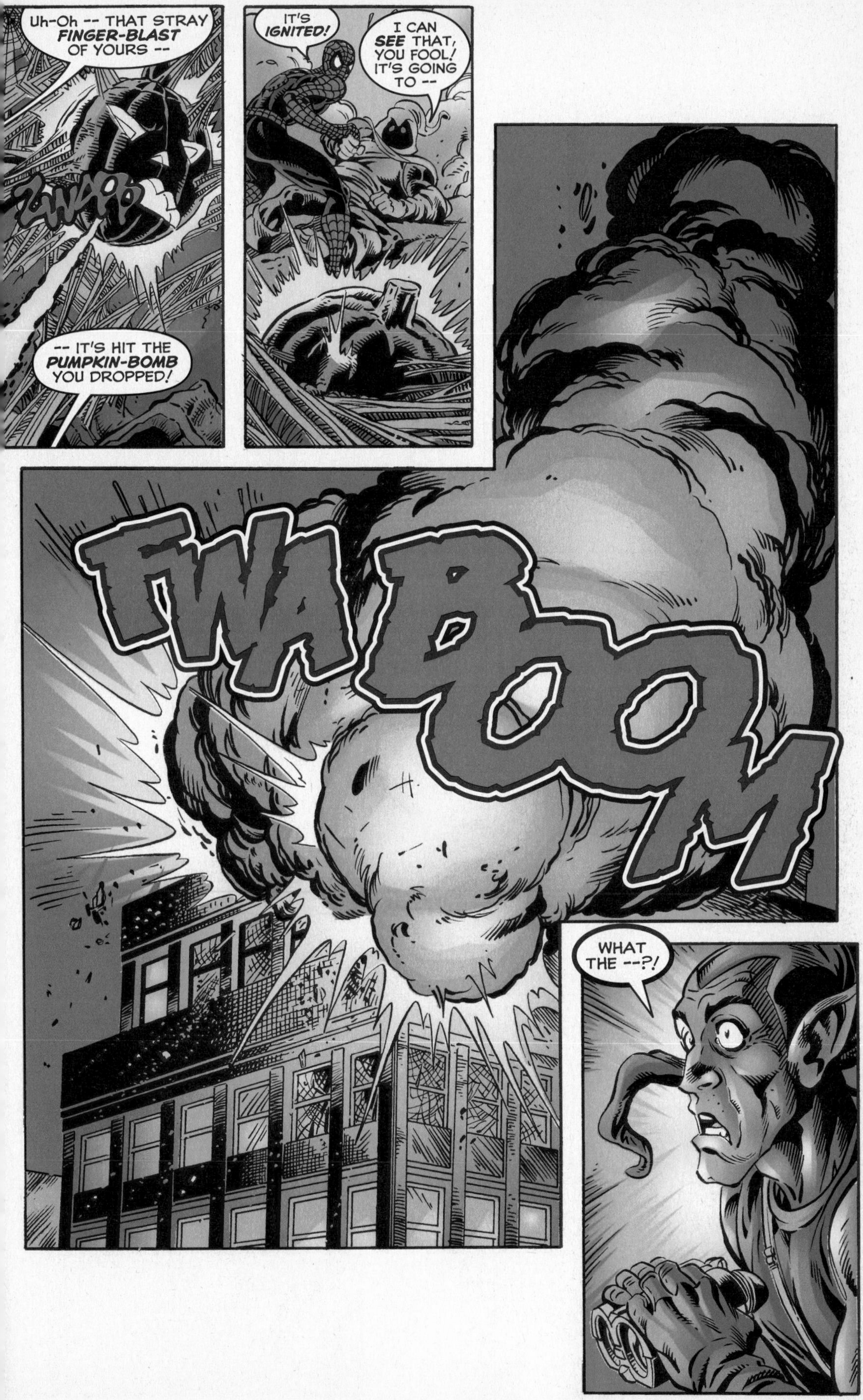
Uh-Oh -- THAT STRAY FINGER-BLAST OF YOURS --
ZWAPP
-- IT'S HIT THE PUMPKIN-BOMB YOU DROPPED!
IT'S IGNITED!
I CAN SEE THAT, YOU FOOL! IT'S GOING TO --
FWABOOM
WHAT THE --?!

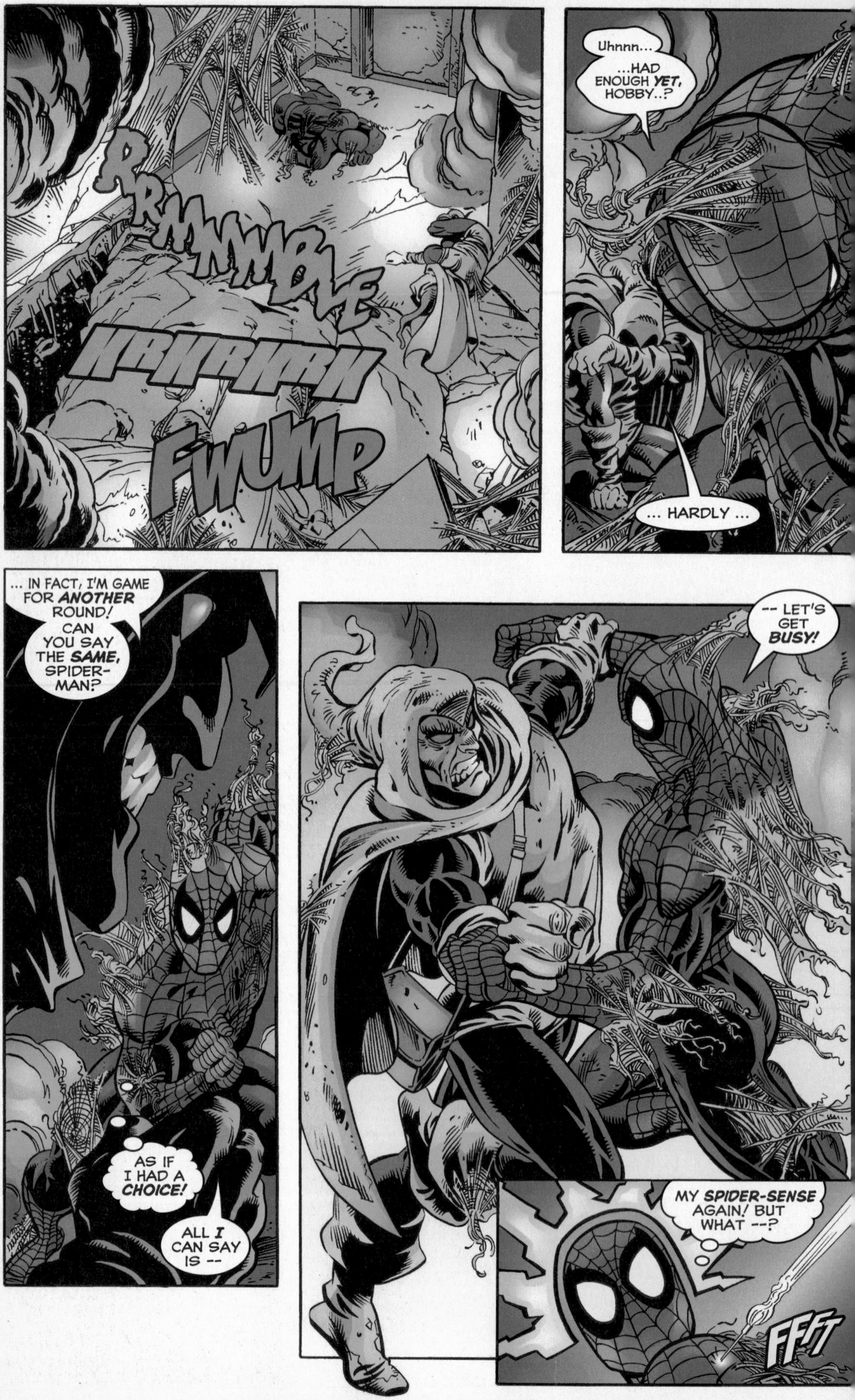
RRMMMBLE
KRKRKRN
FWUMP
Uhhnn...
...HAD ENOUGH YET, HOBBY..?
... HARDLY ...
... IN FACT, I'M GAME FOR ANOTHER ROUND! CAN YOU SAY THE SAME, SPIDER-MAN?
AS IF I HAD A CHOICE!
ALL I CAN SAY IS --
-- LET'S GET BUSY!
MY SPIDER-SENSE AGAIN! BUT WHAT --?
FFFT

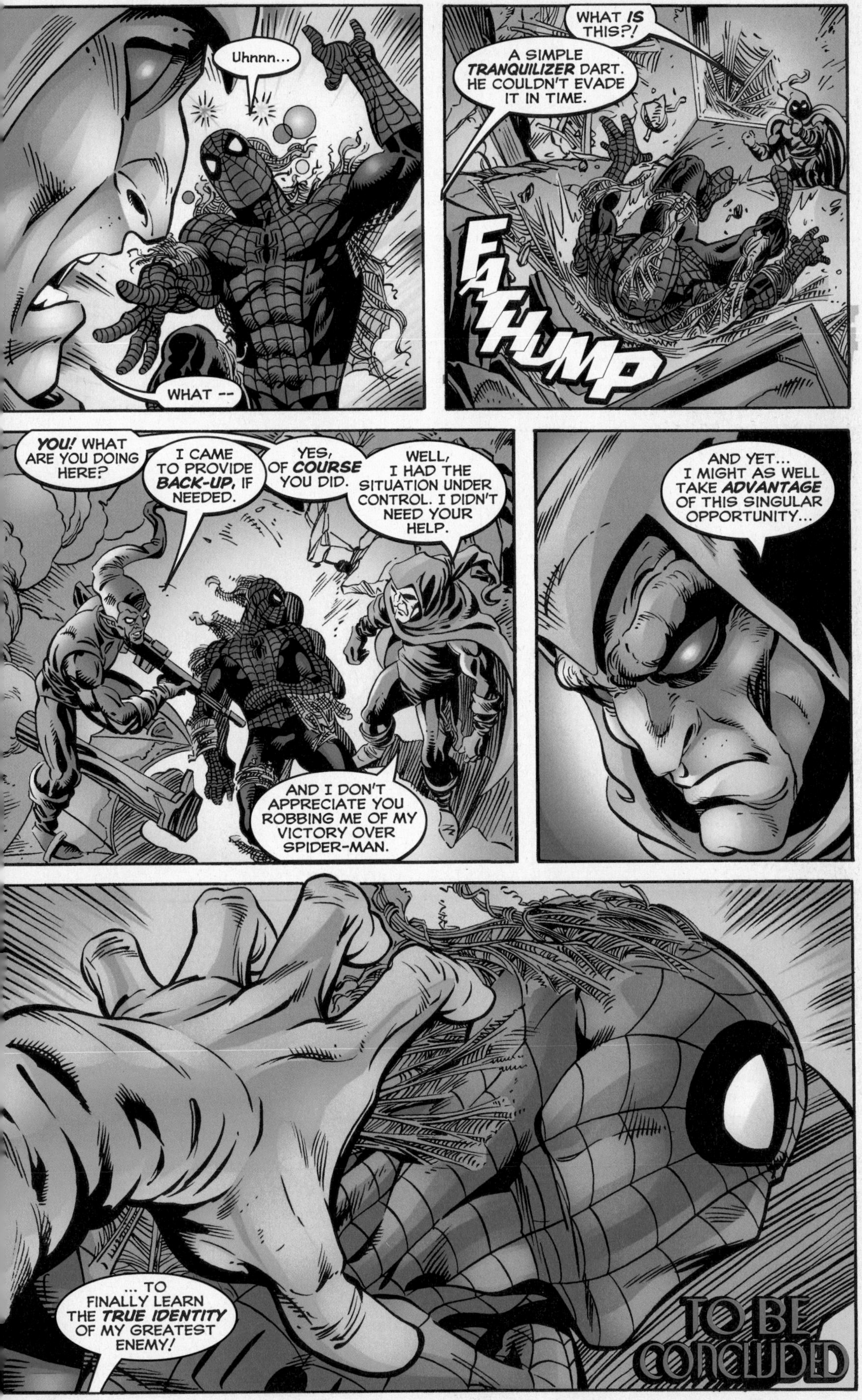
Uhnnn...
WHAT --
WHAT IS THIS?!
A SIMPLE TRANQUILIZER DART. HE COULDN'T EVADE IT IN TIME.
FATHUMP
YOU! WHAT ARE YOU DOING HERE?
I CAME TO PROVIDE BACK-UP, IF NEEDED.
YES, OF COURSE YOU DID.
WELL, I HAD THE SITUATION UNDER CONTROL. I DIDN'T NEED YOUR HELP.
AND I DON'T APPRECIATE YOU ROBBING ME OF MY VICTORY OVER SPIDER-MAN.
AND YET... I MIGHT AS WELL TAKE ADVANTAGE OF THIS SINGULAR OPPORTUNITY...
... TO FINALLY LEARN THE TRUE IDENTITY OF MY GREATEST ENEMY!
TO BE CONCLUDED

MARVEL COMICS
THE SPECTACULAR
SPIDER-MAN
GOBLINS AT THE GATE PART 3
SEPT #261
APPROVED BY THE COMICS CODE AUTHORITY
ROMITA
GREENBERG
ROSS
MILGROM

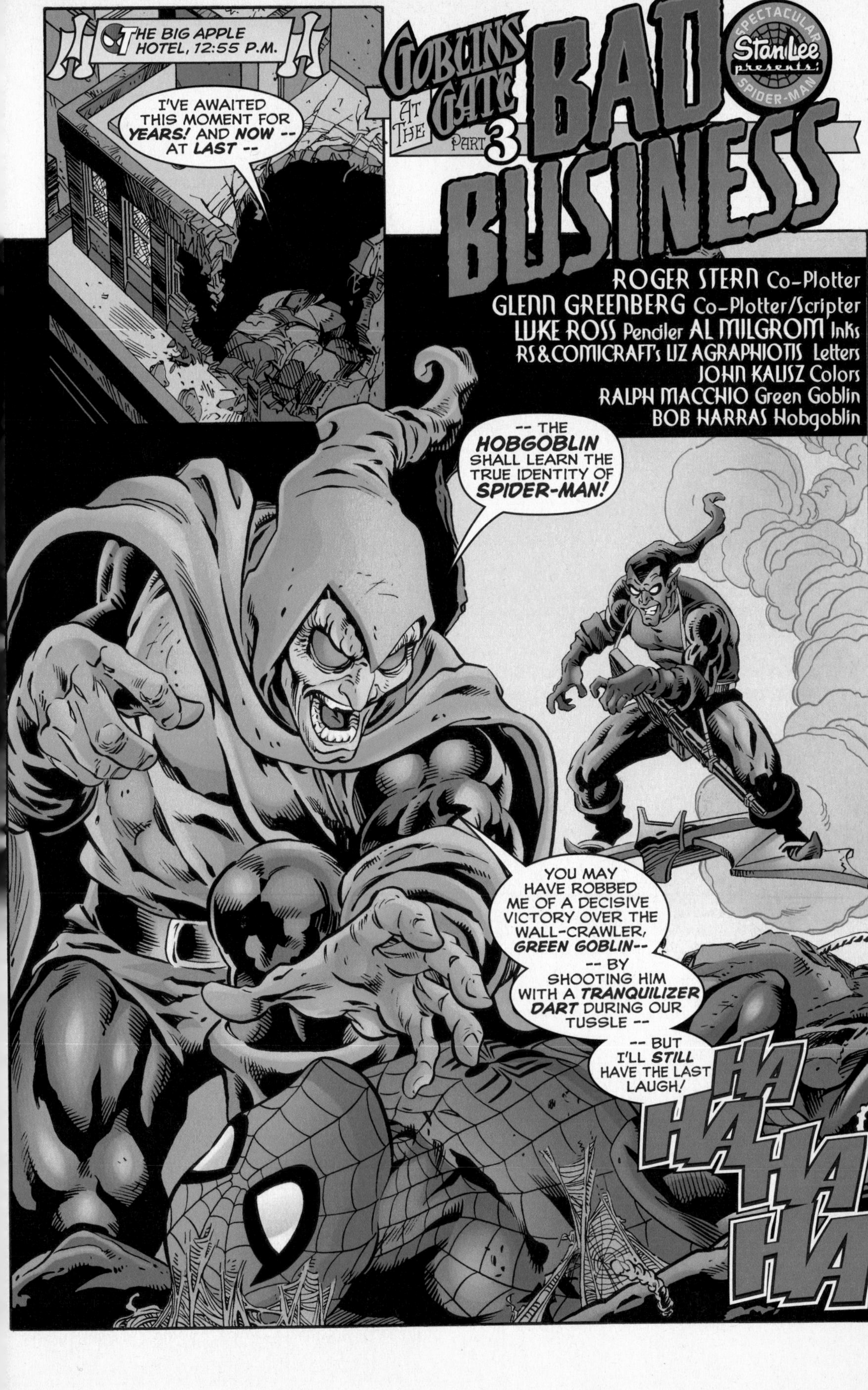
THE BIG APPLE HOTEL, 12:55 P.M.
I'VE AWAITED THIS MOMENT FOR YEARS! AND NOW -- AT LAST --
GOBLINS AT THE GATE PART 3
BAD BUSINESS
SPECTACULAR Stan Lee presents: SPIDER-MAN
ROGER STERN Co-Plotter
GLENN GREENBERG Co-Plotter/Scripter
LUKE ROSS Penciler AL MILGROM Inks
RS&COMICRAFT's LIZ AGRAPHIOTIS Letters
JOHN KALISZ Colors
RALPH MACCHIO Green Goblin
BOB HARRAS Hobgoblin
-- THE HOBGOBLIN SHALL LEARN THE TRUE IDENTITY OF SPIDER-MAN!
YOU MAY HAVE ROBBED ME OF A DECISIVE VICTORY OVER THE WALL-CRAWLER, GREEN GOBLIN--
-- BY SHOOTING HIM WITH A TRANQUILIZER DART DURING OUR TUSSLE --
-- BUT I'LL STILL HAVE THE LAST LAUGH!
HA HA HA HA HA

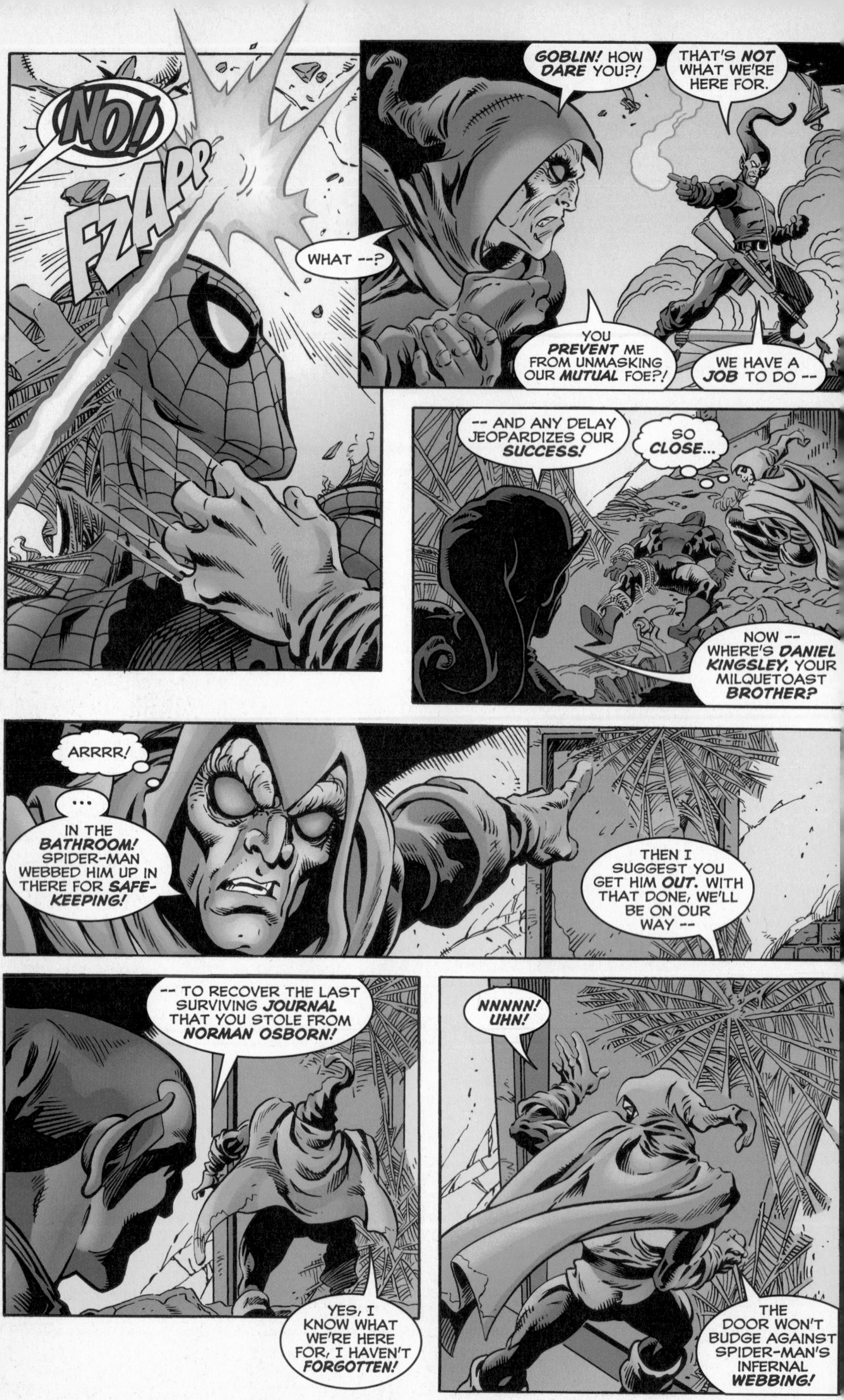
NO!
FZAPP
WHAT --?
GOBLIN! HOW DARE YOU?!
THAT'S NOT WHAT WE'RE HERE FOR.
YOU PREVENT ME FROM UNMASKING OUR MUTUAL FOE?!
WE HAVE A JOB TO DO --
-- AND ANY DELAY JEOPARDIZES OUR SUCCESS!
SO CLOSE...
NOW -- WHERE'S DANIEL KINGSLEY, YOUR MILQUETOAST BROTHER?
ARRRR!
...
IN THE BATHROOM! SPIDER-MAN WEBBED HIM UP IN THERE FOR SAFE-KEEPING!
THEN I SUGGEST YOU GET HIM OUT. WITH THAT DONE, WE'LL BE ON OUR WAY --
-- TO RECOVER THE LAST SURVIVING JOURNAL THAT YOU STOLE FROM NORMAN OSBORN!
YES, I KNOW WHAT WE'RE HERE FOR, I HAVEN'T FORGOTTEN!
NNNNN! UHN!
THE DOOR WON'T BUDGE AGAINST SPIDER-MAN'S INFERNAL WEBBING!

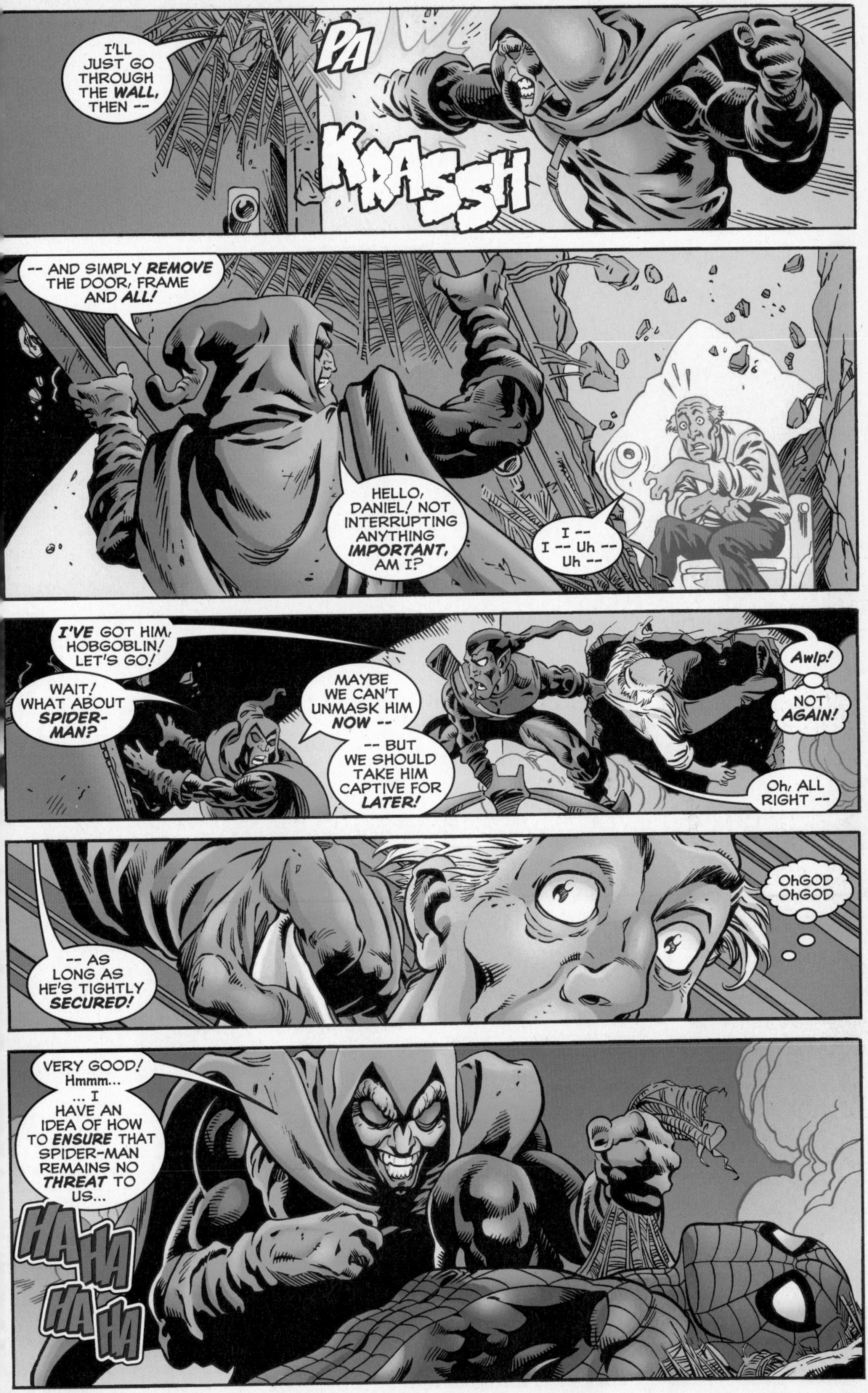
I'LL JUST GO THROUGH THE WALL, THEN --
PA
KRASSH
-- AND SIMPLY REMOVE THE DOOR, FRAME AND ALL!
HELLO, DANIEL! NOT INTERRUPTING ANYTHING IMPORTANT, AM I?
I -- I -- Uh -- Uh --
I'VE GOT HIM, HOBGOBLIN! LET'S GO!
WAIT! WHAT ABOUT SPIDER-MAN?
MAYBE WE CAN'T UNMASK HIM NOW --
-- BUT WE SHOULD TAKE HIM CAPTIVE FOR LATER!
Awlp!
NOT AGAIN!
Oh, ALL RIGHT --
OhGOD OhGOD
-- AS LONG AS HE'S TIGHTLY SECURED!
VERY GOOD! Hmmm... ... I HAVE AN IDEA OF HOW TO ENSURE THAT SPIDER-MAN REMAINS NO THREAT TO US...
HA HA HA HA

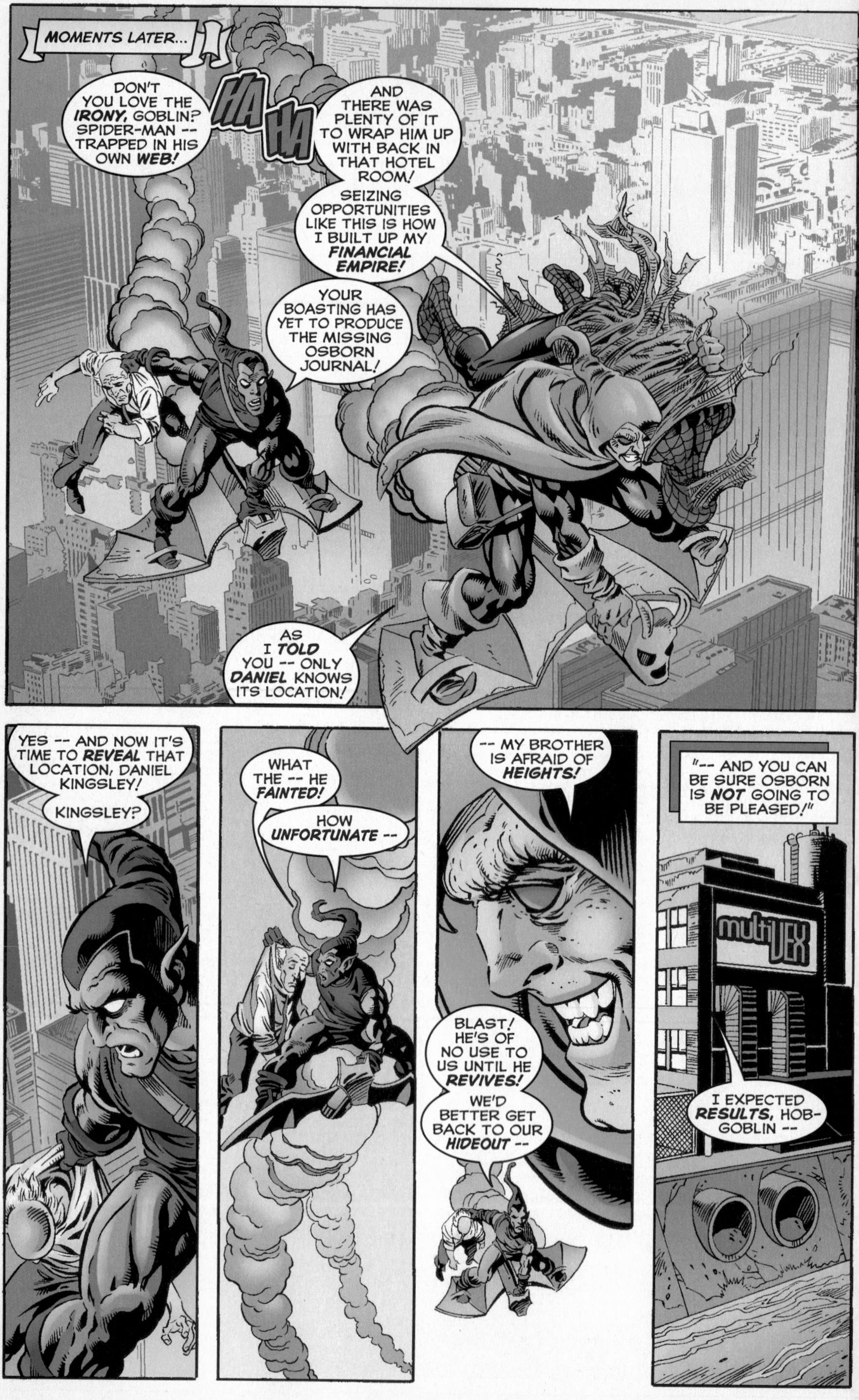
MOMENTS LATER...
DON'T YOU LOVE THE IRONY, GOBLIN? SPIDER-MAN -- TRAPPED IN HIS OWN WEB!
HA HA
AND THERE WAS PLENTY OF IT TO WRAP HIM UP WITH BACK IN THAT HOTEL ROOM!
SEIZING OPPORTUNITIES LIKE THIS IS HOW I BUILT UP MY FINANCIAL EMPIRE!
YOUR BOASTING HAS YET TO PRODUCE THE MISSING OSBORN JOURNAL!
AS I TOLD YOU -- ONLY DANIEL KNOWS ITS LOCATION!
YES -- AND NOW IT'S TIME TO REVEAL THAT LOCATION, DANIEL KINGSLEY!
KINGSLEY?
WHAT THE -- HE FAINTED!
HOW UNFORTUNATE --
-- MY BROTHER IS AFRAID OF HEIGHTS!
BLAST! HE'S OF NO USE TO US UNTIL HE REVIVES!
WE'D BETTER GET BACK TO OUR HIDEOUT --
"-- AND YOU CAN BE SURE OSBORN IS NOT GOING TO BE PLEASED!"
multiVEX
I EXPECTED RESULTS, HOB-GOBLIN --

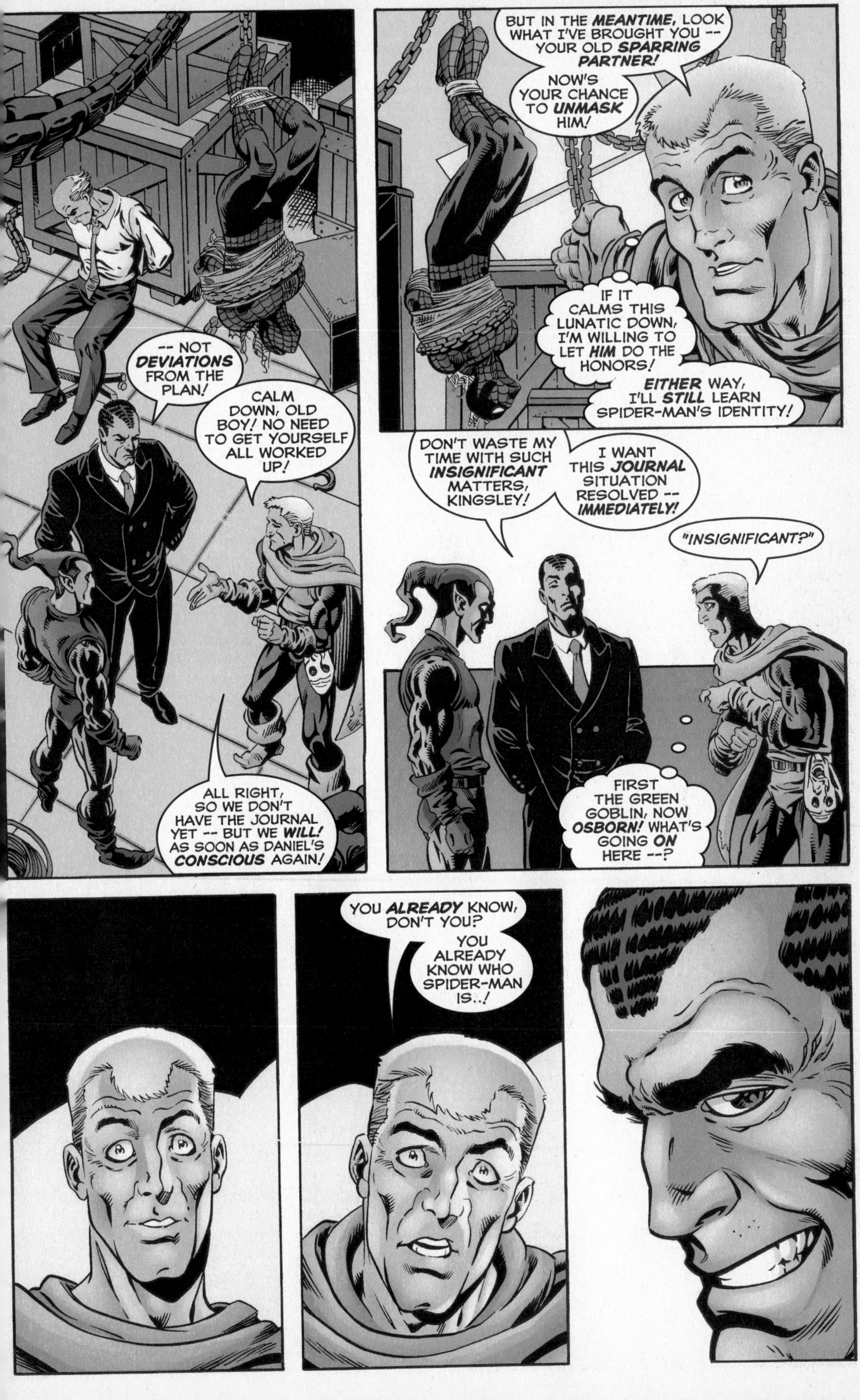
-- NOT DEVIATIONS FROM THE PLAN!
CALM DOWN, OLD BOY! NO NEED TO GET YOURSELF ALL WORKED UP!
ALL RIGHT, SO WE DON'T HAVE THE JOURNAL YET -- BUT WE WILL! AS SOON AS DANIEL'S CONSCIOUS AGAIN!
BUT IN THE MEANTIME, LOOK WHAT I'VE BROUGHT YOU -- YOUR OLD SPARRING PARTNER!
NOW'S YOUR CHANCE TO UNMASK HIM!
IF IT CALMS THIS LUNATIC DOWN, I'M WILLING TO LET HIM DO THE HONORS!
EITHER WAY, I'LL STILL LEARN SPIDER-MAN'S IDENTITY!
DON'T WASTE MY TIME WITH SUCH INSIGNIFICANT MATTERS, KINGSLEY!
I WANT THIS JOURNAL SITUATION RESOLVED -- IMMEDIATELY!
"INSIGNIFICANT?"
FIRST THE GREEN GOBLIN, NOW OSBORN! WHAT'S GOING ON HERE --?
YOU ALREADY KNOW, DON'T YOU?
YOU ALREADY KNOW WHO SPIDER-MAN IS..!

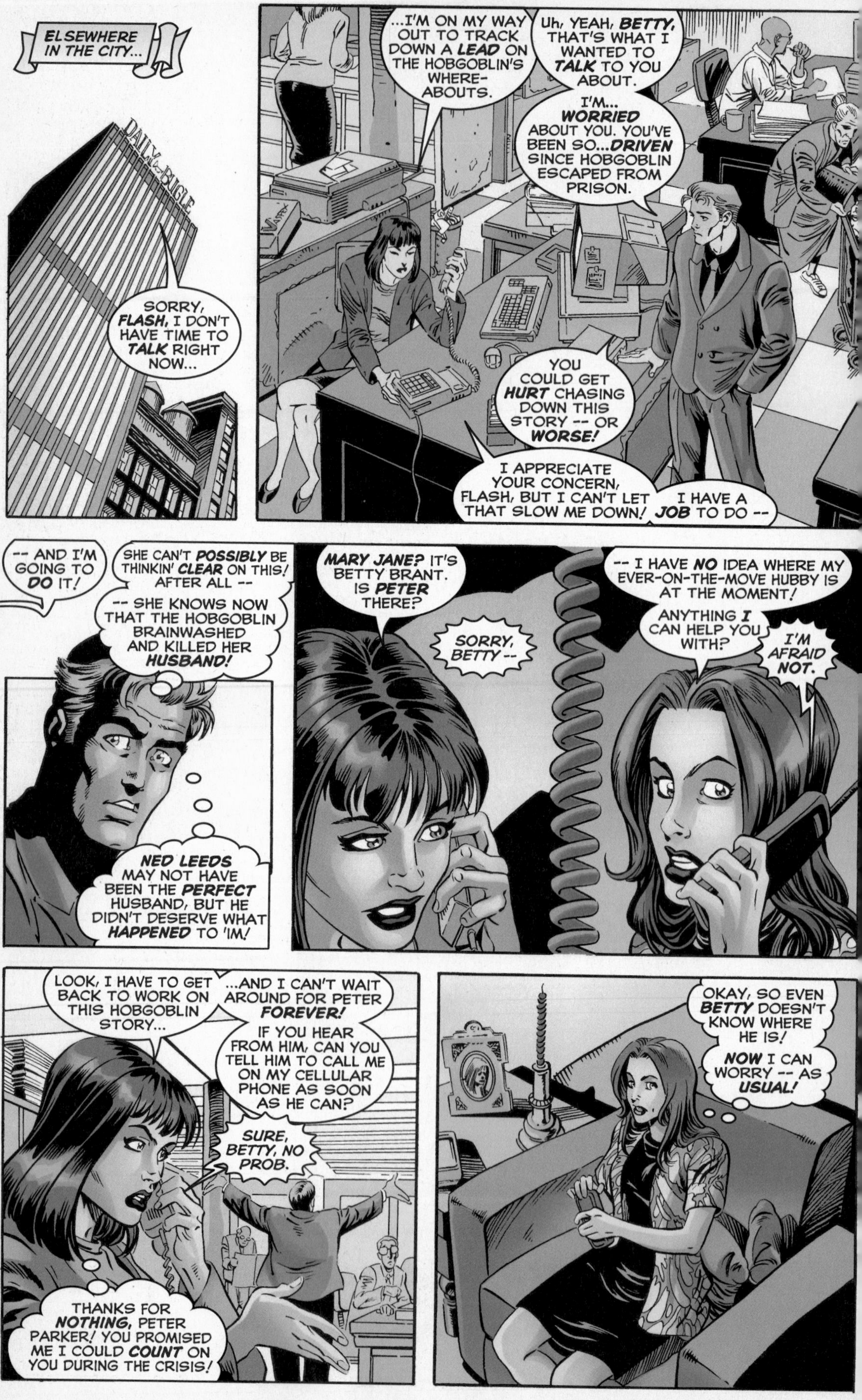
ELSEWHERE IN THE CITY...
DAILY BUGLE
SORRY, FLASH, I DON'T HAVE TIME TO TALK RIGHT NOW...
...I'M ON MY WAY OUT TO TRACK DOWN A LEAD ON THE HOBGOBLIN'S WHERE-ABOUTS.
Uh, YEAH, BETTY, THAT'S WHAT I WANTED TO TALK TO YOU ABOUT.
I'M... WORRIED ABOUT YOU. YOU'VE BEEN SO...DRIVEN SINCE HOBGOBLIN ESCAPED FROM PRISON.
YOU COULD GET HURT CHASING DOWN THIS STORY -- OR WORSE!
I APPRECIATE YOUR CONCERN, FLASH, BUT I CAN'T LET THAT SLOW ME DOWN!
I HAVE A JOB TO DO --
-- AND I'M GOING TO DO IT!
SHE CAN'T POSSIBLY BE THINKIN' CLEAR ON THIS! AFTER ALL --
-- SHE KNOWS NOW THAT THE HOBGOBLIN BRAINWASHED AND KILLED HER HUSBAND!
NED LEEDS MAY NOT HAVE BEEN THE PERFECT HUSBAND, BUT HE DIDN'T DESERVE WHAT HAPPENED TO 'IM!
MARY JANE? IT'S BETTY BRANT. IS PETER THERE?
SORRY, BETTY --
-- I HAVE NO IDEA WHERE MY EVER-ON-THE-MOVE HUBBY IS AT THE MOMENT!
ANYTHING I CAN HELP YOU WITH?
I'M AFRAID NOT.
LOOK, I HAVE TO GET BACK TO WORK ON THIS HOBGOBLIN STORY...
...AND I CAN'T WAIT AROUND FOR PETER FOREVER!
IF YOU HEAR FROM HIM, CAN YOU TELL HIM TO CALL ME ON MY CELLULAR PHONE AS SOON AS HE CAN?
SURE, BETTY, NO PROB.
THANKS FOR NOTHING, PETER PARKER! YOU PROMISED ME I COULD COUNT ON YOU DURING THE CRISIS!
OKAY, SO EVEN BETTY DOESN'T KNOW WHERE HE IS!
NOW I CAN WORRY -- AS USUAL!

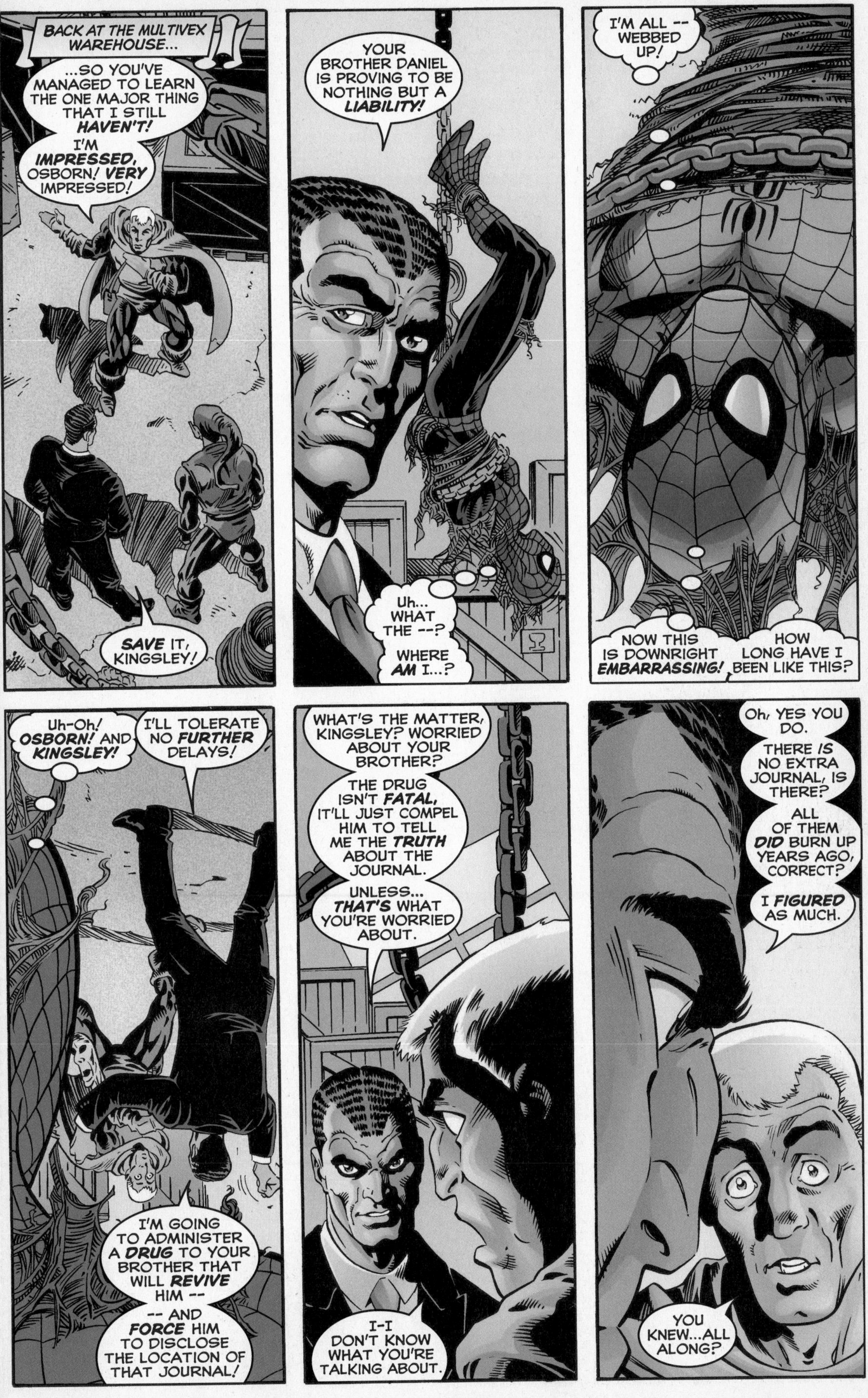
BACK AT THE MULTIVEX WAREHOUSE...
...SO YOU'VE MANAGED TO LEARN THE ONE MAJOR THING THAT I STILL HAVEN'T!
I'M IMPRESSED, OSBORN! VERY IMPRESSED!
SAVE IT, KINGSLEY!
YOUR BROTHER DANIEL IS PROVING TO BE NOTHING BUT A LIABILITY!
Uh... WHAT THE --?
WHERE AM I...?
I'M ALL -- WEBBED UP!
NOW THIS IS DOWNRIGHT EMBARRASSING!
HOW LONG HAVE I BEEN LIKE THIS?
Uh-Oh! OSBORN! AND KINGSLEY!
I'LL TOLERATE NO FURTHER DELAYS!
I'M GOING TO ADMINISTER A DRUG TO YOUR BROTHER THAT WILL REVIVE HIM --
-- AND FORCE HIM TO DISCLOSE THE LOCATION OF THAT JOURNAL!
WHAT'S THE MATTER, KINGSLEY? WORRIED ABOUT YOUR BROTHER?
THE DRUG ISN'T FATAL, IT'LL JUST COMPEL HIM TO TELL ME THE TRUTH ABOUT THE JOURNAL.
UNLESS... THAT'S WHAT YOU'RE WORRIED ABOUT.
I-I DON'T KNOW WHAT YOU'RE TALKING ABOUT.
Oh, YES YOU DO.
THERE IS NO EXTRA JOURNAL, IS THERE?
ALL OF THEM DID BURN UP YEARS AGO, CORRECT?
I FIGURED AS MUCH.
YOU KNEW...ALL ALONG?

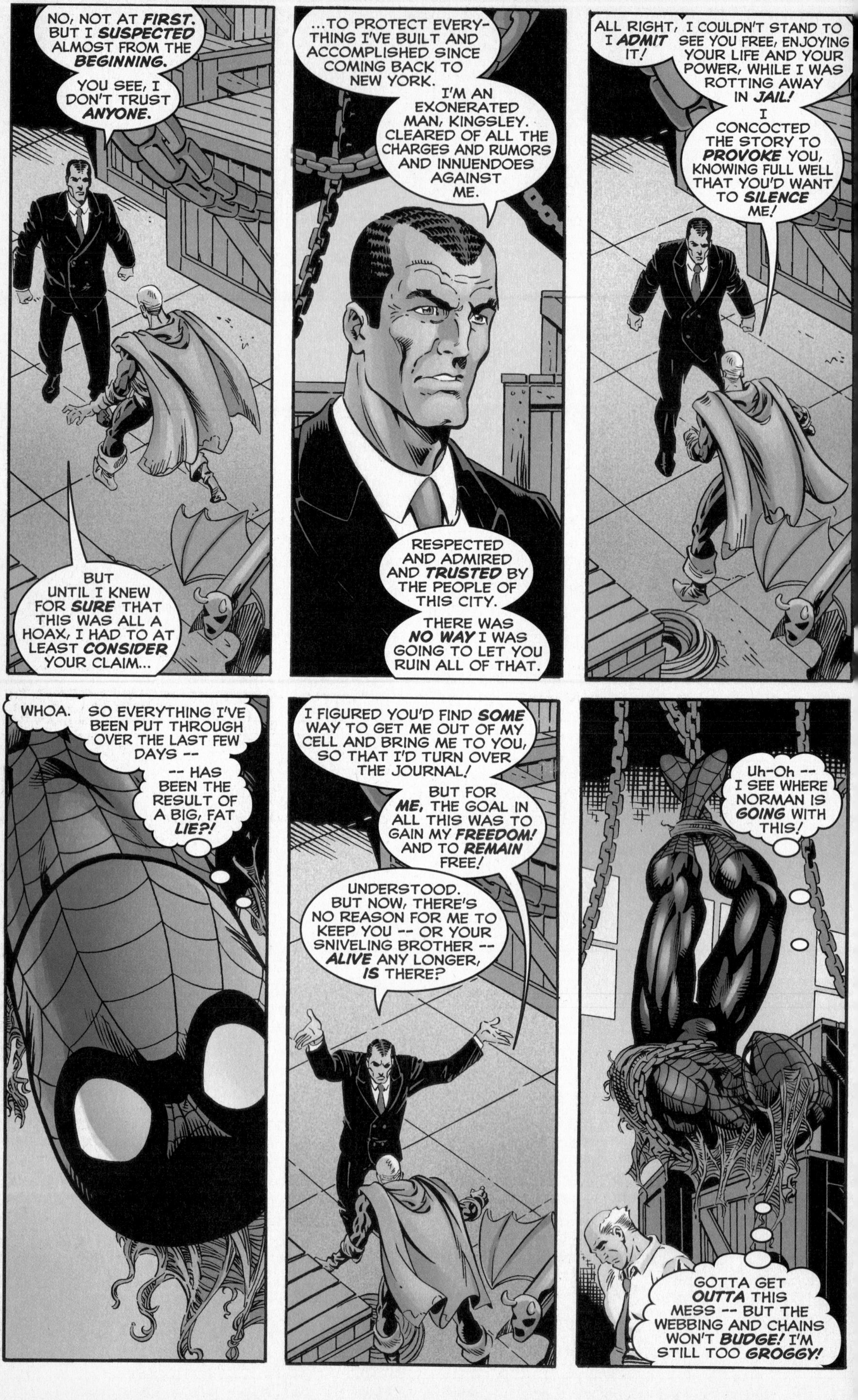
NO, NOT AT FIRST. BUT I SUSPECTED ALMOST FROM THE BEGINNING.
YOU SEE, I DON'T TRUST ANYONE.
BUT UNTIL I KNEW FOR SURE THAT THIS WAS ALL A HOAX, I HAD TO AT LEAST CONSIDER YOUR CLAIM...
...TO PROTECT EVERYTHING I'VE BUILT AND ACCOMPLISHED SINCE COMING BACK TO NEW YORK.
I'M AN EXONERATED MAN, KINGSLEY. CLEARED OF ALL THE CHARGES AND RUMORS AND INNUENDOES AGAINST ME.
RESPECTED AND ADMIRED AND TRUSTED BY THE PEOPLE OF THIS CITY.
THERE WAS NO WAY I WAS GOING TO LET YOU RUIN ALL OF THAT.
ALL RIGHT, I ADMIT IT!
I COULDN'T STAND TO SEE YOU FREE, ENJOYING YOUR LIFE AND YOUR POWER, WHILE I WAS ROTTING AWAY IN JAIL!
I CONCOCTED THE STORY TO PROVOKE YOU, KNOWING FULL WELL THAT YOU'D WANT TO SILENCE ME!
WHOA.
SO EVERYTHING I'VE BEEN PUT THROUGH OVER THE LAST FEW DAYS --
-- HAS BEEN THE RESULT OF A BIG, FAT LIE?!
I FIGURED YOU'D FIND SOME WAY TO GET ME OUT OF MY CELL AND BRING ME TO YOU, SO THAT I'D TURN OVER THE JOURNAL!
BUT FOR ME, THE GOAL IN ALL THIS WAS TO GAIN MY FREEDOM! AND TO REMAIN FREE!
UNDERSTOOD. BUT NOW, THERE'S NO REASON FOR ME TO KEEP YOU -- OR YOUR SNIVELING BROTHER -- ALIVE ANY LONGER, IS THERE?
Uh-Oh -- I SEE WHERE NORMAN IS GOING WITH THIS!
GOTTA GET OUTTA THIS MESS -- BUT THE WEBBING AND CHAINS WON'T BUDGE! I'M STILL TOO GROGGY!

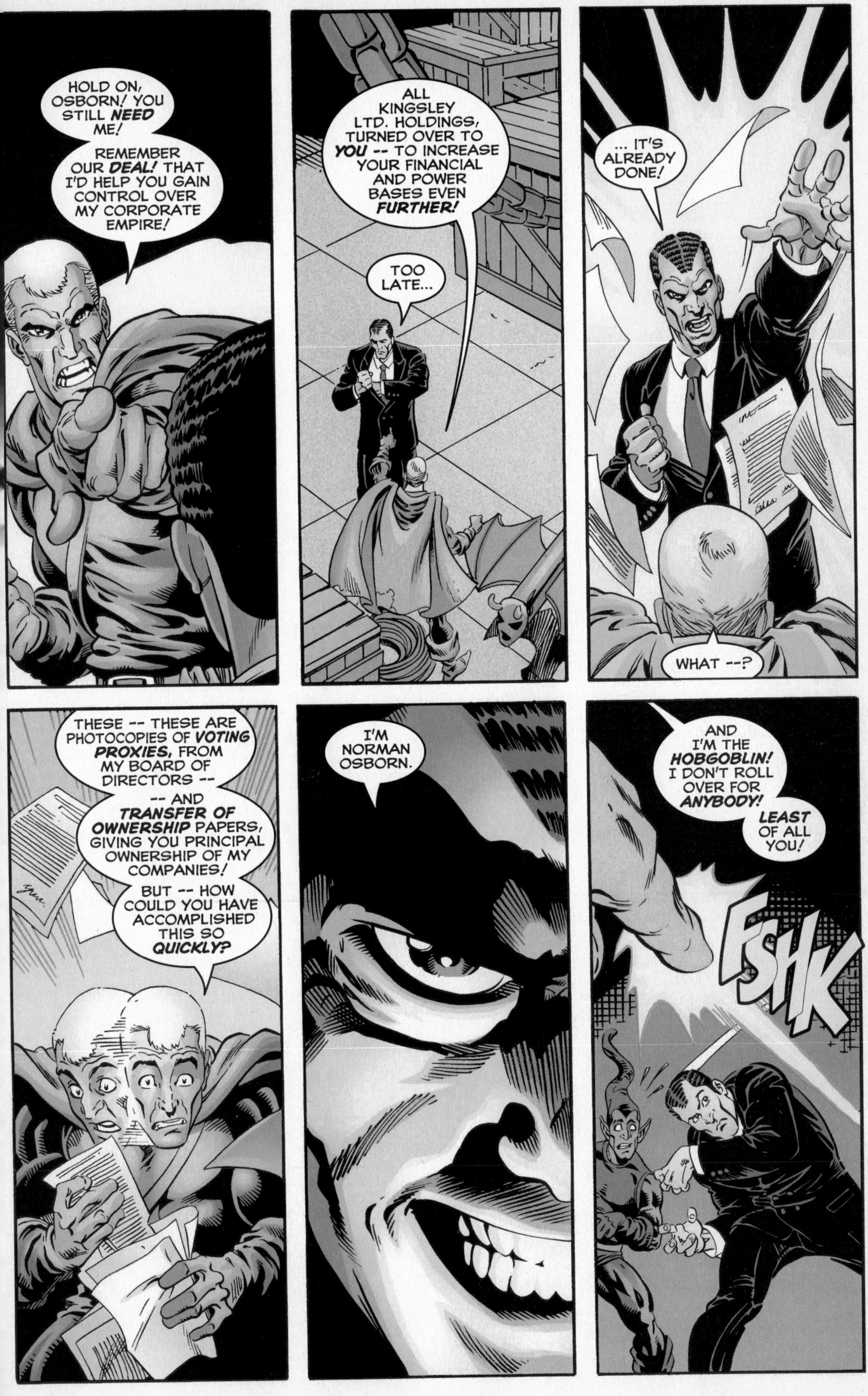
HOLD ON, OSBORN! YOU STILL NEED ME!
REMEMBER OUR DEAL! THAT I'D HELP YOU GAIN CONTROL OVER MY CORPORATE EMPIRE!
ALL KINGSLEY LTD. HOLDINGS, TURNED OVER TO YOU -- TO INCREASE YOUR FINANCIAL AND POWER BASES EVEN FURTHER!
TOO LATE...
... IT'S ALREADY DONE!
WHAT --?
THESE -- THESE ARE PHOTOCOPIES OF VOTING PROXIES, FROM MY BOARD OF DIRECTORS --
-- AND TRANSFER OF OWNERSHIP PAPERS, GIVING YOU PRINCIPAL OWNERSHIP OF MY COMPANIES!
BUT -- HOW COULD YOU HAVE ACCOMPLISHED THIS SO QUICKLY?
I'M NORMAN OSBORN.
AND I'M THE HOBGOBLIN! I DON'T ROLL OVER FOR ANYBODY!
LEAST OF ALL YOU!
FSHK

YOU'RE *FINISHED,* KINGSLEY!

THIS IS GOING TO BE A *PLEASURE!*

FZAPP

NO!

BUT --!

GET *BACK!* HE'S *MINE!*

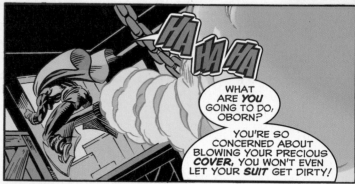

HA HA HA

WHAT ARE *YOU* GOING TO DO, OBORN?

YOU'RE SO CONCERNED ABOUT BLOWING YOUR PRECIOUS *COVER,* YOU WON'T EVEN LET YOUR *SUIT* GET DIRTY!

IN *YOUR CASE,* KINGSLEY, I'M WILLING TO MAKE AN *EXCEPTION!*

Huh?

YOU'RE DRAGGING US BOTH *DOWN!*

UNGHN! NNHNN!

THINGS ARE FALLING APART ALL *AROUND* ME!

GOTTA -- GET -- *OUTTA* -- THIS!

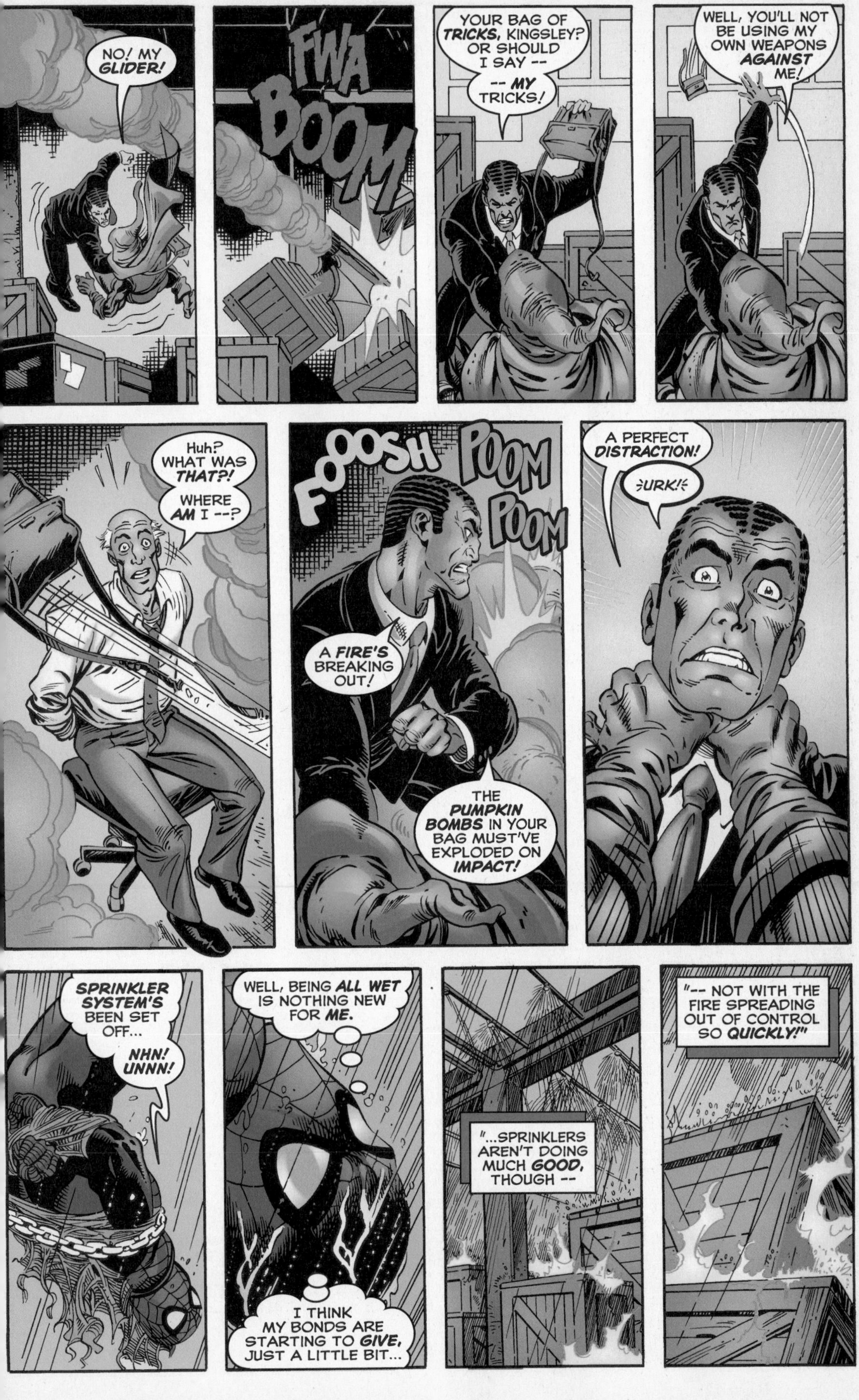
NO! MY GLIDER!
FWA BOOM
YOUR BAG OF TRICKS, KINGSLEY? OR SHOULD I SAY --
-- MY TRICKS!
WELL, YOU'LL NOT BE USING MY OWN WEAPONS AGAINST ME!
Huh? WHAT WAS THAT?!
WHERE AM I --?
FOOOSH POOM POOM
A FIRE'S BREAKING OUT!
THE PUMPKIN BOMBS IN YOUR BAG MUST'VE EXPLODED ON IMPACT!
A PERFECT DISTRACTION!
URK!
SPRINKLER SYSTEM'S BEEN SET OFF...
NHN! UNNN!
WELL, BEING ALL WET IS NOTHING NEW FOR ME.
I THINK MY BONDS ARE STARTING TO GIVE, JUST A LITTLE BIT...
"...SPRINKLERS AREN'T DOING MUCH GOOD, THOUGH --
"-- NOT WITH THE FIRE SPREADING OUT OF CONTROL SO QUICKLY!"

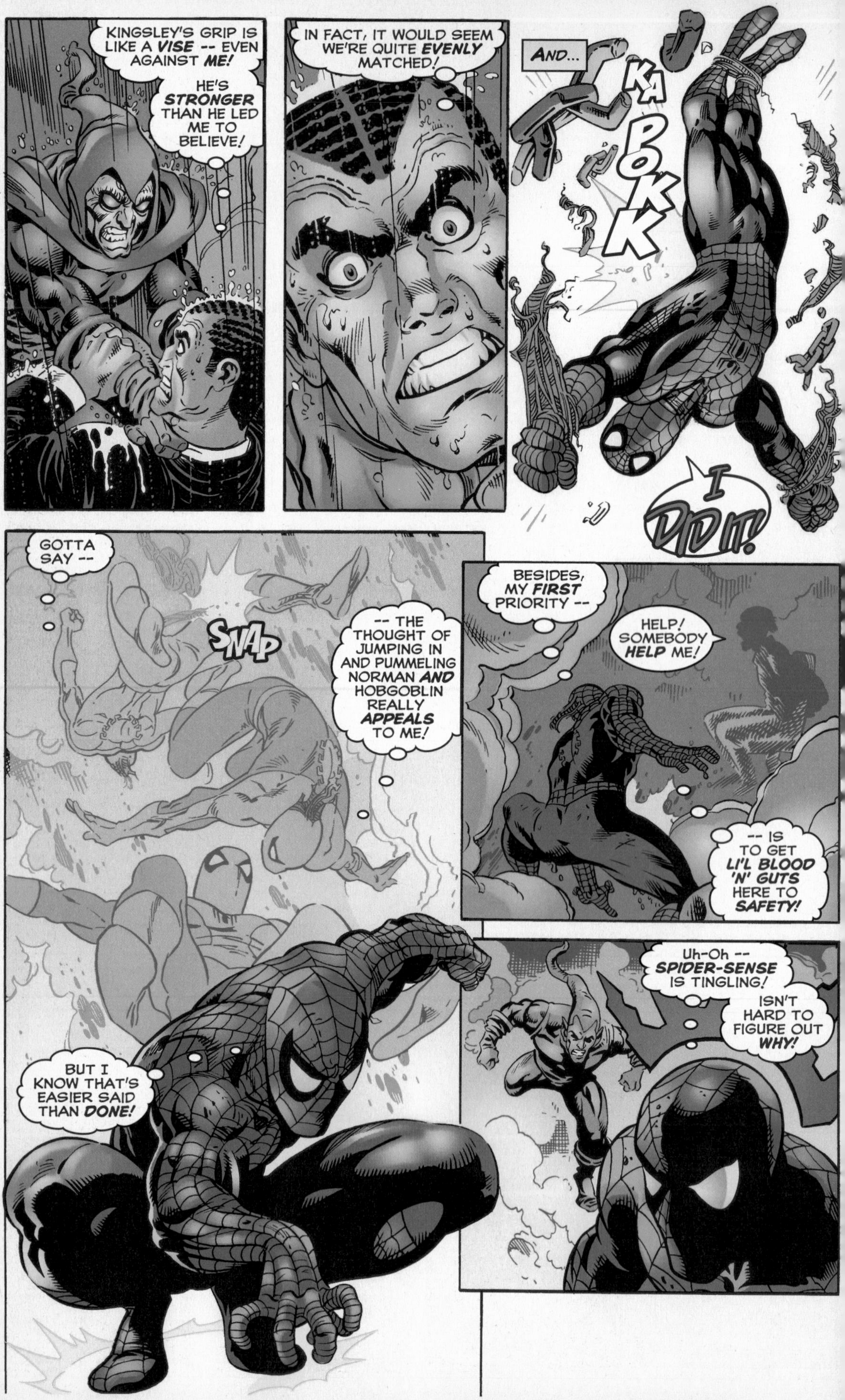
KINGSLEY'S GRIP IS LIKE A VISE -- EVEN AGAINST ME!
HE'S STRONGER THAN HE LED ME TO BELIEVE!
IN FACT, IT WOULD SEEM WE'RE QUITE EVENLY MATCHED!
AND...
KA POKK
I DID IT!
GOTTA SAY --
SNAP
-- THE THOUGHT OF JUMPING IN AND PUMMELING NORMAN AND HOBGOBLIN REALLY APPEALS TO ME!
BUT I KNOW THAT'S EASIER SAID THAN DONE!
BESIDES, MY FIRST PRIORITY --
HELP! SOMEBODY HELP ME!
-- IS TO GET LI'L BLOOD 'N' GUTS HERE TO SAFETY!
Uh-Oh -- SPIDER-SENSE IS TINGLING!
ISN'T HARD TO FIGURE OUT WHY!

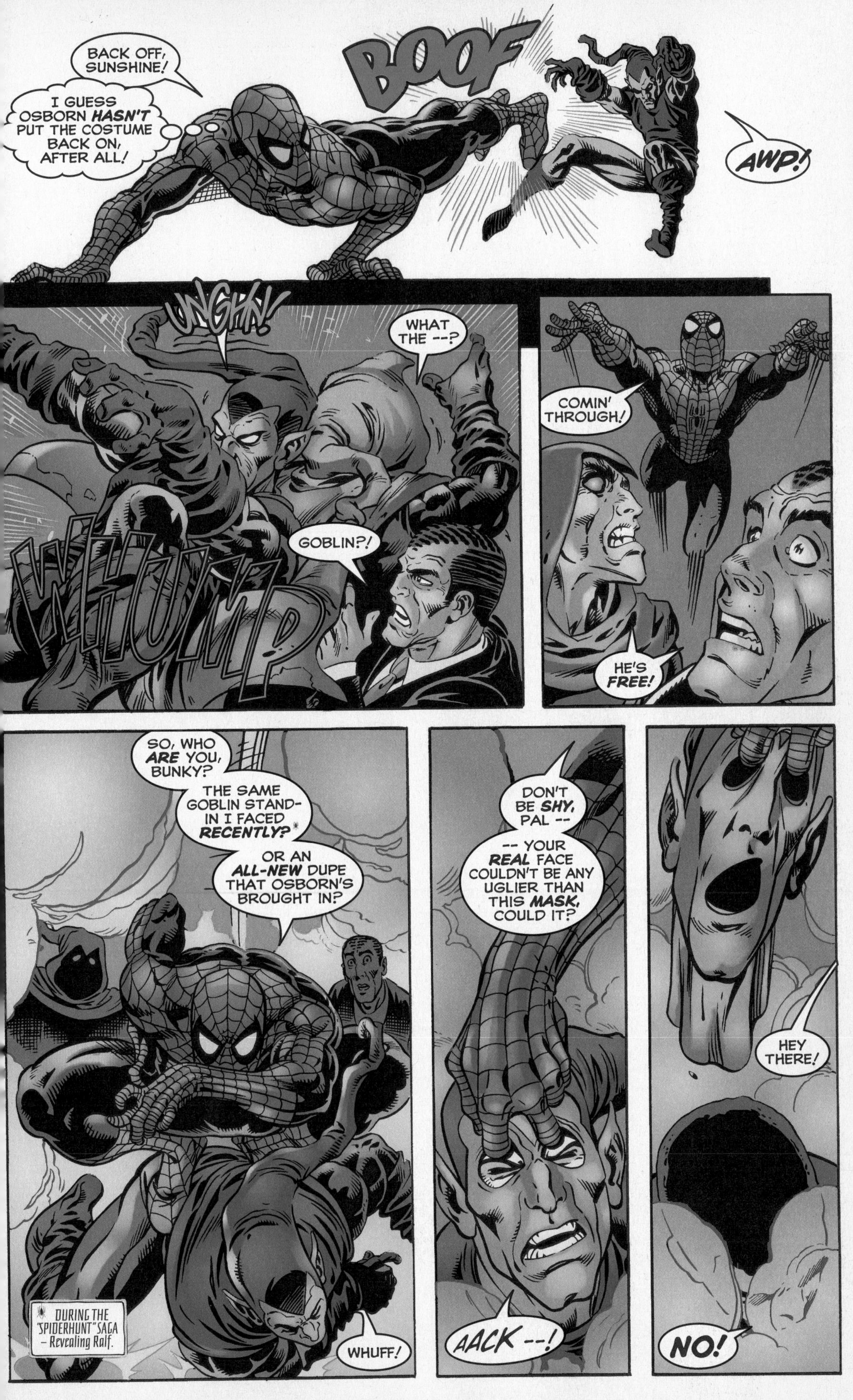
BACK OFF, SUNSHINE!
I GUESS OSBORN HASN'T PUT THE COSTUME BACK ON, AFTER ALL!
BOOF
AWP!
UNGH!
WHAT THE --?
GOBLIN?!
WHUMP
COMIN' THROUGH!
HE'S FREE!
SO, WHO ARE YOU, BUNKY?
THE SAME GOBLIN STAND-IN I FACED RECENTLY?
OR AN ALL-NEW DUPE THAT OSBORN'S BROUGHT IN?
DURING THE "SPIDERHUNT" SAGA – Revealing Ralf.
WHUFF!
DON'T BE SHY, PAL --
-- YOUR REAL FACE COULDN'T BE ANY UGLIER THAN THIS MASK, COULD IT?
AACK --!
HEY THERE!
NO!

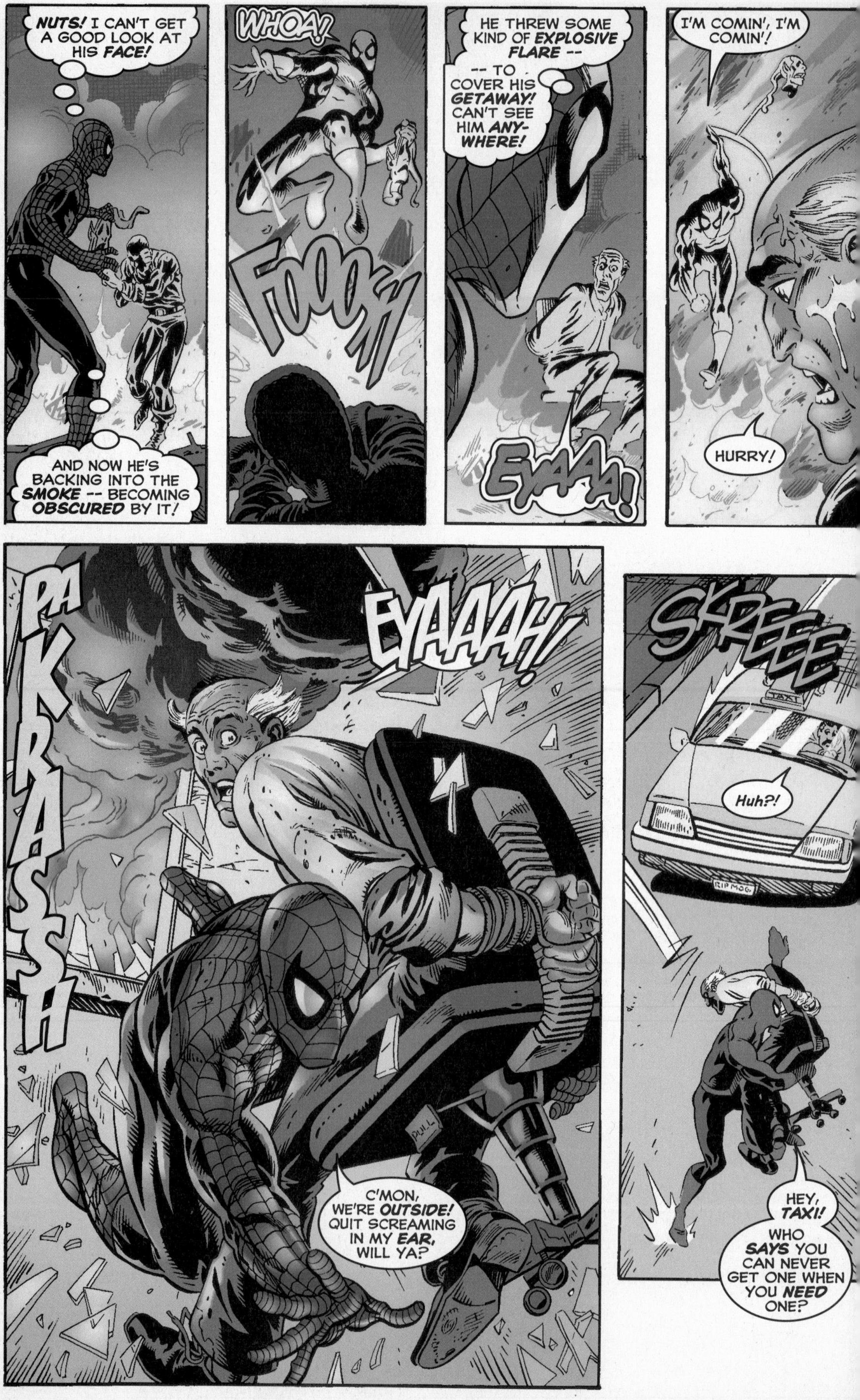

NUTS! I CAN'T GET A GOOD LOOK AT HIS FACE!
AND NOW HE'S BACKING INTO THE SMOKE -- BECOMING OBSCURED BY IT!
WHOA!
FOOOSH
HE THREW SOME KIND OF EXPLOSIVE FLARE --
-- TO COVER HIS GETAWAY! CAN'T SEE HIM ANYWHERE!
EYAAAA!
I'M COMIN', I'M COMIN'!
HURRY!
PAKRASH
EYAAAH!
C'MON, WE'RE OUTSIDE! QUIT SCREAMING IN MY EAR, WILL YA?
SKREEEE
Huh?!
HEY, TAXI!
WHO SAYS YOU CAN NEVER GET ONE WHEN YOU NEED ONE?

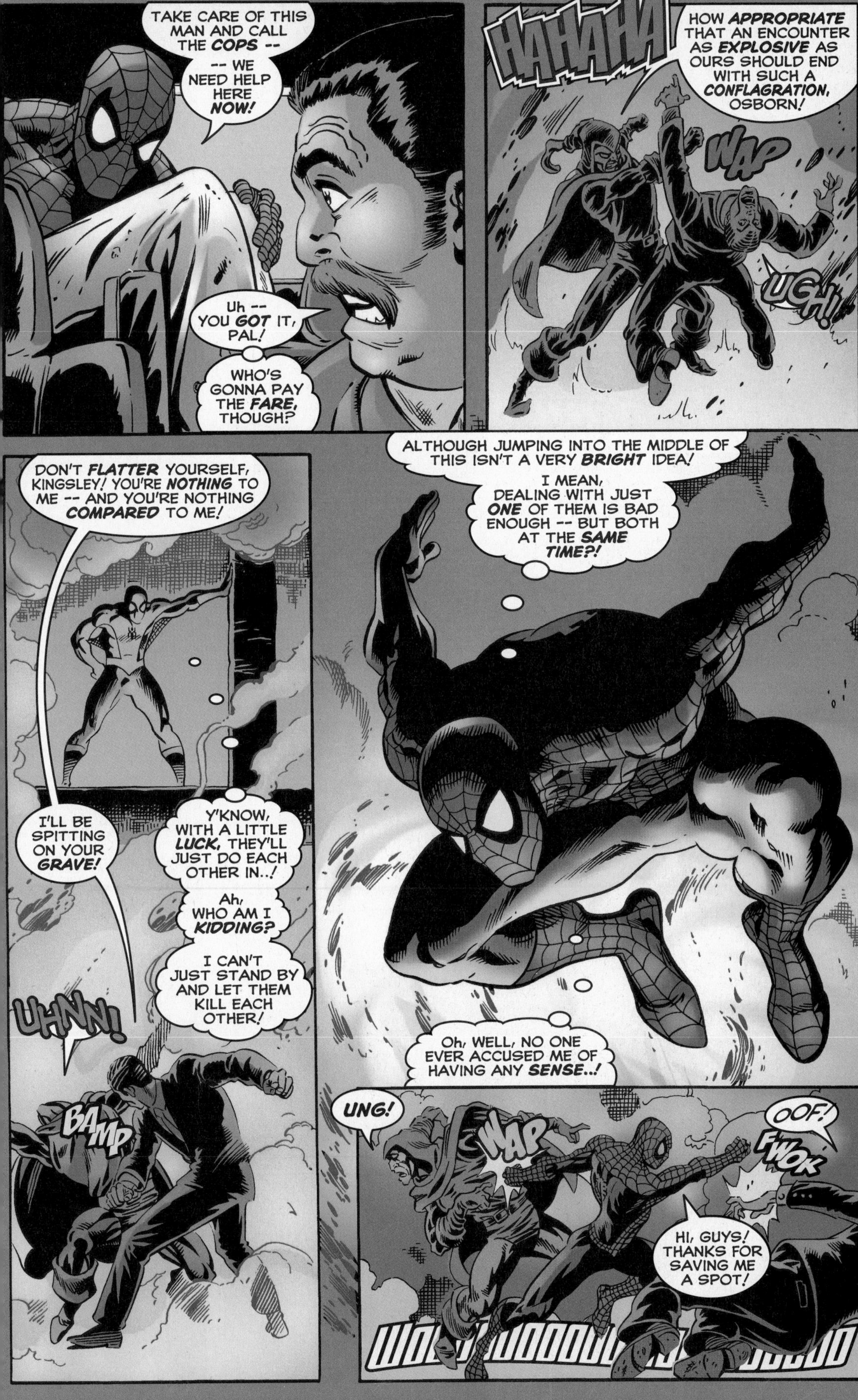
TAKE CARE OF THIS MAN AND CALL THE COPS --
-- WE NEED HELP HERE NOW!
Uh -- YOU GOT IT, PAL!
WHO'S GONNA PAY THE FARE, THOUGH?
HAHAHA
HOW APPROPRIATE THAT AN ENCOUNTER AS EXPLOSIVE AS OURS SHOULD END WITH SUCH A CONFLAGRATION, OSBORN!
WAP
UGH!
DON'T FLATTER YOURSELF, KINGSLEY! YOU'RE NOTHING TO ME -- AND YOU'RE NOTHING COMPARED TO ME!
I'LL BE SPITTING ON YOUR GRAVE!
Y'KNOW, WITH A LITTLE LUCK, THEY'LL JUST DO EACH OTHER IN..!
Ah, WHO AM I KIDDING?
I CAN'T JUST STAND BY AND LET THEM KILL EACH OTHER!
UHNN!
BAMP
ALTHOUGH JUMPING INTO THE MIDDLE OF THIS ISN'T A VERY BRIGHT IDEA!
I MEAN, DEALING WITH JUST ONE OF THEM IS BAD ENOUGH -- BUT BOTH AT THE SAME TIME?!
Oh, WELL, NO ONE EVER ACCUSED ME OF HAVING ANY SENSE..!
UNG!
WAP
OOF!
FWOK
HI, GUYS! THANKS FOR SAVING ME A SPOT!

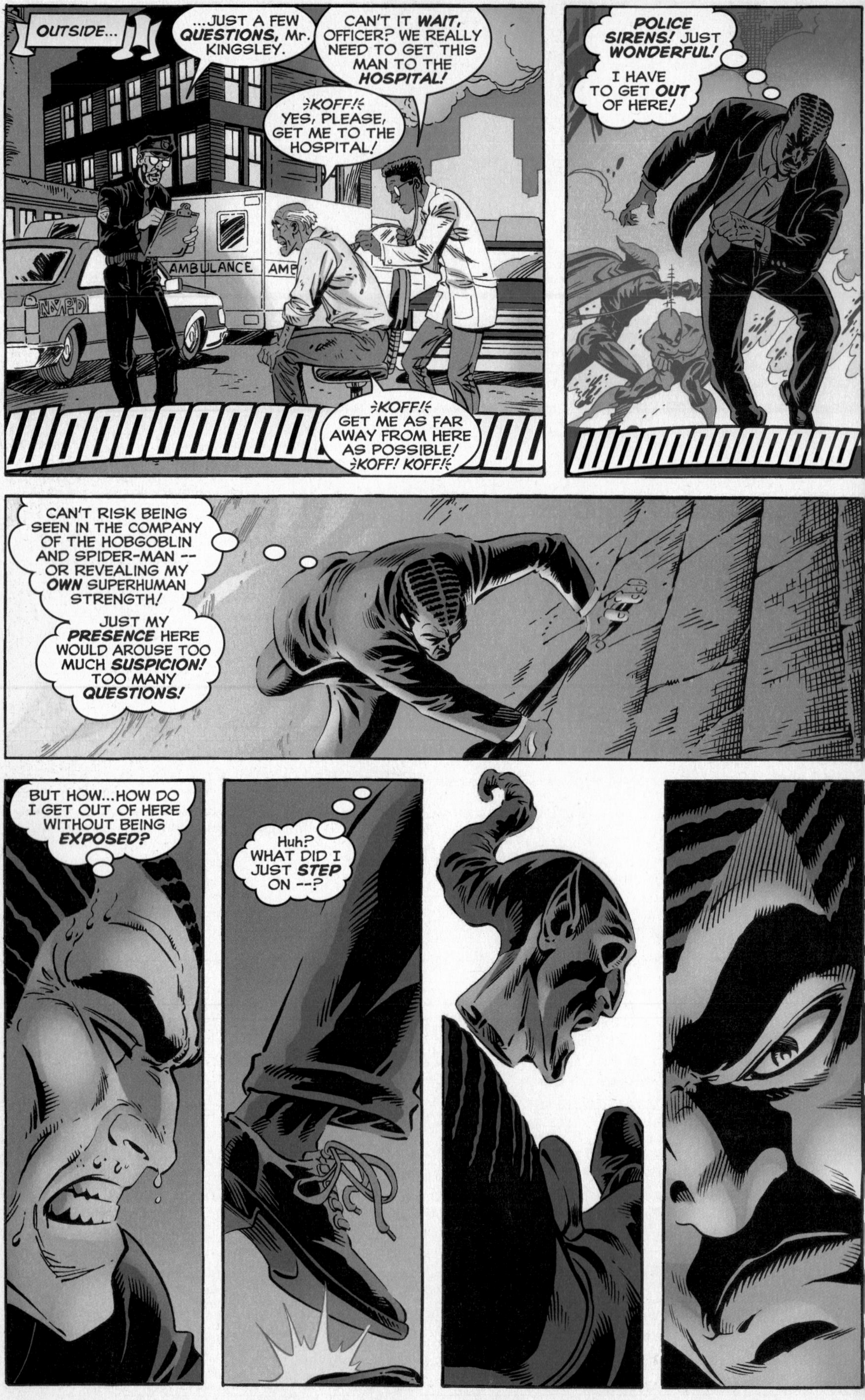
OUTSIDE...
...JUST A FEW QUESTIONS, Mr. KINGSLEY.
CAN'T IT WAIT, OFFICER? WE REALLY NEED TO GET THIS MAN TO THE HOSPITAL!
KOFF! YES, PLEASE, GET ME TO THE HOSPITAL!
AMBULANCE
NYPD
KOFF! GET ME AS FAR AWAY FROM HERE AS POSSIBLE! KOFF! KOFF!
WOOOOOOOOOOOOOO
POLICE SIRENS! JUST WONDERFUL!
I HAVE TO GET OUT OF HERE!
WOOOOOOOOOOO
CAN'T RISK BEING SEEN IN THE COMPANY OF THE HOBGOBLIN AND SPIDER-MAN -- OR REVEALING MY OWN SUPERHUMAN STRENGTH!
JUST MY PRESENCE HERE WOULD AROUSE TOO MUCH SUSPICION! TOO MANY QUESTIONS!
BUT HOW...HOW DO I GET OUT OF HERE WITHOUT BEING EXPOSED?
Huh? WHAT DID I JUST STEP ON --?

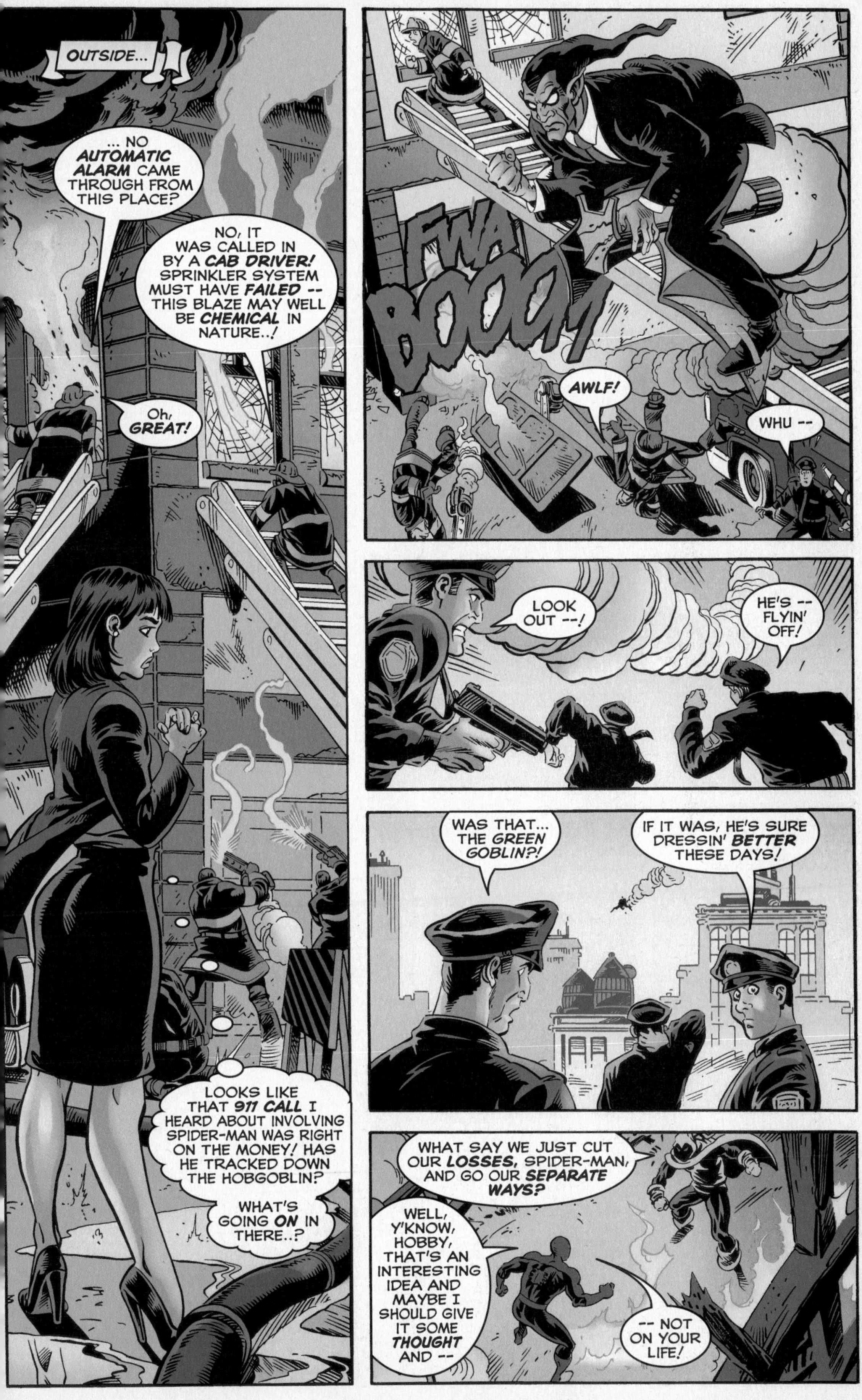
OUTSIDE...
... NO AUTOMATIC ALARM CAME THROUGH FROM THIS PLACE?
NO, IT WAS CALLED IN BY A CAB DRIVER! SPRINKLER SYSTEM MUST HAVE FAILED -- THIS BLAZE MAY WELL BE CHEMICAL IN NATURE..!
Oh, GREAT!
LOOKS LIKE THAT 911 CALL I HEARD ABOUT INVOLVING SPIDER-MAN WAS RIGHT ON THE MONEY! HAS HE TRACKED DOWN THE HOBGOBLIN?
WHAT'S GOING ON IN THERE..?
FWA BOOOM
AWLF!
WHU --
LOOK OUT --!
HE'S -- FLYIN' OFF!
WAS THAT... THE GREEN GOBLIN?!
IF IT WAS, HE'S SURE DRESSIN' BETTER THESE DAYS!
WHAT SAY WE JUST CUT OUR LOSSES, SPIDER-MAN, AND GO OUR SEPARATE WAYS?
WELL, Y'KNOW, HOBBY, THAT'S AN INTERESTING IDEA AND MAYBE I SHOULD GIVE IT SOME THOUGHT AND --
-- NOT ON YOUR LIFE!

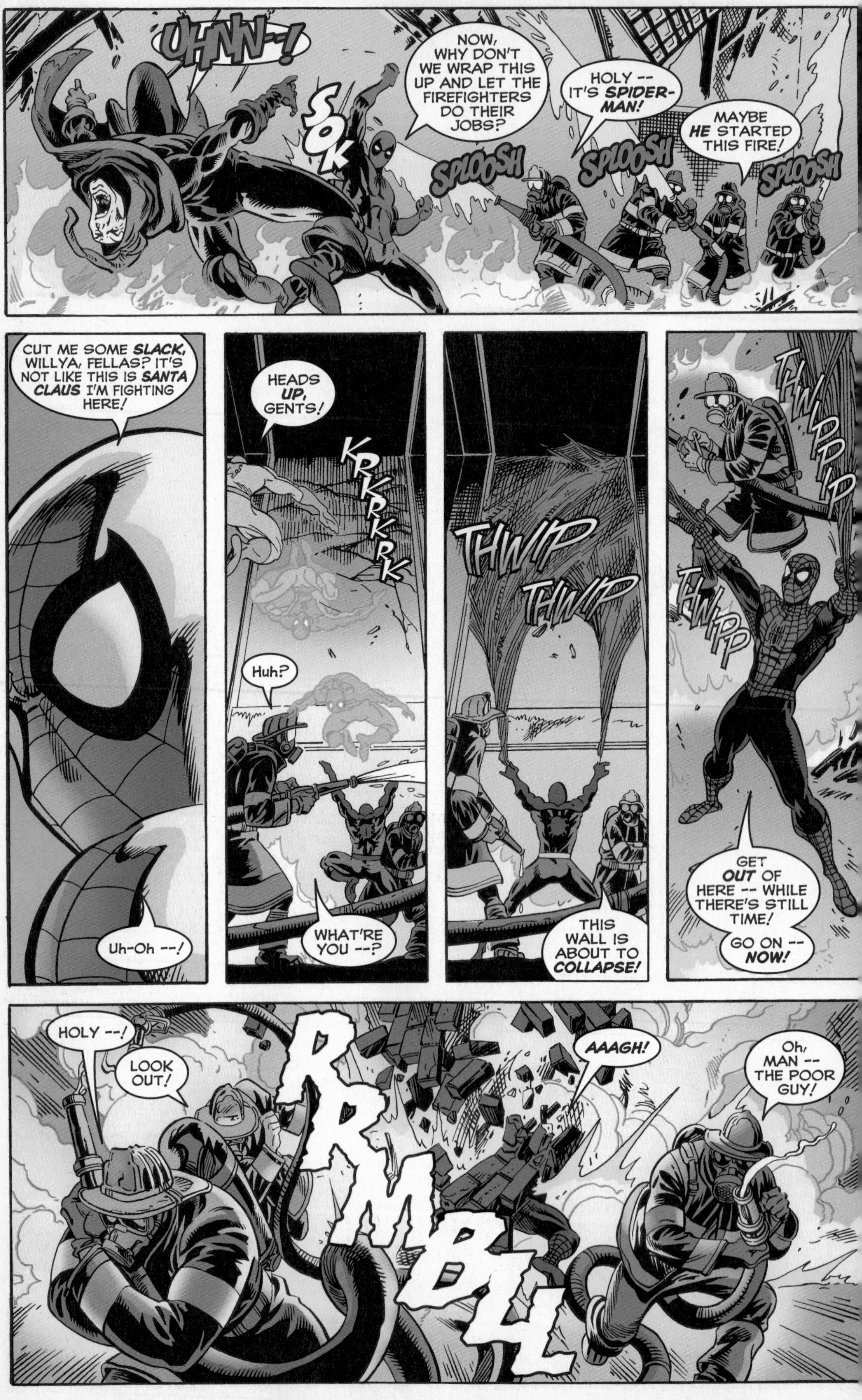
UHNN--!
SOK
NOW, WHY DON'T WE WRAP THIS UP AND LET THE FIREFIGHTERS DO THEIR JOBS?
HOLY -- IT'S SPIDER-MAN!
MAYBE HE STARTED THIS FIRE!
SPLOOSH
SPLOOSH
SPLOOSH
CUT ME SOME SLACK, WILLYA, FELLAS? IT'S NOT LIKE THIS IS SANTA CLAUS I'M FIGHTING HERE!
Uh-Oh --!
HEADS UP, GENTS!
KRKRKRKRK
Huh?
WHAT'RE YOU --?
THWIP
THWIP
THIS WALL IS ABOUT TO COLLAPSE!
THWIPP
THWIPP
GET OUT OF HERE -- WHILE THERE'S STILL TIME!
GO ON -- NOW!
HOLY --!
LOOK OUT!
RRMBLL
AAAGH!
Oh, MAN -- THE POOR GUY!

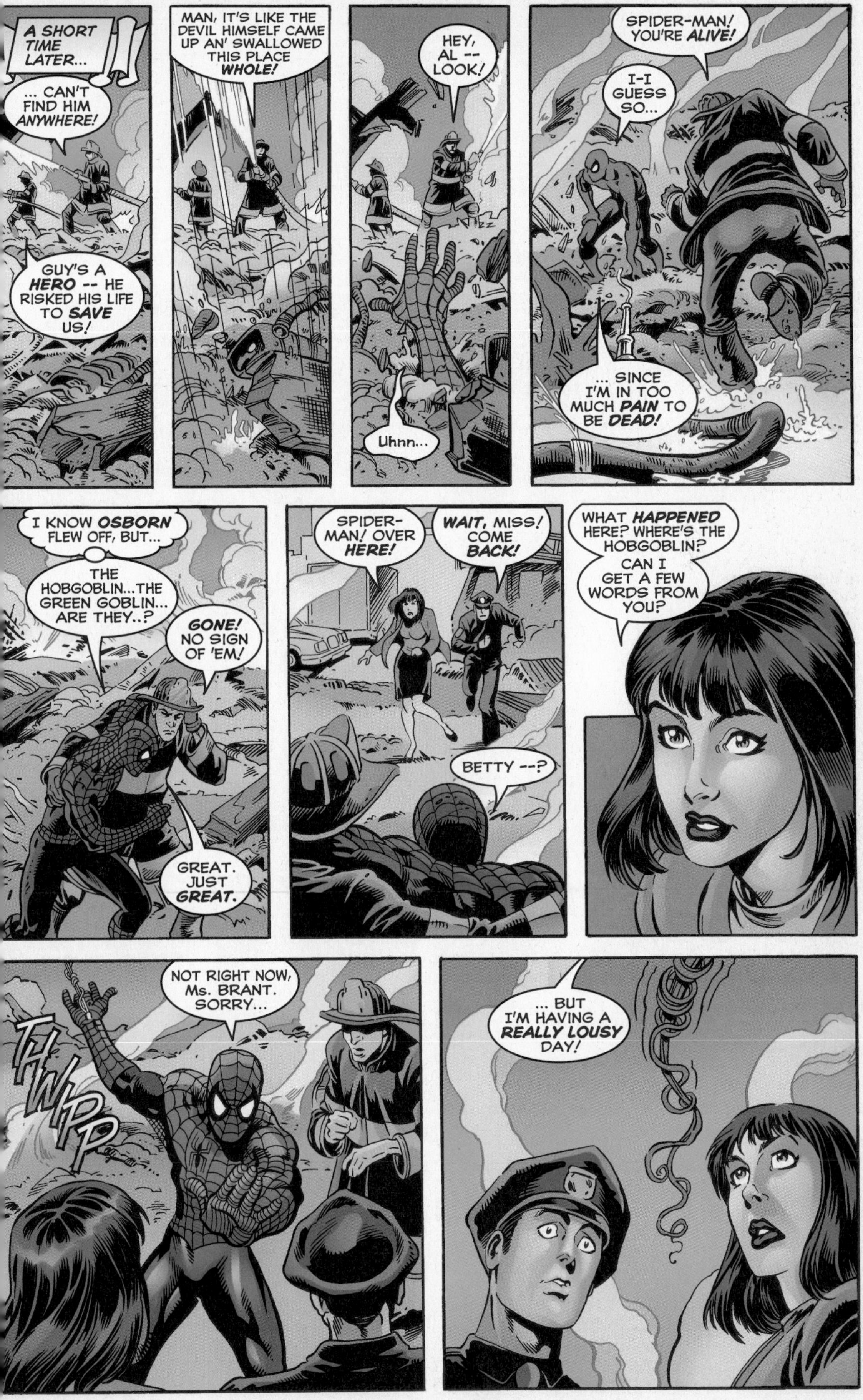
A SHORT TIME LATER...
... CAN'T FIND HIM ANYWHERE!
GUY'S A HERO -- HE RISKED HIS LIFE TO SAVE US!
MAN, IT'S LIKE THE DEVIL HIMSELF CAME UP AN' SWALLOWED THIS PLACE WHOLE!
HEY, AL -- LOOK!
Uhnn...
SPIDER-MAN! YOU'RE ALIVE!
I-I GUESS SO...
... SINCE I'M IN TOO MUCH PAIN TO BE DEAD!
I KNOW OSBORN FLEW OFF, BUT...
THE HOBGOBLIN...THE GREEN GOBLIN... ARE THEY..?
GONE! NO SIGN OF 'EM!
GREAT. JUST GREAT.
SPIDER-MAN! OVER HERE!
WAIT, MISS! COME BACK!
BETTY --?
WHAT HAPPENED HERE? WHERE'S THE HOBGOBLIN?
CAN I GET A FEW WORDS FROM YOU?
NOT RIGHT NOW, Ms. BRANT. SORRY...
THWIPP
... BUT I'M HAVING A REALLY LOUSY DAY!

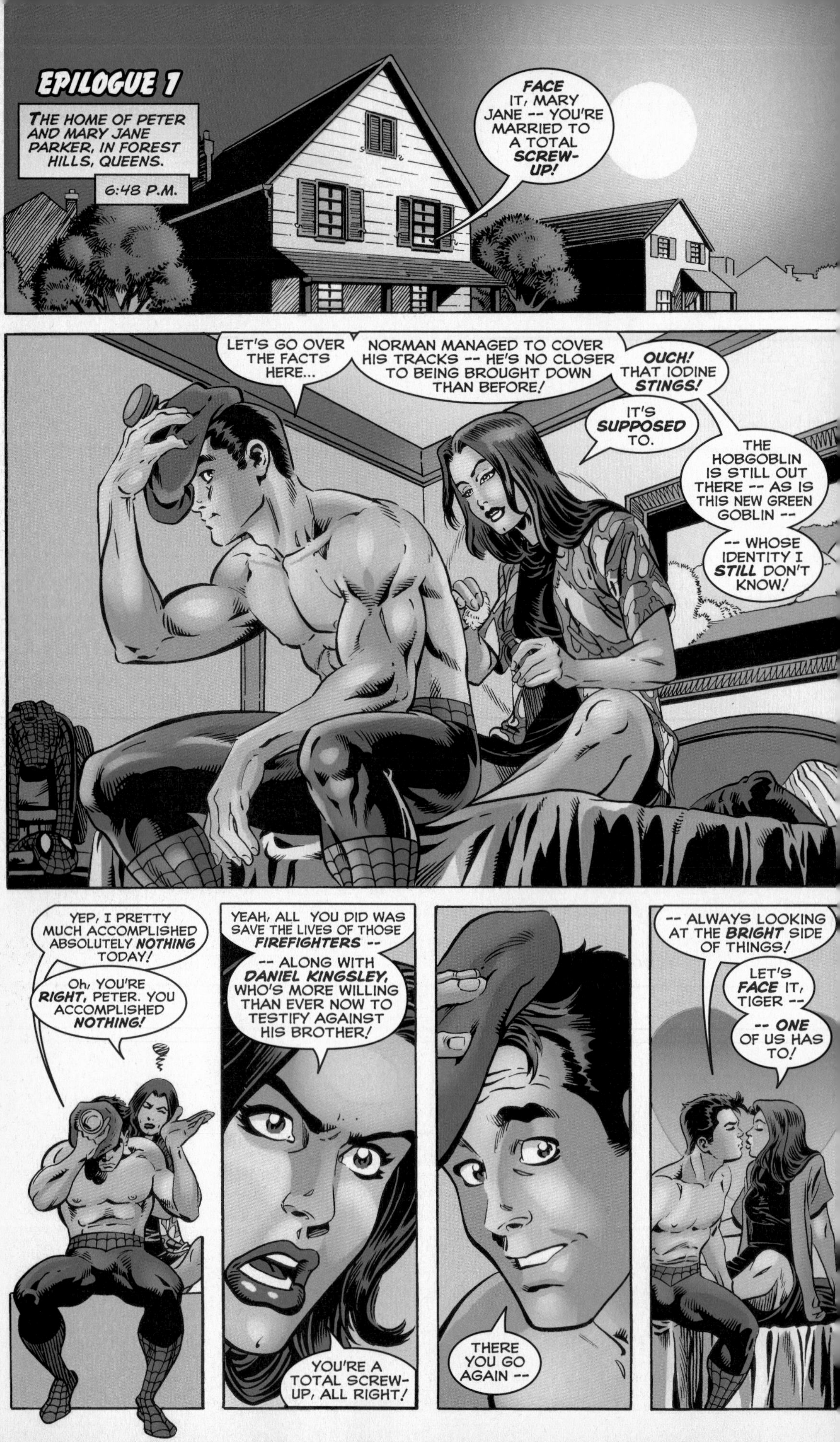
EPILOGUE 1
THE HOME OF PETER AND MARY JANE PARKER, IN FOREST HILLS, QUEENS.
6:48 P.M.
FACE IT, MARY JANE -- YOU'RE MARRIED TO A TOTAL SCREW-UP!
LET'S GO OVER THE FACTS HERE...
NORMAN MANAGED TO COVER HIS TRACKS -- HE'S NO CLOSER TO BEING BROUGHT DOWN THAN BEFORE!
OUCH! THAT IODINE STINGS!
IT'S SUPPOSED TO.
THE HOBGOBLIN IS STILL OUT THERE -- AS IS THIS NEW GREEN GOBLIN --
-- WHOSE IDENTITY I STILL DON'T KNOW!
YEP, I PRETTY MUCH ACCOMPLISHED ABSOLUTELY NOTHING TODAY!
Oh, YOU'RE RIGHT, PETER. YOU ACCOMPLISHED NOTHING!
YEAH, ALL YOU DID WAS SAVE THE LIVES OF THOSE FIREFIGHTERS --
-- ALONG WITH DANIEL KINGSLEY, WHO'S MORE WILLING THAN EVER NOW TO TESTIFY AGAINST HIS BROTHER!
YOU'RE A TOTAL SCREW-UP, ALL RIGHT!
THERE YOU GO AGAIN --
-- ALWAYS LOOKING AT THE BRIGHT SIDE OF THINGS!
LET'S FACE IT, TIGER --
-- ONE OF US HAS TO!

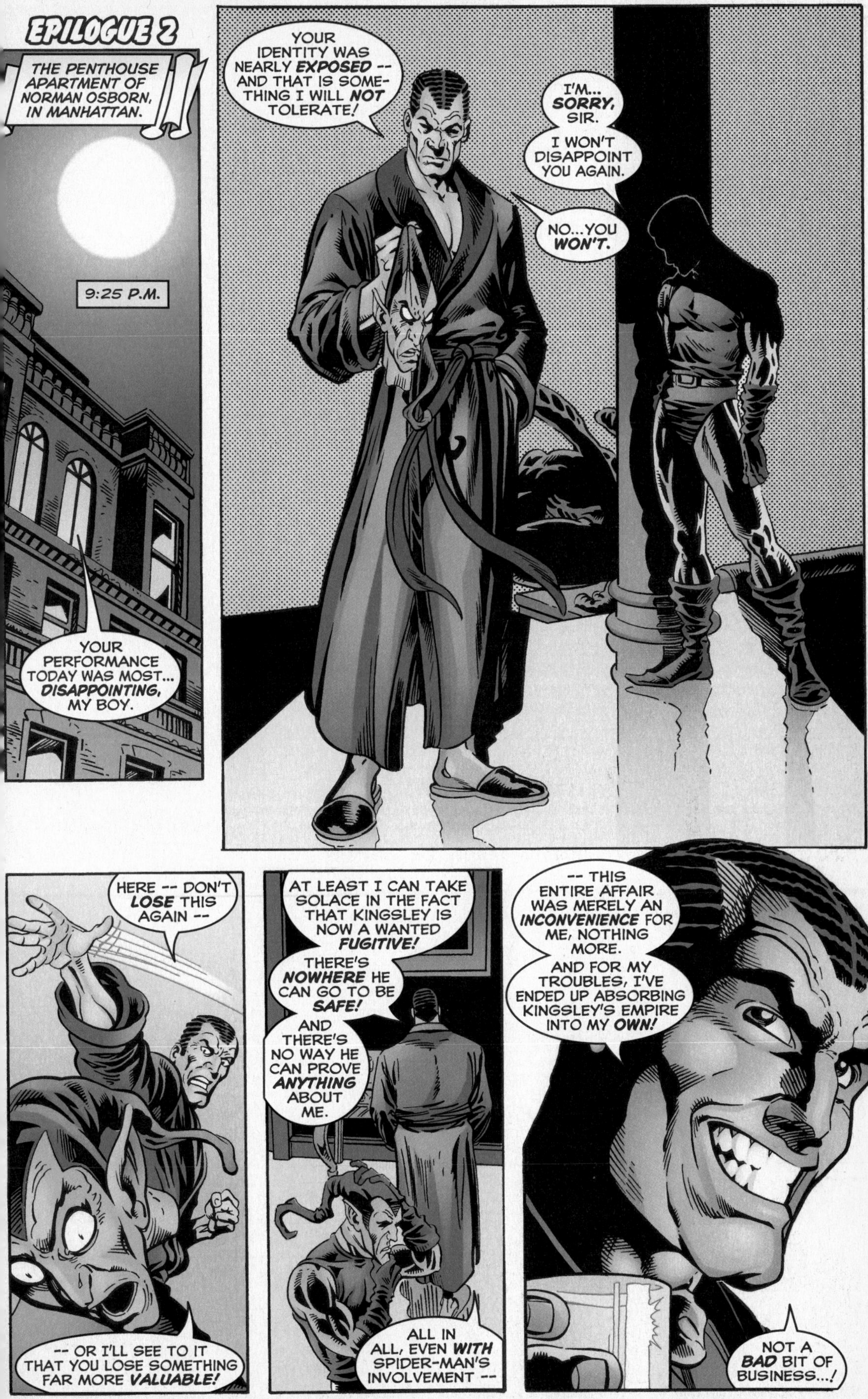
EPILOGUE 2
THE PENTHOUSE APARTMENT OF NORMAN OSBORN, IN MANHATTAN.
9:25 P.M.
YOUR PERFORMANCE TODAY WAS MOST... DISAPPOINTING, MY BOY.
YOUR IDENTITY WAS NEARLY EXPOSED -- AND THAT IS SOMETHING I WILL NOT TOLERATE!
I'M... SORRY, SIR.
I WON'T DISAPPOINT YOU AGAIN.
NO...YOU WON'T.
HERE -- DON'T LOSE THIS AGAIN --
-- OR I'LL SEE TO IT THAT YOU LOSE SOMETHING FAR MORE VALUABLE!
AT LEAST I CAN TAKE SOLACE IN THE FACT THAT KINGSLEY IS NOW A WANTED FUGITIVE!
THERE'S NOWHERE HE CAN GO TO BE SAFE!
AND THERE'S NO WAY HE CAN PROVE ANYTHING ABOUT ME.
ALL IN ALL, EVEN WITH SPIDER-MAN'S INVOLVEMENT --
-- THIS ENTIRE AFFAIR WAS MERELY AN INCONVENIENCE FOR ME, NOTHING MORE.
AND FOR MY TROUBLES, I'VE ENDED UP ABSORBING KINGSLEY'S EMPIRE INTO MY OWN!
NOT A BAD BIT OF BUSINESS...!

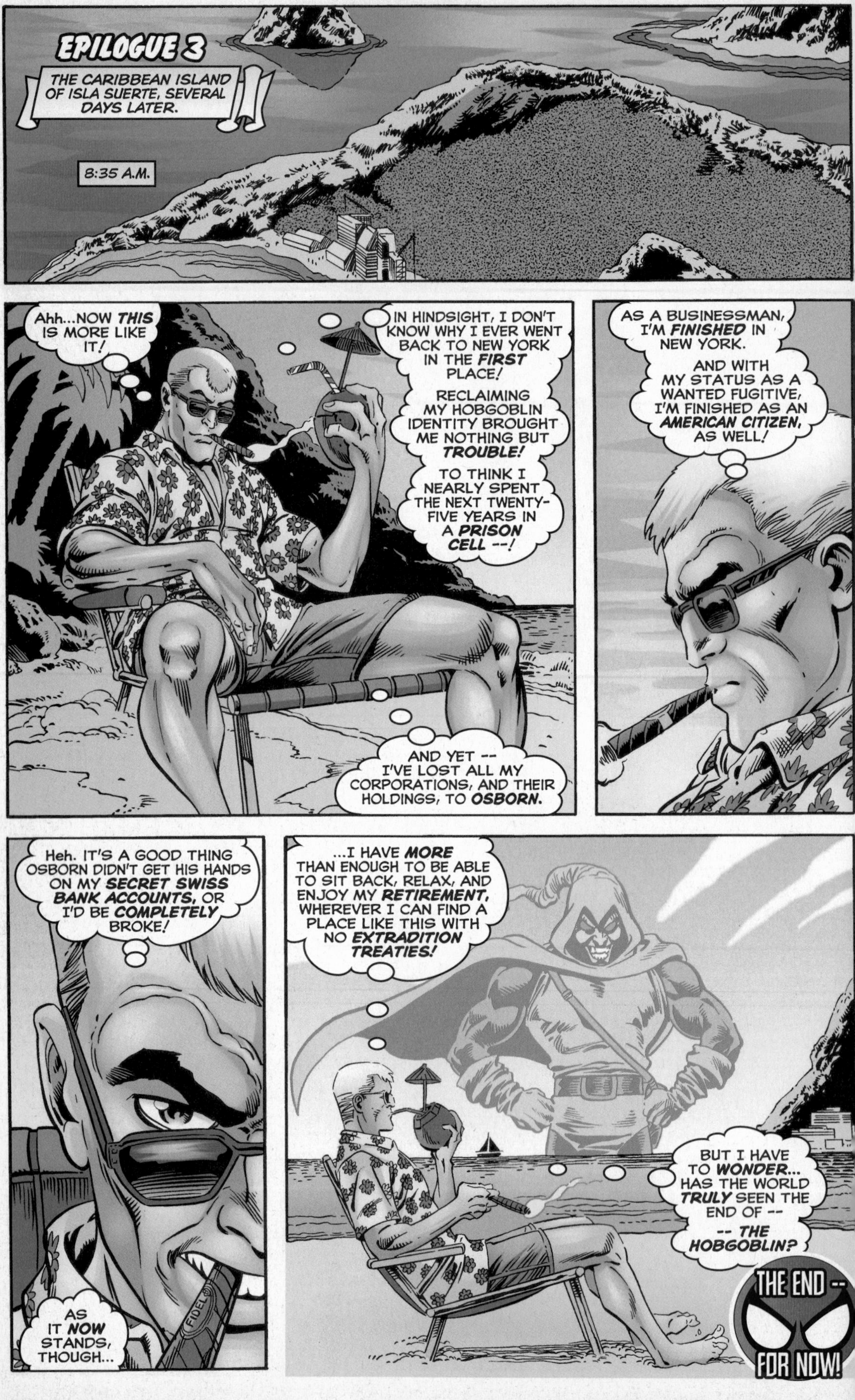
EPILOGUE 3
THE CARIBBEAN ISLAND OF ISLA SUERTE, SEVERAL DAYS LATER.
8:35 A.M.
Ahh...NOW THIS IS MORE LIKE IT!
IN HINDSIGHT, I DON'T KNOW WHY I EVER WENT BACK TO NEW YORK IN THE FIRST PLACE!
RECLAIMING MY HOBGOBLIN IDENTITY BROUGHT ME NOTHING BUT TROUBLE!
TO THINK I NEARLY SPENT THE NEXT TWENTY-FIVE YEARS IN A PRISON CELL --!
AND YET -- I'VE LOST ALL MY CORPORATIONS, AND THEIR HOLDINGS, TO OSBORN.
AS A BUSINESSMAN, I'M FINISHED IN NEW YORK.
AND WITH MY STATUS AS A WANTED FUGITIVE, I'M FINISHED AS AN AMERICAN CITIZEN, AS WELL!
Heh. IT'S A GOOD THING OSBORN DIDN'T GET HIS HANDS ON MY SECRET SWISS BANK ACCOUNTS, OR I'D BE COMPLETELY BROKE!
AS IT NOW STANDS, THOUGH...
FIDEL
...I HAVE MORE THAN ENOUGH TO BE ABLE TO SIT BACK, RELAX, AND ENJOY MY RETIREMENT, WHEREVER I CAN FIND A PLACE LIKE THIS WITH NO EXTRADITION TREATIES!
BUT I HAVE TO WONDER... HAS THE WORLD TRULY SEEN THE END OF --
-- THE HOBGOBLIN?
THE END -- FOR NOW!

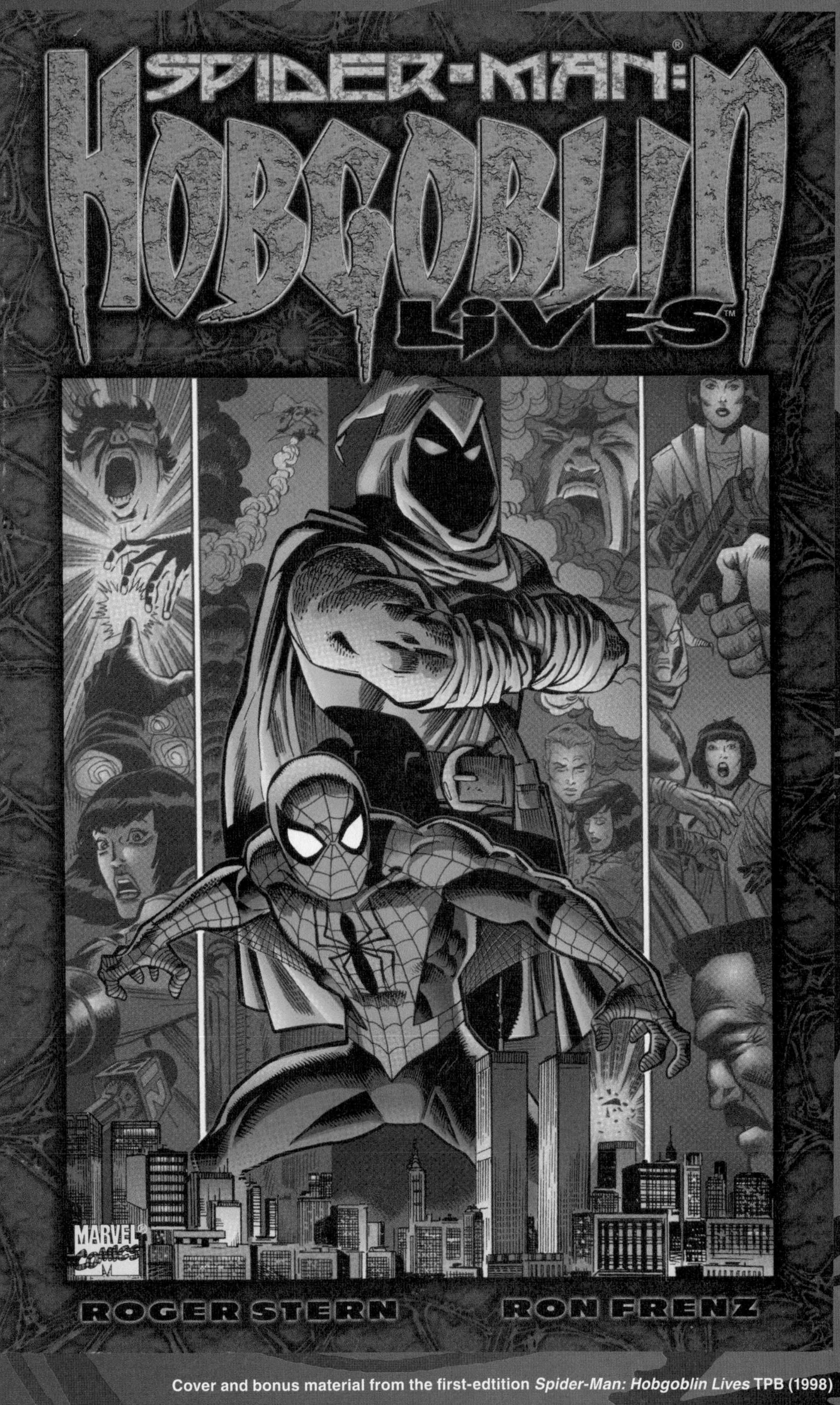
SPIDER-MAN:
HOBGOBLIN
LIVES
MARVEL COMICS
ROGER STERN
RON FRENZ

Cover and bonus material from the first-edtition *Spider-Man: Hobgoblin Lives* TPB (1998)

SPIDER-MAN/HOBGOBLIN TIMELINE

As compiled by Roger Stern

[Note: Previously unrevealed behind-the-scenes actions and related explanations appear in bold.]

AMAZING SPIDER-MAN #238

While fleeing from Spider-Man, Georgie (a small-time hood) stumbles across one of the Green Goblin's old lairs in Queens.

Georgie brings a Mysterious Shadowy Figure to the lair.

The two of them clean out the place and torch it.

The Mysterious Shadowy Figure blows up the van they used, killing Georgie.

The Mysterious Shadowy Figure uses Osborn's gear to create a new identity for himself as the Hobgoblin!

AMAZING SPIDER-MAN #239

Using Osborn's journals, Hobgoblin makes systematic raids on all of the old Green Goblin lairs, taking whatever he finds.

Spider-Man, suspecting the worst, checks out the Goblin lairs he knew about, and comes across the Hobgoblin!

Hobgoblin just barely manages to get away (albeit with cracked ribs); he knows he needs an advantage over Spider-Man.

>>>**Hobgoblin begins his search through Osborn's journals to find the secret formula which had given Norman the super-strength of the Green Goblin. He plans to acquire it himself.**

AMAZING SPIDER-MAN #245

Hobgoblin employs Lefty Donovan to lead a gang of hoodlums in a series of raids on Osborn holdings to acquire the chemicals needed for the secret formula.

The gang is captured, thanks to Spider-Man — but Lefty manages to get away, using gear the Hobgoblin had given him.

Spider-Man suspects that Lefty is the Hobgoblin.

>>>**Using Dr. Winkler's prototype brainwashing gear, recovered from one of Osborn's old lairs, Hobgoblin plants posthypnotic suggestions and instructions in Lefty's mind.**

AMAZING SPIDER-MAN #246

Following instructions, Lefty mixes the chemicals (while Hobgoblin watches from safety).

As Hobgoblin had expected, the chemicals erupt in Lefty's face, burning the poor stooge.

Hobgoblin pulls Lefty to safety, and then retreats unseen back into the building as emergency vehicles approach.

The building erupts in flame (but Hobgoblin is safe within his hidden lair).

Three weeks later, Lefty comes out of a coma, energized by the secret formula.

Reacting to posthypnotic suggestions, Lefty returns to the burned out house. He enters the hidden lair, attaches sensors to himself, and takes off in the guise of the Hobgoblin.

Lefty/Hobgoblin publicly challenges Spider-Man to fight him in Times Square.

Spider-Man stuns Lefty and unmasks him. Lefty's dazed response tells Spider-Man that someone else is his "boss." But before Spider-Man can find out that boss's identity...

Lefty's goblin glider takes off under remote control, slamming him into the side of a building and killing him.

Spider-Man realizes that the real Hobgoblin must have set Lefty up.

And the real Hobgoblin has acquired the data he needs to give himself super-strength!

SPECTACULAR SPIDER-MAN #85

Hobgoblin uses the formula under controlled conditions to give himself super-strength.

Overconfident, the Hobgoblin goes looking for Spider-Man.

Hobgoblin battles Spider-Man and the Black Cat and learns that mere physical strength is not enough,

that Spider-Man is a superior fighter.

Hobgoblin retreats to plan anew.

AMAZING SPIDER-MAN #249

Hobgoblin launches a vast blackmailing scheme against wealthy types who frequent the Century Club, among them: J. Jonah Jameson, Roderick Kingsley **(actually, his brother Daniel in disguise)**, George Vandergill, and Harry Osborn (who's being blackmailed — due to the fact that his father was the Green Goblin).

The blackmail victims gather at the club, where they are greeted by the Hobgoblin, who starts to spell out his conditions.

Harry stands up to the Hobgoblin, who turns out to be a robot stand-in.

The real Hobgoblin attacks and is countered by Spider-Man.

Hobgoblin is ready for him this time, attacking with a gas which deadens Spider-Man's spider-sense.

Spider-Man is saved by the intervention of the Kingpin (a club member).

Hobgoblin taunts Kingpin and departs; Kingpin (not realizing that Spider-Man's spider-sense has been deadened) plants a spider-tracer on the 'goblin's glider as Hobgoblin takes off.

AMAZING SPIDER-MAN #250

Spider-Man searches for the Hobgoblin without his spider-sense...and without luck.

>>>**Jameson asks Ned Leeds to investigate the Hobgoblin.**

Spider-Man discovers that Jameson is going to publicly confess his sins.

Spider-Man tunes up an old tracking gizmo to help locate his spider-tracer.

Spider-Man finds the Hobgoblin's lair.

Battle begins. during which Osborn's journals are destroyed in the ensuing fire and explosion.

Hobgoblin and Spider-Man are knocked unconscious.

AMAZING SPIDER-MAN #251

Hobgoblin regains consciousness first and beats Spider-Man mercilessly.

As fire engulfs the building, Hobgoblin leaves the scene in his battle wagon.

Spider-Man manages to grab hold of the departing battle wagon.

Spider-Man gets inside; he and the Hobgoblin battle as the wagon goes off the pier into the Hudson River.

Another explosion rips through the battle wagon; Spider-Man manages to survive.

Hobgoblin goes missing; there's nothing left behind but his mask.

>>>**A week passes, during which Spider-Man goes missing [*Marvel Super Heroes: Secret Wars*].**

During this time, Ned tracks down the Hobgoblin. Hobgoblin gets the drop on Ned and uses the Winkler process to brainwash him, programming the reporter to handle some of the 'goblin's dirty work.

Hobgoblin decides to play the role of master criminal, using Ned to manipulate Richard Fisk into become the Rose, the better to get back at the Kingpin.

AMAZING SPIDER-MAN #252

Spider-Man returns from the Secret War.

AMAZING SPIDER-MAN #253

The Rose has his operation up and running, and is fixing sporting events.

AMAZING SPIDER-MAN #254

Police dredge up Hobgoblin's battle wagon from the Hudson River.

Jack O'Lantern (Jason Macendale) organizes a team to steal it.

While Spider-Man battles Jack O'Lantern, the battle wagon motors off by itself (under remote control).

AMAZING SPIDER-MAN #255

Hobgoblin, who had moved the battle wagon to lure Spider-Man into a trap, gets tired of waiting and makes other plans.

AMAZING SPIDER-MAN #256

The Rose, tired of Spider-Man's interference, hires the Puma to kill him.

AMAZING SPIDER-MAN #257

The Kingpin learns of the Rose's "hit" on Spider Man. Rose is referred to as being in the Kingpin's employ.

Kingpin forces Rose to call off the hit.

Hobgoblin "introduces" himself to the Rose in front of Rose's top two lieutenants, Johnston and Varley.

AMAZING SPIDER-MAN #258

Rose "puts Hobgoblin to a test" with some of his underlings.

Hobgoblin "passes" and proposes a criminal alliance.

AMAZING SPIDER-MAN #259

Hobgoblin raids an illegal casino, demanding 10% of the take — in competition with the Kingpin.

Hobgoblin makes another such raid.

The Hobgoblin-Rose alliance flourishes.

Hobgoblin plans to use Rose's men against Ha and Liz Osborn.

Spider-Man learns that Hobgoblin is alive and kicking.

AMAZING SPIDER-MAN #260

Spider-Man learns of Hobgoblin-Rose connectio

Rose tells Johnston and Varley that once the Hobgoblin has served his purpose, they are going to kill him.

Harry Osborn catches wind of a takeover bid against his company.

Hobgoblin smashes into Harry's office, demanding more of Norman's journals.

Spider-Man counterattacks, chasing Hobgoblin out of Harry's building.

Rose's men abduct the pregnant Liz Osborn an Mary Jane Watson (who is with Liz at the time of th kidnapping).

AMAZING SPIDER-MAN #261

Rose and Hobgoblin hold Liz and Mary Jane hostage.

Harry searches for and finds another journal.

Spider-Man tails Harry to a meeting with Hobgoblin.

Hobgoblin takes Harry captive; Spider-Man follows.

Spider-Man rescues everyone, but the bad guy get away.

Hobgoblin discovers that the newly discovered journal is useless; it tells him nothing he didn't already know. He vows to make Spider-Man pay.

AMAZING SPIDER-MAN #271

Mary Jane works as a model for the fashion div sion of Kingsley Ltd.

Berry and Ned argue; Pete thinks how Ned has been going undercover for weeks at a time.

AMAZING SPIDER-MAN #273

Betty and Ned argue some more; Pete thinks about how she's been seeing Flash Thompson.

Ned sees Flash and Betty embrace.

AMAZING SPIDER-MAN #275

Hobgoblin has developed new weaponry, appa ently subsidized by the Rose's money.

Hobgoblin brazenly grabs a criminal payoff in

bad daylight.

Sha Shan plans to leave Flash; he hits her. Taken back by his own action, he leaves.

Betty pours her heart out to Joe Robertson about her marital woes; Robbie is surprised to learn about Ned's "undercover assignments."

Looking for Flash, Ned accosts Sha Shan as he's leaving.

Flash and Ned argue; Flash flattens Ned with one punch.

Flash discovers that Sha Shan has left him; he's furious.

Hobgoblin captures Sha Shan — grabbing her at random — to lure Spider-Man out into the open.

Spider-Man goes after Hobgoblin, rescues Sha Shan, and is zapped by Hobgoblin.

AMAZING SPIDER-MAN #276

Spider-Man recovers, and redoubles his efforts against the Hobgoblin.

Hobgoblin is forced to flee.

Flash visits Sha Shan in the hospital, but things do not go well.

Following an explosion, Spider-Man finds an unconscious figure in a Hobgoblin outfit — it's Flash! The Police take Flash away. [Flash has been framed by the real Hobgoblin!]

AMAZING SPIDER-MAN #280

Flash, cooling his heels in jail, is visited (separately) by both Sha Shan and Betty.

Mary Jane continues modeling at Kingsley Ltd; Roderick Kingsley **(actually, a disguised Daniel)** is shown supplying Hobgoblin (as a shadowy, masked figure) with materials.

Jason Macendale (Jack O'Lantern) approaches the Rose about freeing Hobgoblin (whom he believes to be Flash) or taking his place; Rose says he'll consider it.

Mary Jane runs into the civilian identity of Hobgoblin on the street; she doesn't know he's Hobgoblin, and we don't see his face. They walk off together, indicating that she knows him.

AMAZING SPIDER-MAN #281

Joe Robertson discovers visual clues (subtle costume differences) that Flash couldn't be Hobgoblin.

Jack O'Lantern breaks Flash out of jail.

Hobgoblin is enraged by this and goes after Jack O'Lantern. Jack O'Lantern has to flee for his life.

Flash is left a fugitive on the streets.

AMAZING SPIDER-MAN #282

Robertson turns evidence of Flash's innocence over to Flash's lawyer.

AMAZING SPIDER-MAN #283

Flash is still on the run.

Ned is acting flaky.

Pete spots Mary Jane at Kingsley Ltd. and gets a spider-sense tingle. The reason…

Hobgoblin is meeting with **(a disguised Daniel)** Kingsley just one wall away. Kingsley thinks: "I'd better take some special precautions, to make certain he never turns that anger against me…"

AMAZING SPIDER-MAN #284

With the Kingpin out of town, a Gang War erupts.

Hobgoblin is acting strangely, recklessly; he refers to Rose as "my employer." [The reason: it is now brainwashed, programmed Ned Leeds who wears the mask; he's being used by the real Hobgoblin and is not responsible for his actions.]

There's another nasty scene between Ned and Betty.

Jack O'Lantern (on behalf of the Kingpin's Arranger) attacks Silvermane.

The Rose starts bossing the ersatz Ned/Hobgoblin.

NYPD Lt. Kris Keating arrests Johnston and Varley.

Kingsley meets with Keating in a rendezvous — which is observed by a very puzzled Spider-Man.

Hammerhead is bombed, but survives.

Betty returns to her apartment and finds Flash hiding out there.

Ned/Hobgoblin is shot at by the Punisher.

AMAZING SPIDER-MAN #285

Hammerhead approaches the Rose about an alliance (with Hammerhead as #1).

Johnston and Varley — out of jail without explanation — are back working for the Rose.

Ned/Hobgoblin thinks about avoiding contact with the Punisher.

There is a confrontation between Jack O'Lantern and Hammerhead and his men; Jack O'Lantern flees.

In a private meeting with Joe Robertson, Ned claims to have been researching a big story.

The Rose calls in Ned/Hobgoblin; Jack O'Lantern is working for the Arranger; Ned/Hobgoblin and Jack O'Lantern are ordered to shake hands. [The real Hobgoblin, of course, would never have gone for this.]

AMAZING SPIDER-MAN #286

Ned/Hobgoblin provides cover for the Rose and his men during the escalating Gang War.

Richard Fisk picks up a young woman named Dina in Washington Square Park and (over coffee) starts spilling his guts to her; they go back to his place, where he lets her in on the secret that he's the Rose; he claims that he's never killed anyone who didn't deserve it.

Ned/Hobgoblin and Jack O'Lantern attack a bowling alley together.

During an altercation between Spider-Man and Ned/Hobgoblin, Jack O'Lantern bugs out.

Ned/Hobgoblin abandons the Rose in the middle of Gang War.

The Rose is injured; he has to kill a young rookie cop in order to make his getaway.

AMAZING SPIDER-MAN #287

Richard Fisk introduces Dina to his buddy Alfredo.

Peter Parker and Matt Murdock (Daredevil) have a falling out.

Alfredo recovers information from bugs which he'd installed in Kingsley's building.

Ned/Hobgoblin grabs Alfredo, confirms that he (Ned/Hobgoblin) has quit working for the Rose, and — after Alfredo gives him information about the Kingpin — dumps 'fredo in the river.

Ned visits Pete, letting him in on information about Kingpin's planned return to the city.

Kingsley throws Lance Bannon out of his offices; on the way out, Lance sees Mary Jane and says, "Don't ever tell anyone I was ever here!"

Daredevil, Falcon, and others cause a diversion to keep Spider-Man away from the Kingpin, during the Kingpin's return to New York.

Kingpin gives Ned/Hobgoblin a packet of information about overseas spy activities — "As I agreed when you contacted me in Europe" — in return for a packet containing the Rose's identity; Kingpin orders this second packet burnt, unopened, saying that he already knows who the Rose is.

AMAZING SPIDER-MAN #288

Ned visits Lance Bannon, saying that he (Ned) is going to hit Jameson for a European assignment; he offers to take Lance along as photographer; Lance has a bunch of Hobgoblin pics out.

Betty returns to her apartment, only to find Ned/Hobgoblin slapping an unconscious Flash Thompson.

Betty sees Ned/Hobgoblin unmasked and passes out.

Ned/Hobgoblin flees the scene, his goblin glider exhausting a plume of smoky **(hallucinogenic)** gas in his wake.

Ned/Hobgoblin attacks Jack O'Lantern "to make you pay for deserting me" (in *Amazing Spider-Man* #286's battle against Spider-Man).

Alfredo attacks Ned/Hobgoblin; Jack O'Lantern attacks Alfredo, saying "I must be the one who takes the goblin out." Ned/Hobgoblin splits.

Kingpin summons the Rose, revealing that he knows his son is under the mask.

SPIDER-MAN VS. WOLVERINE #1

Ned hits up Jonah for an assignment to Berlin to track down master spy Charlemagne.

Jonah sends Pete along.

Pete gets involved with Wolverine in Berlin.

>>>Behind the scenes — as later shown in *Amazing Spider-Man* #289 — Jason Macendale takes out a contract on Hobgoblin, employing the Foreigner's organization for the hit; Foreigner tells Macendale that the hit was completed.

Pete returns to his hotel to find Ned bound and gagged, his throat cut — dead.

In a funk, Pete returns to the U.S.

AMAZING SPIDER-MAN #289

Ned's body is returned to New York.

Kingpin plays chess with Foreigner; Kingpin acknowledges that "you had the Hobgoblin killed." Kingpin is displeased by this; he puts word out on the street for Spider-Man, "Let him know I have information on the Hobgoblin."

At Ned's graveside services, Betty acts irrationally.

Flash is wandering the streets; he tries to turn himself in to some cops, but they don't recognize him; they tell Flash to buzz off.

>>>Behind the scenes — as later shown in *Web of Spider-Man* #29 — Kingsley has an argument with Keating. Kingsley says that Keating "cooperated with Leeds…kept his secret! You set up Flash Thompson for him!"; Keating insists that "I would've gone after Leeds himself sooner or later! He was my informant! But you manufactured *weapons* for that psycho!" Johnston and Varley interrupt the argument; they shoot Kingsley; Keating escapes.

The Rose returns to his penthouse to find both Johnston and Varley dead, killed by Macendale, who is there in the guise of the (new) Hobgoblin.

The Rose tells Macendale/Hobgoblin that Kingpin has a file that he's turning over to Spider-Man; Macendale/Hobgoblin agrees to let the Rose live and takes off; Rose radios Kingpin that Macendale/Hobgoblin is on his way.

>>>Behind the scenes — as later shown in *Web of Spider-Man* #29 — Alfredo breaks into one of "Ned's secret hideouts" and is attacked by Macendale/Hobgoblin. Alfredo bugs out, with Macendale/Hobgoblin in hot pursuit, and is run off a pier. Alfredo is rescued by Spider-Man; Rose is aware of the attack, but unaware of the rescue.

Spider-Man visits the Kingpin and is given a special file folder.

As Spider-Man goes over the contents of the file, the reader is shown a Spider-Man's mind's-eye flashback in which four of the Foreigner's men surprise Ned in his hotel room, finding him dressed as the Hobgoblin…one of Foreigner's men grabs Ned, breaking his arm and then garroting him.

>>>The Kingpin's file contained photocopies of a journal entry purportedly written by Ned in Berlin…and evidence (in the form of sequential photos of the assassination taken by Foreigner's men) which visually revealed what happened.

The Kingpin tells Spider-Man that Foreigner's men then took his costume and journals, leaving his body — bound and gagged — for Peter Parker to find.

Having digested all this, Spider-Man takes the file and goes off in search of Foreigner, but can't find him.

Spider-Man is attacked by Macendale/Hobgoblin. They have a long battle, during which time the file is destroyed. Flash comes upon the battle and is hurt trying to help Spider-Man. Macendale/Hobgoblin gets away as Spider-Man performs CPR on Flash.

Flash is saved and cleared of all charges.

Kingpin blows up an elevator that the Foreigner is in; Foreigner miraculously survives (albeit slightly singed).

WEB OF SPIDER-MAN #30

Alfredo and Dina get together.

Richard Fisk ducks into a confessional at St. Patrick's, where he tells how…

…Ned had been after him for some time about his father.

…he finally decided to strike back at the Kingpin, after trouble with his mother.

…Alfredo had contacted Leeds [who by this time was under the control of the real Hobgoblin].

…Ned led them to a warehouse lair and "revealed" that he was the Hobgoblin.

…he became the Rose at Ned's suggestion.

Richard finally runs from the church. He winds up going to the Kingpin, saying, "You win, Father. I'll work for you."

>>>Much later —

Betty joins a cult.

Betty infiltrates the Foreigner's organization and finds out that "Ned had been the Hobgoblin" — which the Foreigner still foolishly believes to be true.

Macendale carries on as the new Hobgoblin with uneven success — until he is finally captured by Spider-Man in *Spider-Man* #69.

AFTERWORD

By Roger Stern

Well? Did you guess the Hobgoblin's identity?

If you didn't, don't feel too bad. People have been guessing who the Hobgoblin was for over a decade — and most of them had guessed wrong.

Readers first started trying to solve the mystery of the Hobgoblin shortly after we introduced him in *Amazing Spider-Man #238*. For months, we were inundated with letters from intrigued readers. Guesses ranged from J. Jonah Jameson to dear old Aunt May, from Stan Lee to Steve Ditko! (I'm sure that somebody even guessed Roderick Kingsley, though I don't remember ever seeing a letter to that effect.)

So, for all of you who did guess correctly, congratulations! But you should know that I beat you all to it.

You see, I was the first to guess correctly.

(This is where we segue into the true story about the origins of the Hobgoblin.)

When I first began my tenure as a Spider-Writer, I had a great time pitting Spider-Man against some of his classic enemies (like the Vulture, always one of my faves) and some well-established strangers (like the Juggernaut and Mr. Hyde). But I also wanted to introduce and develop some new antagonists who could really give the ol' Wall-Crawler a hard time. At the time, however, there was a very vocal coterie of readers who wanted to see the same villains back month after month...especially the Green Goblin.

Me, I didn't ever want to see the Goblin again.

Norman Osborn — the real Green Goblin — was dead (or so we thought at the time). And as far as I was concerned, his successors had been little more than pretenders to the throne. But the clamor just wouldn't die down — people wanted a Goblin.

So I decided to meet them halfway. I figured that I'd come up with a new villain — someone who appropriated the Goblin's weaponry and power, but who operated without the Goblin's madness. This Hobgoblin would be a coldly calculating adversary, one who would remain a mystery both to Spider-Man and the readers. Just as with the original Green Goblin, no one would see the Hobgoblin unmasked.

To maintain that air of mystery, I didn't even name him in the plot for *ASM #238*. To be honest, I hadn't really decided who he was when I described him to John Romita Jr. as a mysterious, shadowy figure. But then, a funny thing happened. As I was scripting that first story, searching for the character's proper "voice," I figured out who he was.

I was so happy, I immediately called up my then-Spider-Editor, Tom DeFalco. "Tom, I know who the Hobgoblin is!"

"Oh? Who is he?"

"I'm not going to tell you."

There was a pause at the other end of the line. *"You're not going to tell me?!"*

"It's not that I don't trust you, Tom. But if I don't tell you, you can't accidentally slip and tell someone else. If I'm the only one who knows, the secret of the Hobgoblin can really stay secret!"

There was another studied pause, and then — in that soft and gentle tone that he reserved for talking to small children and addle-headed freelancers — Tom said, *"Okay. I can see that. But when you finally get close to revealing his identity, you **will** let me know?"*

I assured him that I would and merrily went on my way...writing Spider-Man and driving those around me crazy. Everyone, it seemed, wanted to know who the Hobgoblin was — and I wouldn't tell anyone! Readers approached me at conventions, friends called me on the phone, but I wouldn't tell. The secret was mine, and no one — not my artists, not my editors, not even my wife! — would know it until I was ready to let them know.

In the meantime, I sprinkled little clues — all but unnoticeable — here and there in the stories. If you go back and check *Amazing Spider-Man* between issues #238 and #250, you may begin to see them. But be warned, I also planted a few red herrings. (Hey, solving a mystery isn't supposed to be easy!)

My original plan was to keep people guessing at least an issue longer than Stan Lee had kept people guessing about the Green Goblin. Paul Smith (then artist of the *X-Men*) told me that I should **never** reveal the Hobgoblin's identity. And I almost didn't. As things turned out, the secret of Hobgoblin's true identity remained unsolved for over a decade.

Here's how that happened...

John Romita Jr. and I both decided to leave *Amazing Spider-Man* around the same time, and Tom DeFalco — who had stepped down as Spider-Editor to oversee other projects — was offered the writing assignment. The first thing he did was call me up.

"They offered me Spider-Man."

"That's great, Tom! You'd be perfect for it!"

"I'm going to take it, but on one condition."

"What's that?"

"Tell me who the Hobgoblin is!"

I choked back a guffaw and gave Tom a name.

There was a pause at the other end of the line. "Really? Are you telling me the truth?"

"That doesn't matter, Tom. You're the Spider-Writer now, and you can make the Hobgoblin whoever you want."

And so he did. Together with Ron Frenz, Tom wove a series of stories which were everything a *Spider-Man* story should be. I enjoyed them immensely.

I'm told that Tom and Ron were planning to make Ned Leeds the Hobgoblin. Not my choice, but that didn't bother me. As I'd told Tom, the decision was theirs to make.

Then Tom and Ron left *Amazing Spider-Man*. Ned was killed in a *Spider-Man Vs. Wolverine* special. And it was revealed, after the fact, that Ned had been the Hobgoblin.

Unorthodox as that story was, it would have stood the test of time...except for one very important detail.

The super-powerful Hobgoblin could never have been killed the way that Ned Leeds was.

I saw that immediately and was a bit surprised that no one else seemed to notice. So I filed that thought away and waited to see what happened next.

What happened next, of course, was that Jason Macendale took over as the new Hobgoblin. There were new revelations about Ned, of course, but there was something about them that just didn't ring true.

After a while I realized that my original clues, few though they were, had gone unchallenged...and that the clues sown by subsequent writers indicated that the Hobgoblin — the real Hobgoblin — had set Ned up, just as he had set up Lefty Donovan before him! The Hobgoblin had committed the perfect crime and gotten away with it, unless...

...unless someone brought him to justice.

But I was the only one who knew the true identity of the Hobgoblin, and shortly thereafter, I found myself writing stories about reporters for Great Metropolitan Newspapers in a completely different reality. *

Time passed. Seasons changed. Heroes were reborn. **

In the intervening years, I would sometimes cross paths with a Spider-Editor and point out the evidence proving that Ned Leeds was not the Hobgoblin...and that therefore, the original Hobgoblin was still at large.

Some editors seemed dismayed by my revelations, others intrigued. But it wasn't until early in 1996 that I found two editors who were crazy enough to have me write the story you've just read.

And you know what? Writing it was fun!

Oh, sure, it took me awhile to get used to the idea of Peter Parker and Mary Jane Watson being husband and wife — and Aunt May being gone — but once I was over those hurdles, everything seemed to click into place, just like it used to. (At least it did for me. I hope it did for you, too.)

So here's a big thank you to Tom Brevoort and Glenn Greenberg for giving this ol' Spider-writer a chance to set things straight and finish the story that he'd started fourteen years before. Tom and Glenn did an exemplary job of shepherding this project to completion, enlisting mighty Ron Frenz and consortium of talented inkers and colorists to make the art shine.

But, I have to tell you, their help didn't come without a price. I still recall getting that phone call, telling me that the Hobgoblin project had been approved. There was hesitation in Glenn's voice as he said, *"There's just one thing you have to tell us...**who** is the Hobgoblin?!?"* So I told them.

But I didn't tell them what comes next.

Roger Stern
10-16-97

* One of the things I love about this business is the opportunity to say such things with a perfectly straight face.

** Ditto.